Sadlier-Oxford

NEW

PHONICS AND WORD STUDY

GRADES 4-6

biologist

explorer

astronomer

Developing the Skills to Become

SENIOR AUTHORS

Richard T. Vacca
Professor of Education
Kent State University

Lesley Mandel Morrow
Professor of Literacy
Rutgers University

Introducing
Sadlier Word Study

Current reading research suggests that children need to gain automaticity in decoding to become successful at comprehending text. An emphasis on word study at the middle grades builds upon the powerful relationship that exists between accurate, quick decoding and reading comprehension.

Sadlier Word Study, Levels D–F, provides students with the skills and strategies necessary to decode unfamiliar words by extending the development of phonics instruction into the middle grades. The program helps students apply decoding skills and develop word-meaning strategies as they read content-area materials.

The systematic sequence of skills and strategies in *Sadlier Word Study* provides students with a ready knowledge of word parts and the ability to use context clues, leading to better comprehension.

Successful Readers

CONTENT OVERVIEW

Level D

Level E

Level F

Unit Theme	Literature Selection	Skill Focus
1. Athletes	*Beach Volleyball* by Martin Lee and Marcia Miller	Consonant Blends and Consonant Digraphs
2. Explorers	*Meet an Underwater Explorer* by Luise Woelflein	Short, Long, and *r*-controlled Vowels; Vowel Pairs, Vowel Digraphs, Diphthongs, and Phonograms
3. Artists and Composers	*Twisted Trails* from *Time for Kids*	Word Endings, Contractions, Plurals, Possessives, and Compound Words
4. Making a Difference	*It's Our World, Too!* by Phillip Hoose	Prefixes, Roots, and Syllables
5. Scientists	*Your Future in Space* by Alan L. Bean	Suffixes and Syllables
6. People and Government	*Everybody's Uncle Sam* by Lester David	Dictionary and Thesaurus Skills; Synonyms, Antonyms, Homonyms; Clipped, Blended, and Borrowed Words; Idioms and Analogies
1. The Northeast	*Native Peoples of the Northeast* by Trudie Lamb Richmond	Consonant Blends, Consonant Digraphs, and Double Consonant Sounds
2. The Southeast	*Saving the Everglades* from *Time for Kids*	Vowel Pairs, Vowel Digraphs, Diphthongs, and Phonograms
3. The Middle West	*How to Grow a Painting* by Gail Skroback Hennessey	Word Endings, Contractions, Plurals, Possessives, and Compound Words
4. The Southwest	*Deep in the Heart of...Big Bend* by Bud McDonald	Prefixes, Roots, Base Words, and Suffixes
5. The West	*Catching Up with Lewis and Clark* from *Time for Kids*	Context Clues
6. The Northwest and Hawaii	*Hawaii: Then and Now* by Marcie and Rick Carroll	Dictionary and Thesaurus Skills; Synonyms, Antonyms, and Homonyms; Word Origin and Language Development
1. World Regions	*Thinking Big* by Scott Wallace	Consonant Blends and Consonant Digraphs; Vowel Pairs, Vowel Digraphs, Diphthongs, and Phonograms
2. Africa and the Middle East	*Cleopatra's Lost Palace* from *Time for Kids*	Word Endings, Contractions, Plurals, Possessives, and Compound Words
3. India and the Far East	*Science in Ancient China* by George Beshore	Prefixes, Roots, Base Words, and Suffixes
4. Ancient Greece to the Renaissance	*When Clothes Told a Story* by Linda Honan	More Prefixes, Roots, Base Words, and Suffixes
5. The Americas	*Coyote and the Stars* by Tsonakwa	Context Clues
6. The Modern World	*Can We Rescue the Reefs?* from *Time for Kids*	Dictionary and Thesaurus Skills; Synonyms, Antonyms, and Homonyms; Word Origin and Language Development

Using Word Study Skills to

As students move into the middle grades, they are expected to read and respond to a wide variety of content-area reading materials. *Sadlier Word Study* provides students with the word study skills and strategies necessary to tackle challenging texts.

Abundant instructional activities provide the practice and reinforcement students need, developing their confidence as they read to learn. With the systematic instruction provided in *Sadlier Word Study*, students learn to pronounce words and unlock their meanings more quickly and more accurately, leading to better reading comprehension.

Student Texts

Word Study in Context

Nonfiction photo-essays apply word study strategies to reading comprehension and critical thinking skills.

Structural Analysis

Lessons provide students with a clear map to help analyze structural and meaning clues in parts of words.

Critical Thinking

Critical Thinking questions encourage use of higher-order thinking skills.

Home Connection

A *Family Page* encourages family members to become partners in helping children become better readers.

"Chunking" Strategies

The use of phonograms, consonant blends and digraphs, and word endings help students apply their knowledge of phonics to decode difficult words.

Build Comprehension

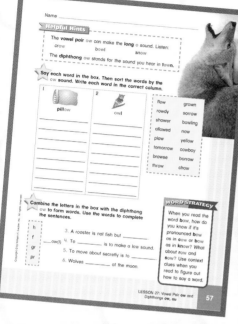

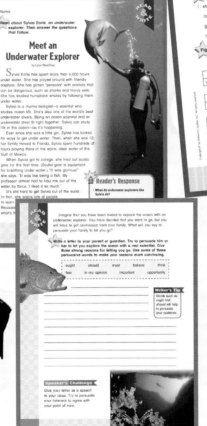

Context Clues

The *Word Strategy* feature shows students how to use specific context clues to unlock the meaning of unfamiliar words.

Dictionary Usage

Practical lessons help students learn to use dictionaries and thesauruses as tools for word study.

Reading and Writing

Engaging thematic lessons help students apply word study strategies in order to better comprehend content-area reading materials.

"Students at the middle grades need to maximize their ability to analyze chunks or letters within words; analyze the structure of words for morphemic or meaning-bearing clues; use context clues not only to pronounce unfamiliar words, but also to figure out their meanings; and use dictionaries and thesauruses as tools for word study. Students develop knowledge and control over these strategies through explicit instructional activities."

(Vacca, 2000)

v

Featuring a Complete

The *Sadlier Word Study* Teacher's Edition provides all of the resources necessary to meet today's challenging standards. Lesson features include systematic, explicit instruction and a wide variety of activities and strategies to meet the needs of all learners.

Teacher's Edition

Objectives
Clearly stated objectives correlate to national reading standards shown on the *Planning Resource* pages.

Warm Up
Each lesson begins with a review of a previously taught skill.

Explicit Instruction
Explicit and systematic instruction helps students master word study skills and strategies.

Supporting All Learners
Activities cater to all students' learning styles and language needs.

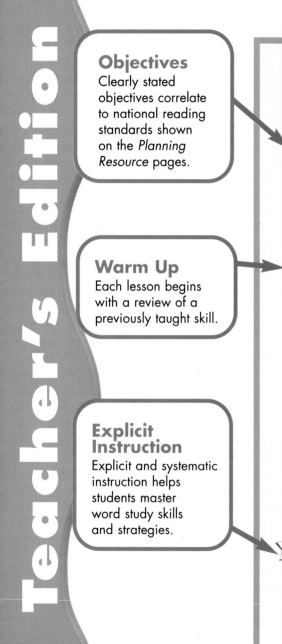

LESSON 49 • UNIT 4
Student Pages 101–102

Prefixes
un-, re-, dis-

Objectives

• To identify the prefixes **un-**, **re-**, and **dis-**

• To identify the meanings of words with these prefixes

• To write words with these prefixes

Warming Up

• Write this rhyme on the board.

Suppose you were a word,
And a prefix came along,
It would change your very meaning.
All you know might now be wrong.
Would you feel glad or **unhappy?**
Would you smile or feel **unkind?**
Would you make it feel **unwelcome?**
Would you mind?

• Read the rhyme aloud with students. Have a volunteer underline the words that contain a prefix (shown in bold type). Ask students to define these words.

• Ask students what these words have in common. (They begin with the letters **un,** and they mean the opposite of the word that follows the letters **un.**)

Teaching the Lesson

• Explain that many words begin with letter combinations called prefixes. Tell students that prefixes are not words by themselves, but they do have meaning. Point out that adding a prefix changes the meaning of the word they are added to.

• Read aloud the Helpful Hints on page 101 as students follow along silently.

Name _____

Helpful Hints

A **prefix** is a word part added to the **beginning** of a base word. Adding a prefix to a word can change the meaning of the word. It can also make a new word.

The prefix un means "not," as in un**afraid.**
The prefix dis means "not" or "opposite of," as in dis**like.**
The prefix re means "again," as in re**write,** or "back," as in re**turn.**

Watch out for words that seem to have prefixes but really do not. When you remove the un from **uncle,** no base word remains.

Add un, re, or dis to each of these base words. Write the new word on the line.

1. not **kind**   2. **pay** back   3. the opposite of **agree**
   unkind   _repay_   _disagree_
4. **fill** again   5. not **known**   6. not **important**
   refill   _unknown_   _unimportant_

Read the base word at the left of each sentence. Add the prefix un, re, or dis to the base word. Write the new word on the line.

welcome 7. The members of the cleanup crew were
   greeted by a(n) _unwelcome_ sight.

safe   8. The amount of trash left over from the
   parade made the street _unsafe_

appear   9. The volunteers quickly went to work to make
   the garbage _disappear_

store   10. They worked long and hard to _restore_
   the street to its original condition.

pleasant 11. We are sorry their task was
   so _unpleasant_

CHALLENGE
Some words have two prefixes. Underline the two prefixes in each of these words. Then tell what each word means.
unresolved
rediscovered

LESSON 49: Prefixes **un-, re-, dis-**   101

UNIVERSAL ACCESS
Meeting Individual Needs

Visual Learners
Write these base words and definitions on the board.

_____ **lucky** (not lucky)
_____ **obey** (not obey)
_____ **pay** (pay back)
_____ **view** (view again)
_____ **cover** (cover again)
_____ **agree** (not agree)

Have students use a different color chalk to write the prefix **un-**, **re-**, or **dis-** before each base word to make a new word.

Kinesthetic Learners
Write these words on index cards: **use, place, fill, comfort, obey, attach, new, healthy, fold, clog,** and **paid.** Place the cards around the classroom. Make another set of cards with the words **reuse, replace, refill, discomfort, disobey, reattach, renew, unhealthy, unfold, unclog,** and **unpaid.** Place these cards in a pile. Have students select a card from the pile and find its "match." Have students say a sentence for each word.

Teacher Support System

Level D Teacher's Edition

Add the prefixes in red to the base words in the box.
Write the new words on the lines.

1	un	2	re	3	dis
familiar	unfamiliar	place	replace	connect	disconnect
opened	unopened	turn	return	honest	dishonest
able	unable	view	review	color	discolor
happy	unhappy	solve	resolve	loyal	disloyal
checked	unchecked	think	rethink	like	dislike
tie	untie	live	relive	approve	disapprove

Use the best word from above to complete each sentence correctly.

4. Some people feel they are ___unable___ to solve community problems.

5. If people are ___unfamiliar___ with the problems in their community, they can do nothing to help solve them.

6. A community must ___resolve___ its problems by finding solutions.

7. If pollution goes ___unchecked___, it can make people and animals sick.

8. Waste in rivers and streams can ___discolor___ the water, turning it from blue to muddy gray.

9. Yet rivers and streams can ___return___ to their original state with just a little help.

10. Scientists must ___review___ all the facts before choosing a plan of action.

11. Sometimes, scientists must ___rethink___ their solutions to problems.

12. Their solutions must not make people sad or ___unhappy___.

102 LESSON 49: Prefixes un-, re-, dis-

Home Involvement Activity *Return of the Jedi* is a movie with a prefix in its title. Underline the prefix in the title of these videos your whole family can enjoy: *Egypt Uncovered Discovering Canada by Rail*

Practicing the Skill

● Read aloud the direction lines on pages 101 and 102. Guide students as needed. You may want to complete the first item in each set together.

● For exercises 4–12 on page 102, have students consider the context in order to choose the most appropriate word.

Curriculum Connections

Spelling Link

Write these scrambled words and sentences on the board. Have students unscramble the words and write them in the blanks to complete each sentence.

plercea
(replace) — It is time to _____ some old library books with new copies.

skildei
(dislike) — I _____ it when book pages are torn or missing.

blenua
(unable) — People are _____ to use very worn books.

weivre
(review) — Please _____ our plan to raise money.

voleser
(resolve) — It should _____ the problem.

Science Link

● Have groups of students do research to find out more about the effects of water pollution and what people can do to help clean up polluted areas. Suggest that students go to the library to find nonfiction books about the subject. Encyclopedias and students' science textbooks may also be useful resources.

● Have group members discuss their findings and prepare a brief written report. Photocopy the report for other students to read. Ask students to circle the words in the report that contain the prefixes **un-**, **re-**, or **dis-** added to a base word.

Observational Assessment

Note how readily students are able to determine which prefix to add to a base word.

Practice
Clear instruction, including modeling and guided practice, enables students to experience success as they practice each new skill in the Student Text.

Curriculum Connections
Cross-curricular activities extend word study skills and strategies into other subject areas, such as Social Studies, Science, and Math.

Assessment
Strategies for observing, recording, and monitoring student progress are frequently highlighted in the Lesson Plans.

English-Language Learners/ESL

Write these sentences on the board and underline as shown.
I am <u>not happy</u> with my garden. I <u>do not like</u> all the weeds. I will <u>again plant</u> the flowers.

Write the words **replant**, **dislike**, and **unhappy** on cards and display them. Have a volunteer read a sentence and find the card that matches the meaning of the underlined words.

Gifted Learners

Display the following list:
dismal, distant, disband, reread, reason, restart, relish, unless, unseen, untitled, under, and **unwise.** Have students circle each word that has been formed by adding a prefix to a base word.
(disband, reread, restart, unseen, untitled, unwise)

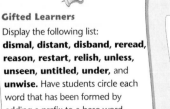

Learners With Special Needs

Additional strategies for supporting learners with special needs can be found on page 99L.

SADLIER READING

**Getting Ready to Read
with Mother Goose**
Level PreK/K

Sadlier Phonics
Levels K, A, B, and C

Sadlier Word Study
Levels D, E, and F

TEACHER'S EDITION

Sadlier
WORD STUDY
Reading

Level D

Senior Authors

Richard T. Vacca

Lesley Mandel Morrow

Contributing Authors

Charles T. Mangrum II, Ed.D.
Professor of Reading Education
University of Miami

Stephen S. Strichart, Ph.D.
Professor of Education
Florida International University

Program Consultants

Raymond P. Kettel, Ed.D.
Associate Professor of Education
University of Michigan
Dearborn, Michigan

Sylvia A. Rendón, Ph.D.
Coordinator for English Language Arts
Cypress-Fairbanks I.S.D.
Houston, Texas

Lisbeth Ceaser, Ph.D.
Dir., Precollegiate Academic Development
California Polytechnic State University
San Luis Obispo, California

Susan Stempleski, M.Ed., M.A.
Lecturer in TESOL
Teachers College, Columbia University
New York, New York

Sadlier-Oxford
A Division of William H. Sadlier, Inc.

Advisors

The publisher wishes to thank the following teachers and administrators who read portions of the series prior to publication for their comments and suggestions.

Rubbie D. Baker
Fifth Grade Teacher
Decatur, Georgia

Margarite K. Beniaris
Assistant Principal
Chicago, Illinois

Trish Bresch
Elementary School Teacher
Westmont, New Jersey

Shaun R. Burke
Fourth Grade Teacher
Rancho Santa Margarita,
California

Margaret Clifford
Principal
Michigan City, Indiana

Veronica Durden
Counselor
Beaumont, Texas

Christine Henschell
Sixth Grade Teacher
Grand Rapids, Michigan

Malini Horiuchi
Fifth Grade Teacher
Hollis Hills, New York

Amy T. Kwock
Principal
Honolulu, Hawaii

Connie Sartori
Sixth Grade L.A. Teacher
Seminole, Florida

Carmen Talavera
Fourth Grade Teacher
Long Beach, California

Acknowledgments

William H. Sadlier, Inc., gratefully acknowledges the following for the use of copyrighted materials:

Dictionary entries and pronunciation keys (text only). Reprinted from Macmillan School Dictionary 1, with the permission of the publisher, The McGraw-Hill Companies, Inc. Copyright © 1990 by Macmillan Publishing Company, a division of Macmillan, Inc.

"Everybody's Uncle Sam" (text only) by Lester David. By Permission of Maggie Rosen. Reprinted from BOYS' LIFE magazine (July 1996), published by Boy Scouts of America.

"It's Our World, Too!" (text only) from IT'S OUR WORLD, TOO! by Phillip Hoose. Copyright © 1993 by Phillip Hoose. Used by permission of Little, Brown and Company (Inc.).

"Meet an Underwater Explorer" (text only) by Luise Woelflein. Reprinted from the June 1994 issue of RANGER RICK magazine, with the permission of the publisher, the National Wildlife Federation. Copyright © 1994 by the National Wildlife Federation.

"Blazing a Twisted Trail" (text only). Reprinted from the October 25, 1996, issue of TIME FOR KIDS magazine, with the permission of the publisher, Time Inc. Copyright © 1996 Time Inc.

"Your Future in Space" (text only) by Alan L. Bean. By permission of the author. Reprinted from BOYS' LIFE magazine (July 1996), published by the Boy Scouts of America.

Photo Credits

ADVENTURE PHOTO & FILM/ Colin Monteath: 46 inset ARCHIVE: 64; American Stock: 105; ART RESOURCE: 34 ALAN L. BEAN: 174; BRIDGEMAN ART LIBRARY/ Royal Society, London, UK: 137; CORBIS: 53, 137, 140, 141, 147, 149, 152, 170, 171, 172, 175, 177 bottom; TempSport: 17 top right; Bettmann: 29, 30, 31, 39 bottom left & right, 45, 60 inset, 77, 103, 110, 112, 113, 113 top & bottom, 122, 162, 177 bottom, 203, 220; Historical Picture Archive: 35; Owen Franken: 41; Jeff Fanuga: 42; Niall MacLeod: 46 right; Wolfgang Kaehler: 48; George Lepp: 57; Philadelphia Museum of Art: 67; North Carolina Museum of Art/ Jacob Lawrence: 70; Hulton-Deutsch Collection: 81; Gregory Clements/Winslow Homer: 88; Ron Austing/Frank Lane Picture Agency: 94; Roger Ressmeyer: 128, 169; Sygma/ Les Stone: 132; Outline/ Timothy Greenfield-Sanders: 136; Paul A. Souders: 144; AFP: 184, 209 inset; Robert Maass: 191; Lake County Museum: 193; Joseph Sohm/ChromoSohm, Inc.: 204, 209; UPI: 208; Ted Spiegel: 214; Craig Lovell: 215; Catherine Karnow: 221 right DIGITAL VISION: 36 ADRIAN FISHER: 95 FPG/ Jim Cummins: 13; Vcg: 62 bottom right; Neil Nissing: 72; AL GIDDINGS: 61; THE GRANGER COLLECTION: 155, 157, 159; Currier & Ives: 91; THE IMAGE BANK: 150 left; Terje Rakke: 5; ActionPix, Inc.: 20; Per Eriksson: 43; THE IMAGE WORKS/ Esbin-Anderson: 75; Jeff Greenberg: 115; M. Greenlar: 118; Michelle Gabel: 134; Steve Rubin: 135; Peter Hvidzak: 177; Bob Daemmrich: 183, 199; J. Greenberg: 207; INDEX STOCK IMAGERY: 179, 222; NASA: 163, 173 right NATIONAL GEOGRAPHIC SOCIETY/ William R. Curtsinger: 31; 60 inset; Raymond Gehman: 68; Marie-Louise Brimberg: 84; Jodi Cobb: 87; Richard Nowitz: 93; PHOTODISC/ 18 top left, top right, 23, 27 inset & right, 52, 62 top left, 65, 139, 143, 150 bottom right, 158, 177 top, 194, 210; Steve Cole: 73, 82 top left; Amanda Clement: 92; Don Farrall: 98; C. Squared Studios: 110; Russell Illig: 111; S. Meltzer/Photolink: 210 top left; SW Productions: 210; Spike Mafford: 217 PHOTOFEST: 97, 116 THE STOCK MARKET: 137, 142, 156, 168; Mark Gamba: 76; Mug Shots: 99; Tom Stewart: 121; Chris Collins: 189; STONE: 65, 154, 160, 164, 176; Blake Little: 5, 9; Paul Rees: 7; Robert Daemmrich: 10; Dennis O'Clair: 12, 17 bottom left; Zigy Kaluzny: 15, 130; David Madison: 16; Steven Peters: 18 bottom right; Alan Levenson: 22; Ian Shaw: 24; Erik Butler: 25; Bob Thomas: 26; John Blaustein: 28; Lois & Bob Schlowsky: 31, 125; John & Eliza Forder: 37; John Lund: 38; Art Wolf: 47; Patrick Ingrand: 54; Darryl Torckler: 55; Ernest Braun: 56; Brad Hitz: 69; Doug Struthers: 73; Ian Shaw: 74; Jon Bradley: 80; Charles Gupton: 82 bottom left; Paul Chesley: 85; Daniel J. Cox: 99; David Woodfall: 99; Roger Tully: 99; Jeffrey Zaruba: 109; Mitch Kezar: 124; Jake Rajs: 129; Will & Deni Mcintyre: 131; Alan Klehr: 153; Doug Struthers: 167; Laurence Dutton: 193; Chris Thomaidis: 196; Ken Fisher: 198; Ed Honowitz: 198; Andrew Olney: 223; SUPERSTOCK: 177, 182, 185, 187, 188, 197, 212, 213, 221 bottom left THE STOCK MARKET: 5; 14; TIME WARNER TRADE PUBLISHING: 133: Phillip Hoose THE UNIVERSITY OF ARIZONA MUSEUM OF ART: Red CaNNa by Georgia O'Keeffe: 71

Illustrators:

Dirk Wunderlich: Cover; Dave Jonason: 8, 18, 40, 90, 96, 114; Mary Power: 5M, 31M, 99M, 177M; Functional Art: Diane Ali, Batelman Illustration, Moffit Cecil, Adam Gordon, Larry Lee, John Quinn, Sintora Regina Vanderhorst, Michael Woo

Dear Teacher,

As students enter the middle grades, their need to become strategic readers increases as they encounter unfamiliar words in content-area reading materials. The instructional core of the Sadlier Word Study program promotes strategic reading by guiding students through a logical sequence of skills and strategies that will enable them to decode difficult words quickly and accurately and will increase their reading comprehension.

Sadlier Word Study reflects current approaches to using word study strategies to improve reading comprehension in grades 4 through 6. Most notably, the program is built upon the following sound principles:

- **Chunking Strategies** extend the use of phonics while helping students develop a knowledge of word parts, such as consonant blends, phonograms, prefixes, suffixes, and roots, that will enable them to decode unfamiliar words.

- **Context Clues** help students build meaning by decoding words in context.

- **Word Study in Context** enables students to contextualize word study strategies by applying them to quality nonfiction photo-essays in content-area reading.

- **Integrated Language Arts** connect speaking, listening, reading, writing, and viewing, and tie nonfiction reading selections to numerous research and inquiry activities, while fostering communication skills.

- **Review and Assessment** provide frequent opportunities to monitor students' knowledge of word study strategies and adapt instruction to student performance.

As educators, we are proud to present a research-based, integrated approach to word study instruction. We are confident that your students will enjoy the content-area literature and the theme-based lessons, both of which provide an exciting context for learning and applying word study strategies.

We hope that you and your class will enjoy using *Sadlier Word Study*.

Sincerely,

Richard T. Vacca

Richard T. Vacca, Ph. D.

Lesley M. Morrow

Lesley Mandel Morrow, Ph. D.

Contents

Consonant Blends and Consonant Digraphs

Theme: Athletes

Short and Long Vowels, r-controlled Vowels, Vowel Pairs, Vowel Digraphs, Diphthongs, and Phonograms

Theme: Explorers

Sadlier WORD STUDY Reading

A Research-Based Program

Sadlier Word Study, Levels D–F, comprises a research-based program for intermediate reading instruction. Today, a growing body of research confirms that a balanced approach to reading instruction is in students' best interests (Morrow, 2001). One way in which teachers achieve balance is to "scaffold" instruction explicitly so that students become competent in the use of skills and strategies of effective readers (Vacca and Vacca, 1999). Sadlier Word Study provides a framework for explicit instruction necessary for developing students' ability to unlock the meaning of words (Vacca, 2000). Based on the program goals listed below you can see that an integrated language arts approach to the teaching of skills is employed.

Program Goals

Sadlier Word Study provides middle-grade students with a solid foundation of word study skills and strategies. The program is designed to extend the development of phonics, while emphasizing strategies that students need to construct meaning for unfamiliar or difficult words. In this way, the relationship between necessary decoding skills and reading comprehension is strengthened. To do this successfully, Sadlier Word Study focuses on the following program goals that are key components in balanced literacy instruction:

▶ Use of Word Study Strategies
▶ **Spelling Instruction**
▶ Reading Comprehension
▶ **Writing Practice**

▶ **Explicit Instruction**
▶ **Modified Instruction for ELL/ESL**
▶ Thematic Instruction
▶ **Mulitple Assessment Strategies**

Use of Word Study Strategies

The Research
Research suggests that word knowledge is a key factor in comprehension (Hennings, 2000). The greater a student's knowledge of word meanings, the better his or her chances of figuring out new or unfamiliar words on a page. For students to be strategic as they to learn new words, they should:

▶ Analyze chunks of letters within words

▶ Analyze the structure of words for morphemic or meaning-bearing clues

▶ Use context clues to pronounce and figure out the meaning of new words

▶ Use dictionaries and thesauruses as word study tools (Vacca, 2000)

Sadlier WORD STUDY Reading

Sadlier Word Study follows through on this research by offering activities designed to help students become proficient in their use of word study strategies. Students build words and divide them into parts. They sort words according to spelling patterns, word parts, or other features. They do cloze exercises, create word walls, and use dictionaries and thesauruses to learn word histories, definitions, and synonyms. Repeated practice enables students to build a strong base of word study strategies.

Spelling Instruction

The Research

The ability to spell well enhances students' writing and vocabulary development (Adams, Treiman, & Pressley, 1996). Spelling instruction supports students as they learn about and confirm their knowledge of the structure of English. Students benefit from the following:

▶ learning the spelling and the meanings of prefixes, suffixes, base words, and roots

▶ recognizing spelling patterns

As suggested by this research, *Sadlier Word Study* offers one or more *Spell and Write* lessons in each unit. In these lessons, students are asked to spell words from the unit and are given instruction in recognizing spelling patterns through sorting activities and word building exercises. Students are then given a writing prompt and are asked to write an original piece using the words in context. In addition, a *Spelling Link* is featured in every lesson. Words and sentences are suggested for dictation to provide additional spelling practice.

Reading Comprehension

The Research

For students to receive the greatest benefit and enjoyment from their reading, they must receive comprehension strategy instruction that builds on their knowledge of the world and of language (Pressley, 1998). *The Report of the National Reading Panel* (National Institute of Child Health and Human Development, 2000) points out that reading comprehension can be improved by teaching students to use specific cognitive strategies or to reason strategically when they encounter problems in understanding what they are reading.

The research on the importance of teaching reading comprehension is clear. To understand what is being read is a primary goal of reading instruction. To this end, *Sadlier Word Study* builds a student's ability to comprehend text through a systematic and focused emphasis on the skills and strategies necessary to unlock meaning. The *Read and Write* lessons in each unit help students develop key comprehension skills such as comparing and contrasting, making inferences, distinguishing between fact and nonfact, identifying main idea and supporting details, summarizing, and synthesizing information. As students read the authentic nonfiction literature selections, their attention is focused on one or more of these comprehension strategies. Through specific questioning and repeated practice, students become more skillful in their ability to comprehend non-fiction literature.

The Research

Many researchers today view reading and writing as skills that build upon each other; when they are cultivated concurrently, each adds to the proficiency in the other (Morrow, 2001). According to Pearson et al. (1992), "Good [reading] instruction includes an environment conducive to learning where the usefulness of reading is constantly seen. Students who interact daily with print, read what others have written, and write to and for others develop conceptual understandings about the value of reading. Writing practice allows students to make this important connection between reading and writing.

The *Sadlier Word Study* program offers both *Read and Write* and *Spell and Write* lessons designed to give students writing practice as suggested by research. Students are asked to use their experiential knowledge as they write letters, descriptions, explanations, directions, journal entries, and creative expressions. The writing activities lead students step-by-step through the writing process and at the end they are asked to add each new piece to their writing portfolios. By the end of the year, students' portfolios will reflect their knowledge of newly learned reading and writing skills.

Explicit Instruction

The Research

Explicit instruction reflects the dynamic interaction between the teacher and the student. The concept of explicit instruction has evolved from research on cognitive and metacognitive processes in reading (Vacca, 2000). When students are taught analytical procedures for learning words, instead of expecting them to figure out the procedures on their own, the efficiency of word-learning is improved (Gaskins & Ehri et al., 1996/1997). Explicit instruction of word study strategies ensures that students are aware of the strategies, and understand how and when to use them.

The *Sadlier Word Study* program has been designed to address the research that calls for explicit instruction. Students develop knowledge and control over skills and strategies through explicit instructional activities. The lesson plans provide for the four major components of explicit instruction: *explanation, demonstration, practice,* and *application.* During *explanation,* teachers direct attention to the *Helpful Hints* that allow students to learn the rules and procedures behind the use of the strategy. Once students understand the rules and procedures, teachers *demonstrate* their use through a "think-aloud" method, allowing them to model the thinking processes used in applying the skill or strategy. Students are then given *practice* activities to develop expertise in the use of the skill or strategy. Finally, students are asked to *apply* the skills and strategies they've learned through regular, ongoing class activities.

ELL/ESL Modified Instruction

The Research

When English is a second language for students, a firm foundation in their first language will support academic achievement in the second language (Cummins, 1979). Teachers encounter students from diverse cultural and language backgrounds. Good teaching strategies that adapt to these differences are those that work best. (Morrow, 1997)

he *Sadlier Word Study* program includes activities specifically designed for English-language learners and ESL students. The activities provide students with opportunities to attach meaning to unfamiliar vocabulary through the use of concrete objects, pictures, photographs, and pantomimed gestures. The lessons allow students whose first language is not English to participate fully in the lessons as they develop their competency in both the language and in cross-curricular content.

Thematic Instruction

The Research

Current research supports thematic instruction. Content-area themes provide a "context" for learning and by their very nature allow for curricular as well as language-arts integration. Students hone their reading skills as they "read to learn" (Vacca, Vacca & Gove, 2000).

Sadlier Word Study teaches strategies and skills in the context of high-interest, motivating themes that integrate all of the language arts, as well as the content areas. As students read about their world, they explore topics through authentic and challenging projects. The convenient two-page thematic lessons provide flexibility for teaching skills based on the needs of the students.

Multiple Assessment Strategies

The Research

Monitoring learners' progress calls for a variety of assessment strategies. Teachers must use keen observation of student development to inform instruction (Braunger and Lewis, 1997). The following types of assessment are recommended: screening assessments, checklists, writing rubrics, tests, comprehensive assessments, and portfolios.

Sadlier Word Study provides many opportunities for both formal and informal assessment. Each unit includes *Review and Assess* lessons. In addition, the Teacher's Edition contains Pretests, Post Tests, writing rubrics, checklists, as well as observational, performance-based, and portfolio assessments. The multiple assessment strategies allow for early detection of difficulties and give a solid determination of what each student has learned.

One Final Note

The *Sadlier Word Study* program reflects the most current research available and supports balanced literacy instruction. We wish you success in helping each and every student continue to become a proficient reader.

Richard T. Vacca   *Lesley M. Morrow*

Word Study Workshop

What Is Word Study?

Word study as a discipline includes phonics and goes beyond it. Whereas phonics focuses on letters and their sounds, word study focuses on words. Word study picks up where phonics leaves off, teaching readers how to use their phonological knowledge to figure out what words mean. *Sadlier Word Study,* a program developed to meet the needs of students in grades 4–6, includes elements of phonics, vocabulary, spelling, and study skills.

The program asks students to study words up close (dissecting them and analyzing their parts) and from a distance (looking at context and determining how it affects meaning). *Sadlier Word Study's* combination of "micro" and "macro" approaches offers a unique support system to teach middle-grade readers strategies for unlocking word meaning.

Richard T. Vacca, Professor of Education at Kent State University identifies the following basic strategies regularly used by competent readers:

▶ using the structure of words, the meaning-bearing clues provided by word parts, to construct meaning

▶ using *context clues* to figure out the meanings of unfamiliar words

▶ knowing how and when to use a dictionary when other strategies fail

These strategies are word-study strategies, and they all have to do with word meaning. So, how does word study bridge the gap between knowing how to pronounce words (where phonics leaves off) to figuring out what they mean? The answer to this question is virtually the explanation of how people learn to read.

Word Study Mirrors Reading Development

Recent studies have isolated four developmental phases in the acquisition of reading. They are *prealphabetic, partial alphabetic, full alphabetic,* and *consolidated alphabetic.* Identifying this sequence has helped educators recognize both the need for and the role of word study.

Prealphabetic

Children in this phase can recognize some words by using nonalphabetic visual cues. For example, a child seeing the octagonal shape of a stop sign might say, "stop," or a child recognizing the label on a box of cereal might say the cereal's name.

Partial Alphabetic

In this phase children know some letters and their sounds and notice these letters and sounds within words. A child at this stage might recognize his or her written name but not necessarily know all the letter-sound relationships within it.

Full Alphabetic

Children who are fully alphabetic know all the letters of the alphabet. They can figure out how to pronounce unfamiliar words by sounding out letters.

Consolidated Alphabetic

Children in the consolidated alphabetic phase approach words by looking at more than one letter—or chunks of words at a time.

Chunks: Bridging Letters and Meaning

Looking at word chunks, or "chunking," is a hallmark word study strategy. The chunks readers recognize are usually predictable letter patterns that contain meaning clues. Prefixes, suffixes, and roots are good examples.

Encountering the word *unimaginable,* a student could look at the chunks *un + imagin + able* and put together their meanings to figure out that the word means, roughly, "not able to be imagined." Other examples of word chunks that contain meaning clues are inflectional endings, comparatives, and superlatives.

Word Study in the Middle Grades

Many middle graders are on the brink of the fourth phase of reading development. Vacca explains that some students may need help sounding out and blending letters. He believes that the challenge of word study programs in the middle grades is to extend instruction in increasingly sophisticated ways into the consolidated alphabetic phase of development.

Explicit Instruction

Middle-grade students need to learn how to use the following word study strategies presented and taught in *Sadlier Word Study*:

▶ analyze chunks of letters within words

▶ analyze the structure of words for morphemic, or meaning-bearing clues

▶ use context clues to pronounce and figure out the meaning of unfamiliar words

▶ use dictionaries and thesauruses as tools for word study

Students practice and develop their ability to use these strategies through explicit instruction.

The goal of explicit instruction is to help students develop strategies for self-regulated, independent use—to cope with the kinds of problems they must solve as they are reading. Explicit instruction includes *explanation, demonstration, practice,* and *application.*

Explanation Through direct explanation of the strategy, students become more aware of *what* the strategy is and *how* and *when* to use it. Explanations help students learn the strategy and develop a rationale for its use.

Demonstration The teacher models the use of the strategy using a *think-aloud,* mirroring the thinking required to use the strategy effectively.

Practice The teacher provides students with practice activities to develop expertise in using the strategy and to discuss students' use of it.

Application Once students have had some practice with the use of a strategy, regular, on-going class activities encourage its application.

Thematic Instruction

Each *Sadlier Word Study* Student Edition is organized by theme. An engaging piece of nonfiction presents each unit's word study strategies within the context of a different theme. The thematic connection is maintained throughout the unit, with individual lessons using theme-related vocabulary, excerpts, and activities to teach word study strategies.

Curriculum Integration

Each unit of *Sadlier Word Study* begins with a nonfiction selection from a content area such as science, social studies, math, health, music, or art. The *Read and Write* lessons also provide selections about subjects appropriate to the students' age and interests.

The support material in both the Student Edition and Teacher's Edition offers opportunities for students to apply word study strategies in their pursuit of knowledge in the content areas. The program's cross-curricular features and follow-up activities give students a relevant context in which to practice the skills they are learning.

Integrating Word Study and Language Arts

Sadlier Word Study integrates the language arts so that students gain practice applying word study strategies to various language experiences.

Listening and Speaking The Teacher's Edition often prompts students to read aloud, listen to oral presentations, and to take part in informal discussions. Features in the Student Edition specifically designed to encourage discussion include the *Critical Thinking* and the *Reader's Response* questions.

Reading The program provides opportunities for students to read authentic literature in the *Unit Openers* and the *Read and Write* lessons. The Student Edition and the Teacher's Edition also offer lists of theme-related books for students to read on their own.

Writing Writing is an integral part of both the *Read and Write* and *Spell and Write* features, which often appear twice in each unit. In addition, the Teacher's Edition includes activities asking students to express themselves through expository and creative writing.

Spelling The *Spell and Write* features in every unit offer word sort activities that help students recognize predictable spelling patterns that often contain clues to meaning. These features also require students to write a composition using the spelling words in context.

Assessment

To help teachers evaluate students' work, each unit in the *Sadlier Word Study* Teacher's Edition contains an overview of strategies for assessment, including blackline masters. In it, unit-specific suggestions are given for how to use each of the assessment tools below.

Pretests and Post Tests Provided in each unit, these two tests are similar in content and can be used in various ways. One may be given as a pretest—a diagnostic tool to identify a starting point for instruction—and the other as a post test—a formal end-of-unit assessment of students' mastery of the unit skills.

Observational Assessment It is important to observe and record students' performance in the classroom frequently. Try to set aside 5–15 minutes a day to observe two or three students, so that you observe each class member about every two to three weeks. Specific instances for doing so are highlighted in the lesson plans.

Review and Assess Appearing in the Student Edition often twice in each unit, these lessons help the teacher ascertain whether students have mastered the unit content. If students need more instruction, the teacher can use the Reteaching activities found in the lesson plans.

Performance Classroom-based projects and activities help teachers determine whether students have correctly assimilated specific word study strategies. Suggestions for such activities can be found in the *Assessment* overview for each unit.

Portfolio Have students keep a portfolio of writing samples and other pieces of work that demonstrate their reading and writing skills. Such samples show how students have improved and where they may still have difficulty.

Universal Access

Sadlier Word Study offers lesson-specific methods for teaching students with a wide range of abilities, including those whose first language is not English, students struggling below grade level, gifted learners, and those with special needs. The pre-unit section labeled *Universal Access: Students*

with Special Needs particularly addresses students who have learning deficits, attention-deficit disorder, or problems with sensory discrimination. This section suggests ways of tailoring the more challenging lessons to meet the needs of these students.

Teaching ELL/ESL Students

Because students for whom English is not the primary language can be at any level of fluency, it is important to select teaching strategies and materials appropriate to the individual. Following are listed the stages, or levels, of second-language acquisition.

Pre-Production This stage of proficiency applies to those who are new to English. Shared-reading activities are appropriate for this level.

Early Production Students at this level are trying out the new language, responding with one- or two-word answers. Errors in grammar and pronunciation are to be expected.

Speech Emergence Learners at this level of proficiency use the new language to engage in conversation. Provide opportunities for these students to work in groups, encouraging communication between group members.

Intermediate Fluency Intermediate-level students may demonstrate fluency in social settings. However, academic language is still limited. Teachers can focus on continuing to build the vocabulary of these students and developing higher levels of language use.

Advanced Fluency Once English learners reach advanced fluency, they understand and speak English almost as well as native speakers. At this point, continue to build literacy skills, broadening vocabulary and developing more sophisticated levels of language use.

The English-Language Learners/ESL activities in the *Sadlier Word Study* Teacher's Edition have been designed with the above five stages in mind. The goal is to help students develop both receptive (listening, reading, viewing) and expressive (speaking, writing) abilities.

Intervention

Early reading failure can be a powerful force in shaping students' visions of themselves. The relationship between reading skills and success in all subject areas is a compelling reason for timely intervention activities.

Determine When to Intervene When a new concept is introduced, students must demonstrate understanding of this concept before moving on to the next step in the process.

Target Students for Intervention Activities that are playful in nature can help you identify students who are having difficulty. Such activities do not single out a student to the rest of the class, but they do provide you with an opportunity for informal evaluation.

Use Intervention Strategies Lesson-specific intervention strategies are recommended on the *Intervention* page in each pre-unit section of the Teacher's Edition.

Consonant Sounds

Theme: Athletes

STANDARDS

✪ Read expository text with grade-appropriate fluency and understand its content

✪ Develop and strengthen vocabulary by reading words in context

✪ Recognize letter-sound correspondence with consonant blends and consonant digraphs

✪ Distinguish initial, medial, and final consonant sounds in single and multi-syllabic words

OBJECTIVES

▶ To appreciate nonfiction works about athletes

▶ To distinguish soft and hard **c** and **g** and the sounds of **s** in words

▶ To distinguish consonant blends and consonant digraphs in words

▶ To write words with the letters **c, g,** and **s,** consonant blends, and consonant digraphs

LESSONS

Assessment Strategies

An overview of assessment strategies appears on page **5C**. It offers suggestions for using unit-specific assessment tools, including **Pretests** and **Post Tests** (pages **5D-5G**), the **Activity Master** (page **5M**), and the **Assessment Checklist** (page **5H**).

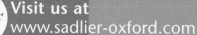
Thematic Teaching

In Unit 1, students learn about consonant blends and consonant digraphs. Students encounter words that contain these elements in the context of nonfiction selections and exercises related to the theme *Athletes*.

Students begin their investigation of *Athletes* by creating a mural of Olympic athletes from different parts of the world. The resource list on this page provides titles of multimedia that celebrate the spirit of sports and athletes. Many of the Teacher's Edition lessons in this unit open with poems, riddles, or tongue twisters related to *Athletes*. These "hooks" can spark students' interest in both the theme and in the play of words.

Curriculum Integration

Writing
Students write compositions on page **26**.

Science
Students search for words related to science and medicine on page **24**.

Social Studies
Students use an almanac, a map, or a globe on page **6**, hunt for place names and words related to social studies on page **8**, and identify countries on page **14**.

Math
Students write simple equations using words to represent numbers on page **16**.

Literature
Students select excerpts from stories, poems, or songs on page **10**.

Optional Learning Activities

Meeting Individual Needs
Most of the Teacher's Edition lessons offer activities for students with distinct learning styles or particular intellectual or sensory strengths. The activities are labeled for learners with the following "styles": **Auditory, Visual, Kinesthetic, Musical, Tactile,** and **Logical.**

Multicultural Connections
Students research an athlete from another culture on page **6** and they learn about Pelé, the Brazilian soccer star on page **22**.

Word Study Strategies
Pages **5I–5J** offer an array of activities that give students practice using strategies such as word sorting, word building, and dividing words into syllables.

Universal Access
Exercises tailored to meet the needs of **English-Language Learners** and **Gifted Learners** can be found in almost every Teacher's Edition lesson. Strategies designed to help **Learners with Special Needs,** such as students with Spatial Discrimination Deficits can be found on page **5L**.

Intervention
Page **5K** offers **Intervention Strategies** designed to help students performing below grade level understand the concepts taught in **Lessons 6, 9,** and **10**.

Reteaching
Students combine blends and phonograms on page **20**, and write words that contain digraphs on page **30**.

Technology
Page **5N** offers activities for students who enjoy working with computers or audio/video equipment. In addition, **Computer Connections**—tips designed to support students who use a word processor—can be found on pages **18** and **28**.

R E S O U R C E S

Books
Kamisky, Marty
  Uncommon Champions: Fifteen Athletes Who Battled Back, Boyds Mills Press, 2000
Rudeen, Kenneth and Hays, Michael. *Jackie Robinson,* HarperTrophy, 1996.

Videos
The Mighty Ducks, Walt Disney Video.
The Sandlot, CBS, Fox Video.

CDs
Catch a Wave: Beach Songs for Kids, Rhino Records.
World Playground: Musical Adventure for Kids, Putumayo World Music

In Unit 1, students study consonant blends and consonant digraphs. To evaluate students' mastery of these skills, use any or all of the assessment methods suggested below.

Pretests and Post Tests

The tests on pages **5D–5G** objectively assess how well students understand consonant blends and consonant digraphs. These tests may be used at the beginning of the unit as an informal diagnostic tool or at the end of the unit as a more formal measure of students' progress.

Observational Assessment

Opportunities for observing students as they work are suggested throughout the unit. Lesson-specific recommendations are also included for assessing students' work. Check students' work on a regular basis to see whether they are using what they learn correctly in their writing.

Using Technology

The Technology activities on page **5N** may also help to evaluate students whose language skills are best shown when using computers or audio/video equipment.

Performance Assessment

Have students copy the following words on a sheet of paper: **graph, triumph, shield, thunder,** and **cartwheel.** Have them circle the consonant blend and underline the consonant digraph in each word. Then have students list an additional word for each of the five blends and five digraphs.

Portfolio Assessment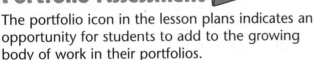

The portfolio icon in the lesson plans indicates an opportunity for students to add to the growing body of work in their portfolios.

Each student's portfolio will be different and should contain pieces that the student feels represent his or her best work. You may wish to give students additional opportunities to add to their portfolios.

Rubric for Writing

	Always	Sometimes	Never
Uses capitalization, punctuation, spelling, and grammar appropriately			
Creates a variety of sentences containing words with consonant blends and initial, medial, and final consonant digraphs			
Uses letters **c**, **g**, and **s** to stand for more than one sound			
Conveys meaning through writing			

Answer Key

Page 5D
1. engine
2. local
3. golf
4. sentence
5. clam
6. crash
7. think
8. sock
9. switch
10. belt
11. whistle
12. cheese
13. three
14. spray
15. drum
16. chick
17. street
18. sugar
19. coast
20. whisk
21. 2
22. 3
23. 2
24. 1
25. 1
26. 3
27. 3
28. 2
29. 3
30. 1

Page 5E
1. flimsy
2. present
3. twinkle

4. chrome
5. strict
6. plant
7. mice
8. budge
9. center
10. guitar
11. whale
12. porch
13. toothache
14. elephant
15. thimble
16. 3
17. 2
18. 2
19. 1
20. 3

Page 5F
1. basic
2. tag
3. ceiling
4. goose
5. touch
6. sunshine
7. swing
8. rough
9. sleep
10. noise
11. spend
12. smile
13. grass
14. graph
15. broken
16. split
17. cloth

18. pumpkin
19. shrimp
20. month
21. 2
22. 3
23. 1
24. 2
25. 2
26. 1
27. 2
28. 3
29. 3
30. 2

Page 5G
1. skill
2. propose
3. wasp
4. tank
5. slender
6. credit
7. gesture
8. decide
9. legal
10. culture
11. spinach
12. splash
13. path
14. wharf
15. stack
16. 3
17. 2
18. 3
19. 1
20. 1

Name _____

Fill in the circle next to the word that has the same sound of *c* or *g* as in the boldfaced word.

1. **fudge**	○ right	○ gopher	○ engine
2. **cone**	○ local	○ spicy	○ celery
3. **goal**	○ gentle	○ golf	○ judge
4. **cereal**	○ canal	○ comb	○ sentence

Fill in the circle next to the word that has the same sound as the underlined letter, blend, or digraph.

5. <u>c</u>lock	○ splash	○ collect	○ clam
6. fla<u>sh</u>	○ crash	○ clasp	○ sand
7. tru<u>nk</u>	○ damp	○ branch	○ think
8. <u>s</u>alad	○ please	○ sock	○ sugar
9. <u>sw</u>ing	○ slipper	○ smoke	○ switch
10. me<u>lt</u>	○ bell	○ belt	○ mitt
11. <u>wh</u>ale	○ wall	○ with	○ whistle
12. tea<u>s</u>e	○ cheese	○ release	○ suit
13. <u>thr</u>ead	○ think	○ twelve	○ three
14. <u>spr</u>ing	○ speed	○ spray	○ string
15. <u>dr</u>ip	○ trip	○ drum	○ grip
16. sa<u>ck</u>	○ patch	○ send	○ chick
17. <u>str</u>ong	○ screen	○ street	○ spring
18. <u>s</u>ure	○ sore	○ sugar	○ sweep
19. la<u>st</u>	○ coast	○ salt	○ toss
20. ta<u>sk</u>	○ fast	○ whisk	○ wish

Write the number of syllables in each word.

21. flower ____	22. together ____
23. surely ____	24. twin ____
25. glide ____	26. property ____
27. champion ____	28. blister ____
29. physical ____	30. laugh ____

Possible score on Unit 1 Pretest 1 is 30. Score _____

Fill in the circle next to the word that has the same consonant blend as in the boldfaced word.

1. **flipper**	○ finish	○ find	○ flimsy
2. **pretend**	○ people	○ perfect	○ present
3. **twice**	○ twinkle	○ tickle	○ timid
4. **chronicle**	○ churn	○ chrome	○ chocolate
5. **stretch**	○ strict	○ steady	○ step
6. **planet**	○ palm	○ pattern	○ plant

Fill in the circle next to the word that has the same sound of *c* or *g* as in the boldfaced word.

7. **space**	○ mice	○ candy	○ comb
8. **huge**	○ guess	○ budge	○ govern
9. **cider**	○ company	○ chorus	○ center
10. **gallon**	○ guitar	○ generous	○ giant

Fill in the circle next to the word that has the same consonant digraph as in the boldfaced word.

11. **whiskers**	○ wallet	○ whale	○ dishwasher
12. **bunch**	○ porch	○ story	○ lucky
13. **bathtub**	○ triple	○ hotel	○ toothache
14. **telephone**	○ pencil	○ helpful	○ elephant
15. **thumbtack**	○ triangle	○ thimble	○ trousers

Fill in the circle next to the correct number of syllables in each word.

16. grandfather	○ 1	○ 2	○ 3
17. receive	○ 1	○ 2	○ 3
18. nephew	○ 1	○ 2	○ 3
19. smooth	○ 1	○ 2	○ 3
20. chemical	○ 1	○ 2	○ 3

Possible score on Unit 1 Pretest 2 is 20. Score _____

Fill in the circle next to the word that contains the same sound of _c_ or _g_ as the boldfaced word.

1. canoe	○ decide	○ basic	○ voice
2. garden	○ wedge	○ tag	○ energy
3. face	○ camera	○ candle	○ ceiling
4. gutter	○ goose	○ gym	○ judge

Fill in the circle next to the word that has the same sound as the underlined letter, blend, or digraph.

5. pea<u>ch</u>	○ chute	○ touch	○ chord
6. <u>sh</u>ovel	○ think	○ choose	○ sunshine
7. ri<u>ng</u>	○ swing	○ rich	○ rink
8. cou<u>gh</u>	○ through	○ rough	○ thought
9. <u>sl</u>ipper	○ whisper	○ blend	○ sleep
10. sea<u>s</u>on	○ switch	○ dream	○ noise
11. <u>sp</u>eech	○ reach	○ screech	○ spend
12. <u>sm</u>all	○ mast	○ stall	○ smile
13. <u>gr</u>ape	○ garage	○ grass	○ gerbil
14. tro<u>ph</u>y	○ graph	○ plate	○ hope
15. <u>br</u>eakfast	○ beak	○ broken	○ treat
16. <u>spl</u>inter	○ spill	○ slip	○ split
17. <u>cl</u>ean	○ shear	○ cloth	○ cell
18. da<u>mp</u>	○ pumpkin	○ map	○ demand
19. <u>shr</u>ink	○ ship	○ shrimp	○ shingle
20. tee<u>th</u>	○ month	○ shelf	○ teen

Write the number of syllables in each word.

21. drama _____	**22.** president _____
23. class _____	**24.** clothesline _____
25. second _____	**26.** train _____
27. flashlight _____	**28.** capital _____
29. general _____	**30.** bridegroom _____

Possible score on Unit 1 Post Test 1 is 30. Score _____

Name _____

Fill in the circle next to the word that has the same consonant blend as in the boldfaced word.

1. sketch	○ simple	○ skill	○ settle
2. provide	○ portrait	○ possible	○ propose
3. grasp	○ test	○ past	○ wasp
4. pink	○ tank	○ chimp	○ tilt
5. slice	○ silly	○ slender	○ sell
6. create	○ credit	○ camera	○ cement

Fill in the circle next to the word that has the same sound of *c* or *g* as in the boldfaced word.

7. agent	○ guard	○ gather	○ gesture
8. dancer	○ vocal	○ cable	○ decide
9. bargain	○ legal	○ germ	○ pledge
10. collar	○ culture	○ citizen	○ cinnamon

Fill in the circle next to the word that has the same consonant digraph as in the boldfaced word.

11. sandwich	○ garnish	○ spinach	○ tooth
12. crash	○ splash	○ clap	○ tramp
13. broth	○ bottom	○ path	○ party
14. wheat	○ wharf	○ weasel	○ weather
15. check	○ cash	○ cloth	○ stack

Fill in the circle next to the correct number of syllables in each word.

16. scholarship	○ 1	○ 2	○ 3
17. clumsy	○ 1	○ 2	○ 3
18. cereal	○ 1	○ 2	○ 3
19. please	○ 1	○ 2	○ 3
20. tribe	○ 1	○ 2	○ 3

Possible score on Unit 1 Post Test 2 is 20. Score _____

Student Name _____

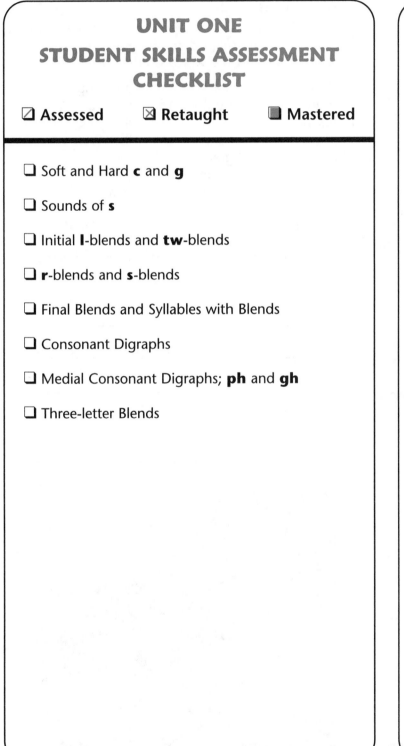

UNIT ONE
STUDENT SKILLS ASSESSMENT CHECKLIST

☑ **Assessed**   ☒ **Retaught**   ▦ **Mastered**

- ❑ Soft and Hard **c** and **g**
- ❑ Sounds of **s**
- ❑ Initial **l**-blends and **tw**-blends
- ❑ **r**-blends and **s**-blends
- ❑ Final Blends and Syllables with Blends
- ❑ Consonant Digraphs
- ❑ Medial Consonant Digraphs; **ph** and **gh**
- ❑ Three-letter Blends

TEACHER COMMENTS

WORD STUDY STRATEGIES

In Unit 1, students study consonant blends and consonant digraphs. To give students opportunities to master word study strategies, use any or all of the activities suggested below.

Build on Phonograms

Add a consonant blend from the box to each phonogram to complete each sentence.

sl	cl	st	tw	br
cr	sp	pl	sw	fl

1. There was ___ **eam** coming out of the kettle.

2. Did you notice the ___ **ack** in the vase?

3. He watched the ___ **ock** until the bell rang.

4. The colors on the ___ **ag** are red, white, and blue.

5. He is not just my brother, he is also my ___ **in.**

6. The alligator was found near the ___ **amp.**

7. I am acting in the school ___ **ay.**

8. The rocket soared into ___ **ace.**

9. Could you ___ **ing** me a napkin?

10. Did you see the runner ___ **ide** at second base?

11. The chocolate cake was too ___ **eet.**

12. Be careful not to ___ **eak** the new camera.

13. Use a dictionary to learn how to ___ **ell** that word.

14. I could teach you how to ___ **ing** a bat.

15. Please remember to ___ **ose** the window if it rains.

Digraph Search

Circle the consonant digraph in each word. Determine where the consonant digraph appears in each word. Then sort the words on the chart.

shovel	math	anything
rough	trophy	whistle
teacher	thirty	fish
pickle	chin	lock
bench	graph	tackle
thumb	while	bashful
author	laugh	phase

Initial	Medial	Final
_____	_____	_____
_____	_____	_____
_____	_____	_____
_____	_____	_____
_____	_____	_____
_____	_____	_____
_____	_____	_____

Blend-Digraph Search

Circle the consonant blend and underline the consonant digraph in each word. Then write the consonant blend and the consonant digraph in the correct columns.

	Consonant Blend	Consonant Digraph
blush	——	——
thunder	——	——
track	——	——
branch	——	——
shoulder	——	——
chord	——	——
flask	——	——
whimper	——	——
length	——	——
paragraph	——	——
breath	——	——
splash	——	——
tricked	——	——
whistle	——	——
brother	——	——
squash	——	——
think	——	——
stick	——	——
smooth	——	——
triumph	——	——

Word Selection

Listen for the sound that the underlined letter(s) make in each word. Then cross out the word in each line that does not contain the same sound.

chain	checkers	cashier	march
chute	channel	chandelier	chef
chemical	such	chaos	cast
gentle	charge	giant	goalie
camel	ceiling	basic	contest
gear	general	gaze	golden
decimal	dance	cedar	curve
salad	single	pose	suit
insurance	saddle	sugar	sure
cheese	desert	wise	inside

Word Sort

Circle the consonant blend or consonant digraph in each word. Then sort the words by the number of syllables.

project	wish	sneaker
gravel	whale	physical
alphabet	rough	glitter
chocolate	flame	dragon
glide	together	skeleton
tackle	champion	craft

One Syllable	Two Syllables	Three Syllables
————	————	————
————	————	————
————	————	————
————	————	————
————	————	————
————	————	————

LESSONS	6 Final Blends	9 Consonant Digraphs	10 Medial Consonant Digraphs
Problem	Students confuse words that contain final consonant blends with words that do not contain final consonant blends.	Students pronounce or write the digraph **th** as **t** or **d**.	Students use the letter **f** instead of **ph** or **gh**.
Intervention Strategies	• Have students identify and list the words with final consonant blends they find confusing, such as **wild** and **wide**. • Have students focus on the consonants in the blend by asking them to highlight each consonant in the blend with a different color ink. • Ask students to say the highlighted consonants aloud and emphasize the blend.	• Model for students how to position mouth and tongue to pronounce /th/. Say the following: **mad, math, mat,** and **pad, path, pat.** Have students repeat, emphasizing final /d/, /th/, and /t/. Have students note the position of the mouth and tongue for each word. • To clarify when the /th/ sound is used, have students practice writing and reading sentences such as: The **bad bat** refused to take a **bath**.	• Tell students that there are only a few words with **ph** or **gh**. • Encourage students to keep a word study notebook. Have them make a list of words in which **ph** or **gh** stands for the sound /f/. • Encourage students to write a mnemonic sentence for each listed **ph** or **gh** word. For example: **Dolphins** have **fins,** but they're not **dolfins.** Cream **puffs** are not **tough**.

The following activities offer strategies for helping students with special needs to participate in selected exercises in Unit 1.

Visual Perceptual Deficits

Soft and Hard c and g

Students who have difficulty recognizing visual cues may be unable to determine when the letters **c** and **g** are soft or hard.

- Begin by writing the words **city** and **cap** on the board. Underneath, write: *Pam visited the _____.* and *Carl wears his _____ backwards.* Ask a volunteer to circle the word that belongs in the first sentence and underline the word that belongs in the second sentence. Have the student say each word.

- Then have students identify the letter common to both words. Ask: *What is different about the way it is pronounced in each word?* Explain that the **c** in **city** is soft because it is followed by **i.** At this point, teach the rule for pronouncing the letter **c.** *Say: c is pronounced like the letter **k. Ce, ci,** and **cy** are pronounced like the letter **s.***

- Then give students cards with words containing hard and soft **c** written in large letters. Also give them the letter **c** cut from velvet and the letter **c** cut from cardboard. Ask them to read the words on the cards aloud. Have them place the velvet **c** on the words with a soft **c** sound and the cardboard **c** on the words with a hard **c** sound.

Spatial Discrimination

Children who have difficulty locating positions may have difficulty with the second activity on page 9. For example, they may forget to write the answers horizontally instead of vertically. Discuss this with students and ask them what they might do to avoid this mistake.

Guide them to see that when they have sorted the words by the proper **s** sound, they can list each category on a separate index card. To copy the words in the proper column, they can work from only one index card at a time, covering up the rows in which those words do not belong.

Attention Deficit Disorder (ADD)

Consonant Blends

Using demonstration can help focus students with ADD and motivate them to discriminate between words with an initial consonant blend and those without. For example, use a tube of glitter and some crumpled papers to demonstrate the different meanings of the words **glitter** and **litter.**

- Hold up the tube of glitter for students to see and write a sentence such as the following on the board: *There is **glitter** in this tube.* Then show students the crumpled papers and write a sentence like the following: *There is **litter** on my desk.* Explain that adding a **g** before the **l** changes one word into the other.

- Actively involve students in the lesson by asking them to read the sentences aloud, emphasizing both the initial **l** and the initial **gl.** Then have them use magnetic letters to make the word **glitter** from the word **litter.** (To prevent over-stimulation, give them only the letters needed to make the two words.)

- When you feel that students are able to discriminate between the two words, do another demonstration—one with some glitter sprinkled on a piece of paper and the other with crumpled papers in a wastebasket. Write these sentences on the board: *There is _____ on the paper. Now the _____ is in the basket.* Have them fill in the missing words or spell them out with the magnetic letters.

Use the words in the box to match the sounds.
Write the words on the lines.

chalk	gold	also	resident	chaperon	person	lunch
insure	elect	chef	decide	tissue	regular	percent
danger	wise	general	country	chameleon	chord	

I. /s/   spelled as **s**

_____

_____

6. /k/   spelled as **c**

_____

_____

2. /z/   spelled as **s**

_____

_____

7. /sh/   spelled as **s**

_____

_____

3. /ch/   spelled as **ch**

_____

_____

8. /j/   spelled as **g**

_____

_____

4. /g/   spelled as **g**

_____

_____

9. /s/   spelled as **c**

_____

_____

5. /sh/   spelled as **ch**

_____

_____

10. /k/   spelled as **ch**

_____

_____

Videotape an Interview with an Athlete

Invite students to videotape an interview with an athlete on a school team. During the interview, the athlete should demonstrate his or her role on the team. If a video camera is not available, students can tape-record the interview and photograph the athlete's demonstration.

- When students have selected an athlete and enlisted his or her cooperation, they should make a list of the tasks the project requires (research, operating the camera, interviewing, and so on). Most of the tasks should be assigned to groups. The whole class should generate the interview questions.

- Compile examples of interviews from sports magazines and show students videos of sports stars being interviewed by a television host. Be sure to set aside time for students to work on the project and to present the final product to another class.

- To give students practice with the different sounds of **c, g,** and **s,** have them list sports-related words that use the letters and their different sounds. **(announce, basic, local, record, score, gym, game, energy, goal, sport, muscle, exercise, advise, problems)** Encourage students to include these words when writing their interview questions.

Design a School Sports Web Page

Tell students that web pages organize information about a specific topic and make it accessible to people connected to the Internet. Encourage students to design a web page about school sports.

- Show students various web sites. Point out that names and phrases on the pages are links to pertinent information. For example, they might include a bulleted list of sports names on their own page. The viewer can click on each sport to learn what opportunities the school offers in that sport. Other links might lead to the names and e-mail addresses of the physical education teacher and school coaches, as well as game schedules and sports equipment.

- Divide the project's tasks among small groups. For example, several students might research the sports opportunities in their school, another group might study web pages to get ideas about how to design their page, another might create graphics for the page, and so on.

- Brainstorm a list of words that includes initial **l**-blends, **s**-blends, and **r**-blends. **(glove, skate, track, swim, spin, slide, drill, stadium, sport, ski, trophy, practice, score, protect)**

- Encourage students to include as many words from the list as possible in the web page text. Tell students that once their page is on the World Wide Web, they should update the information when necessary.

Tape-Record Team Songs and Cheers

Have students make an audiocassette of the songs and cheers they use at school sports events.

- Encourage the class to list their favorite songs and cheers. Have the class vote for the songs or cheers to be recorded.

- Write the words for the songs and cheers on the board. Point out how the syllables of the words affect the rhythm of the selections. Have volunteers divide the words in various lines of the cheers or song lyrics into syllables.

- Students may want to choose someone to announce the selections. Ask for a volunteer to operate the tape-recording machine. The entire class can perform the songs and cheers. Encourage students to take a copy of the tape to pep rallies to teach or inspire the participants.

Introduction to
Consonant Sounds

Objectives

- **To enjoy a piece of nonfiction related to the theme *Athletes***

- **To identify the sounds of c, g, and s and to study consonant blends and consonant digraphs**

Starting with Literature

Ask a student to read "Opening the Olympics" aloud for the class. On the board, write these words from the story's first sentence: **Cheers, explode, crowd.** Have students say **Cheers** aloud. Mask the **eers** and ask a volunteer to pronounce the **ch.** Repeat this process with **pl** and **cr** in the other two words.

Critical Thinking

- For the first two questions, ask students to read the selection carefully to find the answers.

- Encourage students to share their own opinions in response to the third question.

Introducing the Skill

Have students reread the selection to find words with the consonant pairs **pl** and **fl.** Write these words on the board. **(explode, flag, people, flap, flame)** Circle the consonant pairs and ask students what sounds the letters stand for.

Practicing the Skill

- Arrange students in groups. Give each group a different consonant pair to find in the selection.

- Then have each group think of additional words with the same consonant pair.

Opening the Olympics

Cheers explode from the excited crowd. The Olympic torch has entered the packed stadium. The proud runner holds the torch high. She runs past teams of athletes on the field. The opening ceremony has begun.

The Olympic flag waves. It has five linked rings on a white background. The rings stand for the friendship of people in the world's five major regions: Africa, the Americas, Asia, Australia, and Europe. The rings are blue, yellow, black, green, and red. Each country's flag has at least one of these colors.

Thousands of athletes stand with their teams. Their national flags flap in the breeze. The runner glides by, carrying the torch. Its flame was lit in Olympia, Greece. That is where the Olympics were first held nearly three thousand years ago. Now that is where the flame begins its journey each Olympic year.

When the runner lights the great Olympic flame, there is another loud roar. For the next two weeks, athletes from nearly two hundred countries will challenge each other's strength, speed, and skill. They will compete in the name of peace, good will, and understanding.

Let the Games begin!

? Critical Thinking

1. How are the Olympic Games different from other sports events?

2. What might athletes learn at the Olympic Games?

3. Do you think the Olympic Games are important? Explain.

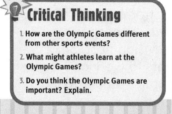

1. Athletes play for their countries.
2. peace, good will, and understanding
3. Answers will vary.

LESSON 1: Introduction to Consonant Blends and Consonant Digraphs **5**

Theme Activity

OLYMPIC MURAL FOR PEACE Invite students to create a mural showing athletes and their country's flags from different parts of the world. Encourage students to do research to find pictures of the athletes and information about their country's flag. Students may wish to include athletes from countries of personal interest or significance. Make sure that both male and female athletes are represented.

Students can draw or post pictures of the athletes performing in their events, the medal ceremonies, or spectators in the stands. Suggest that students label details of the mural with "Unit 1" words: words with **c, g,** or **s** or with consonant blends or consonant digraphs. Remind students to add words to the "Olympic Mural for Peace" as they continue working through the unit.

Visit us at
www.sadlier-oxford.com

Dear Family,

Welcome to Sadlier's *Word Study* program. Each unit presents strategies and exercises to help your child become a better reader. In Unit 1, your child will review the different sounds of **c**, **g**, and **s** and will explore consonant blends and consonant digraphs. The theme of this unit is *athletes*.

A **consonant blend** is two or three consonants sounded together so that each letter is heard (**sp**eed, **spl**atter, jum**per**). Notice that the word **blend** begins and ends with a consonant blend!

A **consonant digraph** is two consonants that together stand for one sound (**ch**air, a**th**lete, ru**sh**). The word digra**ph** ends with the digraph **ph**, which makes the sound of **f**.

Opening the Olympics

Cheers explode from the excited crowd. The Olympic torch has entered the packed stadium. The proud runner holds the torch high. She runs past teams of athletes on the field. The opening ceremony has begun.

The Olympic flag waves. It has five linked rings in a white background. The rings stand for the friendship of people in the world's five major regions: Africa, the Americas, Asia, Australia, and Europe. The rings are blue, yellow, black, green, and red. Each country's flag has at least one of these colors.

Thousands of athletes stand with their teams. Their national flags fly in the breeze. The runner glides by, carrying the torch. Its flame was lit in Olympia, Greece. That is where the Olympics were first held nearly three thousand years ago. Now that is where the flame begins its journey each Olympic year.

When the runner lights the great Olympic flame, there is another loud roar. For the next two weeks, athletes from nearly two hundred countries will challenge each other's strength, speed, and skill. They will compete in the name of peace, good will, and understanding. Let the Games begin!

Critical Thinking
1. How are the Olympic Games different from other sports events?
2. What might athletes learn at the Olympic Games?
3. Do you think the Olympic Games are important? Explain.

LESSON 1: Introduction to Consonant Blends and Consonant Digraphs

5

Family Focus

- Read together the passage on page 5 or an article from the sports page of your local newspaper. Discuss the article with your child. Have your child circle words with consonant blends and consonant digraphs. Offer your support by going over the work.

- Talk about sports or Olympic events that your family enjoys watching. Make a list of these events. Have each family member discuss his or her favorite. Ask what he or she likes most about the sport. Is it the players, the excitement, the competition—or all three?

LINKS TO LEARNING

To extend learning together, you might explore:

Web Sites
www.olympic-usa.org
www.devlab.dartmouth.edu/
olympic/history

Video
Atlanta's Olympic Glory,
PBS Home Video.

Literature
100 Unforgettable Moments in the Summer Olympics
by Robert Italia, ©1996.
Hour of the Olympics
by Mary P. Osborne, ©1998.

Multicultural Connection

Have students research an Olympic athlete from a country other than the United States. Include information about the athlete, his or her sport, and his or her country. Have students discuss how athletes from various nations might feel about competing against one another. Ask: *Can people from different countries compete against one another and still work toward peace, good will, and understanding among nations?*

Social Studies Link

Using an almanac, look up Olympic winners. Encourage students to find these winners' countries on a map or globe. Students might also make an Olympics map, with countries labeled according to the names of their gold medalists.

Word Study at Home

- The Word-Study-at-Home page provides an opportunity for students and their families to work together as students practice their language skills.

- On the Word-Study-at-Home page for Unit 1, students and their families will find activities that relate to the theme *Athletes* and focus on consonant blends and consonant digraphs.

- Have students remove page 6 from their books. Direct them to take the page home so that their families may share in the Word-Study-at-Home activities.

- Encourage students to talk about the sports and Olympics events their families enjoy watching. Students may wish to discuss their own favorites as well, explaining why certain sports appeal to them more than others.

- Invite students to find out about lesser-known Olympic sports as well as those with which they are already familiar. You might assign each student an unusual event—the shot put, javelin toss, decathlon, and so on—and ask him or her to prepare a brief oral report.

Theme-Related Resources

Books

Olympic Summer Games 2000, by Meredith Costain, Puffin, 2000

The Summer Olympics, by Bob Knotts, Children's Press, 2000

Going for the Gold by Melissa Lowell, Bantam Skylark, 1994

Always Dream by Kristi Yamaguchi, illustrated by Doug Keith, Taylor Publishers, 1998

Soft and Hard c and g

Objectives

- **To recognize soft and hard c and g sounds**
- **To associate these sounds with the letters c and g**
- **To decode and write words with soft and hard c and g**

Warming Up

- Write this rhyme on the board and read it aloud with students, emphasizing the sounds of the letters shown in bold type.

    The **c**eremony has be**g**un;

    The **g**ames are under way.

    Coaches pa**c**e as ra**c**ers run,

    And ju**dg**es rule the day.

- Have a volunteer underline the words that have **c** or **g** sounds. Ask the same student to circle the letter or letters representing each sound, saying the sound as he or she does so.

Teaching the Lesson

- Write **center** and **coach** on the board. Read them aloud and ask how the **c** sounds are different. Point out that soft **c** (in **center**) has the sound of the letter **s**. Hard **c** (in **coach**) has the sound of **k**.
- Write the words **gym** and **game** on the board. Read them aloud and ask how the **g** sounds differ. Explain that soft **g** (in **gym**) has the sound of **j**. Hard **g** is the sound heard in **game** and **gum**.
- Have a student read aloud the Helpful Hints as others follow along silently. Then ask: *When does c have a soft sound? A hard sound? When does g have a soft sound? A hard sound?*

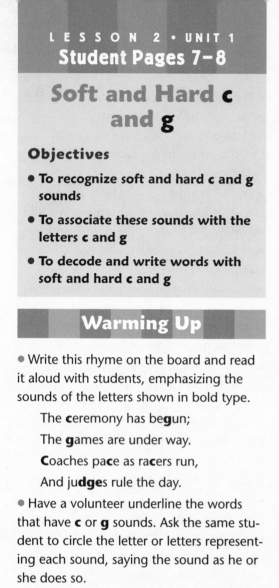

Name _____

Helpful Hint

The letter c usually has a soft sound when it is followed by **e, i,** or **y.** Otherwise, c has a hard sound.

    police   celery   city   lacy   cable   comma   cute

Say each word in the box below.
Does it have a soft c or a hard c?

| announce | basic | canoe | center | cereal | career |
| record | decide | local | score | spicy | voice |

1. Write the soft c words on the lines below.

    announce   center   cereal

    decide   spicy   voice

2. Write the hard c words on the lines below.

    basic   canoe   career

    record   local   score

Complete each sentence with a word from the box above.

3. They'll _____announce_____ the players over the loudspeaker.

4. The _____basic_____ idea of the game is to earn points.

5. The coach will _____decide_____ on the batting order.

6. Our _____local_____ park has a swimming pool.

7. I want to learn how to paddle a _____canoe_____.

8. That player broke the home-run _____record_____.

9. What was the final _____score_____ of the game?

10. Did Jason lose his _____voice_____ cheering for the team?

CHALLENGE

Each of the words below has a hard c *and* a soft c sound. Circle the soft c. Color the hard c.

    bicycle
    calcium
    concert
    currency

UNIVERSAL ACCESS
Meeting Individual Needs

Auditory Learners

To help students distinguish between soft and hard **c** and **g** sounds, write the following mnemonic jingle on chart paper and display it in the classroom. Invite volunteers to sing or chant the words and clap out the rhythm as they walk around the room.

City has a soft **c**;
Country's **c** is hard.
Genius has a soft **g**,
Unlike **goat** or **guard**.

Visual Learners

The chart below can help students remember when a **c** or **g** is soft and when it is hard. Draw the chart on the board for students to copy. Have them add words to each list of examples.

	SOFT: followed by e, i, y	HARD: followed by a, o, u
c	cereal circle lacy	car corn cuddly
g	fudge magic gym	game gone gull

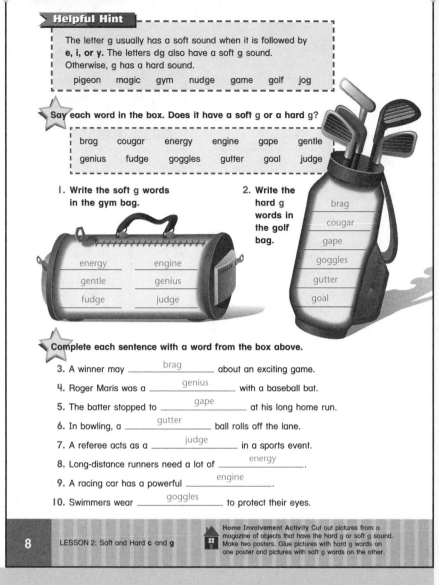

Say each word in the box. Does it have a soft g or a hard g?

brag   cougar   energy   engine   gape   gentle
genius   fudge   goggles   gutter   goal   judge

1. Write the soft g words in the gym bag.

energy   engine
gentle   genius
fudge   judge

2. Write the hard g words in the golf bag.

brag
cougar
gape
goggles
gutter
goal

Complete each sentence with a word from the box above.

3. A winner may _____ brag _____ about an exciting game.

4. Roger Maris was a _____ genius _____ with a baseball bat.

5. The batter stopped to _____ gape _____ at his long home run.

6. In bowling, a _____ gutter _____ ball rolls off the lane.

7. A referee acts as a _____ judge _____ in a sports event.

8. Long-distance runners need a lot of _____ energy _____.

9. A racing car has a powerful _____ engine _____.

10. Swimmers wear _____ goggles _____ to protect their eyes.

Home Involvement Activity Cut out pictures from a magazine of objects that have the hard g or soft g sound. Make two posters. Glue pictures with hard g words on one poster and pictures with soft g words on the other.

English-Language Learners/ESL

Using magazine cutouts and cards, make word/picture cards for words with soft or hard **c** or **g.** Choose words whose meanings can be conveyed by pictures, such as **car** or **goat.** Display each card and say the word, stressing the **c** or **g** sound. Have students repeat. Then tell them to sort the cards according to the **c** or **g** sound in each word.

Gifted Learners

Suggest that students write a poem, story, or newspaper article about athletes or the Olympics. Have students use words with soft and hard **c** and **g** to name important people, places, and things. Ask volunteers to share their work with the class.

Learners with Special Needs

Additional strategies for supporting learners with special needs can be found on page 5L.

Practicing the Skill

- Read aloud the direction lines on pages 7–8 and complete the first item in each exercise with students.
- Remind students to use the process of elimination to narrow down their choices in exercises 3–10 on pages 7 and 8.

Curriculum Connections

Spelling Link

- The following words contain hard or soft **c** or **g** sounds. List the words on the board and read them aloud with students:

celery	goggles	record
engine	decide	cougar
canoe	fudge	basic

- Then have students take turns writing one of these words on the board in scrambled form. Invite volunteers to unscramble the word, check its spelling, and circle the letter or letters in it that represent the **c** or **g** sound.

Social Studies Link

- Have students review pages 5, 7–8 to find words that have soft or hard **c** or **g** and that name a place they might read about in a social studies textbook. Turn this exercise into a game by timing students as they list their words.
- Whoever finds the most words matching both criteria in that time period wins. Possible answers include **regions, Africa, Americas, Greece, countries,** and **city.**

Observational Assessment

*Check to see that students correctly distinguish between the soft and hard sounds of the letters **c** and **g.***

Sounds of s

Objectives

- **To recognize the sounds of s**
- **To associate these sounds with the letter s**
- **To sort and write words with different sounds of s**

Warming Up

- Write the following rhyme on the board. Have a student read it aloud, emphasizing each occurrence of **s** (shown in bold type below).

> Game**s** with ball**s** and **s**pecial shoe**s**
> Are great for tho**s**e competing.
> But, **s**urely, there are other**s** who**s**e
> Idea of fun i**s** reading!

- Ask students to identify the words that have an **s**. Underline the words and circle the letter **s** in each. Ask a volunteer to identify words in which the letter **s** is pronounced like the letter **z**. **(games, balls, shoes, those, others, whose, is)** Ask: *Which word contains an s that is pronounced like the letters sh?* **(surely)**

Teaching the Lesson

- Write the words **salt**, **peas**, and **sugar** on the board. Read the words aloud, stressing the **s** in each. Ask how the **s** sounds differ in each word. Explain that **s** can have different sounds: **s** as in **salt**, **z** as in **peas**, and **sh** as in **sugar**.

- Do the following activity with the class: Point to any of the three words written on the board **(salt, peas, or sugar)** and have students suggest words that contain the same sound. Alternate words and list students' suggestions in columns under the words.

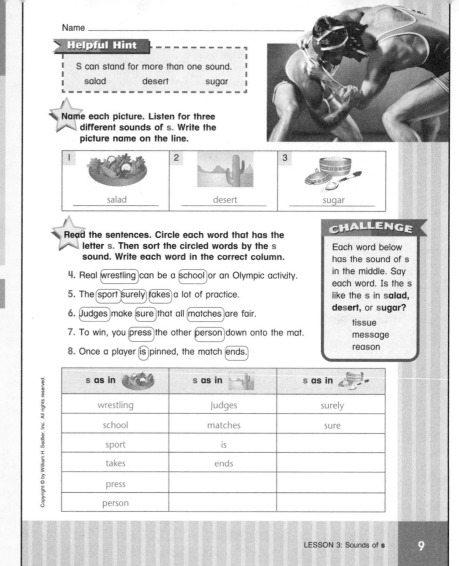

Name _____

> **Helpful Hint**
>
> S can stand for more than one sound.
> salad   desert   sugar

☆ **Name each picture. Listen for three different sounds of s. Write the picture name on the line.**

1	2	3
salad	desert	sugar

☆ **Read the sentences. Circle each word that has the letter s. Then sort the circled words by the s sound. Write each word in the correct column.**

4. Real (wrestling) can be a (school) or an Olympic activity.
5. The (sport) (surely) (takes) a lot of practice.
6. (Judges) make (sure) that all (matches) are fair.
7. To win, you (press) the other (person) down onto the mat.
8. Once a player (is) pinned, the match (ends).

CHALLENGE

Each word below has the sound of s in the middle. Say each word. Is the s like the s in s**a**lad, d**e**sert, or s**u**gar?

tissue
message
reason

s as in 	s as in	s as in
wrestling	Judges	surely
school	matches	sure
sport	is	
takes	ends	
press		
person		

UNIVERSAL ACCESS
Meeting Individual Needs

Auditory Learners

To help students recognize the three different sounds of **s**, write the following rhyme on chart paper and display it in front of the classroom. Have students sing or chant the rhyme as they clap out the rhythm. Encourage them to exaggerate the **s** sounds as they say the words.

> Sugar and spice,
> Daisies and cheese,
> The sounds of **s**
> We say with ease.

Visual Learners

Have students work in pairs. Give each pair a page from a magazine. Direct students to find as many examples as they can of words with the different sounds of **s.** Have students write the words on a sheet of paper, sorting them into three columns as on page 9.

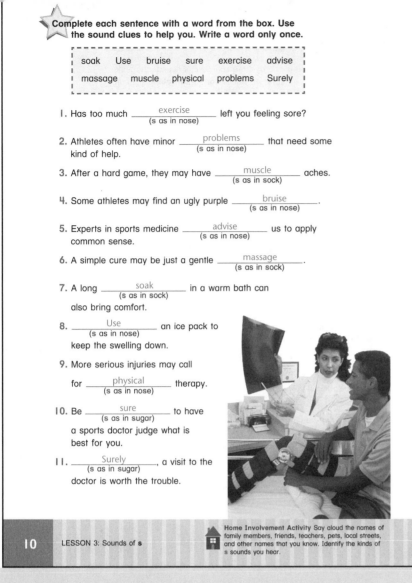

⭐ **Complete each sentence with a word from the box. Use the sound clues to help you. Write a word only once.**

> soak   Use   bruise   sure   exercise   advise
> massage   muscle   physical   problems   Surely

1. Has too much ___exercise___ left you feeling sore?
   (s as in nose)

2. Athletes often have minor ___problems___ that need some kind of help.
   (s as in nose)

3. After a hard game, they may have ___muscle___ aches.
   (s as in sock)

4. Some athletes may find an ugly purple ___bruise___.
   (s as in nose)

5. Experts in sports medicine ___advise___ us to apply common sense.
   (s as in nose)

6. A simple cure may be just a gentle ___massage___.
   (s as in sock)

7. A long ___soak___ in a warm bath can also bring comfort.
   (s as in sock)

8. ___Use___ an ice pack to keep the swelling down.
   (s as in nose)

9. More serious injuries may call for ___physical___ therapy.
   (s as in nose)

10. Be ___sure___ to have a sports doctor judge what is best for you.
    (s as in sugar)

11. ___Surely___, a visit to the doctor is worth the trouble.
    (s as in sugar)

10   LESSON 3: Sounds of s

🏠 **Home Involvement Activity** Say aloud the names of family members, friends, teachers, pets, local streets, and other names that you know. Identify the kinds of s sounds you hear.

English-Language Learners/ESL

Find pictures of items whose names include one of the three different **s** sounds, such as **sugar, soccer, rose, cheese, seven,** and **tissue.** Paste each picture on an index card. Help students identify each item and correctly pronounce the word. Then help them write the word on the card. Finally, have students sort the cards according to their **s** sound.

Gifted Learners

Challenge students to create riddles that can be answered by pairs of rhyming words with **s** sounds. For example: *What animal can be described as a "hose nose"? Answer: an elephant.*

Learners with Special Needs

Additional strategies for supporting learners with special needs can be found on page 5L.

- Read aloud the direction lines on pages 9–10 and complete the first item in each exercise with students.

- Point out that each sentence on page 9 contains more than one word with an **s** sound. Remind students that the **s** sound may appear at the beginning, middle, or end of a word.

- Encourage students to use the sound clues to help them choose the correct words for exercises 1–11 on page 10.

Curriculum Connections

Spelling Link

- Read the following words aloud. For each one, have a volunteer make up a silly sentence. Here is an example for the word **advise:** *I **advise** you not to eat that sneaker!*

bruise	**exercise**	**advise**
massage	**muscle**	**surely**
physical	**problems**	**soak**

- Then have the volunteer spell the word orally and write it on the board.

Literature Link

- Explain that writers often use words with **s** sounds to create a calm or peaceful mood. For example, words such as **soft, whisper,** and **silent** often appear in bedtime stories for children.

- Have students find or suggest examples from stories, poems, or songs in which **s** sounds create a calm or peaceful feeling. Examples include the children's book *Goodnight Moon* and the song "Silent Night."

Observational Assessment

Note whether students pronounce the different s sounds correctly, especially when the sounds occur in the middle or at the end of a word.

Initial **l**-blends and **tw**-blends

Objectives

- **To recognize the sounds of initial l-blends and tw-blends**
- **To associate these sounds with their letters**
- **To read and write words with initial l-blends and tw-blends**

Warming Up

- Write the following poem on the board and have a student read it aloud slowly.

    Twice the batter swung and missed,
    Which made some **pl**ayers **tw**itter.
    But then he **sl**ammed a mighty **bl**ast
    And they yelled, "What a hitter!"

- Have students identify the words that begin with a consonant plus **l**. Underline the words as students say them and circle the **l**-blend.

- Have a volunteer identify the words that begin with a **tw**-blend. He or she should say the words, underline them, and circle the **tw**-blend in each.

Teaching the Lesson

- Write the words **blue, clerk,** and **plum** on the board. Read the words aloud and ask students how they are alike. Explain that each word begins with a blend of a consonant plus the letter **l**.

- Write the words **twice, twin,** and **twelve** on the board. Read them aloud and ask students what letters are common to all three words. (Each word begins with a **tw**-blend.)

- Have volunteers read aloud the Helpful Hints on pages 11 and 12 as others follow along silently.

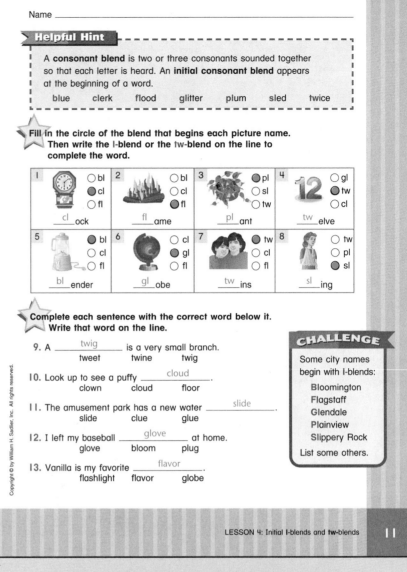

Name _____

Helpful Hint

A **consonant blend** is two or three consonants sounded together so that each letter is heard. An **initial consonant blend** appears at the beginning of a word.

blue   clerk   flood   glitter   plum   sled   twice

Fill in the circle of the blend that begins each picture name. Then write the l-blend or the tw-blend on the line to complete the word.

1. ○ bl ● cl ○ fl — **cl**_ock
2. ○ bl ○ cl ● fl — **fl**_ame
3. ● pl ○ sl ○ tw — **pl**_ant
4. ○ gl ● tw ○ cl — **tw**_elve
5. ● bl ○ cl ○ fl — **bl**_ender
6. ○ cl ● gl ○ fl — **gl**_obe
7. ● tw ○ cl ○ fl — **tw**_ins
8. ○ tw ○ pl ● sl — **sl**_ing

Complete each sentence with the correct word below it. Write that word on the line.

9. A ___twig___ is a very small branch.
    tweet   twine   twig

10. Look up to see a puffy ___cloud___.
    clown   cloud   floor

11. The amusement park has a new water ___slide___.
    slide   clue   glue

12. I left my baseball ___glove___ at home.
    glove   bloom   plug

13. Vanilla is my favorite ___flavor___.
    flashlight   flavor   globe

CHALLENGE

Some city names begin with l-blends:

Bloomington
Flagstaff
Glendale
Plainview
Slippery Rock

List some others.

LESSON 4: Initial l-blends and tw-blends   11

UNIVERSAL ACCESS
Meeting Individual Needs

Visual Learners

Write the blends **cl, fl,** and **sl** on the board. Underneath each blend, have volunteers write a word that combines the blend with the phonogram **ap**. Next, have students write words that combine the same three blends with the phonogram **ip**. Read aloud the finished list, which will look like this:

cl	**fl**	**sl**
clap	flap	slap
clip	flip	slip

Kinesthetic Learners

Write each of the following words on index cards: **cluck, flap, twirl, slide, twist, clap, slim, blow, glue, play, twitch, blink,** and **clown.** Have a volunteer choose a card and try to convey its meaning through body movement, facial expression, and sound effects. The classmate who figures out the word writes it on the board, circles the initial consonant blend, and chooses the next card.

A **phonogram** is a syllable that has a vowel and any letters that follow. Usually, a phonogram has a vowel followed by one or more consonants. Here are some phonograms:

ace   ack   ay   eam   ide   ing   irl   ist   ock

⭐ **Each box has four initial l-blends and four phonograms. Match the blends and the phonograms to form words. Write the words on the lines.**

1	bl	ay		2	cl	ace
	pl	eam			gl	irl
	tw	ack			tw	ock
	gl	ist			pl	ide

black   clock

play   glide

twist   twirl

gleam   place

⭐ **Choose the best word from the two boxes above to complete each sentence. Write the word on the line.**

3. High jumpers can _____ twist _____ their bodies like pretzels to jump over the bar.

4. That baseball team can really _____ play _____ ball.

5. The karate champion has a _____ black _____ belt.

6. Ice skaters _____ glide _____ across the ice.

7. Some ice skaters can spin or _____ twirl _____ so fast that you can barely see their eyes.

8. There were only two minutes left to play on the _____ clock _____ .

9. That basketball player has a _____ gleam _____ in his eye.

10. The winning team will _____ place _____ first in the league.

12   LESSON 4: Initial l-blends and tw-blends

🏠 **Home Involvement Activity** Make some l-blend cards to play a game. Mix the cards and place them face down. Take turns picking a card. Then say words that begin with the blend on the card. Play through the whole deck.

English-Language Learners/ESL

Write each **l**-blend in large letters on a card. Then write the phonograms **ay, ock, ant, ed, ame, at, um,** and **ide** on the board. Hold the blend cards in front of the phonograms one at a time to make words. For each word, say the blend, the phonogram, and then the word they create. Have students repeat each step after you.

Gifted Learners

Challenge students to list as many initial **tw**-blend words as they can. Possible words include **twilight, tweezer, twine,** and **tweet.** Have students choose at least three words from their list to use in an original poem, song, or descriptive paragraph.

Learners with Special Needs

Additional strategies for supporting learners with special needs can be found on page 5L.

● Read aloud the direction lines on pages 11–12 and complete the first item in each exercise with students.

● Encourage students to use the picture clues to help them write the correct words for exercises 1–8 on page 11.

● For exercises 1 and 2 on page 12, point out that students will use each phonogram only once.

Curriculum Connections

Spelling Link

The following words contain initial **l**-blends or **tw**-blends. Read the words aloud. Ask students to write the words on the board and circle their initial consonant blends. Then erase the consonant blends and have volunteers add other **l**- or **tw**-blends to create new words.

glide	**twice**	**clock**
blue	**sling**	**flame**

Social Studies Link

● The first Olympic Games were held in a beautiful stadium built in Olympia, Greece. Later, the ancient Romans held events in the Colosseum in Rome. Today, many sports and other events are held in huge stadiums around the world. There is a soccer stadium in Brazil that can hold 200,000 spectators and one in Czechoslovakia that can hold 240,000.

● Have students write a paragraph about stadiums they have visited or seen on TV. Then ask them to look over their writing and circle examples of words with initial **l**-blends or **tw**-blends.

Observational Assessment

Check to see that students understand how various combinations of initial blends and phonograms form different words.

Student Pages 13–14

r-blends and s-blends

Objectives

- **To recognize the sounds of r-blends and s-blends**
- **To associate these sounds with their letters**
- **To read and write words with initial r-blends and s-blends**

Warming Up

- Write the following poem on the board. Ask a student to read it aloud slowly.

  Around the **tr**ack the runners **sp**ed,

  The **cr**owd's excitement **gr**ew.

  The **sm**iling winner **cr**ossed the line.

  With that, her **dr**eam came **tr**ue.

- Have students identify the words that begin with a consonant and **r**. Underline the words as students say them and circle the **r**-blends. Then have volunteers underline the words that begin with an **s** and a consonant, say each word aloud, and circle the **s**-blends.

★ Teaching the Lesson

- Write the words **trim, grim,** and **brim** on the board and read them aloud. Ask students how the initial consonant blends in the three words are similar. (The second letter in each blend is **r**.) Ask how they are different. (They each begin with a different consonant.)

- Write the words **sly, spy,** and **sky** on the board and read them aloud. Have students compare the initial blends in these words. Point out that the first letter in each blend is **s**. In **s**-blends, the second consonant—not the first—changes from word to word.

- Have a student read aloud both of the Helpful Hints from Lesson 5 as others follow along silently.

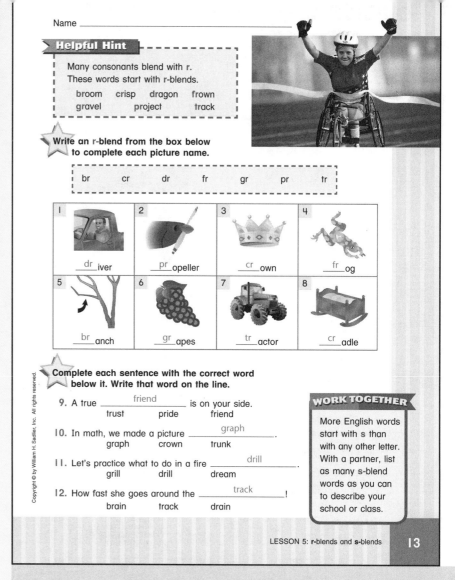

Name _____

Helpful Hint

Many consonants blend with **r**. These words start with r-blends.

| broom | crisp | dragon | frown |
| gravel | | project | track |

★ Write an r-blend from the box below to complete each picture name.

| br | cr | dr | fr | gr | pr | tr |

1. **dr**_iver
2. **pr**_opeller
3. **cr**_own
4. **fr**_og
5. **br**_anch
6. **gr**_apes
7. **tr**_actor
8. **cr**_adle

★ Complete each sentence with the correct word below it. Write that word on the line.

9. A true ___friend___ is on your side.
   trust   pride   friend

10. In math, we made a picture ___graph___.
    graph   crown   trunk

11. Let's practice what to do in a fire ___drill___.
    grill   drill   dream

12. How fast she goes around the ___track___!
    brain   track   drain

WORK TOGETHER

More English words start with s than with any other letter. With a partner, list as many s-blend words as you can to describe your school or class.

LESSON 5: r-blends and s-blends   **13**

UNIVERSAL ACCESS
Meeting Individual Needs

Auditory Learners

Challenge students to create tongue twisters using words with the same initial **r**-blends, such as "**Br**enda **br**ought **br**own **br**ushes." Have students write their tongue twisters on the board and say them rapidly five times. Repeat the activity with **s**-blends, as in "**St**an **st**ood **st**ill, **st**aring at **St**eve."

Musical Learners

Ask students to find examples of words with initial **r**-blends and **s**-blends in the lyrics of songs they know. Compile a class list and discuss which letter combinations and which words are most common in song lyrics. You may wish to have CD jackets or songbooks available for students to use as reference.

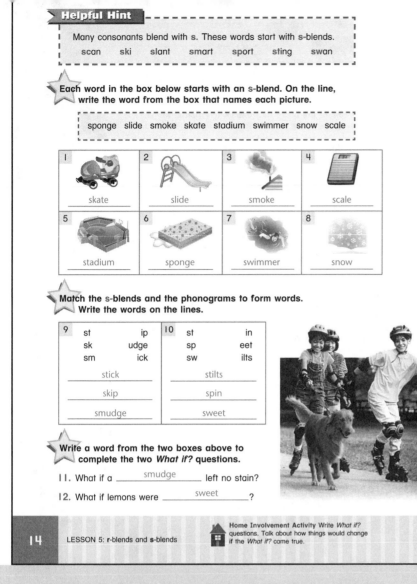

Each word in the box below starts with an s-blend. On the line, write the word from the box that names each picture.

sponge   slide   smoke   skate   stadium   swimmer   snow   scale

1	2	3	4
skate	slide	smoke	scale

5	6	7	8
stadium	sponge	swimmer	snow

Match the s-blends and the phonograms to form words. Write the words on the lines.

9		10	
st	ip	st	in
sk	udge	sp	eet
sm	ick	sw	ilts

stick   stilts

skip   spin

smudge   sweet

Write a word from the two boxes above to complete the two *What if?* questions.

11. What if a _____smudge_____ left no stain?

12. What if lemons were _____sweet_____ ?

14   LESSON 5: r-blends and s-blends

🏠 **Home Involvement Activity** Write *What if?* questions. Talk about how things would change if the *What if?* came true.

Practicing the Skill

- Read aloud the direction lines on pages 13 and 14. Then have students complete the exercises on their own.

- For items 11 and 12 on page 14, explain that students should use context—the surrounding words—to figure out the answers.

Curriculum Connections

Spelling Link

The following pairs of words contain initial **r**-blends and **s**-blends. Read the word pairs aloud. Have students spell both words in each pair and use the words together in an oral sentence.

broom	and	**sponge**
gravel	and	**slide**
crisp	and	**snow**
dragon	and	**smoke**
frown	and	**skate**

Social Studies Link

Many countries have names that begin with **r**-blends and **s**-blends. Using a map of the world, have students identify these blends in the names of as many countries as they can. Possible answers include **France, Greece, Great Britain, Spain, Sweden, Brazil, Scotland, Switzerland,** and **Swaziland.**

Observational Assessment

*Check to make sure students understand that the changing consonant comes before the **r** in **r**-blends (and before the **l** in **l**-blends) but after the **s** in the **s**-blends.*

English-Language Learners/ESL

Write the words **skate, skateboard, stickball, ski, swim, sled,** and **snorkel** on the board. Act out the sports one at a time. Have students take turns circling the word that names the sport, underlining the consonants in the **s**-blend, and reading the word aloud.

Gifted Learners

Have students write a cheer for their favorite team or their favorite activity. Challenge them to use at least three or four words with initial **r**-blends or initial **s**-blends in their cheers.

Learners with Special Needs

Additional strategies for supporting learners with special needs can be found on page 5L.

14

Final Blends and Syllables with Blends

Objectives

- To recognize final consonant blends

- To recognize and write one-, two-, and three-syllable words with consonant blends

Warming Up

- Write the following paragraph on the board. Have a student read it aloud.

   Wilma Rudolph had tremendous **talent**. As a **young** girl, she was often **sick.** But it did not **prevent** her from becoming a great runner. At the 1960 Olympics, she won three **gold** medals!

- Have students identify the words that end with consonant blends (shown in bold type). Underline the words as students say them and circle the final consonant blends.

- Ask a volunteer to identify the underlined words that have more than one syllable. (pre/ve**nt**, tal/e**nt**) Can students find a word in the paragraph that has three syllables and two consonant blends? (**tr**e/me**n**/**d**ous)

Teaching the Lesson

- Write the words **damp, lend, wink,** and **task** on the board. Read the words aloud and ask students how they are alike. Students may say that all the words have four letters or that they have the same pattern of letters (consonant-vowel-consonant-consonant). Point out that the words all end in a consonant blend. Ask a volunteer to circle the blends.

- Have a student read aloud the Helpful Hints on pages 15 and 16 for the class.

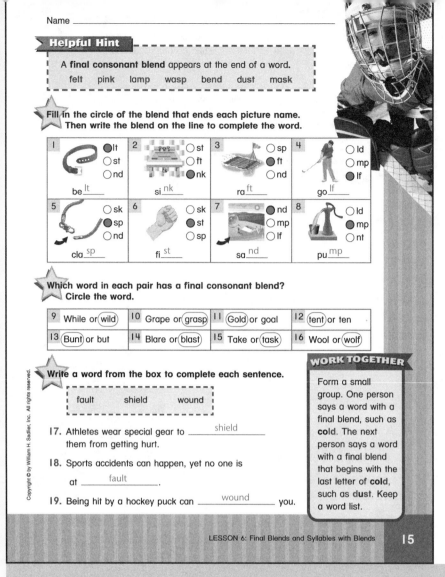

Name _____

Helpful Hint

A **final consonant blend** appears at the end of a word.
felt   pink   lamp   wasp   bend   dust   mask

Fill in the circle of the blend that ends each picture name. Then write the blend on the line to complete the word.

1. ● lt ○ st ○ nd — be **lt**
2. ○ st ○ ft ● nk — si **nk**
3. ○ sp ● ft ○ nd — ra **ft**
4. ○ ld ○ mp ● lf — go **lf**
5. ○ sk ● sp ○ nd — cla **sp**
6. ○ sk ● st ○ sp — fi **st**
7. ● nd ○ mp ○ lf — sa **nd**
8. ○ ld ● mp ○ nt — pu **mp**

Which word in each pair has a final consonant blend? Circle the word.

9. While or (wild)
10. Grape or (grasp)
11. (Gold) or goal
12. (tent) or ten
13. (Bunt) or but
14. Blare or (blast)
15. Take or (task)
16. Wool or (wolf)

Write a word from the box to complete each sentence.

fault   shield   wound

17. Athletes wear special gear to ____**shield**____ them from getting hurt.

18. Sports accidents can happen, yet no one is at ____**fault**____.

19. Being hit by a hockey puck can ____**wound**____ you.

WORK TOGETHER

Form a small group. One person says a word with a final blend, such as **col**d. The next person says a word with a final blend that begins with the last letter of col**d**, such as **d**ust. Keep a word list.

LESSON 6: Final Blends and Syllables with Blends   15

UNIVERSAL ACCESS
Meeting Individual Needs

Kinesthetic Learners

Write the words **sand, gasp, belt, sink, cold, pump, hunt, bank, mask,** and **limp** each on a card. Volunteers choose a card, write the consonant blend in the word on the board, and act out the word for the class. Whoever guesses the correct word writes another final-blend word on a card, adds it to the deck, and becomes the next player.

Visual Learners

Have students list words that have one of the consonant blends found on pages 15–16. The blend can be anywhere within the word, and the word can have more than one syllable. Tell students to list the words so that the letters in the blend line up, as in the example shown below:

stadium

mi**st**ake

fa**st**

A **syllable** is any of the parts into which a word may be divided at the end of a line. Many words with **consonant blends** have more than one syllable.

play-er   pri-va-cy   snow-board

⭐ Say each word in the box. Sort the words by how many syllables they have. Write each word in the correct column.

grasp	drama	sneaker	sport	statistics
dart	creative	flag	president	platform
mound	probably	request	trainer	uniform

1	2	3
One Syllable	**Two Syllables**	**Three Syllables**
grasp	drama	statistics
class	sneaker	creative
sport	frequent	president
dart	platform	probably
flag	request	uniform

⭐ Each team below has one consonant blend. Circle each one-syllable name. Draw one line under each two-syllable name. Draw two lines under the three-syllable names.

4. (Clippers)   5. Blues   6. (Sliders)
7. Predators   8. (Stingrays)   9. Twins
10. Colts   11. (Dragons)   12. Yellowhawks

16   LESSON 6: Final Blends and Syllables with Blends

🏠 **Home Involvement Activity** Work together to list words that rhyme with these words: **bend, camp, tent, gold, mist, pink, task.** Try to find at least two rhymes for each word.

Practicing the Skill

● Review with students the definition of a consonant blend (see page 11).

● Read aloud the direction lines on pages 15 and 16. Complete the first item in each exercise with students.

 Turn to page 5K for an Intervention Strategy designed to help students who need extra support with this lesson.

Curriculum Connections

Spelling Link

Read the following words aloud and have students write them. Then ask volunteers to choose a word, spell it, and identify the consonant blends.

felt	sport	frequent
raft	grasp	president
lamp	golf	platform

Math Link

Invite students to write simple equations using words to represent numbers. The number each word represents should be the number of syllables it has. The word **flag,** for example, would stand for a 1. Here is a sample equation: **grasp + drama = 3.** The number of syllables in **grasp** (1) + the number of syllables in **drama** (2) = 3. Another example is **consonant – blend = 2.** See whether students can solve one another's "syllable-math" problems.

Observational Assessment

*Check that students pronounce each letter in a final consonant blend, especially when saying words ending in **d** or **t**, such as **cold, stand, dust,** and **tent.***

English-Language Learners/ESL

On the board, write **felt, pink, lamp, bend, dust,** and **mask.** Say the words and have students repeat after you. Ask students to change the first letter of each word to create new words. Volunteers can write the new words on the board underneath the original words. Answers include **belt, melt; wink, sink; damp, ramp; lend, send; gust, rust;** and **task.**

Gifted Learners

Challenge students to expand the chart on page 16 by adding words with four or more syllables. You may wish to suggest the words **transportation** and **stegosaurus** to get students started. Urge them to use a dictionary for reference.

Learners with Special Needs

Additional strategies for supporting learners with special needs can be found on page 5L.

Connecting Reading and Writing

Objectives

- **To read a nonfiction piece and respond to it in writing**
- **To practice comparing, contrasting, and synthesizing information**
- **To write a list of rules for playing a sport or a game**

Warming Up

Comprehension Skills

- Ask students to name two sports or games to **compare** and **contrast**. Ask: *In what ways are these two sports or games alike? In what ways are they different?*

- Explain that **synthesizing** is a reading skill. When you synthesize, you put together the ideas within a piece of writing and make sense of them.

Teaching the Lesson

- Suggest that students make a compare/ contrast chart or a Venn diagram to help them answer the first two Reader's Response questions. You might create such a chart on the board and work on it with students.

- For the third question, remind students to give specific reasons for their choice of which type of volleyball they would prefer to play.

Practicing the Skill

- Read the directions on page 18 together. Choose a familiar game and discuss the exercise with students before they begin working independently.

- Ask students why it might be important to list rules in an order that makes sense.

Name _____

Read about a new Olympic sport. Then answer the questions that follow.

Beach Volleyball
by Martin Lee and Marcia Miller

At the 1992 Summer Olympics, a new event was introduced. Fans flocked to see the exciting game of beach volleyball. Beach volleyball is—you got it—volleyball played outdoors on sand.

Beach volleyball began on the beaches of California about 75 years ago. Yet the first tournament wasn't held until 1948. The winners got a case of soda. Now the game is a professional sport. Today's winners get big prize money. In the 1996 Olympics, 24 men's teams and 16 women's teams played for their countries. The U.S. men's and women's teams won gold medals.

The rules for playing beach volleyball are much like those for playing the indoor game. The court is about the same size. It is a flat rectangle 59 feet long and 29 1/2 feet wide. The big difference is in the surface. The sand for beach volleyball must be at least 12 inches deep.

Beach volleyball teams may have two, three, four, or six players. Unlike indoor players, beach volleyball team members can wear clothing with different colors and designs. They can wear sunglasses, hats, or visors. They can even play barefoot.

Beach volleyball takes a lot of energy. Yet players can tumble without getting scraped. Sand softens every fall. If you enjoy playing in the sun, beach volleyball may be your sport.

1. Both are professional sports with big prize money; both are Olympic events; the rules are similar.
2. Beach volleyball is played on sand; there are differences in the number of players and the clothing worn.
3. Answers will vary.

Reader's Response

1. How is beach volleyball like volleyball played indoors?
2. How are the two games different?
3. Which type of volleyball would you rather play? Why?

LESSON 7: Connecting Reading and Writing
Comprehension—Compare and Contrast;
Synthesize

17

UNIVERSAL ACCESS
Meeting Individual Needs

Kinesthetic Learners

Have students form small groups and choose a sport or game. The group identifies the rules and writes them down. One student reads the rules aloud while the others act them out. Ask students to decide if the group's rules are in the correct order.

Learners with Special Needs

Additional strategies for supporting learners with special needs can be found on page 5L.

Visual Learners

Show photographs or illustrations of a sport or a game. Have pairs of students choose a photograph or illustration and brainstorm rules for the sport or game shown. Students might check to make sure they have listed all the game's rules by creating a small cartoon strip that shows each rule in the correct order.

Every sport has its rules. Choose a sport or a game that you enjoy. What is the object of the game? Think about its rules. For example, how many players are needed? What does each player do? How does the game begin? How do you keep score?

⭐ **Make a list of rules for playing the sport you choose. Use at least two of these words to help you write your list of rules.**

block	contest	first	second	last	point
swing	protect	score	sport	twice	triumph

Answers will vary but should include a list of rules written in the order in which the sport is played.

Writer's Tips
Jot down the name of the sport at the top of your list. Write the rules in an order that makes sense.

Writer's Challenge
Use the sport you wrote about or another sport you like. Imagine playing it in a totally different way. For example, how would you play soccer on ice? How would you play softball with a beach ball? Write a list of rules for this new game. Have fun!

18   LESSON 7: Connecting Reading and Writing
Comprehension—Compare and Contrast; Synthesize

The Writing Process

Discuss the purpose of rules in sports and games (to make sure that everyone is playing the same way). Then read aloud the directions at the top of page 18.

Prewrite Have students begin by choosing a sport or game. Suggest that they visualize playing it, look at photographs, act it out, draw cartoon panels—whatever will help them recall how the sport or game is played.

Write Remind students that the list of rules should be clear and easy to follow.

Revise Have students read their rules aloud to a partner. Invite the partner to pretend he or she does not know how to play the game. Encourage the partner to identify places where the rules are not clear.

Proofread Have students read their work slowly and carefully to check for errors in grammar, punctuation, and spelling.

Publish Have students copy their final drafts onto page 18 or a separate sheet of paper. Invite students to read their rules aloud for their classmates.

 **Computer Connection** Suggest that students who write on word processors explore ways of creating bulleted and numbered lists. In some programs, they are created automatically as soon as you indent in a certain way. In other programs, you must highlight the copy you would like bulleted or numbered. Then click on the "bulleted-list" or "numbered-list" icon located on the Toolbar.

Portfolio Have students add their lists of rules about a sport or a game to their portfolios.

English-Language Learners/ESL
Display pictures that show different types of athletes engaged in playing sports or games. Have English-language learners work with fluent speakers to build vocabulary while talking about the pictures or about other subjects related to the theme *Athletes*.

Gifted Learners
Encourage students to create a new kind of volleyball, to be played in a completely different environment—in outer space, on a planet with its own gravity and atmosphere, undersea, or in some other place. Have students explain this new game by writing a list of rules, a play-by-play description of the game, a short story about it, or by creating a comic strip about it. Have students provide an illustration of the game being played. Ask volunteers to share their work with the class.

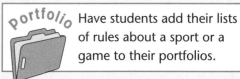

Reviewing and Assessing
Consonant Blends

Objective

To review and assess consonant blends

Warming Up

- List these words on the board: **globe, basic, twig, goal, crow, skate, takes, magic, wink, sure, his, cereal.**

- Say the following clues aloud. Have volunteers identify the word or words that match each clue and circle the letter or letters.

soft **c**	hard **c**
soft **g**	hard **g**
s sound as in **salad**	initial **s**-blend
s sound as in **desert**	initial **tw**-blend
s sound as in **sugar**	initial **l**-blend
final consonant blend	initial **r**-blend

Teaching the Lesson

- Review with students when the letters **c** and **g** have a soft sound. (usually when followed by **e, i,** or **y**) Ask volunteers for examples of hard and soft **c** and **g** words.

- Review the different sounds of **s** and elicit examples of each.

- Have volunteers explain what a consonant blend is and give examples of both initial and final consonant blends. Remind students that a consonant blend may consist of either two or three consonants.

- Ask students to suggest words with a variety of consonant blends. Have students write the words on the board and use them in sentences. Encourage students to include words with more than one syllable.

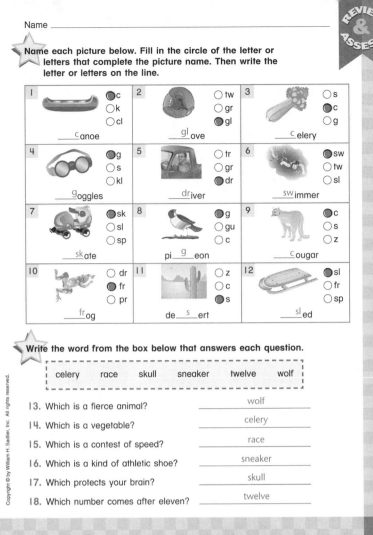

Name each picture below. Fill in the circle of the letter or letters that complete the picture name. Then write the letter or letters on the line.

1. ● c ○ k ○ cl — __c__anoe
2. ○ tw ○ gr ● gl — __gl__ove
3. ○ s ● c ○ g — __c__elery
4. ● g ○ s ○ kl — __g__oggles
5. ○ tr ○ gr ● dr — __dr__iver
6. ● sw ○ tw ○ sl — __sw__immer
7. ● sk ○ sl ○ sp — __sk__ate
8. ● g ○ gu ○ c — pi__g__eon
9. ● c ○ s ○ z — __c__ougar
10. ○ dr ● fr ○ pr — __fr__og
11. ○ z ○ c ● s — de__s__ert
12. ● sl ○ fr ○ sp — __sl__ed

Write the word from the box below that answers each question.

| celery | race | skull | sneaker | twelve | wolf |

13. Which is a fierce animal? __wolf__
14. Which is a vegetable? __celery__
15. Which is a contest of speed? __race__
16. Which is a kind of athletic shoe? __sneaker__
17. Which protects your brain? __skull__
18. Which number comes after eleven? __twelve__

LESSON 8: Review and Assess 19

UNIVERSAL ACCESS
Meeting Individual Needs

Musical Learners

Ask pairs of students to write several lines of a song on a sheet of paper. Have them identify words that contain initial or final consonant blends, underlining initial blends once and final blends twice. Then have students sort the words by blend. Extend the activity by asking the class to compile a master list of sorted words.

Learners with Special Needs

Additional strategies for supporting students with special needs can be found on page 5L.

Kinesthetic Learners

Write the words below on the board. Read each one aloud. After you read the word, have students do one of the following: clap if the word contains an **r**-blend; stamp their feet if it contains an **s**-blend; raise one arm if it contains an **l**-blend; raise two arms if it contains a **tw**-blend.

blame	smoke
mask	twin
flavor	dream
graph	fast
spill	twelve

Fill in the circle of the word that completes each sentence. Then write the word on the line.

1. People who like to fish enjoy the ___pleasure___ of waiting.
   ○ trance ● pleasure ○ price

2. They can ___spend___ hours waiting for a fish to bite.
   ○ blend ○ train ● spend

3. Yet fishing is not just a warm weather ___sport___.
   ○ spirit ● sport ○ sponge

4. Even on frozen lakes, some people have a ___clever___ way to fish.
   ● clever ○ craft ○ cleaner

5. They use tools to ___drill___ holes in the solid ice covering the water.
   ○ twirl ○ grill ● drill

6. They ___drop___ fishing lines down the holes into the cold water.
   ● drop ○ draw ○ drip

7. Ice fishing calls for ___great___ patience.
   ○ gravy ○ green ● great

8. It also requires ice fishers to ___dress___ warmly.
   ● dress ○ dream ○ press

9. Some ice fishers build ___small___ huts over their fishing holes.
   ○ spell ● small ○ still

10. This allows them to ___stay___ warm and dry.
    ○ stand ○ sway ● stay

Extend & Apply — Possible answers are given.

Think of a sports word that fits each clue. Write the word on the line.

11. It begins with a blend. ___sled___
12. It has an s-blend. ___skate___
13. It has a hard g sound. ___game___
14. It has one syllable. ___pool___
15. It ends with a blend. ___golf___
16. It has an r-blend. ___sport___
17. It has a soft c sound. ___racing___
18. It has two syllables. ___baseball___

20 LESSON 8: Review and Assess

Reteaching Activities

Match-Up

List the word parts below on the board. Have students make words by combining initial blends with different phonograms. Encourage students to use a dictionary to check their work.

Initial blend	Phonogram
sp	in
st	ay
tw	ack
bl	eam
pl	ing
dr	ace
sl	ice

Rhyme Time

Write the words below on the board. Underline the final consonant blends. Below each word, have students list rhyming words that have the same final blend.

belt   wink   fast
send   bold   dump

Assessing the Skill

Check Up Read aloud the directions for the exercises on page 19. Then have students complete the page.

Page 20 will help you assess students' ability to identify appropriate consonant-blend words for particular contexts. Make sure students understand the directions. Then have them complete the page.

Observational Assessment As students complete the exercises, try to identify specific areas in which they may benefit from additional instruction. Review and compare your observational notes from previous lessons in the unit. Evaluate both individual student improvement and overall class progress.

Student Skills Assessment Keep track of each student's progress in understanding consonant blends using the checklist on page 5H.

Writing Conference Meet with students individually to discuss written work they have completed in this unit, such as their list of rules on page 18. Ask students to show you a favorite piece of writing from their Home Portfolios as well. Have students look through their own written work for words with initial or final consonant blends, words with soft or hard **c** or **g** sounds, and words that have one of the three sounds of **s**. Make sure all words are correctly spelled.

Group together students who need further instruction in consonant blends and have them complete the *Reteaching Activities*. Turn to page 5C for alternative assessment methods.

Consonant Digraphs

Objectives

- **To associate the sounds of consonant digraphs with their letters**
- **To recognize and write words with initial and final consonant digraphs**

Warming Up

- Write the following rhyme on the board:

  Chu**ck** was playing basketball
  And aimed before he **sh**ot,
  But missed the basket after all
  For lu**ck** was with him not!

- Ask students to identify words in which two consonants stand for one sound. Point out that **Chuck** and **shot** begin with two consonants that make one sound. Then draw students' attention to the **ck** at the end of **Chuck** and **luck**. Finally, underline the words **Chuck, shot,** and **luck** and circle their initial and final digraphs.

Teaching the Lesson

- Have a volunteer read aloud the Helpful Hints on pages 21–22.
- Make sure students understand the difference between consonant blends and consonant digraphs. Explain that the sound of each letter in a consonant blend is heard, whereas the letters that make up a consonant digraph stand for one sound. Have students say the words **flow** (blend) and **thaw** (digraph) aloud.
- Say the words **chalk, chef,** and **chaos,** emphasizing the three different sounds of **ch.**

21

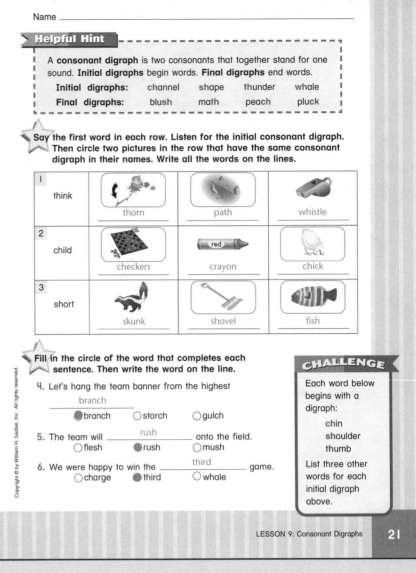

Name _____

> **Helpful Hint**

A **consonant digraph** is two consonants that together stand for one sound. **Initial digraphs** begin words. **Final digraphs** end words.

| Initial digraphs: | channel | shape | thunder | whale |
| Final digraphs: | blush | math | peach | pluck |

Say the first word in each row. Listen for the initial consonant digraph. Then circle two pictures in the row that have the same consonant digraph in their names. Write all the words on the lines.

1	think	thorn	path	whistle
2	child	checkers	crayon	chick
3	short	skunk	shovel	fish

Fill in the circle of the word that completes each sentence. Then write the word on the line.

4. Let's hang the team banner from the highest _____
   branch
   ● branch   ○ starch   ○ gulch

5. The team will _____ rush _____ onto the field.
   ○ flesh   ● rush   ○ mush

6. We were happy to win the _____ third _____ game.
   ○ charge   ● third   ○ whale

> **CHALLENGE**

Each word below begins with a digraph:

   chin
   shoulder
   thumb

List three other words for each initial digraph above.

UNIVERSAL ACCESS
Meeting Individual Needs

Visual Learners

Draw the chart below on the board. Have students form words that begin with the initial digraphs and the vowels listed. Students may wish to look for words in books or magazines.

Digraph	Vowel	Word
ch	a	
ch	i	
sh	o	
th	e	
th	i	
wh	e	
wh	i	

Tactile Learners

Using magnetic letters or letter tiles, have students work in pairs to spell words with initial and final consonant digraphs. Challenge them to include words that have the sounds of **ch** found in **chauffeur** and **chemical.**

21

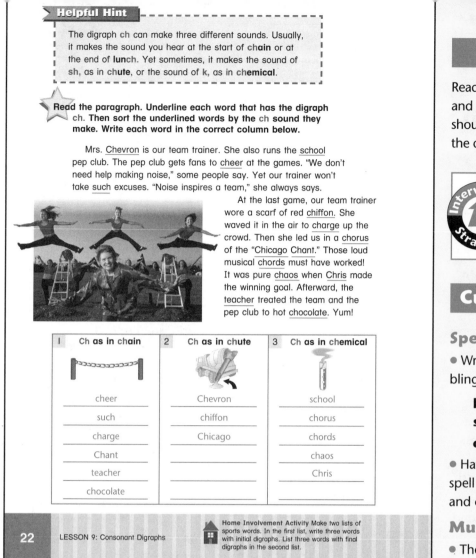

Helpful Hint

The digraph **ch** can make three different sounds. Usually, it makes the sound you hear at the start of **ch**ain or at the end of lun**ch**. Yet sometimes, it makes the sound of **sh**, as in **ch**ute, or the sound of **k**, as in **ch**emical.

⭐ **Read the paragraph. Underline each word that has the digraph ch. Then sort the underlined words by the ch sound they make. Write each word in the correct column below.**

Mrs. Chevron is our team trainer. She also runs the school pep club. The pep club gets fans to cheer at the games. "We don't need help making noise," some people say. Yet our trainer won't take such excuses. "Noise inspires a team," she always says.

At the last game, our team trainer wore a scarf of red chiffon. She waved it in the air to charge up the crowd. Then she led us in a chorus of the "Chicago Chant." Those loud musical chords must have worked! It was pure chaos when Chris made the winning goal. Afterward, the teacher treated the team and the pep club to hot chocolate. Yum!

1 Ch as in chain	2 Ch as in chute	3 Ch as in chemical
cheer	Chevron	school
such	chiffon	chorus
charge	Chicago	chords
Chant		chaos
teacher		Chris
chocolate		

 Home Involvement Activity Make two lists of sports words. In the first list, write three words with initial digraphs. List three words with final digraphs in the second list.

English-Language Learners/ESL

Write these words on the board: **whale, chick, school, peach, fish, moth, sheep,** and **wheel.** Show students a picture of each item, pointing to its name on the board and saying it. Have students repeat after you. Then have them make labeled picture cards for each word. Ask them to read their cards aloud.

Gifted Learners

Ask students to make up riddles for words with digraphs, such as *What ends with **th,** and gets you clean?* (*a **bath***) Have students write their riddles on cards and share them with their classmates.

Learners with Special Needs

Additional strategies for supporting learners with special needs can be found on page 5L.

Practicing the Skill

Read aloud the direction lines on pages 21 and 22. Tell students that on page 22 they should find a total of 14 words containing the digraph **ch.**

Intervention Strategy

Turn to page 5K for an Intervention Strategy designed to help students who need extra support with this lesson.

Curriculum Connections

Spelling Link

● Write these words on the board, scrambling the letters.

path	**whistle**	**chick**
shovel	**fish**	**branch**
chorus	**such**	**rush**

● Have students unscramble the words, spell them orally, write them on the board, and circle each consonant digraph.

Multicultural Connection

● The great Brazilian soccer player Pelé helped his nation's team win the World Cup in 1958 (when he was just 17) and again in 1962 and 1970. Later he played professional soccer in the United States. Pelé is credited with making soccer popular in this country.

● Have students write a paragraph about an athlete they admire. Ask them to circle all the consonant digraphs they find in the paragraph.

Observational Assessment

*Check to see that students understand the difference between a consonant digraph and a consonant blend and that they can distinguish between the three sounds of the digraph **ch.***

Medial Consonant Digraphs; **ph** and **gh**

Objectives

- **To recognize and write words with medial consonant digraphs**

- **To associate the sounds of consonant digraphs ph and gh with their letters**

- **To recognize and write words with consonant digraphs ph and gh**

Warming Up

- Write this paragraph on the board:

  My bro**th**er wanted to try some**th**ing new. He wanted to para**ch**ute from a plane. But my sister Ra**ch**el told him not to be a knu**ck**lehead. She said, "Leave flying to our fea**th**ered friends!"

- Review the fact that a consonant digraph is two consonants that stand for one sound. Explain that digraphs can appear at the beginning, middle, or end of words.

- Ask a volunteer to read aloud the paragraph on the board. Have students underline the words that have digraphs, say the words, and circle the digraphs.

Teaching the Lesson

- Ask a student to read the Helpful Hint on page 23 and identify the digraph in each word. Then have students suggest other words containing the same digraphs.

- Have a student read aloud the Helpful Hint on page 24. Have students say the words **phrase** and **cough** aloud, listening for the **f** sounds. Provide other examples of words that have the digraphs **ph** and **gh**, such as **orphan** and **enough**.

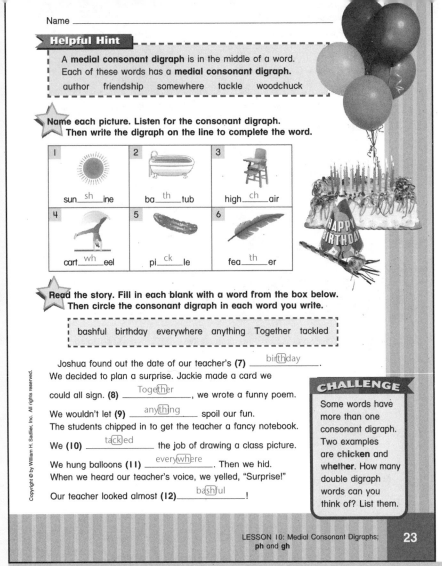

Name _____

Helpful Hint

A **medial consonant digraph** is in the middle of a word. Each of these words has a **medial consonant digraph**.

author   friendship   somewhere   tackle   woodchuck

Name each picture. Listen for the consonant digraph. Then write the digraph on the line to complete the word.

1	2	3
sun__sh__ine	ba__th__tub	high__ch__air
4	**5**	**6**
cart__wh__eel	pi__ck__le	fea__th__er

Read the story. Fill in each blank with a word from the box below. Then circle the consonant digraph in each word you write.

> bashful   birthday   everywhere   anything   Together   tackled

Joshua found out the date of our teacher's (7) __bir(th)day__.
We decided to plan a surprise. Jackie made a card we could all sign. (8) __Toge(th)er__, we wrote a funny poem.
We wouldn't let (9) __any(th)ing__ spoil our fun.
The students chipped in to get the teacher a fancy notebook.
We (10) __ta(ck)led__ the job of drawing a class picture.
We hung balloons (11) __every(wh)ere__. Then we hid.
When we heard our teacher's voice, we yelled, "Surprise!"
Our teacher looked almost (12)__ba(sh)ful__!

CHALLENGE

Some words have more than one consonant digraph. Two examples are **chicken** and **whether**. How many double digraph words can you think of? List them.

LESSON 10: Medial Consonant Digraphs;
ph and gh

23

U N I V E R S A L   A C C E S S
Meeting Individual Needs

Visual Learners

Write the following on the board, leaving two blank spaces in place of each digraph:

> ni_ _el
>
> pit_ _er
>
> friend_ _ip
>
> some_ _ing
>
> al_ _abet
>
> lau_ _
>
> every_ _ere

Have students complete the words by writing the correct digraph in each set of blanks.

Logical Learners

Write these words on the board: **weather, graph, pickle, anchor, wheel, cough, selfish, chief,** and **thimble.** Have students copy these words onto cards and circle the consonant digraphs. Then ask students to sort the cards according to whether the digraph in each word is **initial, medial,** or **final.**

Helpful Hint

The **consonant digraphs** ph and gh can stand for the same sound. In p**h**oto and lau**gh**, the consonant digraphs both make the sound of f.

⭐ Each word in the box has the consonant digraph **ph** or **gh**. Write the word on the line that best completes each sentence.

> alphabet   dolphin   laugh   Phoenix   rough   triumph   trophy

1. A funny joke can cause you to _____laugh_____ out loud.

2. The winner of the contest will get a silver _____trophy_____.

3. The _____dolphin_____ is a mammal that lives in the sea.

4. The opposite of *smooth* is _____rough_____.

5. Another word for *victory* or *success* is _____triumph_____.

6. The _____alphabet_____ is another name for the ABCs.

7. The capital of Arizona is _____Phoenix_____.

⭐ Say each word. Listen for the consonant digraph. Then sort the words according to where the consonant digraph appears in the word: at the beginning, in the middle, or at the end.

> bench   leather   theater   footpath   shovel   paragraph
> physical   cashier   tickle   telephone   whimper   attach

8 Initial Digraph	9 Medial Digraph	10 Final Digraph
theater	leather	bench
shovel	cashier	footpath
physical	tickle	paragraph
whimper	telephone	attach

Home Involvement Activity Brainstorm a list of names of people that have consonant digraphs. The digraphs can be at the beginning, as in **Sharon**, at the end, as in **Joseph**, or in the middle, as in **Rachel**.

24   LESSON 10: Medial Consonant Digraphs; ph and gh

Practicing the Skill

● Read aloud the direction lines on pages 23 and 24. Complete the first item in each exercise with students.

● Point out that for exercises 7–12 on page 23 and exercises 1–7 on page 24, students will need to consider the context in order to complete the sentence correctly.

 Intervention Strategy Turn to page 5K for an Intervention Strategy designed to help students who need extra support with this lesson.

Curriculum Connections

Spelling Link

The following pairs of words contain initial, medial, or final digraphs. Read each pair of words aloud. Then have volunteers repeat the two words, spell each one, and use the pair together in a sentence.

birthday	and	**telephone**
tickle	and	**laugh**
tackled	and	**together**
triumph	and	**trophy**
physical	and	**anything**

Science Link

Many words relating to science and medicine begin with the digraph **ph**, such as **physician** and **pharmacy.** Have students use a dictionary or an encyclopedia to find similar words having to do with science or medicine that contain the digraph **ph.** Ask volunteers to share their findings with the class.

Observational Assessment

*Check that students correctly pronounce words containing medial **ph** and **gh** digraphs, such as **dolphin, trophy, laugh,** and **rough.***

English-Language Learners/ESL

Display items whose names contain digraphs, such as a **feather,** a **dishcloth,** a **pickle,** a **phone,** a **pitcher,** a **trophy,** or a **mushroom.** Write each item's name on a label. Pick up each object, say its name, and have students identify and attach the correct label.

Gifted Learners

Ask students to find examples of proper nouns that contain digraphs. Make the activity a contest by giving 1 point for proper nouns containing initial or final digraphs (**Phoenix**), 2 points for proper nouns with medial digraphs (**Richard**), and 5 points for proper nouns containing more than one digraph (**Shoshone**).

Learners with Special Needs

Additional strategies for supporting learners with special needs can be found on page 5L.

Three-letter Blends

Objectives

- **To recognize the sounds of three-letter blends**
- **To associate the sound of each three-letter blend with its letters**
- **To read and write words with three-letter blends**

Warming Up

- Write the following poem on the board, and have a student read it aloud slowly.

  I got there right on **schedule**

  And **scrambled** to my seat.

  A **splendid** day for baseball,

  A **thrill** that can't be beat!

- Have students identify the words that begin with a combination of three consonants (shown in boldface type above). Underline the words as students say them, and circle the consonant blends in each one.

Teaching the Lesson

- Explain that a consonant blend can be made up of three letters. In the blends that begin the words **scrambled** and **splendid,** all three letter sounds can be heard. On the other hand, in the blends that begin the words **schedule** and **thrill,** only two sounds can be heard. These blends are made up of a consonant digraph (which stands for one sound) and a letter. In **schedule,** the **s** sound blends with the sound of the digraph **ch;** in **thrill,** the sound of the digraph **th** blends with the **r** sound.

- Have a volunteer read aloud the Helpful Hint on page 25. Ask volunteers to suggest words that begin with the consonant blends shown. Write the words on the board, and circle the three-letter blends.

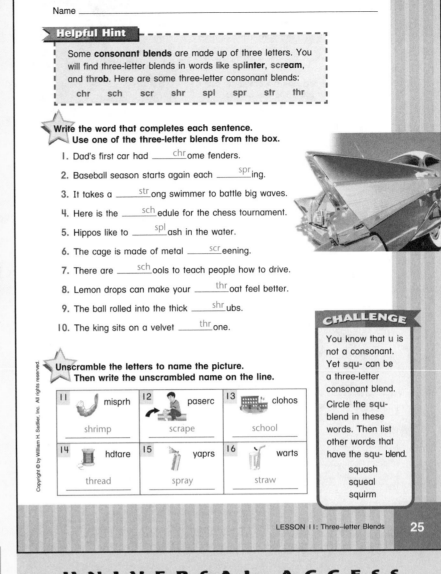

Name _____

Helpful Hint

Some **consonant blends** are made up of three letters. You will find three-letter blends in words like **spl**inter, **scr**eam, and **thr**ob. Here are some three-letter consonant blends:

chr   sch   scr   shr   spl   spr   str   thr

Write the word that completes each sentence.
Use one of the three-letter blends from the box.

1. Dad's first car had _____chr_____ome fenders.
2. Baseball season starts again each _____spr_____ing.
3. It takes a _____str_____ong swimmer to battle big waves.
4. Here is the _____sch_____edule for the chess tournament.
5. Hippos like to _____spl_____ash in the water.
6. The cage is made of metal _____scr_____eening.
7. There are _____sch_____ools to teach people how to drive.
8. Lemon drops can make your _____thr_____oat feel better.
9. The ball rolled into the thick _____shr_____ubs.
10. The king sits on a velvet _____thr_____one.

Unscramble the letters to name the picture.
Then write the unscrambled name on the line.

11	misprh	12	paserc	13	clohos
	shrimp		scrape		school

14	hdtrae	15	yaprs	16	warts
	thread		spray		straw

CHALLENGE

You know that u is not a consonant. Yet squ- can be a three-letter consonant blend.

Circle the squ- blend in these words. Then list other words that have the squ- blend.

squash
squeal
squirm

LESSON 11: Three–letter Blends   **25**

U N I V E R S A L   A C C E S S
Meeting Individual Needs

Logical Learners

Have pairs of students look through books to find words that have three-letter blends. Have them write down the words and sort them according to their blend. Finally, have partners read the words aloud to each other to identify which of the three-letter blends contain consonant digraphs.

Kinesthetic Learners

Have students write each of these three-letter blends on an index card: **spr, scr, str, shr.** Then read aloud the words listed below. For each word, have students hold up the card that shows the correct three-letter blend.

spray	**shrink**	**scrap**
shrub	**stripe**	**script**
stride	**sprang**	**stroll**
shriek	**scream**	**spry**

Use a word from the box for each clue. Write one letter in each space. Read down the shaded column to answer the question. Hint: The answer below has a digraph in the middle.

> Christopher dolphin split spread scheme screech
> shredded laughter sprinkle strength thread shrink

1. a gentle, short rainfall — s p r i n k l e
2. power or force — s t r e n g t h
3. torn into narrow strips or pieces — s h r e d d e d
4. a fancy bed cover — s p r e a d
5. a friendly sea mammal — d o l p h i n
6. to separate into parts — s p l i t
7. a wild or crazy plan — s c h e m e
8. a kind of owl that makes a loud noise — s c r e e c h
9. to get smaller — s h r i n k
10. a sound that shows humor or joy — l a u g h t e r
11. the first name of Mr. Columbus — C h r i s t o p h e r
12. very thin string for sewing — t h r e a d

Question: In this race, horses jump over ditches, hedges, and hurdles. A form of this race is for humans, too. What is this race called?

Answer: _____ steeplechase

Home Involvement Activity Look through newspapers or magazines for words that have three-letter blends. List them. Write a sentence for each word.

- Read aloud the direction lines on pages 25 and 26. Guide students as needed in completing the exercises.
- For items 1–10 on page 25, encourage students to use the context of the sentences to help them figure out the correct word.
- Make sure that students understand the meaning of the words **chrome** (page 25) and **scheme** (page 26).

Curriculum Connections

Spelling Link

- The following words contain different three-letter blends.

straw	thread	sprinkle
laughter	scheme	strength
shrimp	scrape	shredded

- Read the words aloud, and have a volunteer use each one in an original sentence. Then have the student spell the word orally and write it on the board.

Writing Link

- Many verbs (action words) start with three-letter blends. Here are some examples to add to those in the lesson: **scrub, scratch, splash, sprout, scrunch, threaten,** and **throw.**
- Ask students to write a composition describing an activity. Tell them to use as many verbs as they can. When they finish, have them underline verbs that begin with a two-letter blend and circle verbs that begin with a three-letter blend.

Observational Assessment

Check to make sure that students understand the difference between three-letter blends that have three letter sounds and blends (made up of a consonant and a digraph) that have two letter sounds.

English-Language Learners/ESL

Display pictures of items whose names begin with three-letter blends, such as **schedule, school, throat, shrub, throne, shrimp, straw,** and **thread.** Help students identify each item, pronounce its name correctly, and write the name on a label. Shuffle the labels and challenge students to attach each label to the picture of the item it names.

Gifted Learners

Have students create a puzzle like the one on page 26. They should choose words with three-letter blends and write clues describing the words. Remind students that letters in the answers should align vertically to spell a word.

Learners with Special Needs

Additional strategies for supporting learners with special needs can be found on page 5L.

Connecting Spelling and Writing

Objectives

- **To say, spell, sort, and write words with consonant digraphs**
- **To write a letter using spelling words**

Warming Up

- Write the following poem on the board. Have a student read it aloud.

  Physical fitness is our goal.

  Let's get into **sh**ape today.

  Do a sport toge**th**er wi**th** friends.

  Ru**sh** out to the sun**sh**ine and play!

- Ask volunteers to underline words that contain consonant digraphs and circle the digraphs. Remind students that digraphs can appear at the beginning, middle, and end of words.

Teaching the Lesson

- List the following words on the board: **thunder, chain, weather, dolphin, tough, bench, whole, chute, peach, luck, school, pickle.** Have students identify the consonant digraph in each word.
- Review with students the three sounds the digraph **ch** can make. (**ch**ain, **ch**ute, s**ch**ool) Then ask what sound the digraphs **ph** and **gh** can stand for. (the sound of **f**, as in dol**ph**in and tou**gh**) Elicit or provide other examples of various digraphs.

Practicing the Skill

- Read together the directions on page 27. Call on students to read each phrase aloud.
- Tell students to circle the digraphs before sorting and writing the words.

Read each group of words. Say and spell each word in bold print. Repeat the word. Then sort the words according to where the digraph appears in the word. Write each word in the correct column below.

- play in the **sunshine**
- soccer **champion**
- **crouch** behind the plate
- **tackle** the player
- the **north** field
- by an unknown **athlete**
- our favorite **teacher**
- **rather** than wait
- **astonish** the fans
- cast a **shadow**

- a team **photo**
- won a **tough** game
- a silver **trophy**
- wait over **there**
- celebrate a **triumph**
- a **chorus** of smiles

Initial Consonant Digraph	Medial Consonant Digraph	Final Consonant Digraph
champion	sunshine	crouch
shadow	tackle	north
photo	athlete	astonish
there	teacher	tough
chorus	rather	triumph
	trophy	

UNIVERSAL ACCESS
Meeting Individual Needs

Auditory Learners

Have students write each of the following digraphs on a separate index card: **gh, wh, ck, ch.** Then say the words below aloud. For each word, have students hold up the card that shows the correct digraph.

Chicago	**buckle**	**laugh**
enough	**chorus**	**wheel**
rough	**where**	**tackle**
chore	**tickle**	**whether**

Visual Learners

Draw the chart below on the board for students to copy. Have students fill in a word for each digraph in each of the possible positions: **I = Initial, M = Medial, F = Final.**

Digraph	I	M	F
ch			
sh			
th			
wh			
ph			

Learners with Special Needs

Additional strategies for supporting learners with special needs can be found on page 5L.

Many of today's athletes are modern-day heroes. These people are superstars on and off the field. Today, many sports figures are more than super athletes. They are also super people who help the people in their community.

Choose an athlete you admire. Write this athlete a letter. Give three strong reasons to explain why you admire him or her. Ask the athlete some questions. Use at least two of these spelling words in your letter.

sunshine	champion	crouch	tackle	north	athlete	teacher	rather
astonish	shadow	photo	tough	trophy	there	triumph	chorus

_____ [Your address]

_____

_____ [Date]

[Greeting] **Dear** _____,

[Body] _____

_____

_____

_____

_____

_____

Letters will vary but should include the correct form of a friendly letter.

Sincerely, [Closing]

_____ [Signature]

Writer's Tip

Use letter parts correctly. Write your address, the date, and the name of your athlete. Include your reasons and questions in the body. Close with "Sincerely," and sign your name.

Speaker's Challenge

Imagine that you are a sportscaster on the local TV news. Give a description of a real or an imaginary game in which the athlete you wrote about was the star. Vary the tone of your voice to give facts and to stress the excitement of the game.

28 LESSON 12: Connecting Spelling and Writing

English-Language Learners/ESL

Display magazine and newspaper photographs of athletes around the classroom. Have students write labels or captions for each picture. Then have students identify consonant digraphs in their labels or captions.

Gifted Learners

Have students work in pairs. Challenge each pair to write an imaginative or humorous story that includes all of the spelling words on page 28. You may want to provide a story-starter, such as: *Once upon a time **there** was an **athlete** who...* Have volunteers share their stories with the class. Then have students identify and sort words with consonant digraphs in their stories.

The Writing Process

Tell students that on page 28 they will write a letter to an athlete they admire. Go over the directions and spelling words at the top of the page.

Prewrite Have students talk about athletes they admire, from professional ballplayers to Olympic stars. Encourage them to think of specific reasons why a particular athlete deserves admiration.

Write Encourage students to identify their three reasons before starting to write. Suggest that they first get their ideas down on paper without worrying about the spelling words. They can figure out how to include the words afterward.

Revise Ask students to reread their letters carefully. Ask: *Have you included three reasons? Have you asked the athlete some questions? Have you used at least two spelling words? What can you do to make your letter better?*

Proofread Have students check for errors in spelling, grammar, and punctuation.

Publish Have students copy their final drafts onto page 28. Ask volunteers to read their letters aloud to the class.

Computer Connection

Share the following tip with students who use a word processor to do their writing.

● Word processing programs generally include a spelling checker. Explain that this is a useful feature, but not one to become overly dependent on. For example, a spell checker will not distinguish between **their** and **there,** as long as the word is spelled correctly.

● Encourage students to pay attention to misspellings the computer catches, so that they can learn from their mistakes.

Portfolio Suggest that students add their finished letters to their portfolios.

Reviewing and Assessing

Consonant Blends and Consonant Digraphs

Objective

To review and assess consonant blends and consonant digraphs

Warming Up

● Ask: *How is a consonant digraph different from a consonant blend?* Explain that a blend is two or three consonants sounded together so that each letter is heard; a digraph is two consonants that together stand for one sound.

● Write these words on the board: **branch, chant, triumph, splash.** Tell students that each word contains both a consonant blend and a consonant digraph. Have volunteers say each word aloud and circle the blend and the digraph. Point out that **splash** contains a three-letter blend.

Teaching the Lesson

● Remind students that a consonant digraph may appear at the beginning, middle, or end of a word. Elicit examples and write them on the board.

● Make three columns on the board and label them **Initial, Medial,** and **Final.** Have a student write a word with an initial digraph in the first column. The next student can write a word with a medial digraph in the second column, and so on. Underline the digraphs and have students say each word.

● Review the sounds of **ch, ph,** and **gh** and elicit examples of each. Add these to the chart on the board.

29

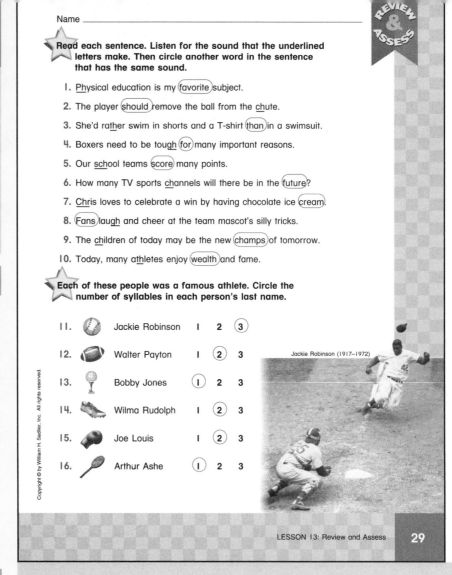

Name _____

⭐ Read each sentence. Listen for the sound that the underlined letters make. Then circle another word in the sentence that has the same sound.

1. Physical education is my (favorite) subject.
2. The player (should) remove the ball from the chute.
3. She'd rather swim in shorts and a T-shirt (than) in a swimsuit.
4. Boxers need to be tough (for) many important reasons.
5. Our school teams (score) many points.
6. How many TV sports channels will there be in the (future)?
7. Chris loves to celebrate a win by having chocolate ice (cream).
8. (Fans) laugh and cheer at the team mascot's silly tricks.
9. The children of today may be the new (champs) of tomorrow.
10. Today, many athletes enjoy (wealth) and fame.

⭐ Each of these people was a famous athlete. Circle the number of syllables in each person's last name.

11.	Jackie Robinson	1	2	③
12.	Walter Payton	1	②	3
13.	Bobby Jones	①	2	3
14.	Wilma Rudolph	1	②	3
15.	Joe Louis	1	②	3
16.	Arthur Ashe	①	2	3

Jackie Robinson (1917–1972)

LESSON 13: Review and Assess   **29**

UNIVERSAL ACCESS
Meeting Individual Needs

Logical Learners

Give each student a magazine. Tell students to find examples of words containing consonant digraphs. Have students sort the words by digraph position: initial, medial, final. Then have students combine their words into a class list, also sorted by digraph position. Write the list on chart paper, highlighting the digraphs in red.

Learners with Special Needs

Additional strategies for supporting learners with special needs can be found on page 5L.

Kinesthetic Learners

Write each of the following words containing consonant digraphs on a separate piece of paper: **fish, whistle, shovel, skunk, cheer, feather, laugh, telephone, bench, thorn.** Have volunteers draw the pieces of paper from a bag. Offer each player a choice of pantomiming the word or giving verbal clues to help classmates guess the word. As each word is identified, write it on the board and circle the digraph.

Read about a wonderful athlete. For each numbered blank, there is a choice of words below. Fill in the circle of the word that best completes the sentence.

Mildred Didrikson Zaharias was the **1** female athlete of her day. She was born in Texas in 1914 and was called "Babe." Babe won more **2** and set more records in more sports than any other athlete. This includes both women *and* men! She was the star of her high school basketball team. Babe also played on track-and-field teams in college. She played eight other sports, too. Babe even **3** a whole inning of a major league baseball game. Then she decided to play golf. Of course, she <u>had a knack for</u> that sport, too! As a golfer, she lost only one **4** in seven years! Babe died in 1956. Yet she was one of the best athletes of the twentieth century.

1. ● greatest   ○ closest   ○ clearest   ○ strictest
2. ○ benches   ○ splits   ● trophies   ○ scrapes
3. ○ graphed   ○ roughed   ○ blushed   ● pitched
4. ○ month   ○ mesh   ● match   ○ march

Read the passage again to answer these questions. Circle the letter of the answer.

5. What made Babe Didrikson Zaharias such a great athlete?
   a. She was born in Texas.
   b. She played basketball in high school.
   (c.) She starred in many different sports.
   d. She took part in a baseball game.

6. What does the phrase <u>had a knack for</u> mean?
   a. liked to collect things
   (b.) was good at
   c. tried to learn
   d. wanted to avoid

Extend & Apply

Suppose you could ask Babe Didrikson Zaharias a question. What would you want to know? Write your question here.
Answers will vary.

Reteaching Activities

Beginning, Middle, End

Draw the chart below on the board for students to copy. Have students complete the chart by filling in words that contain the digraphs in each of the positions indicated:
I = Initial, M = Medial, F = Final.

Digraph	I	M	F
ch			
sh			
th			
wh			
ph			

Digraph Hunting

Arrange students in groups. Assign each group two digraphs. Have groups hunt for objects with names that contain their digraphs. Tell students to keep a list of the objects they find, circling the digraph in each word. The group with the most objects wins.

Assessing the Skills

Check Up Go over the directions for the exercises on page 29. Be sure students understand that they have to circle a word that has the same sound—but not necessarily the same letters—as the underlined digraph. Then have students complete the page.

Page 30 will help you assess students' ability to choose appropriate words with consonant blends and consonant digraphs for a given context. Encourage students to read the passage more than once.

Observational Assessment As students work, watch for areas in which extra help is needed to strengthen skills or eliminate confusion. Review and compare observations you made during previous lessons. Evaluate the progress of individual students as well as that of the whole class.

Student Skills Assessment Keep track of each student's progress in understanding consonant blends and digraphs using the checklist on page 5H.

Writing Conference As you finish the unit, meet with students individually. Review their portfolio samples and other written work and point out examples that show improvement. Encourage students to share favorite pieces of writing from their Home Portfolios with the class. Draw students' attention to words with consonant digraphs and words with three-letter blends in their own writing.

Group together students who need further instruction in consonant digraphs and have them complete the *Reteaching Activities*. Turn to page 5C for alternative assessment methods.

Vowel Sounds

Theme: Explorers

STANDARDS

- Read expository text with grade-appropriate fluency and understand its content
- Develop and strengthen vocabulary by reading words in context
- Recognize letter-sound correspondence in vowel digraphs and vowel pairs
- Identify and pronounce vowel sounds in words

OBJECTIVES

▶ To appreciate nonfiction works about explorers and exploration

▶ To identify and pronounce **r**-controlled vowels

▶ To decode and write words with vowel digraphs, vowel pairs, and diphthongs

▶ To divide words into syllables

LESSONS

Lesson 14 . . . . Introduction to Short and Long Vowels, **r**-controlled Vowels, Vowel Pairs, Vowel Digraphs, Diphthongs, and Phonograms
Lesson 15 . . . . Short and Long Vowels; **y** as a Vowel
Lesson 16 . . . . **r**-controlled Vowels **ar, er, ir, or, ur**
Lesson 17 . . . . **r**-controlled Vowels **air, are, ear, eer**
Lesson 18 . . . . Connecting Reading and Writing—Comprehension: Problem and Solution, Synthesize
Lesson 19 . . . . Vowel Pairs **ai, ay, ee, ea** and Vowel Digraph **ea**
Lesson 20 . . . . Vowel Pairs **ei** and **ie**; Vowel Digraphs **ei, ey, ie**
Lesson 21 . . . . Syllables with Short and Long Vowels, **r**-controlled Vowels, Vowel Pairs, and Vowel Digraphs
Lesson 22 . . . . Connecting Spelling and Writing
Lesson 23 . . . . Review and Assess
Lesson 24 . . . . Vowel Digraphs **au** and **aw; al**
Lesson 25 . . . . Vowel Digraph **oo** and Vowel Pairs **oa, oe**
Lesson 26 . . . . Diphthongs **oi, oy, ew**
Lesson 27 . . . . Vowel Pair **ow** and Diphthongs **ow, ou**
Lesson 28 . . . . Syllables with Vowel Pairs, Vowel Digraphs, and Diphthongs
Lesson 29 . . . . Connecting Reading and Writing—Comprehension: Make Decisions, Synthesize
Lesson 30 . . . . Review and Assess

Assessment Strategies

An overview of assessment strategies appears on page **31C**. It offers suggestions for using unit-specific assessment tools, including **Pretests** and **Post Tests** (pages **31D–31G**), the **Activity Master** (page **31M**), and the **Assessment Checklist** (page **31H**).

Thematic Teaching

In Unit 2, students learn about vowel sounds and the letters that represent them. Students encounter words with these sounds and letters in the context of nonfiction selections and exercises related to the theme *Explorers*.

Students begin their investigation of the *Explorers* theme by creating an illustrated time line showing explorers' movement into the American West during the 18th and 19th centuries. The resource list on this page offers titles of books, videos, and other materials that celebrate the discoveries and the spirit of explorers, then and now. Many of the Teacher's Edition lessons in this unit open with poems, riddles, or tongue twisters related to *Explorers*. These "hooks" can spark students' interest both in the theme and in the play of words.

Curriculum Integration

Science

Students make a list of animals on page **34,** look through science books on page **46,** write questions about animals on page **52,** and research the topic of snow on page **58.**

Social Studies

Students will make a map on page **32** and find out more about explorers on pages **36** and **60.** On page **44,** they match words that tell about Lewis and Clark.

Drama

Students create a skit on page **38** and write dialogues on page **56.**

Music

Students find songs with rhyming lyrics on page **42.**

Art

Students describe their favorite work of art on page **54.**

Optional Learning Activities

Meeting Individual Needs

Most Teacher's Edition lessons offer activities for students with distinct learning styles or particular intellectual or sensory strengths. The activities are labeled for learners with the following "styles": **Visual, Kinesthetic, Auditory, Logical, Musical,** and **Tactile.**

Multicultural Connections

Students research Creole culture on page **32.**

Word Study Strategies

Pages **31I–31J** offer an array of activities that give students practice using strategies such as word sorting, word building, and dividing words into syllables.

Universal Access

Exercises tailored to meet the needs of **English-Language Learners** and **Gifted Learners** can be found in almost every Teacher's Edition lesson. Strategies designed to help **Learners with Special Needs,** such as students with Attention Deficit Hyperactivity Disorder, can be found on page **31L.**

Intervention

Page **31K** offers **Intervention Strategies** designed to help students understand the concepts taught in **Lessons 16, 20,** and **28.**

Reteaching

On page **50** students identify vowel sounds, and on page **64** students identify digraphs, diphthongs, and vowel pairs.

Technology

Page **31N** offers activities for students who enjoy working with computers or audio/video equipment. In addition, **Computer Connections**—tips designed to support students who use a word processor—can be found on pages **40, 48** and **62.**

RESOURCES

Books
Armstrong, Jennifer. *Shipwreck at the Bottom of the World: Shackleton's Amazing Voyage,* NY: Crown Publishing, 1998.
Jenkins, Steve. *The Top of the World: Climbing Mount Everest,* NY: Houghton Mifflin Co., 1999.

Videos
Everest, Imax.
The Explorers: A Century of Discovery, National Geographic Video.

CDs
25 Fun Adventure Songs, Twin Sister Records.

UNIT 2 ✓ ASSESSMENT

In Unit 2, students study short and long vowels, **r**-controlled vowels, vowel pairs, vowel digraphs, diphthongs, and phonograms. To evaluate students' mastery of these skills, use any or all of the assessment methods suggested below.

Pretests and Post Tests

The tests on pages **31D–31G** objectively assess how well students understand **r**-controlled vowels, vowel pairs, vowel digraphs, diphthongs, and phonograms. These tests may be used at the beginning of the unit as an informal diagnostic tool or at the end of the unit as a more formal measure of students' progress.

Observational Assessment

Each lesson includes a reminder to observe students at work in the classroom. Lesson–specific recommendations are included for assessing students' work. Check students' written work on a regular basis to see whether they are successfully applying what they learn.

Using Technology

The Technology activities on page **31N** may also help to evaluate students' whose language skills are best shown when using computers or audio/video equipment.

Performance Assessment

Using the following words, have students make a chart for sorting vowel sounds: **look, sweat, lawn, new, town, spoil, group, year.** Then, have students sort the following words in the correct rows: **through, allow, toil, jewel, stood, yawn, measure.** Then ask each student to add two new words with the same vowel sound to each row.

Portfolio Assessment

The portfolio icon in the lesson plans indicates an opportunity for students to add to the growing body of work in their portfolios.

Each student's portfolio will be different and should contain pieces that the student feels represent his or her best work. You may wish to give students additional opportunities to add to their portfolios.

Rubric for Writing

	Always	Sometimes	Never
Uses capitalization, punctuation, spelling, and grammar appropriately			
Creates a variety of sentences containing words with vowel pairs, vowel digraphs, diphthongs, and **r**-controlled vowels			
Uses vivid verbs and adjectives appropriate for intended purpose			
Uses persuasive words to convey meaning through writing			

Answer Key

Page 31D
1. short
2. long
3. short
4. long
5. short
6. ar
7. or
8. ir
9. er
10. ai
11. air
12. ea
13. al
14. oa
15. ie
16. mea-dow
17. poi-son
18. be-ware
19. tun-nel
20. cor-ner
21. pi-lot
22. laun-dry
23. cheer
24. la-dy
25. ur-gent

Page 31E
1. last
2. torch
3. share
4. sky
5. law

6. lie
7. toy
8. lean
9. chain
10. allow
11. tie
12. fear
13. circus
14. rope
15. new
16. thief
17. car-pet
18. dai-ly
19. o-bey
20. sad-dle

Page 31F
1. long
2. short
3. long
4. short
5. short
6. ur
7. or
8. ar
9. er
10. ai
11. are
12. ei
13. aw
14. oy
15. ou
16. di-et

17. sheep
18. ter-ror
19. ta-ble
20. rea-dy
21. show-er
22. sea-son
23. thun-der
24. tur-key
25. loy-al

Page 31G
1. dime
2. bee
3. mark
4. author
5. fork
6. shade
7. soon
8. coat
9. knew
10. show
11. couch
12. saw
13. piece
14. steer
15. cheese
16. har-poon
17. re-ceive
18. plas-tic
19. ear-ring
20. scout

Name _____

Fill in the circle that tells whether the vowel sound in each word is long or short.

1. send	○ short	○ long
2. fly	○ short	○ long
3. hand	○ short	○ long
4. coat	○ short	○ long
5. sing	○ short	○ long

Fill in the circle next to the letters that complete each word.

6. sh___k	○ uir	○ ar	○ er	○ or
7. t___ch	○ ir	○ ar	○ ur	○ or
8. b___d	○ ir	○ ur	○ er	○ or
9. f___n	○ ir	○ ur	○ ar	○ er
10. tr___n	○ ay	○ ee	○ ai	○ ea
11. ch___	○ uar	○ ear	○ are	○ air
12. f___ther	○ oe	○ ei	○ ea	○ ie
13. s___t	○ au	○ al	○ aw	○ oa
14. l___n	○ oa	○ oe	○ or	○ oy
15. br___f	○ ei	○ ie	○ ey	○ ee

Write each word and use a hyphen (-) to divide it into syllables.

16. meadow _____	**17.** poison _____
18. beware _____	**19.** tunnel _____
20. corner _____	**21.** pilot _____
22. laundry _____	**23.** cheer _____
24. lady _____	**25.** urgent _____

Possible score on Unit 2 Pretest 1 is 25. Score _____

Pretest 2

Name _____

Fill in the circle next to the word with the same vowel sound as in the first word in each row.

1. map	○ paper	○ fair	○ last
2. form	○ torch	○ term	○ finish
3. hair	○ share	○ deer	○ pier
4. pie	○ sky	○ brief	○ piece
5. chalk	○ same	○ main	○ law
6. time	○ help	○ lie	○ fir
7. coin	○ toy	○ boat	○ note
8. team	○ weather	○ lean	○ lane
9. play	○ side	○ hurt	○ chain
10. cloud	○ coat	○ allow	○ show
11. shy	○ may	○ key	○ tie
12. sheer	○ fear	○ mean	○ three
13. fir	○ fire	○ circus	○ right
14. cold	○ hot	○ shoot	○ rope
15. boot	○ new	○ choice	○ knot

Fill in the circle next to the word that is correctly divided into syllables.

16. thief	○ thi-ef	○ thief
17. carpet	○ car-pet	○ carp-et
18. daily	○ da-ily	○ dai-ly
19. obey	○ o-bey	○ ob-ey
20. saddle	○ sadd-le	○ sad-dle

Possible score on Unit 2 Pretest 2 is 20. Score _____

Name _____

Fill in the circle that tells whether the vowel sound in each word is long or short.

1. cane	○ short	○ long
2. top	○ short	○ long
3. bean	○ short	○ long
4. punch	○ short	○ long
5. list	○ short	○ long

Fill in the circle next to the letters that complete each word.

6. c__b	○ ur	○ ar	○ er	○ or
7. f__t	○ ir	○ ur	○ er	○ or
8. h__p	○ ir	○ ar	○ er	○ or
9. g__m	○ ir	○ ur	○ ar	○ er
10. w__t	○ ay	○ ee	○ ai	○ ea
11. sc__	○ eer	○ ear	○ are	○ air
12. __ther	○ ee	○ ei	○ ea	○ ie
13. cl__	○ au	○ al	○ aw	○ oa
14. j__	○ oa	○ oe	○ oi	○ oy
15. l__d	○ oy	○ ow	○ ou	○ oi

Write each word and use a hyphen (-) to divide it into syllables.

16. diet _____	**17.** sheep _____
18. terror _____	**19.** table _____
20. ready _____	**21.** shower _____
22. season _____	**23.** thunder _____
24. turkey _____	**25.** loyal _____

Possible score on Unit 2 Post Test 1 is 25. Score _____

Post Test 2

Name _____

Fill in the circle next to the word with the same vowel sound as in the first word in each row.

1. five	○ chief	○ plain	○ dime
2. beat	○ mate	○ hole	○ bee
3. hard	○ mark	○ beard	○ torn
4. taught	○ laughter	○ author	○ await
5. shore	○ fork	○ toast	○ lost
6. hay	○ hat	○ she	○ shade
7. moon	○ stone	○ look	○ soon
8. doe	○ cot	○ shoe	○ coat
9. chew	○ went	○ knew	○ tell
10. throw	○ town	○ allow	○ show
11. house	○ touch	○ cough	○ couch
12. false	○ sea	○ saw	○ flea
13. weep	○ piece	○ shell	○ leather
14. near	○ steer	○ stare	○ stir
15. please	○ jealous	○ cheese	○ melt

Fill in the circle next to the word that is correctly divided into syllables.

16. harpoon	○ harp-oon	○ har-poon
17. receive	○ rec-eive	○ re-ceive
18. plastic	○ plast-ic	○ plas-tic
19. earring	○ ear-ring	○ earr-ing
20. scout	○ scout	○ sco-ut

Possible score on Unit 2 Post Test 2 is 20. Score _____

UNIT 2

STUDENT PROGRESS CHECKLIST

Student Name ____________________

UNIT TWO
STUDENT SKILLS ASSESSMENT CHECKLIST

☐ Assessed ☒ Retaught ■ Mastered

- ❑ Short and Long Vowels; **y** as a Vowel
- ❑ **r**-controlled Vowels **ar, er, ir, or, ur**
- ❑ **r**-controlled Vowels **air, are, ear, eer**
- ❑ Vowel Pairs **ai, ay, ee, ea** and Vowel Digraph **ea**
- ❑ Vowel Pairs **ei** and **ie;** Vowel Digraphs **ei, ey, ie**
- ❑ Syllables with Short and Long Vowels, **r**-controlled Vowels, Vowel Pairs, and Vowel Digraphs
- ❑ Vowel Digraphs **au** and **aw; al**
- ❑ Vowel Digraph **oo** and Vowel Pairs **oa, oe**
- ❑ Diphthongs **oi, oy, ew**
- ❑ Vowel Pair **ow** and Diphthongs **ow, ou**
- ❑ Syllables with Vowel Pairs, Vowel Digraphs, and Diphthongs

TEACHER COMMENTS

In Unit 2, students study short and long vowels, **r**-controlled vowels, vowel pairs, vowel digraphs, diphthongs, and phonograms. To give students opportunities to master word study strategies, use any or all of the activities suggested below.

Vowel Sort

Read each word. Determine whether the underlined letter has a short or long vowel sound then sort the words as directed below.

s<u>e</u>ll	p<u>u</u>pil	t<u>i</u>n	fl<u>y</u>
k<u>i</u>te	h<u>a</u>nd	b<u>u</u>mp	s<u>y</u>stem
stor<u>y</u>	g<u>y</u>m	pl<u>a</u>ne	g<u>o</u>

1. Write the words with **short** vowel sounds.

_____ _____ _____

_____ _____ _____

2. Write the words with **long** vowel sounds.

_____ _____ _____

_____ _____ _____

Word Building

Build words that contain the same vowel sound as each numbered word below. Write the two letters to complete each word. Then write an additional word on the line that contains the same vowel sound.

1. park   ch __ t   h __ m   _____

2. form   p __ ch   sp __ t   _____

3. bird   d __ ty   tw __ l   _____

4. fern   s __ ve   g __ bil   _____

5. turn   c __ ve   t __ tle   _____

6. word   w __ k   w __ m   _____

7. care   v __ y   sh __ e   _____

8. lawn   h __ k   y __ n   _____

9. claim   afr __ d   f __ nt   _____

10. thread   ah __ d   m __ dow   _____

Word Selection

Underline the word in each pair that has the same vowel sound as the numbered word.

1. **pair**   bear/bird   share/sharp

2. **hare**   harm/hair   air/aim

3. **leer**   swear/shear   steer/stair

4. **bear**   spare/spear   deer/hair

5. **learn**   gear/girl   pearl/pear

6. **smear**   cheer/chair   rare/rear

7. **spread**   please/chest   chief/leather

8. **snow**   loud/note   follow/allow

9. **royal**   choice/post   toll/annoy

10. **sleigh**   obey/seize   sneeze/eight

11. **chief**   leaf/thread   meadow/speed

12. **walk**   lawn/yarn   sauce/carrot

13. **toast**   rope/shoe   toe/canoe

14. **pie**   listen/sky   brief/pile

15. **train**   cast/make   stay/cabin

Word Meaning

Circle the word that completes each sentence. Then write the word on the line.

1. A _____ is a juicy fruit.

   pail   **peach**   **peel**

2. I hooked the _____ at the end of the fishing line.

   bait   **bay**   **bake**

3. One slice of cherry _____ was left.

   pie   **piece**   **price**

4. We rode on the _____ in the snow.

   survey   **sky**   **sleigh**

5. My _____ have no pockets.

   jets   **jails**   **jeans**

6. The baby _____ all night.

   crime   **cried**   **chief**

7. The shape of my _____ is round.

   head   **heed**   **hay**

8. Do you _____ when you have a cold?

   sneeze   **seize**   **sneak**

Rhyming Words

Find a word from the box that rhymes with each numbered word and write it on the line.

claw	crow	through	crowd	toy
toil	code	thought	cook	town

1. loud _____   2. blew _____

3. low _____   4. brown _____

5. load _____   6. bought _____

7. look _____   8. broil _____

9. law _____   10. boy _____

Syllables in Words

Answer each question with a word from the box. Write the word on the line.

fifty	over	neighbor
tomorrow	daisy	bicycle
bird	thief	circle
never		

1. What one-syllable word names someone who steals?

   _____

2. What two-syllable word names a person who lives next door to you?

   _____

3. What two-syllable word names a shape?

   _____

4. What three-syllable word names something you steer?

   _____

5. What two-syllable word names a number?

   _____

6. What two-syllable word means "not ever"?

   _____

7. What two-syllable word means the opposite of under?

   _____

8. What two-syllable word names a flower?

   _____

9. What one-syllable word names an animal?

   _____

10. What three-syllable word means "the day after today"?

    _____

UNIT 2 INTERVENTION STRATEGIES

LESSONS	**16** r-controlled Vowels	**20** Vowel Pairs and Vowel Digraphs	**28** Syllables
Problem	Student has difficulty spelling words with **r-**controlled vowels that sound alike.	Student has difficulty reading and spelling words with vowel pairs **ei** and **ie** and vowel digraphs **ei, ey, ie.**	Student has difficulty dividing words into syllables.
Intervention Strategies	• Have students make a section for **r**-controlled vowels in their word-study notebook. Encourage students to list the words with **r-**controlled vowel sounds by their spelling patterns. Have students refer to the list when completing the exercises. • Have the student scan a page for words with **r**-controlled vowels that have the same vowel sound as the word **fern**. Have the student sort the words in separate columns according to whether the vowel sound as in the word **fern** is spelled **ir, ur,** or **er.**	• Encourage students to make a section in their word-study notebook for words with **ei, ey, ie.** • Have them create a column for each spelling pattern: long **e,** spelled **ei, ey, ie;** long **i** spelled **ie;** long **a** spelled **ei.** • Then have them label each column with an illustration of a word that represents the vowel sound and spelling pattern. For example: **pie.** • Whenever students learn a new word with these vowel sounds and spelling patterns, they can enter it in the appropriate column.	• As students read multisyllabic words, have them use their fingers to tap the number of syllables. • Review the rule that every syllable contains a vowel sound. Remind students that some words have a syllable with more than one vowel, for example: **audience.** Point out to them that vowel pairs and vowel digraphs are pronounced as one vowel and are not divided, **au-di-ence.**

The following activities offer strategies for helping students with special needs to participate in selected exercises in Unit 2.

Auditory/Oral Discrimination
r-Controlled Vowels

Students who have difficulty with pronunciation and/or sound discrimination may need help with **r**-controlled vowels. Because the **r** sound is dominant, it may be the only sound students can identify in combinations such as **or** (as in **bore**) or **ar** (as in **bar**).

- To help students distinguish between these **r**-controlled vowel sounds, enlist both their prior knowledge and their kinesthetic sense. Say these sentences: *The little pig barred the door against the wolf. The handyman bored a hole through the door.* Ask students to explain what was done to the door in each sentence. Then ask them which verb **(bar** or **bore)** rhymes with **door,** a word that many students will know well.

- If students still have trouble pronouncing or distinguishing the sounds from one another, have them watch your mouth as you say the words **bar** and **bore.** Point out that, in the first case, your mouth is open and relaxed. In the second case, your mouth is not open as wide and is more rounded. Have them imitate your mouth positions as they say the words.

Attention Deficit Hyperactivity Disorder (ADHD)
Phonograms

The first activity in Lesson 15 asks students to pick out words that contain a particular phonogram from a row of many words. Students with ADHD may become restless if required to do this activity quietly on their own. To enable these students to discharge some of their extra energy, invite them to copy items 1–4 on page **33** onto the board. Ask them to lead the class in doing the activity together. They can call on their classmates, record their answers, and read the answers aloud.

Auditory Perceptual Deficits
Vowel Pairs and Diphthongs

Some students may have difficulty understanding that the same combination of vowels may be both a vowel pair and a diphthong—as in the case of **cr<u>ow</u>** and **c<u>ow</u>.** An exercise containing familiar elements contrasting these sounds may help these students.

- Make two lists of words, one in which the letters **ow** are pronounced as a diphthong and one in which the letters **ow** are pronounced as a vowel pair.

- Then write sentences using one word from the diphthong list and one word from the vowel pair list on the board. Here is an example: *Tie a pretty <u>bow</u> around the <u>cow's</u> neck.* Have volunteers underline the words containing the letters **ow,** and read the sentences aloud.

- When students recognize that this combination of letters has two different pronunciations, invite them to use the words in each list to make up similar sentences.

Name _____

Find the words that contain the same vowel sound as the underlined vowels. Write the words on the lines.

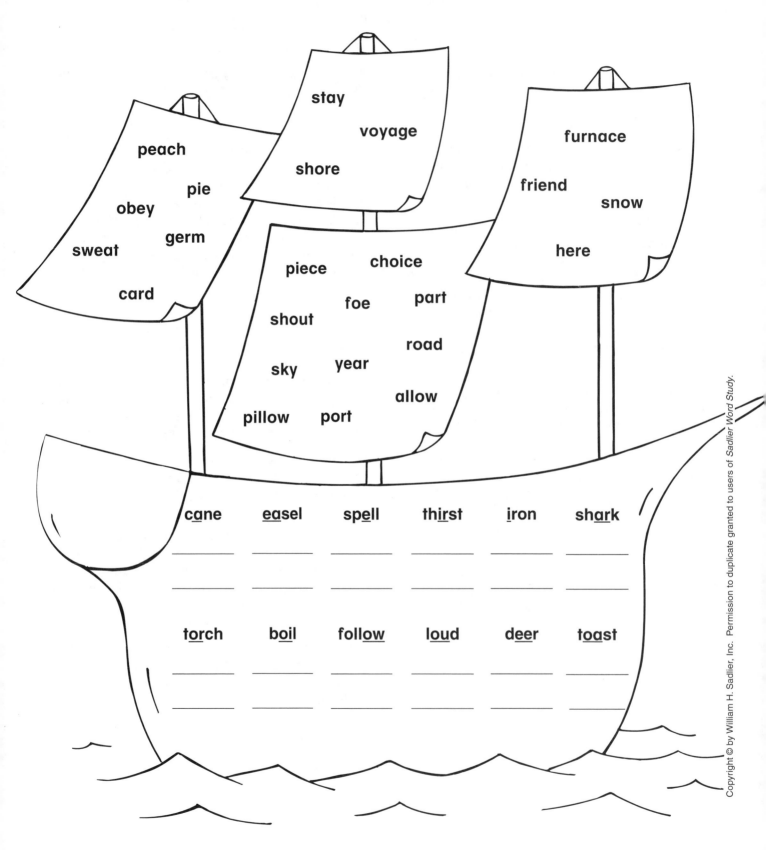

peach

pie

obey

germ

sweat

card

stay

voyage

shore

furnace

friend

snow

here

piece

choice

foe

part

shout

road

sky

year

allow

pillow

port

c**a**ne   **ea**sel   sp**e**ll   th**i**rst   **i**ron   sh**a**rk

_____ _____ _____ _____ _____ _____

_____ _____ _____ _____ _____ _____

t**o**rch   b**oi**l   foll**ow**   l**ou**d   d**ee**r   t**oa**st

_____ _____ _____ _____ _____ _____

_____ _____ _____ _____ _____ _____

Exploring the Familiar with a Camera

Ask students to photograph places in their community. Tell them that they are going to organize the pictures into a photo essay.

- Once students have chosen an area to be explored, help them plan the project. They may want to form committees for such tasks as researching the area, interviewing the inhabitants, writing captions for the pictures, and taking the pictures.

- Have students use professional photo essays as models. Set aside time for class trips to the area to be photographed and to the local historical society. If possible, invite an expert on the area to talk to your class about it.

- During the presentation, have a different student talk about each picture. Compile a list of **r**-controlled vowel words and help students write scripts that include some of them. A possible list might include: **farm, fort, park, foreign, porch, explore, born, barn, work, world, bird, squirrel.** Give each student a chance to practice pronouncing **r**-controlled vowel words.

Videotape an Explorers' Club Meeting

Ask students to pretend that they are all explorers who have just returned from expeditions to foreign countries. Ask each student to select a culture that interests him or her and to research some aspect of it (such as a dance, a ceremony, or a costume) that they would enjoy preparing and presenting on a video. (The presentations can be done "live" if no camera is available.)

- Help students choose someone to introduce the different presentations and someone to operate the camera. Set aside time for them to work on the project and to present the final product to another class.

- Once students have selected their contribution to the club meeting and researched it, have them write a brief description or explanation about it.

- After they have written their explanations, have them do the following: draw a single line under words with **ea** as short **e,** draw a double line under words with **ea** as long **e,** highlight words with **ei** as long **e,** and circle words with **ei** as long **a** Then have them check to make sure they can identify the vowel sounds.

Tape Record a Play about an Exploratory Expedition

Encourage students to write and record a one-act play that is based on a journal kept by an explorer.

- One group of students can write the script, another can decide how the sound effects should be handled, and still another can act it out. Set aside time for students to work on the project and to present it to their classmates.

- Read students selections from travel journals, such as those written by Christopher Columbus and William Clark.

- Suggest to the writing group that they set the scene by having the leader read from his or her journal. Then the other characters can act it out. For example: *When we landed on the planet Orchidia, we couldn't believe its beauty. We sat down by a stream, marveling at the flowers and fruits that hung from the trees. Suddenly, we heard a strange grinding sound. Lieutenant Sanchez turned to me . . .Lieutenant Sanchez: Shall I check that out, Captain?*

- Give students copies of the script and have them underline examples of digraphs and circle examples of diphthongs.

Introduction to
Vowel Sounds

Objectives

- **To enjoy a piece of nonfiction related to the theme *Explorers***
- **To study long and short vowels, r-controlled vowels, vowel pairs, vowel digraphs, diphthongs, and phonograms**

Starting with Literature

- Ask a student to read "What a Deal!" aloud for the class.
- On the board, write some words from the story with long and short vowels.

west	**places**	**Gap**
lived	**these**	**just**
price	**Ocean**	**United**

- Invite students to say the words aloud. Encourage them to suggest other words with the same vowel sounds, modeling with some examples if necessary.

Critical Thinking

- Suggest that students review the story to find answers to the first two questions.
- Encourage students to explain the reasons for their answers to the third question.

Introducing the Skill

Have students reread "What a Deal!" to find words in which the letter **r** follows a vowel. Write these words on the board. Ask volunteers to circle the vowel-plus-**r** combinations and say the sounds they represent.

Practicing the Skill

Have students work in five groups. Give each group a different vowel. Invite the groups to search through books to find words that include their vowels. Suggest that students select familiar words.

What a Deal!

People have been exploring new places for centuries. North America is just one place that adventurers have explored.

Few American colonists lived west of the Appalachian Mountains before 1776. Yet some people did cross these mountains. One of these early explorers was Daniel Boone. Boone followed old Native American trails to a pass in the mountains. This pass was called the Cumberland Gap. From there, he led families west to settle on land in Kentucky.

Soon, the United States owned the land as far west as the Mississippi River. Yet the country needed more land for its many settlers. France owned all the land west of the Mississippi River. Would France sell some of this land?

The year was 1803. President Thomas Jefferson wanted to buy the port of New Orleans from France. To his surprise, France wanted to sell more than just New Orleans. "How much will you give for the whole of Louisiana?" a French official asked. Jefferson said just $15 million. France agreed to his price. For just four cents an acre, the President had doubled the size of the United States! This land deal is called the Louisiana Purchase. A year later, Lewis and Clark would begin to explore this land. Their journey would lead the way for the pioneers to go west—all the way to the Pacific Ocean.

Critical Thinking

1. Why did people want to go west?
2. What made the Louisiana Purchase such a "good deal"?
3. Would you have gone west with the pioneers? Why or why not?

1. People went west to explore and settle.
2. It doubled the size of the U.S. for only $15,000,000.
3. Answers will vary.

LESSON 14: Introduction to Short and Long Vowels, r-controlled Vowels, Vowel Pairs, Vowel Digraphs, Diphthongs, and Phonograms   **31**

Theme Activity

EXPLORERS TIME LINE Invite students to create a time line showing the expeditions of various explorers who moved into the American West during the 18th and 19th centuries. Encourage students to illustrate their time line with pictures of the explorers and the places they traveled through.

Students might also want to include information about the Native American peoples who lived in the places that the explorers visited. Ask students to include drawings illustrating the lives of the Native Americans who inhabited these lands.

Then have students label various items in their illustrations with "Unit 2" words: words containing short and long vowels, **r**-controlled vowels, vowel pairs, vowel digraphs, diphthongs, and phonograms. Invite students to add to their "Explorers Time Line" throughout the unit.

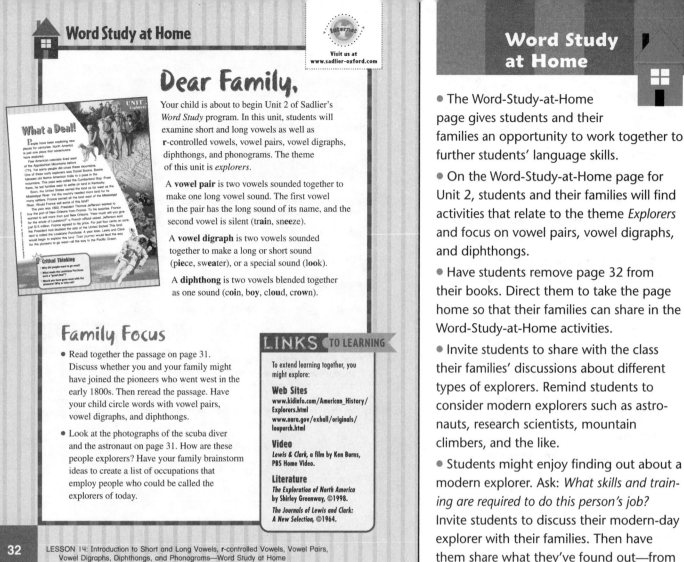

Dear Family,

Your child is about to begin Unit 2 of Sadlier's *Word Study* program. In this unit, students will examine short and long vowels as well as **r**-controlled vowels, vowel pairs, vowel digraphs, diphthongs, and phonograms. The theme of this unit is *explorers*.

A **vowel pair** is two vowels sounded together to make one long vowel sound. The first vowel in the pair has the long sound of its name, and the second vowel is silent (tr**ai**n, sn**ee**ze).

A **vowel digraph** is two vowels sounded together to make a long or short sound (p**ie**ce, sw**ea**ter), or a special sound (l**oo**k).

A **diphthong** is two vowels blended together as one sound (c**oi**n, b**oy**, cl**ou**d, cr**ow**n).

Family Focus

- Read together the passage on page 31. Discuss whether you and your family might have joined the pioneers who went west in the early 1800s. Then reread the passage. Have your child circle words with vowel pairs, vowel digraphs, and diphthongs.

- Look at the photographs of the scuba diver and the astronaut on page 31. How are these people explorers? Have your family brainstorm ideas to create a list of occupations that employ people who could be called the explorers of today.

LINKS TO LEARNING

To extend learning together, you might explore:

Web Sites
www.kidinfo.com/American_History/
Explorers.html
www.nara.gov/exhall/originals/
loupurch.html

Video
Lewis & Clark, a film by Ken Burns,
PBS Home Video.

Literature
The Exploration of North America
by Shirley Greenway, ©1998.

The Journals of Lewis and Clark:
A New Selection, ©1964.

Word Study at Home

- The Word-Study-at-Home page gives students and their families an opportunity to work together to further students' language skills.

- On the Word-Study-at-Home page for Unit 2, students and their families will find activities that relate to the theme *Explorers* and focus on vowel pairs, vowel digraphs, and diphthongs.

- Have students remove page 32 from their books. Direct them to take the page home so that their families can share in the Word-Study-at-Home activities.

- Invite students to share with the class their families' discussions about different types of explorers. Remind students to consider modern explorers such as astronauts, research scientists, mountain climbers, and the like.

- Students might enjoy finding out about a modern explorer. Ask: *What skills and training are required to do this person's job?* Invite students to discuss their modern-day explorer with their families. Then have them share what they've found out—from research and at home—with the rest of the class.

Multicultural Connection

Tell students that New Orleans was once ruled by Spain, whose influence has contributed to the city's cultural heritage. For instance, the word **Creole,** referring to people or things from New Orleans, comes from the Spanish word **criollo,** meaning "native to the place." The city is known for **creole** food, **creole** architecture, and **creole** folklore. Have students find out more about the culture of this unique city.

Social Studies Link

Ask students to make a map of North America showing different expeditions led by European and European-American explorers. Have students label the map with the explorers' names, their countries of origin, and the dates of their journeys.

Theme-Related Resources

Videos
Lewis & Clark, Explorers of the New Frontier, Biography, 1999

Books
Meriwether Lewis: Boy Explorer, by Charlotta Bebenroth, illustrated by Al Fiorentino, Econo-Clad Books, 1999

Lewis & Clark for Kids: Their Journey of Discovery with 21 Activities, by Janis Herbert, Chicago: Chicago Review Press, 2000.

How We Crossed the West: The Adventures of Lewis & Clark, by Rosalyn Schanzer, National Geographic Society, 1997

Short and Long Vowels; **y** as a Vowel

Objectives

- To recognize short and long vowel sounds and the use of **y** as a vowel
- To associate these sounds with various letter combinations
- To decode and write words with short and long vowel sounds and with **y** used as a vowel

Warming Up

- Write the following sentences on the board and say them with students.

  When the **cat's away**, the **mice will play.**

  The **squeaky wheel gets** the **grease.**

  The **sky's** the **limit.**

- Ask a volunteer to underline the words that have long vowel sounds. (**away, mice, play, squeaky, wheel, grease, sky's**) Ask another student to circle the words whose long vowel sound is long **a.** (**away, play**) Repeat the exercise with the words that have short vowel sounds. (**When, cat's, will, gets, limit**) Have the student circle words whose short vowel sound is the short **i.** (**will, limit**)

- Then ask a volunteer to identify the words with **y** used as a vowel. Have the student draw a square around the **y** with the long **i** sound and a triangle around the **y** with the long **e** sound.

Teaching the Lesson

- Write **spin, spine,** and **spiny** on the board and read them aloud. Ask how the vowel sounds differ. Explain that vowel sounds can be short or long. Point out that **y** as a vowel can have three sounds—short **i,** long **e,** and long **i.**

- Have a student read the Helpful Hints aloud as the rest of the class follows along.

33

Name _____

Helpful Hints

If a word or syllable has only one vowel, either at the beginning of the word or syllable or between two consonants, the vowel usually has the **short** sound.

hand   sell   sick   fin   hop   bump

Note: The words above contain phonograms.
A **phonogram** is a syllable that has a vowel and any letters that follow. Look at these phonograms:

and   ell   ick   in   op   ump

Read each picture name. Underline the words in the row that have the same phonogram as the name of the picture.

1. **pin** <u>spin</u> chip plan <u>tin</u> <u>grin</u> pen <u>fin</u>

2. **bell** <u>fell</u> ball <u>sell</u> stall <u>tell</u> <u>swell</u> bend

3. **stump** <u>dump</u> damp <u>lump</u> <u>bump</u> bum stamp drum

4. **stand** <u>land</u> ramp <u>sand</u> <u>hand</u> <u>band</u> sing <u>and</u>

Helpful Hint

Y can stand for **short i, long i,** and **long e.**
short i: system   **long i:** fly   **long e:** story

Say the words in the box below. Then sort the words.

dry   penny   gym

5 Short i sound	6 Long i sound	7 Long e sound
gym	dry	penny

WORK TOGETHER

Use phonograms to write a short poem about exploring. Have a partner circle the phonograms you use.

UNIVERSAL ACCESS
Meeting Individual Needs

Kinesthetic Learners

Have students stand with their arms at their sides. Read a list of words with different vowel sounds, such as **fin, coat, mane, gym, lump, seat, race, fly, spell, bite, mill,** and **try.** Have students put their hands on their heads when they hear short vowel sounds and extend their arms straight out when they hear long vowel sounds.

Visual Learners

The chart below will help students distinguish between long and short vowel sounds. Draw it on the board for students to copy. Then have students add words of their own to the chart.

Letter	Short	Long
a	bat	bait
e	bed	bead
i	kit	kite
o	cot	coat
u	cut	cute

Aztec-Puebla mask

★ **Read each word. Write S if the vowel or vowels in red have a short sound. Write L if the vowel or vowels in red have a long sound.**

1. he _L_   2. plane _L_   3. pupil _S_   4. moat _L_   5. pony _L_

6. legal _L_   7. piper _S_   8. meat _L_   9. stable _L_   10. wait _L_

★ **Underline each word that has the same phonogram as the word at the top of the list.**

11. **pray**	12. **rice**	13. **sing**	14. **pick**	15. **neat**
stay	price	sang	sick	creep
spray	glide	ring	pack	seat
plane	race	pill	pluck	heat
hay	twice	wing	click	beat

★ **Read each sentence. Underline the word with the same vowel sound as the word in bold print.**

16. Explorers crossed the seas in ships made from **trees**.

17. Some people **set** out looking for goods to sell and to trade.

18. Explorers brought slaves all the **way** from West Africa.

19. For other explorers, the plan was to try to **find** land for their countries.

20. As a **rule**, sailors stayed cool by resting below deck.

21. Some of these sailors were **bold** and boastful.

22. After many months at sea, most sailors were glad to be **home** again.

23. Those who **stayed** at sea faced many hardships.

34   LESSON 15: Short and Long Vowels; y as a Vowel

Home Involvement Activity List the titles of favorite books, movies, songs, magazines, or TV shows. Circle each short vowel sound. Underline each long vowel sound.

Practicing the Skill

● Read aloud the direction lines on pages 33–34 and complete the first item in each exercise with students.

● Remind students that saying words aloud can help them identify various vowel sounds.

● Invite students to work with partners to complete the pages.

Curriculum Connections

Spelling Link

Write the lists below on the board. Encourage students to think of as many different letters as possible to complete each word. Tell students that words in the first list have a short vowel sound, while words in the second list need one or two vowels to make a long vowel sound. See if they can guess which letter completes the words in the third list.

s_ng	p_ne	penn_
p_n	m_ _t	s_stem
t_n	r_le	g_m
b_ll	b_ _t	fl_
b_nd	r_ce	dr_

Science Link

Invite students to make a list of six animals they would like to know more about. Ask students to review the list, circling short vowel sounds in red ink and long vowel sounds in a different color ink. Then have them write a few sentences about the animal of their choice, continuing to color-code the vowel sounds in their written words.

Observational Assessment

Check to see that students can properly identify short and long vowel sounds and the long and short sounds of **y** *as a vowel.*

English-Language Learners/ESL

Find items whose names include short vowels, long vowels, and **y**s. Use items that you can hold or point to, such as **cup**, **coat**, **pin**, **ball**, **bell**, **nose**, **fly**, **stamp**, **stone**, **lace**, and **penny**. Write the word for each item on the board. Point to each word, pick up the item, and say the word. Then have students pick up an item and point to its name on the board as they say it.

Gifted Learners

Invite students to write a rhyming poem using as many different kinds of vowel sounds as they can. Ask them to recite their poems aloud, stressing the various vowel sounds. Then have students say their poems to a partner, leaving out the rhyming words, allowing the partner to fill in the blanks.

Learners with Special Needs

Additional strategies for supporting learners with special needs can be found on page 31L.

r-controlled Vowels
ar, er, ir, or, ur

Objectives

- To recognize the sounds of ar, er, ir, or, ur
- To associate the sounds of ar, er, ir, or, ur with their letters
- To decode and write words with r-controlled vowels

Warming Up

- Write the letters **ar** and **or** on the board and say the sounds the letters make. Then write this rhyme on the board:

  You won't meet a **shark**

  If you stay on the **shore**.

  But you'll stay in the **dark**

  If you do not **explore!**

- Ask a volunteer to underline the words with the sound of **ar** or **or** (shown in bold-face type above). Have the same student identify the two phonograms in the words. **(ark** and **ore)**

Teaching the Lesson

- Write these words on the board.

part	sort	dirt
dark	fork	perk
barn	corn	turn
harm	storm	worm

- Work with students to identify the sound that the words in each column have in common and the letters that make the sound.
- Ask what happens to a vowel sound when **r** follows the vowel. (The sound of the vowel changes.)
- Point out that the words in the third column all have the same vowel sound, yet it is made by different letters in each case. Have students identify both the sound and the letters.

35

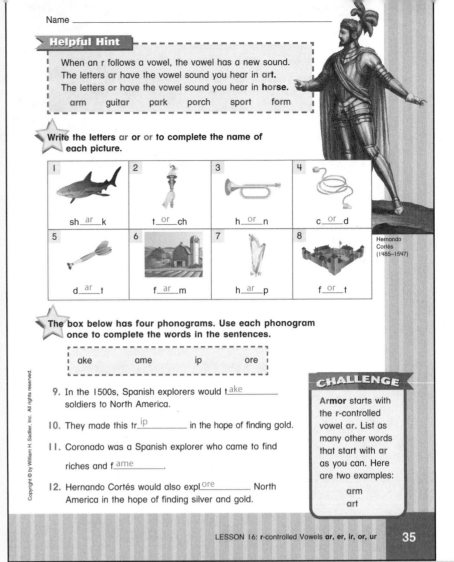

Name _____

Helpful Hint

When an r follows a vowel, the vowel has a new sound. The letters ar have the vowel sound you hear in art. The letters or have the vowel sound you hear in horse.

arm   guitar   park   porch   sport   form

Write the letters ar or or to complete the name of each picture.

1. sh__ar__k
2. t__or__ch
3. h__or__n
4. c__or__d
5. d__ar__t
6. f__ar__m
7. h__ar__p
8. f__or__t

Hernando Cortés (1485–1547)

The box below has four phonograms. Use each phonogram once to complete the words in the sentences.

ake	ame	ip	ore

9. In the 1500s, Spanish explorers would t__ake__ soldiers to North America.

10. They made this tr__ip__ in the hope of finding gold.

11. Coronado was a Spanish explorer who came to find riches and f__ame__.

12. Hernando Cortés would also expl__ore__ North America in the hope of finding silver and gold.

CHALLENGE

Armor starts with the r-controlled vowel ar. List as many other words that start with ar as you can. Here are two examples:

arm

art

LESSON 16: r-controlled Vowels **ar, er, ir, or, ur**   35

UNIVERSAL ACCESS
Meeting Individual Needs

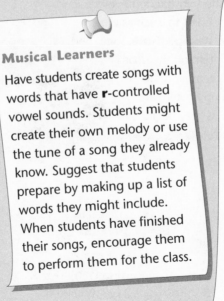

Musical Learners

Have students create songs with words that have **r**-controlled vowel sounds. Students might create their own melody or use the tune of a song they already know. Suggest that students prepare by making up a list of words they might include. When students have finished their songs, encourage them to perform them for the class.

Kinesthetic Learners

Write phonograms with **r**-controlled vowels on cards. Have students form teams and stand near the board. Place some cards in front of each team. Have the first player on each team pick a card and write three words containing the phonogram. This student passes the chalk to the next player. After one team finishes, stop the game and count each team's words. The team with the most correct words wins.

Helpful Hint

Look at these different spellings for the same vowel sound.

whirl   fern   blurb   world

Notice that or can stand for this sound, too.

⭐ **Underline the word that names each picture. Then write the word on the line.**

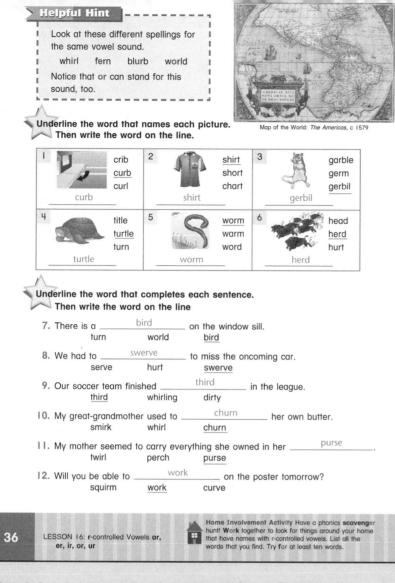

1	crib <u>curb</u> curl curb	2	<u>shirt</u> short chart shirt	3	garble germ <u>gerbil</u> gerbil
4	title <u>turtle</u> turn turtle	5	<u>worm</u> warm word worm	6	head <u>herd</u> hurt herd

⭐ **Underline the word that completes each sentence. Then write the word on the line**

7. There is a _____bird_____ on the window sill.
   turn   world   <u>bird</u>

8. We had to _____swerve_____ to miss the oncoming car.
   serve   hurt   <u>swerve</u>

9. Our soccer team finished _____third_____ in the league.
   <u>third</u>   whirling   dirty

10. My great-grandmother used to _____churn_____ her own butter.
    smirk   whirl   <u>churn</u>

11. My mother seemed to carry everything she owned in her _____purse_____.
    twirl   perch   <u>purse</u>

12. Will you be able to _____work_____ on the poster tomorrow?
    squirm   <u>work</u>   curve

36   LESSON 16: r-controlled Vowels **ar, er, ir, or, ur**

Home Involvement Activity Have a phonics **scavenger** hunt! **Work** together to look for things around your home that have names with r-controlled vowels. List all the words that you find. Try for at least ten words.

English-Language Learners/ESL

On the board, write words with **r**-controlled vowels. Point to each word, say it, and have students repeat after you. Hand out magazine cutouts of items named by the words on the board. Work with students to match the pictures to the words. Have students write the word at the bottom of a sheet of paper and paste the picture above it.

Gifted Learners

Ask students to write and illustrate a story about exploration. It could take place at any time and in any setting. It could be based on real or imagined events. When students have finished their drafts, they should underline words with **r**-controlled vowels. Have volunteers read their stories aloud.

Learners with Special Needs

Additional strategies for supporting learners with special needs can be found on page 31L.

Practicing the Skill

● Read aloud the direction lines on pages 35–36. Complete the first item in each exercise with students.

● Suggest that students say words aloud to help them identify their vowel sounds.

Intervention Strategy

Turn to page 31K for an Intervention Strategy designed to help students who need extra support with this lesson.

Curriculum Connections

Spelling Link

Have students listen carefully as you read aloud the words and sentences below. Then have a volunteer spell the word orally and write it on the board.

shirt	Why don't you wear a red **shirt?**
hurt	I fell down and **hurt** my knee.
swerve	I had to **swerve** to get out of the way.
curve	There was a **curve** in the road.
squirm	Do not **squirm** in your seat.
worm	I saw a **worm** in the garden.
third	Sandra was the **third** person on the cafeteria line.
work	There is so much **work** to do!

Social Studies Link

Organize students into groups and invite them to talk about explorers. Ask the members of each group to do research about the explorer of their choice. Have group members work together to write about the explorer, using at least five words with **r**-controlled vowels. Then invite the groups to share their work.

Observational Assessment

*Check to see that students understand how vowel sounds change when the vowels are followed by **r**. Make sure they understand that **ir, er, ur,** and **or** can stand for the same vowel sound.*

r-controlled Vowels
air, are, ear, eer

Objectives

- **To recognize the sounds of r-controlled vowels in the phonograms air, are, ear, eer**

- **To associate the sounds of the phonograms air, are, ear, eer with the letters than make them up**

- **To decode and write words with the phonograms air, are, ear, eer**

Warming Up

- Write the following poem on the board:

  In fourteen hundred ninety-two,

  Give or take a **year,**

  Christopher Columbus knew

  The **earth** to be a sphere.

- Ask a volunteer to underline the words in the rhyme with the letters **ear. (year, earth)** Ask him or her to say the words and identify the different sounds the letters **ear** represent.

Teaching the Lesson

- Write the following words on the board: **pair, pare,** and **pear.** Read them aloud with students. Point out that the words sound alike but are spelled differently and have different meanings. Have a volunteer define the three words.

- Explain that the letters **ear** do not always sound as they do in **pear** and **bear.** On the board, write the words **dear** and **year** and have a volunteer say them. Then write the words **search** and **pearl** and ask a student to read them aloud. Ask: *What three different sounds can the letters **ear** stand for?*

- Finally, call on a student to circle any words on the board that rhyme with the words **peer** and **cheer. (dear** and **year)** Then read aloud the Helpful Hints.

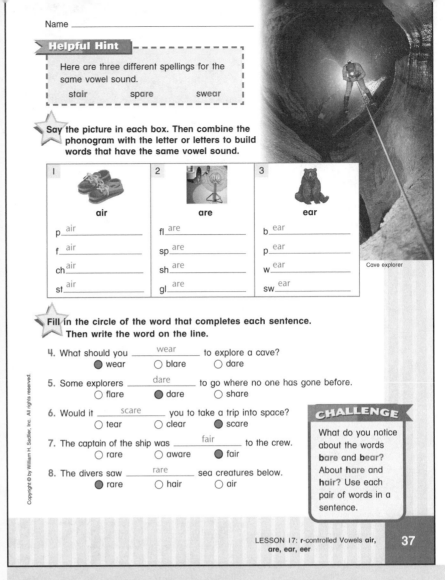

Name _____

Helpful Hint

Here are three different spellings for the same vowel sound.

stair   spare   swear

Say the picture in each box. Then combine the phonogram with the letter or letters to build words that have the same vowel sound.

1 air	2 are	3 ear
p air	fl are	b ear
f air	sp are	p ear
ch air	sh are	w ear
st air	gl are	sw ear

Fill in the circle of the word that completes each sentence. Then write the word on the line.

4. What should you ___wear___ to explore a cave?
   ● wear   ○ blare   ○ dare

5. Some explorers ___dare___ to go where no one has gone before.
   ○ flare   ● dare   ○ share

6. Would it ___scare___ you to take a trip into space?
   ○ tear   ○ clear   ● scare

7. The captain of the ship was ___fair___ to the crew.
   ○ rare   ○ aware   ● fair

8. The divers saw ___rare___ sea creatures below.
   ● rare   ○ hair   ○ air

CHALLENGE

What do you notice about the words **bare** and **bear?** About **hare** and **hair?** Use each pair of words in a sentence.

Cave explorer

UNIVERSAL ACCESS
Meeting Individual Needs

Auditory Learners

Write the following rhyme on the board and read it aloud for students and again with them:

I had a little nut-tree,

nothing would it **bear.**

But a silver nutmeg

and a golden **pear.**

Have students make up their own rhymes using a similar rhyme pattern and words with **r**-controlled vowel sounds. Invite them to read their work aloud.

Logical Learners

Draw a word-sort chart like the following on the board for students to copy. Have a volunteer explain the logic behind the way the words are grouped. Encourage students to add words to each box on the chart.

pearl		
heard		
fear	peer	
dear	deer	
fair	fare	wear
stair	stare	swear

The letters **ear** and **eer** can stand for the same vowel sound.

| year | clear | deer | sneer |

Ear can also stand for the sound you hear in **earl.**

Say the picture in each box. Then combine the phonogram with the letter or letters to build words that have the same vowel sound.

1	2	3
ear	**eer**	**ear**
g ear _____	st eer _____	p ear _____ l
y ear _____	l eer _____	_____ ear th
sm ear _____	p eer _____	l ear _____ n
sp ear _____	ch eer _____	_____ ear ly

Complete each sentence with a word from the boxes above.

4. The divers found a _____pearl_____ in that oyster shell.

5. The captain found it hard to _____steer_____ the ship.

6. We put on our scuba _____gear_____ and dove into the water.

7. We got an _____early_____ start in order to reach shore before nightfall.

8. Sailors used to _____smear_____ mud on themselves to protect their skin from the sun.

9. The captain can _____peer_____ through his spyglass.

10. When we reached dry land, we let out a loud _____sheer_____.

11. People have explored nearly every corner of the _____earth_____.

12. Last _____year_____, the shuttle explored outer space.

Home Involvement Activity Make word webs for the r-controlled vowel sounds air, are, ear, and eer. List as many words for each sound as you can.

English-Language Learners/ESL

Write the following words on the board and read them aloud for students: **ear, hear, tear, beard, steer, near, fear, stair, pair, wear, search,** and **early.** Point to a word, say it again, and demonstrate its meaning by using pantomime. Then have students change one or two letters of any word on the board, say it, and act it out for the class.

Gifted Learners

Invite students to write a story whose plot depends upon the confusion caused by a character mistaking one word for another, such as **bear** for **bare, hare** for **hair,** or **deer** for **dear.**

Learners with Special Needs

Additional strategies for supporting learners with special needs can be found on page 31L.

● Read aloud the direction lines on pages 37–38 and complete the first item in each exercise with students.

● Invite students to say the words to themselves as they work.

Curriculum Connections

Spelling Link

Read aloud the words and the sentences below. Have students listen carefully to the context of each sentence before writing the word to make sure they spell it correctly.

fair	We won a prize at the **fair.**
stair	Stand on the **stair** to see better.
bear	Tom saw a **bear** in the woods.
spare	There's a **spare** tire in the trunk.
share	Delia and I will **share** the candy.
chair	Ralph prefers the **chair** to the sofa.
earth	The sun warmed the cold **earth.**
pearl	Doug found a **pearl** in an oyster.
wear	Shelly refused to **wear** her boots.
learn	I'd like to **learn** how to ski.

Drama Link

Have students create a skit based on the words taught in this lesson and additional words that have the same **r**-controlled vowel sounds. Suggest that they begin by brainstorming a list of words. Then have students circle words that lend themselves to a story. For example, the skit might be set in a forest, where **bears, hares, deer,** and **fairies** live. The plot might revolve around a **search** for a precious **pearl.** Encourage students to be creative as they write their skit and make costumes, props, and scenery. Invite students to present their skit to their classmates.

Observational Assessment

*Check to see that students can correctly pronounce and spell each of the vowel sounds represented by the letters **air, are, ear, eer.***

Connecting Reading and Writing

Objectives

- To read a nonfiction piece and respond to it in writing
- To practice identifying problems and solutions and synthesizing ideas in a piece of writing
- To write an entry in a journal

Warming Up

Comprehension Skills

- Tell students they will be identifying and writing about **problems and solutions** in this lesson. As an example, tell them you need the phone number for a local hardware store. Write on the board: *Problem: Need telephone number.* Invite suggestions from students as to what you should do and write them on the board as follows: *Solutions: Call directory assistance. Look up number in phone book.* Ask students to suggest other examples of problems and their solutions.

- Remind students that **synthesizing** is putting together the ideas within a piece of writing and making sense of them.

Teaching the Lesson

Students might use colored markers to identify information from the selection that could help them answer the first two Reader's Response questions. For the second question, have students use logic and imagination to speculate about how Lewis and Clark solved their problems.

Practicing the Skill

Read the directions on page 40. Have volunteers read aloud the words in the box. Ask students why vivid details are important in travel journals.

Name _____

⭐ **Read about the journey of the explorers Lewis and Clark. Then answer the questions that follow.**

The Journey of Lewis and Clark

Now that the United States had made the Louisiana Purchase, President Thomas Jefferson wanted to know more about the land. What did it look like? Who lived on it? What plants grew there? What animals made it their home? To get answers, Jefferson sent his friend Meriwether Lewis to explore the Louisiana Purchase.

In 1804, Lewis and his friend William Clark began their trip through the West. They had about forty men with them. The group left from St. Louis and sailed up the Missouri River. The explorers got help from the people they met. For example, they met Sacajawea (sah kah jah WEE uh), a young Shoshone woman. She spoke to the Shoshone and to other groups for them. She also guided the explorers part of the way. Her brother, a Shoshone chief, gave the group horses for crossing the Rocky Mountains. From there, the explorers would follow the Columbia River to the Pacific Ocean. Along the way, Lewis mapped all the routes.

The journey of Lewis and Clark was not easy. Yet, Lewis and Clark wrote down in their journals all that they saw. Today, you can still read what they wrote. You can also see what they saw by following the Lewis and Clark Trail.

Sacajawea Leading Lewis and Clark
by Alfred Russell

1. To learn more about the land.
2. language barriers, transportation; they got help from the people they met
3. Answers will vary.

Reader's Response

1. Why did Thomas Jefferson want Lewis to explore the Louisiana Purchase?

2. What kinds of problems did Lewis and Clark face on their journey? How do you think they solved them?

3. Would you like to follow the Lewis and Clark Trail? Give three reasons.

LESSON 18: Connecting Reading and Writing
Comprehension—Problem and Solution;
Synthesize

39

UNIVERSAL ACCESS
Meeting Individual Needs

Auditory Learners

Some students might prefer an oral description to a written one. Encourage these students to use vivid language so that their listeners can picture their descriptions. Invite partners to help these students recall what they have said so that they can turn their oral work into a written composition.

Visual Learners

If students have difficulty thinking of a writing topic, encourage them to choose a place and make a chart listing the problems that might arise there. Here is an example:

Problems in the Woods
• get lost
• meet dangerous animals
• run out of food

Seeing ideas listed may help students remember a similar event in their own lives to write about.

Learners with Special Needs

Additional strategies for supporting learners with special needs can be found on page 31L.

Like Lewis and Clark, many explorers have described their travels in a journal. Good descriptions in a journal help a writer to remember an experience. They also help readers to picture what the writer has seen and felt on the trip.

Now it's your turn to write in a travel journal. Describe a trip you have taken. Write an entry for a day in which you solved a problem on the trip. Include strong details. Use at least two of these words in your journal entry.

| careful | dare | share | plane | peer | boat |
| world | trip | explore | car | problem | solve |

Writer's Tip

Use vivid verbs and vivid adjectives in your details to let your readers see and feel what you saw, did, and felt.

Date: _____

Place: _____ *Answers will vary.*

Problem: _____

_____

_____

Solution: _____

_____

_____

_____

_____

Writer's Challenge

Imagine that you are Meriwether Lewis or William Clark. Write a journal entry for a day on which you solved a difficult problem. Use vivid details to describe the experience.

40 LESSON 18: Connecting Reading and Writing
Comprehension—Problem and Solution; Synthesize

English-Language Learners/ESL

Work with students individually to help them identify problems that have occurred during trips they have taken. Encourage them to describe these experiences orally. Invite fluent speakers to help English learners transcribe their stories.

Gifted Learners

Invite students to think of the most fantastic trip they can. It might be a trip inside a human body or a voyage back into the past. Ask students to create illustrated journals describing places, problems, and solutions from their journeys. Encourage them to share their journals with the rest of the class.

The Writing Process

Discuss the purpose of a travel journal—to tell others about interesting events that occurred during your trip. Ask students to identify what elements go into a good travel journal. Point out that vivid language helps readers picture places and events more easily. Then read aloud the directions at the top of page 40.

Prewrite Have students brainstorm a list of places they've visited or problems they've encountered while traveling.

Write Tell students to read the words in the box and choose two to include in their journals. Have them consider how they will use these words as they write their drafts.

Revise Encourage students to let a partner read their journal entries. Have students share feedback.

Proofread Remind students to read their work slowly and carefully to check for errors in grammar, punctuation, and spelling.

Publish Have students copy their final drafts onto page 40 or a separate sheet of paper. Invite volunteers to read their journals aloud.

Computer Connection Suggest that students who use word processors explore different ways of creating boldface and italic type. In most programs, the combination of control plus **B** for bold and control plus **I** for italic will change the typeface to bold or italic and back again. Most programs also have "Toolbar" options labeled **B** and **I**. Remind students that italics are used for emphasis as well as for the titles of ships, trains, and books. Boldface type is used to set off special words.

Portfolio Suggest that students add their finished travel journals to their portfolios.

Vowel Pairs **ai, ay, ee, ea** and Vowel Digraph **ea**

Objectives

- **To recognize the sounds of the vowel pairs ai, ay, ee, ea and the digraph ea**
- **To associate the sounds of the vowel pairs and the digraph with their letters**

Warming Up

- Display this rhyme and read it aloud:

  Magellan **hailed** from Portugal
  But later **sailed** for **Spain.**
  He led his **fleet** around the world
  And gave a **strait** his name.

- Have a volunteer underline words with the long **a** sound. (**hailed, later, sailed, Spain, gave, strait, name**) Ask: *Which of these words contain the vowel pair ai?* (**hailed, sailed, Spain, strait**)

- Then ask a student to identify words with the long **e** sound. (**He, fleet**) Which word has the vowel pair **ee**? (**fleet**)

Teaching the Lesson

- Write these words on the board:

maid	may	meet	meat	meadow
pail	pay	peel	peal	pleasant
rain	ray	reed	read	ready

- Have a volunteer read aloud the words in the first row and then say their vowel sounds. Repeat with the remaining rows.

- Have a volunteer look at the words in each column and identify the two letters they have in common. (**ai, ay, ee, ea, ea**) Ask: *How are the vowel sounds of the words in the last column different from the others?* (The vowel sounds of the words in the last last column are short.)

Name _____

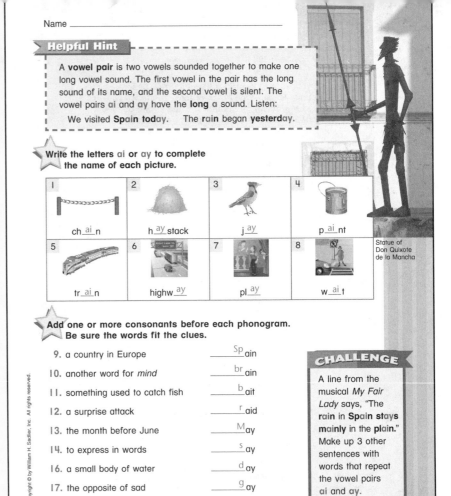

> **Helpful Hint**
>
> A **vowel pair** is two vowels sounded together to make one long vowel sound. The first vowel in the pair has the long sound of its name, and the second vowel is silent. The vowel pairs **ai** and **ay** have the **long a** sound. Listen:
>
> We visited **Spain today.**   The **rain** began **yesterday.**

⭐ Write the letters **ai** or **ay** to complete the name of each picture.

1	2	3	4
ch_ai_n	h_ay_stack	j_ay_	p_ai_nt
5	6	7	8
tr_ai_n	highw_ay_	pl_ay_	w_ai_t

Statue of Don Quixote de la Mancha

⭐ Add one or more consonants before each phonogram. Be sure the words fit the clues.

9. a country in Europe — _Sp_ain
10. another word for *mind* — _br_ain
11. something used to catch fish — _b_ait
12. a surprise attack — _r_aid
13. the month before June — _M_ay
14. to express in words — _s_ay
16. a small body of water — _d_ay
17. the opposite of sad — _g_ay

> **CHALLENGE**
>
> A line from the musical *My Fair Lady* says, "The **rain** in **Spain** stays **mainly** in the **plain**." Make up 3 other sentences with words that repeat the vowel pairs **ai** and **ay.**

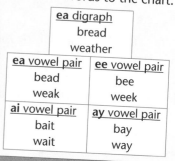

UNIVERSAL ACCESS
Meeting Individual Needs

Auditory Learners

Write the following tongue twisters on the board:

She sells s**ea**shells by the s**ea**shore.

Is there a pl**ea**sant p**ea**sant present?

Have a student read them aloud. Ask a volunteer to underline and say the words that contain the vowel pair **ea** or the digraph **ea**. Ask what distinguishes the vowel pair from the digraph.

Visual Learners

Draw the following chart on the board for students to refer to as they complete this lesson. Invite students to add their own words to the chart.

ea digraph	
bread	
weather	

ea vowel pair	**ee** vowel pair
bead	bee
weak	week

ai vowel pair	**ay** vowel pair
bait	bay
wait	way

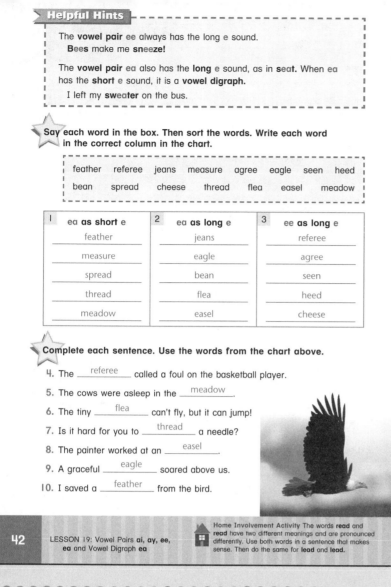

The **vowel pair** ee always has the long e sound.
   Bees make me **sneeze!**

The **vowel pair** ea also has the **long** e sound, as in s**ea**t. When ea
has the **short** e sound, it is a **vowel digraph**.
   I left my sw**ea**ter on the bus.

★ Say each word in the box. Then sort the words. Write each word
in the correct column in the chart.

| feather | referee | jeans | measure | agree | eagle | seen | heed |
| bean | spread | cheese | thread | flea | easel | meadow |

1 ea as short e	2 ea as long e	3 ee as long e
feather	jeans	referee
measure	eagle	agree
spread	bean	seen
thread	flea	heed
meadow	easel	cheese

★ Complete each sentence. Use the words from the chart above.

4. The _____referee_____ called a foul on the basketball player.

5. The cows were asleep in the _____meadow_____.

6. The tiny _____flea_____ can't fly, but it can jump!

7. Is it hard for you to _____thread_____ a needle?

8. The painter worked at an _____easel_____.

9. A graceful _____eagle_____ soared above us.

10. I saved a _____feather_____ from the bird.

42   LESSON 19: Vowel Pairs **ai, ay, ee,**
    ea and Vowel Digraph **ea**

Home Involvement Activity The words **read** and
read have two different meanings and are pronounced
differently. Use both words in a sentence that makes
sense. Then do the same for **lead** and **lead**.

42

Vowel Pairs **ei** and **ie**; Vowel Digraphs **ei, ie, ey**

Objectives

- To recognize the vowel pairs **ei** and **ie** and the digraphs **ei, ie,** and **ey**
- To distinguish between the vowel pair **ei** and the digraph **ei** and between the vowel pair **ie** and the digraph **ie**

Warming Up

- Write this poem on the board, underlining the words in boldface type:

A pirate's crew **seized** pieces of **eight**,
Thieves of the ocean were **they**.
But **neither** the captain nor his first mate
Saw their ship sinking under the **weight**,
Until a shark **seized** them as **prey**!

- Read the poem aloud with students. Ask a volunteer to identify and say the underlined words with the long **e** sound. (**seized, neither**) Have another student identify and say the underlined words with the long **a** sound. (**eight, they, weight, prey**)
- Tell students that the letters **ei** in **seized** and **neither** are a vowel pair. The letters **ei** in **eight** and **weight** and **ey** in **they** and **prey** are vowel digraphs.

Teaching the Lesson

- Review with students the difference between vowel pairs and vowel digraphs.
- Explain that vowel pairs always have a long vowel sound, and they take that sound from the first letter in the pair.
- Vowel digraphs are pairs of letters that have either a long or short vowel sound. The vowel sound of a digraph can come from either letter, or it can be different from either letter, as in the long **a** sound of **ey** in **they** and **prey**.

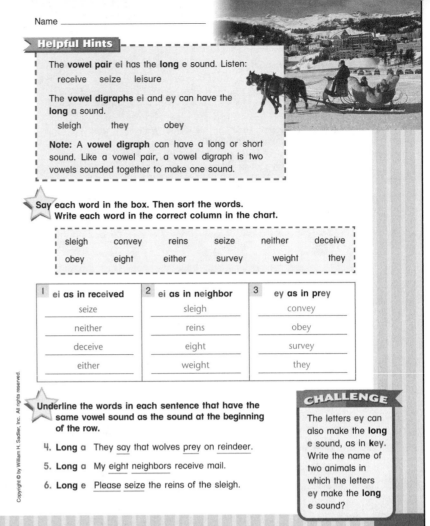

Name _____

Helpful Hints

The **vowel pair** ei has the **long** e sound. Listen:
receive   seize   leisure

The **vowel digraphs** ei and ey can have the **long** a sound.
sleigh   they   obey

Note: A **vowel digraph** can have a long or short sound. Like a vowel pair, a vowel digraph is two vowels sounded together to make one sound.

Say each word in the box. Then sort the words. Write each word in the correct column in the chart.

| sleigh | convey | reins | seize | neither | deceive |
| obey | eight | either | survey | weight | they |

1 ei as in received	2 ei as in neighbor	3 ey as in prey
seize	sleigh	convey
neither	reins	obey
deceive	eight	survey
either	weight	they

Underline the words in each sentence that have the same vowel sound as the sound at the beginning of the row.

4. **Long** a   They <u>say</u> that wolves <u>prey</u> on <u>reindeer</u>.

5. **Long** a   My <u>eight</u> <u>neighbors</u> receive mail.

6. **Long** e   Please <u>seize</u> the reins of the sleigh.

CHALLENGE

The letters ey can also make the **long** e sound, as in **key**. Write the name of two animals in which the letters ey make the **long** e sound?

LESSON 20: Vowel Pairs **ei** and **ie**;
Vowel Digraphs **ei, ey, ie**

43

UNIVERSAL ACCESS
Meeting Individual Needs

Auditory Learners

To help students keep track of the different vowel pairs and vowel digraphs they are learning, write the following mnemonic jingle on the board. Keep it displayed throughout the lesson and suggest that students refer to it as they complete the exercises.

I before **e**, except after **c**
Or when sounding like **a**,
As in **neighbor** and **weigh**,
Or when sounding like **e**'s,
As in **leisure** and **seize**.

Visual Learners

The chart below can help students organize the information taught in this lesson. Draw it on the board for students to copy. Have volunteers suggest additional words for each category.

Vowel Pairs	ei	ie	
	seize either	pie tie	
Vowel Digraphs	ei	ie	ey
	eight reins	piece chief	they prey

Helpful Hints

The **vowel pair** ie has the **long i** sound, as in p**ie**.
The **vowel digraph** ie can stand for the **long e** sound, as in pi**e**ce.

Add ie to the letters in the boxes to form words. Then write the words to complete the sentences.

cr_**ie**_d
tr_**ie**_d
sp_**ie**_d
fr_**ie**_d

— ie —

ch_**ie**_f
th_**ie**_f
br_**ie**_f
gr_**ie**_f

— ie —

1. This means "attempted." _____tried_____
2. This means "cooked in oil." _____fried_____
3. This means "wept." _____cried_____
4. This means "watched secretly." _____spied_____
5. This means "sadness." _____grief_____
6. This is a robber. _____thief_____
7. This is a leader. _____chief_____
8. This means "short." _____brief_____

Use a word from the box below to complete each sentence.

pie believe shriek untied piece die dried achieve

9. To accept as true is to _____believe_____.
10. Riding a roller coaster causes most people to _____shriek_____.
11. Can I have a large _____piece_____ of that chocolate cake?
12. To accomplish is to _____achieve_____.
13. As soon as Dad got home, he _____untied_____ his necktie.
14. I placed _____dried_____ flowers in a vase.
15. I think apple _____pie_____ is my favorite dessert.
16. The plants will _____die_____ if we do not water them.

44 LESSON 20: Vowel Pairs **ei** and **ie**;
Vowel Digraphs **ei**, **ey**, **ie**

Home Involvement Activity Recite the old rhyme that helps us remember how to spell some tricky words. *Use i before e, except after c, or when sounded like a, as in n**ei**ghbor and w**ei**gh.*

Practicing the Skill

Read aloud the direction lines on pages 43–44 and complete the first item in each exercise with students. Suggest that students say the words quietly to themselves as they work.

Turn to page 31K for an Intervention Strategy designed to help students who need extra support with this lesson.

Curriculum Connections

Spelling Link

On the board, write the sentences below. Have students write the correct letter combination in each blank.

Santa Claus travels in a **sl__gh.**
It is pulled by **__ght r__ndeer.**
Children **bel__ve** that Santa brings gifts.
Some leave him a **p__ce** of cake or **p__.**
Our **n__ghbors** call Santa "St. Nick."
Every year **th__** make a chain of **dr__d** cranberries to decorate their tree.

Social Studies Link

Have students match the words below with the sentences about Lewis and Clark.

tried   convey   achieve
received   chief

1. Lewis and Clark ____ help from Sacajawea.
2. They ____ to reach the Pacific Ocean.
3. They accepted horses from Sacajawea's brother, a Shoshone ____.
4. Lewis and Clark kept journals in order to ____ to others all they did and saw.
5. What did President Jefferson want to ____ by sending Lewis on this journey?

Observational Assessment

*Check to see that students know when to use **ei** and when to use **ie**.*

English-Language Learners/ESL

On the board, make a list words in which **ei** has the long **a** sound and another of words in which **ei** has the long **e** sound. Show pictures or act out the words' meanings as you say the words. Ask students to circle the letters **ei** as you say each word together. Repeat the exercise with two lists of words that contain the letters **ie.**

Gifted Learners

Have students look in a social studies textbook or an encyclopedia to find ten words that they can use in a passage from an explorer's log. Explain that the words must include the vowel pairs **ei** and **ie** or the vowel digraphs **ei**, **ie**, and **ey.**

Learners with Special Needs

Additional strategies for supporting learners with special needs can be found on page 31L.

Syllables with Short and Long Vowels, r-controlled Vowels, Vowel Pairs, and Vowel Digraphs

Objectives

- **To divide into syllables words with short and long vowels, r-controlled vowels, vowel pairs, and vowel digraphs**

- **To divide compound words into syllables**

Warming Up

- Write the following Christina Rossetti poem on the board. Read it aloud with students.

An
emerald
is as green
as grass, A **ru-
by** red as blood, A **sap-
phire** shines as blue as **hea-
ven,** But a flint lies in the mud.
A diamond is a brilliant stone
to catch the world's desire, An
opal holds a **rain-
bow's** light, but
a flint holds
fire.

- Invite students to identify the places where words are divided. Have a volunteer circle each hyphen while pronouncing the syllables it divides.

Teaching the Lesson

Explain that there are rules for dividing words into syllables. Discuss why it might be important to know how to divide a word into syllables. Then have a student read aloud the Helpful Hints. Ask: *When would you divide two vowels that are found together in a word? Would you ever split vowel pairs or vowel digraphs? Explain.*

45

Name _____

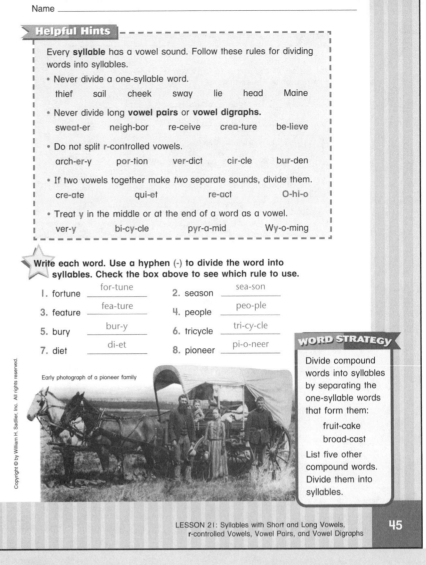

> **Helpful Hints**
>
> Every **syllable** has a vowel sound. Follow these rules for dividing words into syllables.
>
> - Never divide a one-syllable word.
>
>   thief   sail   cheek   sway   lie   head   Maine
>
> - Never divide long **vowel pairs** or **vowel digraphs**.
>
>   sweat-er   neigh-bor   re-ceive   crea-ture   be-lieve
>
> - Do not split r-controlled vowels.
>
>   arch-er-y   por-tion   ver-dict   cir-cle   bur-den
>
> - If two vowels together make *two* separate sounds, divide them.
>
>   cre-ate   qui-et   re-act   O-hi-o
>
> - Treat y in the middle or at the end of a word as a vowel.
>
>   ver-y   bi-cy-cle   pyr-a-mid   Wy-o-ming

Write each word. Use a hyphen (-) to divide the word into syllables. Check the box above to see which rule to use.

1. fortune ___for-tune___
2. season ___sea-son___
3. feature ___fea-ture___
4. people ___peo-ple___
5. bury ___bur-y___
6. tricycle ___tri-cy-cle___
7. diet ___di-et___
8. pioneer ___pi-o-neer___

Early photograph of a pioneer family

WORD STRATEGY

Divide compound words into syllables by separating the one-syllable words that form them:

fruit-cake
broad-cast

List five other compound words. Divide them into syllables.

LESSON 21: Syllables with Short and Long Vowels, r-controlled Vowels, Vowel Pairs, and Vowel Digraphs

45

UNIVERSAL ACCESS
Meeting Individual Needs

Tactile Learners

Arrange students in groups. Give each group five cards with three-syllable words written on them. Have students cut the cards to separate the syllables of the words. Ask a member of each group to place the card pieces in a bag and mix them up. When you say "Go!" students should empty the bags and reassemble the syllables to recreate the original five words.

Kinesthetic Learners

Make large letter cards for **a, b, c, e, f, i, l, n, o, r, s, t** and **y.** Distribute the cards. Direct students to hold up the letters in front of the room to spell **feature, bury, fortune, season, tricycle, terror,** and **rabbit.** Have other students hold up one or more hyphen cards between the letters of each word following the rules for dividing words into syllables.

Here are more rules to help you divide words into syllables.

• If a word has two consonants between two vowels (VCCV), divide between consonants. BUT—do *not* split **consonant blends** or **consonant digraphs**.

sun-ny   fel-low   can-vas   fif-ty   mon-key   ush-er   lath-er

• If a word has one consonant between two vowels (VCV), divide *after* the consonant if the first vowel is short.

shad-ow   nev-er   hab-it   trav-el   riv-er

• If a word has one consonant between two vowels (VCV), divide *before* the consonant if the first vowel is long.

pi-lot   re-gal   ba-sic   o-ver   cra-zy

★ Write each word. Use a hyphen (-) to divide the word into syllables. Check the box above to see which rule to use.

1. terror — ter-ror
2. washer — wash-er
3. pillow — pil-low
4. gravel — grav-el
5. robot — ro-bot
6. donkey — don-key
7. basis — ba-sis
8. rabbit — rab-bit
9. under — un-der
10. sixty — six-ty
11. closet — clos-et
12. ever — ev-er
13. wagon — wag-on
14. favor — fav-or
15. rather — rath-er
16. lazy — la-zy

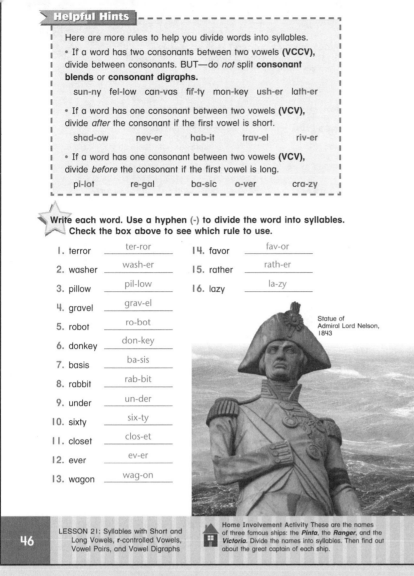

Statue of Admiral Lord Nelson, 1843

Home Involvement Activity These are the names of three famous ships: the *Pinta*, the *Ranger*, and the *Victoria*. Divide the names into syllables. Then find out about the great captain of each ship.

46   LESSON 21: Syllables with Short and Long Vowels, r-controlled Vowels, Vowel Pairs, and Vowel Digraphs

Practicing the Skill

• Read aloud the direction lines on pages 45–46 and complete the first item in each exercise with students.

• Suggest that students first identify what category the word falls into and then look up the rule for that type of word.

Curriculum Connections

Spelling Link

Read these sentences aloud. Repeat the word shown in bold type, and have students write it down, correctly dividing it into syllables.

She had good **fortune** in her life.

What kind of **creature** is that?

He had a **donkey** and a cart.

We need lots of fruit in our **diet**.

That remark was not **fair!**

Her **heartbeat** was strong.

Raul will create a new **painting**.

Have you seen my white **rabbit?**

Brushing your teeth is a good **habit**.

I'd like to learn **archery**.

Science Link

Invite students to look through science books and articles and write down the longest words they can find. Chemical names or technical terms are perfect for this. Then challenge students to divide these words into syllables, applying what they have learned. Stress that it is not necessary to know a word's meaning in order to divide it into syllables correctly.

Observational Assessment

Check to see that students grasp the principle that vowel pairs and vowel digraphs cannot be broken.

English-Language Learners/ESL

Help students understand the relationship between a visual syllable and the sound of a word part. Write on the board some familiar two-syllable words, using hyphens to divide them into syllables. Have students say each syllable as you point to it. Repeat with some familiar three-syllable words.

Gifted Learners

Give students cards and have them write a multisyllable word on each one. Collect the cards and have two students at a time each take an equal number of cards from the deck. Time them to see who can divide the words into syllables more quickly.

Learners with Special Needs

Additional strategies for supporting learners with special needs can be found on page 31L.

Connecting Spelling and Writing

Objectives

- **To say, spell, sort, and write words with r-controlled vowels, vowel pairs, vowel digraphs, and y as a vowel**

- **To write an essay using spelling words**

Warming Up

● Write the following paragraph on the board. Have a student read it aloud.

> The old expl**or**er told his st**or**y. He had left Sp**ai**n **ei**ght y**ear**s ago and had s**ee**n man**y** things. His w**or**ds conv**ey**ed his excitement.

● Ask volunteers to find and circle **r**-controlled vowels, vowel pairs, vowel digraphs, and **y** as a vowel. Together with the class, read aloud the words that contain the circled items.

Teaching the Lesson

● List the following words on the board. Next to each, have volunteers write and say aloud other words that have the same **r**-controlled vowel sound: **bark, sport, herd, clear, girl.**

● Next, list the following words on the board: **brain, play, bread, tree, bean, prey, either.** Have volunteers write and say aloud other words that have the same vowel pairs or vowel digraphs.

Practicing the Skill

Read together the directions on page 47. Have students read each phrase aloud and then complete the page.

Name _____

☆ **Read each group of words. Say and spell each word in bold print. Repeat the word. Then sort the words. Write each word in the correct column below.**

- **explore** the unknown
- **heed** the warning
- a group of **rare** birds
- hold the **reins**
- the earth's water **cycle**
- on a **daring** voyage
- **seize** the moment
- in the **chilly** breeze
- **endure** harsh conditions
- a **typical** day
- shaped like a **pyramid**
- a **nature** walk

- might **freeze** solid
- just like **poetry**
- will **remain** for a year
- **disagree** with the leader

Words with r-controlled Vowels	Words with Vowel Pairs or Vowel Digraphs	Words with y as a Vowel
explore	heed	cycle
rare	seize	chilly
daring	freeze	typical
endure	remain	pyramid
nature	disagree	poetry
	reins	

UNIVERSAL ACCESS
Meeting Individual Needs

Auditory Learners

Say aloud a series of one-syllable words from Lessons 16, 17, 19, and 20. For each word, have students tell whether they hear a vowel-**r** combination, a vowel pair, or a vowel digraph. Then have students write the word on the board. Extend the activity by having students suggest additional words and write them on the board.

Visual Learners

Write each of the following words on an index card: **cry, heavy, butterfly, bicycle, sky, windy, pyramid, dizzy,** and **pony.** Tell the class they are going to play "**Y**-Word Charades." Give out cards to volunteers and have them act out the words. As students figure out each word, write it on the board. Ask whether the **y** in the word has a short **i** sound (as in **gym**), a long **i** sound (as in **fly**), or a long **e** sound (as in **penny**).

Learners with Special Needs

Additional strategies for supporting learners with special needs can be found on page 31L.

Antarctica is the coldest spot on Earth. Almost all of this continent is covered with ice all year long. No animals or plants can survive there year-round. Yet explorers have risked their lives to learn about this cold and lonely place. Today, people use Antarctica only for scientific research.

★ Think about why explorers may have risked their lives to go to Antarctica. Write your ideas in a brief essay. End your essay by telling whether you would ever visit this cold, lonely place. Use two or more of these spelling words.

explore	heed	rare	reins	cycle	daring
seize	chilly	endure	typical		
pyramid	nature	freeze	poetry	remain	disagree

Answers will vary.

Writer's Tip

Before you begin to write, find out facts about Antarctica in a reference book, such as an atlas. Choose the best information. You can also research Antarctica on the Internet.

_____
_____
_____
_____
_____
_____
_____
_____

Writer's Challenge

Write an eyewitness account to describe what you saw when a group of explorers came to Antarctica. Take the point of view of a penguin who saw the explorers arrive and who watched them struggle. Keep the same point of view throughout.

English-Language Learners/ESL

Have students make up riddles for words with **r**-controlled vowels, vowel pairs, vowel digraphs, or **y** as a vowel. For example: *Sea explorers don't want to get bitten by this. It has five letters and an **r**-controlled vowel. What is it? (a **shark**)* Have volunteers write their riddles on the board and read them aloud. As students solve the riddles, have them write the answers on the board. Give additional clues as needed.

Gifted Learners

Have students research and write a composition about an explorer, taking the first person ("I") point of view. Encourage students to make their narrative exciting. Students should illustrate and design a cover for their composition.

The Writing Process

Tell students that on page 48 they will write a brief essay relating to the continent of Antarctica. Go over the directions and spelling words at the top of the page.

Prewrite Discuss with the class what factors motivate people to explore the unknown. Ask students whether they would ever be tempted to be explorers. Why or why not? Also have students think about how the world might be different if, in the past, no one had explored the unknown.

Write Encourage students to plan what they wish to say before they start to write. Suggest that they write the first draft of their essay without worrying about the spelling words. They can determine how best to put in the words afterward.

Revise Have students reread their essays carefully. Ask: *Have you put in specific reasons why explorers may have risked their lives? Have you told whether you would ever visit Antarctica and given reasons to support your opinion?*

Proofread Have students check for errors in spelling, grammar, and punctuation.

Publish Have students copy their final drafts onto page 48. Ask volunteers to read their essays aloud.

Computer Connection

Share the following tip with students who use a word processor to do their writing.

● Many word-processing programs have a grammar checker. This feature can be helpful, but grammar checkers won't catch every error. They can suggest undesirable or unnecessary changes. Students should use their judgment.

● Grammar checkers can help spot passive constructions, which students may wish to change to active constructions.

Portfolio Suggest that students add their finished essays to their portfolios.

Reviewing and Assessing

Short and Long Vowels, y as a Vowel, r-controlled Vowels, Vowel Pairs, and Vowel Digraphs

Objective

To review and assess short and long vowels, r-controlled vowels, vowel pairs, and vowel digraphs

Warming Up

● Write the following lists on the board. Have volunteers draw lines connecting pairs of words that have the same vowel sound. Say the words aloud.

bell	**cry**
ramp	**free**
gym	**weigh**
shark	**sneer**
girl	**stare**
bear	**world**
ear	**tin**
pie	**send**
flea	**tan**
they	**arm**

● Have students suggest additional pairs of words having the same sounds. Compare how the words are spelled.

Teaching the Lesson

● Direct students' attention to the first exercise on page 49. Stress that students will be looking for words with the same vowel sound but not necessarily the same vowels. Look back at examples from *Warming Up*. Also point out that students will need to underline two or more words in each row.

● For both exercises on page 49, encourage students to say the words softly to themselves to help them hear the sounds.

49

Name _____

☆ Say the word next to the number. Underline the words in the row that have the same vowel sound as the numbered word.

1	art	heart	dark	chair	steep	worm
2	flat	great	grab	brag	jar	wrap
3	try	my	play	sky	rye	knife
4	whirl	which	squirrel	worried	girl	turn
5	stair	chair	stain	steer	mare	dryer
6	head	greed	leaf	led	health	bread
7	rein	stain	being	plane	veil	height
8	peach	stream	crease	pause	swear	Greek
9	word	born	work	fork	birch	churn
10	sleigh	sway	bright	prey	sweat	clay
11	prune	rule	grape	truce	drum	church
12	form	color	stork	worm	home	porch

☆ Underline the word in each pair that has the same vowel sound as the sound at the beginning of the row.

13.	**Long i**	thief or pie?	rhyme or sixty?	speed or spied?
14.	**Long e**	meat or pearl?	early or green?	meant or cheat?
15.	**Long a**	weigh or grieve?	peach or paint?	sweat or stray?
16.	**Short e**	break or thread?	clear or wealth?	bread or braid?
17.	**Short i**	sprint or sprite?	trail or gym?	fright or wrist?
18.	**Short o**	flop or chore?	nose or nozzle?	low or log?

LESSON 23: Review and Assess **49**

UNIVERSAL ACCESS
Meeting Individual Needs

Auditory Learners

Write these words across the board, using a different color chalk for each: **cane, bare, day, raid, fern.** Have volunteers list words underneath these words that have the same vowel sound. If the sound is spelled the same, use matching colored chalk. If not, use white chalk. For example, students would print **lane** in the same color as **cane,** but **pain** would require white chalk.

Learners with Special Needs

Additional strategies for supporting students with special needs can be found on page 31L.

Visual Learners

On chart paper, draw two large trees, each with six or seven branches. Label the branches: *short a sound, long a sound, short e, long e, short i, long i, short o, long o, short u, long u, vowel pairs, vowel digraphs, r-controlled vowels.* Have students draw and cut out paper leaves. Then have them print a word on each cutout and tape it to an appropriate branch. Try to fill all the branches. Discuss which words could be attached to more than one branch.

Fill in the circle of the word that completes each sentence. Then write the word on the line.

1. Christopher Columbus lived for a time in ___Spain___.
   ○ Maine ● Spain ○ Baytown

2. He wished to explore unknown parts of the ___world___
   ○ weird ○ whirl ● world

3. He hoped to get money to ___seek___ new lands.
   ● seek ○ eke ○ sheik

4. It took more than a ___week___ to get ready for the voyage.
   ● week ○ weak ○ wreck

5. The journey in 1492 was long and ___hard___.
   ○ heard ○ herd ● hard

6. The crew was thrilled to spot ___dry___ land.
   ○ dray ○ dried ● dry

★ A *hink-pink* is a pair of one-syllable words that rhyme. Complete each hink-pink with a word that rhymes with the word in bold print. Watch out! Just because the words rhyme doesn't mean that they are spelled alike!

7. If you think too hard, you might get ___brain___ **strain**.

8. I raised a robin. Then I raised a wren. Now I'm raising my **third** ___bird___.

9. The king's wicked wife is called the ___mean___ **queen**.

10. If you fear that your wig will fall off, you'll have a ___hair___ **scare**!

Extend & Apply

Make up your own hink-pinks. To help, write at least one rhyming word on each blank line.

11. clay ___day, hay___   12. head ___bed, red___

13. dare ___care, spare___   14. splash ___dash, mash___

50   LESSON 23: Review and Assess

Reteaching Activities

Single-Syllable Sounds

Write the following sentences on the board.

> **We sailed for days.**
> **The bread is stale.**
> **He tore his green jeans.**
> **My hair turned gray.**
> **I fear the boat leaks.**

Have students read each sentence aloud. Then have them identify short and long vowel sounds, **r**-controlled vowels, vowel pairs, and vowel digraphs. Ask students to write the words on cards and sort them by vowel sound.

Sound Thinking

Have students write these phrases on cards: *short **a**, long **a**, short **e**, long **e**, short **i**, long **i**, short **o**, long **o**, short **u**, long **u**, vowel pair, vowel digraph, **r**-controlled vowel.* Choose a sampling of words from the unit. Say each word aloud and have students hold up the card(s) that name the word's vowel sound.

Then have a volunteer write the word on the board and circle the letters that represent the vowel sound.

Assessing the Skill

Check Up If you have not yet assigned the exercises on page 49, as discussed in *Teaching the Lesson,* do so now.

Page 50 will help you assess students' understanding of vowels, vowel pairs, and vowel digraphs. Read aloud the directions for the exercises. Then have students complete the page. For items 1–6, tell students to consider all three choices before choosing one. For items 7–10, encourage students to use context clues to help them figure out what words to fill in.

Observational Assessment As students do the exercises, try to identify any areas of difficulty or confusion. For items 7–10, note whether students are able to make effective use of context clues when filling in their words. Review earlier observational notes to help you evaluate students' progress.

Student Skills Assessment Keep track of student's progress in understanding vowels, vowel pairs, and vowel digraphs using the checklist on page 31H.

Writing Conference Set aside time to meet with students individually to talk over their recent writing, such as the essay on page 48 and the travel journal on page 40. Discuss how the student's work has improved and what the student can do to make his or her writing even better. Ask students what they have added to their Home Portfolios.

Group together students who need further instruction in vowels, vowel pairs, and vowel digraphs and have them complete the *Reteaching Activities.* Turn to page 31C for alternative assessment methods.

Vowel Digraphs
au and aw; al

Objectives

- To associate the vowel digraphs **au** and **aw** and the digraph **al** with the **aw** sound

- To pronounce and write words with the vowel digraphs **au** and **aw** and the digraph **al**

- To build vocabulary by identifying words with the vowel digraphs **au** and **aw** and the digraph **al**

Warming Up

- Write the following poem on the board. Have a student read it aloud.

    On a newly mowed **lawn,**

    Maudie and **Shawna** and **Dawn** and **Paul**

    Saw a **hawk** and a **fawn** and an **autumn** leaf **fall.**

- Ask a volunteer to underline the words in the poem that have the **aw** sound. Then have the student say that sound while circling the two letters that make the **aw** sound in each word.

- Point out to students the different ways of spelling the **aw** sound.

Teaching the Lesson

- Write these words on the board.

caution	draw	talk
launch	brawl	walk
haunt	paw	stalk
taught	raw	chalk

- Say the words with students and help them identify the vowel digraph or letters that represent the **aw** sound. Ask them to add more examples to the list.

- Have a student read the Helpful Hint aloud. Then ask: *How many ways can we spell words having the **aw** sound?*

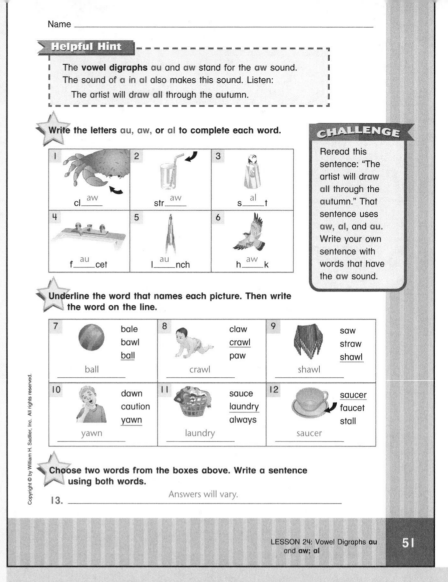

Name _____

Helpful Hint

The **vowel digraphs** au and aw stand for the aw sound. The sound of a in al also makes this sound. Listen:
    The artist will draw all through the autumn.

Write the letters au, aw, or al to complete each word.

1	2	3
cl__aw__	str__aw__	s__al__t
4	5	6
f__au__cet	l__au__nch	h__aw__k

CHALLENGE

Reread this sentence: "The artist will draw all through the autumn." That sentence uses aw, al, and au. Write your own sentence with words that have the aw sound.

Underline the word that names each picture. Then write the word on the line.

7		8		9	
	bale bawl <u>ball</u>		claw <u>crawl</u> paw		saw straw <u>shawl</u>
	ball		crawl		shawl
10		11		12	
	dawn caution <u>yawn</u>		sauce laundry always		saucer faucet stall
	yawn		laundry		saucer

Choose two words from the boxes above. Write a sentence using both words.

13. _____ Answers will vary. _____

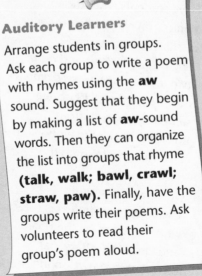

UNIVERSAL ACCESS
Meeting Individual Needs

Auditory Learners

Arrange students in groups. Ask each group to write a poem with rhymes using the **aw** sound. Suggest that they begin by making a list of **aw**-sound words. Then they can organize the list into groups that rhyme **(talk, walk; bawl, crawl; straw, paw).** Finally, have the groups write their poems. Ask volunteers to read their group's poem aloud.

Kinesthetic Learners

Choose three students to hold signs with the letters **au, aw,** and **al.** On index cards, write words that have the **aw** sound. Place the cards face down in the middle of the room. Have students—one at a time—choose a card, say the word, and line up behind the student with the sign **au, aw,** or **al.**

⭐ **Choose a word from the box to complete each sentence. Write the word on the line. Use the hints in parentheses ( ).**

> walking   shawl   sprawled   yawning   caught
>
> launch   dawn   lawn   small   tall   talk

⭐ **Complete each sentence with a word from the box.**

1. The ___launch___ was planned for that Tuesday morning. (rhymes with *staunch*)

2. Everyone was ___caught___ up in the excitement. (rhymes with *taught*)

3. Whenever people got together they would ___talk___ about the mission. (rhymes with *walk*)

4. We left our home early in order to arrive at the launch before ___dawn___. (rhymes with *lawn*)

5. Many people were already there, and some were sleepy and ___yawning___. (rhymes with *awning*)

6. Others were ___walking___ toward the rocket to get a closer look. (rhymes with *squawking*)

7. Some people were standing, but others were ___sprawled___ on the grass. (rhymes with *hauled*)

8. A few families spread blankets on the ___lawn___ and had breakfast. (rhymes with *fawn*)

9. My mother was cold, so she put on her ___shawl___. (rhymes with *ball*)

10. I looked up when the ___tall___ rocket began to lift off. (rhymes with *crawl*)

11. Even ___small___ children began to cheer. (rhymes with *stall*)

52   LESSON 24: Vowel Digraphs **au** and **aw**; **al**

🏠 **Home Involvement Activity** Austin, Texas, is a city that has the vowel digraph au in its name. Brainstorm to create a list of other place names that have the vowel digraph au or aw.

English-Language Learners/ESL

On the board, make a list of words that include the letter pair **au**, leaving blanks for the vowels: **f_ _cet, h_ _l,** and so on. Invite students to fill in the blanks as they say each word. Review the lists and help students identify each word's meaning. Repeat the process with **aw** and **al.**

Gifted Learners

Have students write a poem about autumn or a subject of their choice. Suggest that they write the poems in a shape that relates to the subject.

Reddish-brown are autumn leaves.
Wheat grows tall in golden sheaves.

Learners with Special Needs

Additional strategies for supporting learners with special needs can be found on page 31L.

Practicing the Skill

● Read aloud the direction lines on pages 51–52 and complete the first item in each exercise with students.

● Remind students that they can use the process of elimination to narrow down their choices, checking off the words in the box as they answer items 1–11 on page 52.

● Encourage students to say the rhyming words aloud to help them hear the answers.

Curriculum Connections

Spelling Link

Write these scrambled words on the board and have students unscramble them, spelling them correctly.

> **wakusq**   **slaprewd**   **khaw**
>
> **awrst**   **tals**   **was**
>
> **wand**   **cesau**   **cesaur**

(Answers: **squawk, sprawled, hawk, straw, salt, saw, dawn, sauce, saucer**)

Science Link

Work with students to think of birds and other animals whose names have an **aw** sound, such as **macaw, fawn, prawn,** and **hawk.** Have students work in groups to choose an animal, write three questions about it, and then look for the answers in an encyclopedia or science textbook. Students may want to create an illustration of the animal. Have volunteers present their work to the class, perhaps as an informal oral report.

Observational Assessment

*Check to see that students can properly pronounce the vowel digraphs **au** and **aw** and the digraph **al**.*

52

Vowel Digraph **oo** and Vowel Pairs **oa, oe**

Objectives

- **To distinguish between the two pronunciations of the vowel digraph oo**
- **To recognize that the vowel pairs oa and oe have the long o sound**
- **To decode, pronounce, and write words with the vowel digraph oo and the vowel pairs oa and oe**

Warming Up

- Write this rhyme on the board. Have a student read it aloud.

  They'll come a time **soon**

  When I'll walk on the **moon**.

  But now I'll just have

  a **look** in this **book**.

- Have students clap their hands when they hear the **oon** sound and drum on their desks when they hear the **ook** sound. Then have two volunteers go to the board, each with a different color chalk. One can underline the **oon** words, saying the **oo** sound heard in the words. The other can repeat the process with the **ook** words.

⭐ Teaching the Lesson

- Write these words on the board.

mood	hood	loan	hoe
scoop	brook	soak	toe
loon	nook	cloak	woe

- Have a volunteer read aloud the words in the first row and then say the different vowel sounds. Repeat with the remaining rows. Have students add to the lists with words having the same vowel sounds.

- Have a student read aloud the Helpful Hints as others follow along silently.

Name _____

▸ Helpful Hint

> The **vowel digraph oo** can have two different sounds. It can stand for the vowel sound you hear in **moon** or the vowel sound you hear in **book**. Listen:
> Read this **book** about exploring the **moon**.

⭐ Complete each sentence with a word from the box. Then *circle* the *moon* (🌙) or the *book* (📖) to show the oo sound in the word you wrote.

lagoon	looked	cook	food	stood
smooth	swooped	took	shook	drooped

1. We sailed the ship into the __lagoon__.
2. A pelican __swooped__ down and landed on the deck.
3. The flag __drooped__ in the hot and still evening.
4. I __stood__ on deck to watch the sunset.
5. I __looked__ at the amazing colors in the sky.
6. While there was still light, I __took__ a picture.
7. I ate some __food__ while on deck.
8. The calm but steady winds made for __smooth__ sailing.
9. Yet the ship __shook__ when the winds picked up.
10. The ship's __cook__ served dinner when the sea became calm.

◂ CHALLENGE

Write a long sentence that includes words with the oo vowel digraph. Here's an example: **Look** in **school** for **cool boots**, **wooden stools**, or **good books**.

UNIVERSAL ACCESS
Meeting Individual Needs

Kinesthetic Learners

Make flash cards of words that have the letters **oo, oa,** or **oe.** Have students form a line. Direct them to different parts of the room depending upon what flash card they read (left for words with the letters **oo,** right for the letters **oa,** and the center for the letters **oe.**) Hold up the flash cards one at a time. As students reach the head of the line, have them say the word and then go to the correct place in the room.

Visual Learners

Have students look through magazines and cut out pictures of items named by words with the digraph **oo** or the vowel pairs **oa** or **oe,** such as **moon, book, road, toes,** and **doe.** Ask students to make a collage incorporating both the cut-out images and written words. Post the collages on a bulletin board.

53

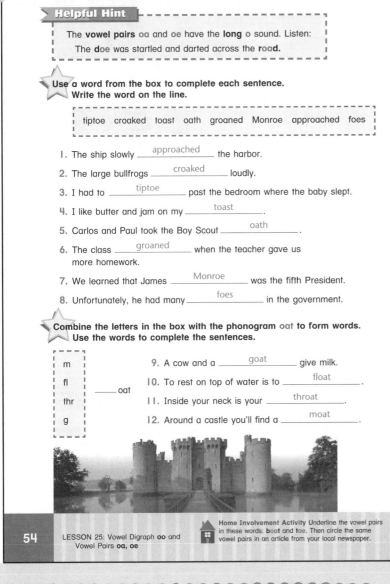

Helpful Hint

The **vowel pairs** oa and oe have the **long** o sound. Listen:
The **doe** was startled and darted across the **road**.

⭐ Use a word from the box to complete each sentence.
Write the word on the line.

tiptoe   croaked   toast   oath   groaned   Monroe   approached   foes

1. The ship slowly ___approached___ the harbor.

2. The large bullfrogs ___croaked___ loudly.

3. I had to ___tiptoe___ past the bedroom where the baby slept.

4. I like butter and jam on my ___toast___.

5. Carlos and Paul took the Boy Scout ___oath___.

6. The class ___groaned___ when the teacher gave us more homework.

7. We learned that James ___Monroe___ was the fifth President.

8. Unfortunately, he had many ___foes___ in the government.

⭐ Combine the letters in the box with the phonogram oat to form words.
Use the words to complete the sentences.

m
fl
thr   ___ oat
g

9. A cow and a ___goat___ give milk.

10. To rest on top of water is to ___float___.

11. Inside your neck is your ___throat___.

12. Around a castle you'll find a ___moat___.

54   LESSON 25: Vowel Digraph **oo** and Vowel Pairs **oa, oe**

🏠 **Home Involvement Activity** Underline the vowel pairs in these words: b**oa**t and t**oe**. Then circle the same vowel pairs in an article from your local newspaper.

Practicing the Skill

● Read aloud the direction lines on pages 53–54 and complete the first item in each exercise with students.

● Make sure students understand both parts of questions 1–10 on page 53.

● Remind students to use the process of elimination throughout.

Curriculum Connections

Spelling Link

● Write these words from the lesson on the board, aligning the blank spaces vertically. Have students fill in the blanks.

_iptoe
sw_oped
_ath
shoo_
to_st
f_oat
sm_oth
gr_aned
croa_ed

● Ask the students what the missing letters spell. Tell them to read the words vertically. (Answer: **took a look**)

Art Link

Provide students with art books or magazines and ask them to find a piece of art work that they especially like. Have them write five sentences describing what they see and how they feel about it, using at least five **oo, oa,** or **oe** words. Suggest that they begin their paragraph with the following words: "When I **look** at this work of art, I notice . . ."

Observational Assessment

*Check to see that students know which way to pronounce the **oo** words they use. Make sure they pronounce **oa** and **oe** words with a long **o** sound.*

English-Language Learners/ESL

Remind students that one combination of letters can make two different sounds. On the board, make two lists: one of words in which **oo** is pronounced as in **moon** and one of words in which **oo** is pronounced as in **book.** Show pictures illustrating the words as you say each word together.

Gifted Learners

Encourage students to create an illustrated story about traveling to the moon. It could be a nonfiction piece based on facts they have researched, a fictional story, or a fantasy. Have students circle all **oo** vowel digraphs and **oa** and **oe** vowel pairs. Ask students to read their stories aloud.

Learners with Special Needs

Additional strategies for supporting learners with special needs can be found on page 31L.

Diphthongs oi, oy, and ew

Objectives

- To recognize that the diphthongs oi and oy are pronounced "oy," while the diphthong ew is pronounced as in new
- To decode and write words with the diphthongs oi, oy, and ew

Warming Up

- Write this dialogue on the board, to be read by two volunteers.

Terry: Hi, Gerry. What's **new?**

Gerry: What's **new?** I just got back from a **voyage** at sea!

Terry: **Whew!** Did you **enjoy** it?

Gerry: Well, we had to **avoid** a huge storm that could have **destroyed** the ship.

Terry: Did that **spoil** the trip?

Gerry: No, but we had to eat **oyster stew** that was hard to **chew.**

Terry: Did that **annoy** you?

Gerry: Not really. Maybe next time you could **join** us?

- Have a volunteer go the board and underline words with the **oy** sound. Circle the letters that represent that sound and then say the sound out loud. Repeat the process for the **ew** sound as in **new**.

Teaching the Lesson

- Write these words on the board.

coin—join   soy—coy   blew—drew

Encourage students to read the words aloud and identify the letters that represent the vowel sounds they contain. Then ask students to add more examples using the same diphthongs.

- Have a student read aloud the Helpful Hints. Then ask: *How many ways can we spell the **oy** sound?*

55

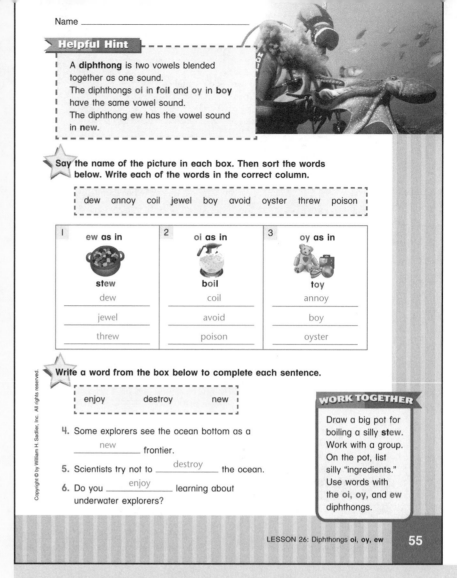

Name _____

Helpful Hint

A **diphthong** is two vowels blended together as one sound.
The diphthongs oi in **foil** and oy in **boy** have the same vowel sound.
The diphthong ew has the vowel sound in **new**.

⭐ Say the name of the picture in each box. Then sort the words below. Write each of the words in the correct column.

dew annoy coil jewel boy avoid oyster threw poison

1 ew as in stew	2 oi as in boil	3 oy as in toy
dew	coil	annoy
jewel	avoid	boy
threw	poison	oyster

⭐ Write a word from the box below to complete each sentence.

enjoy   destroy   new

4. Some explorers see the ocean bottom as a _____new_____ frontier.

5. Scientists try not to ___destroy___ the ocean.

6. Do you ___enjoy___ learning about underwater explorers?

WORK TOGETHER

Draw a big pot for boiling a silly st**ew**. Work with a group. On the pot, list silly "ingredients." Use words with the oi, oy, and ew diphthongs.

LESSON 26: Diphthongs oi, oy, ew   **55**

UNIVERSAL ACCESS
Meeting Individual Needs

Visual Learners

Pair students to play Tic-Tac-Toe using words with diphthongs **oi, oy,** or **ew** instead of **x**'s and **o**'s. Each player chooses a diphthong. The first player writes a word with his or her diphthong in a space. The other player blocks with his or her word. The first player to get three words with the same diphthong in a row wins.

Kinesthetic Learners

Write the letters **o, y, i, e,** and **w** on cards. (Include twice as many **o**'s). Make enough cards so that you can give one to each student. Have students mingle. When you say, "Stop!" students should pair up as quickly as possible to form an **oi, oy,** or **ew** diphthong. Then each pair of students must call out two words that include their diphthong.

⭐ Combine the letters in the boxes with the diphthongs **oi, oy, and ew** to form words. Use the words to complete the sentences.

| c |
| sp |
| br |
| t |

—— oi(l)

1. To grill at high heat is to _____ broil _____.
2. To rot is to _____ spoil _____.
3. To wind around is to _____ coil _____.
4. To work hard is to _____ toil _____.

| ann |
| empl |
| enj |
| destr |

—— oy

5. To give a job to is to _____ employ _____.
6. To ruin is to _____ destroy _____.
7. To like something is to _____ enjoy _____.
8. To bother is to _____ annoy _____.

| n |
| d |
| st |
| ch |

—— ew

9. To chomp is to _____ chew _____.
11. A meat dish with vegetables is a _____ stew _____.
10. Something not old is _____ new _____.
12. Droplets of water form _____ dew _____.

⭐ Choose one word from each of the three groups above. Write a sentence for each word.

Answers will vary.

13. _____
14. _____
15. _____

56 LESSON 26: Diphthongs **oi, oy, ew**

🏠 **Home Involvement Activity** Try this tongue twister: "A noisy noise annoys an oyster." Then make up tongue twisters of your own. Use diphthongs.

English-Language Learners/ESL

Write pairs of the diphthongs **oi, oy,** and **ew** on the board. Add consonants to make rhyming words. Say the words aloud, and then have the students say them.

boil/toil   boy/toy   dew/few

Help students add words to these examples.

Gifted Learners

Have students create a catalog for a toy shop that sells toys whose names include the diphthongs **oi, oy,** and **ew**. Encourage students to include magical toys in their collection, in addition to toys from other countries and other planets. Have students illustrate their catalog with drawings of the toys.

Learners with Special Needs

Additional strategies for supporting learners with special needs can be found on page 31L.

Practicing the Skill

● Read aloud the direction lines on pages 55–56 and complete the first item in each exercise with students.

● Remind students to take special care when writing the diphthongs **oi** and **oy**. They sound exactly alike and the only way to know which diphthong to use is by memorization.

● Students can use the process of elimination to answer all items except the last three on page 56.

Curriculum Connections

Spelling Link

Read the words and sentences aloud. Have students write the words in their notebooks.

enjoy   Do you **enjoy** playing baseball?

annoy   Would it **annoy** you if I shut the window?

destroy We had to **destroy** our elm tree.

toy   I got a new **toy** for my birthday.

boil   We had to **boil** water for tea.

jewel   There was a **jewel** in the bracelet.

spoil   Those pears may **spoil** in the sun.

avoid   He wanted to **avoid** the test.

threw   Lissa **threw** the ball to Jose.

dew   The **dew** made the grass damp.

Drama Link

Invite students to create their own dialogues like the one that began the lesson, using **oi, oy,** and **ew** words. Encourage them to develop their dialogues into skits with costumes, props, music, and sound effects. Give students time to rehearse and have them present their work to the class.

Observational Assessment

*Check to see that students can correctly pronounce the diphthongs **oi, oy,** and **ew**. Make sure students can spell the words that have the **oi** and **oy** diphthongs.*

Vowel Pair **ow** and Diphthongs **ow, ou**

Objectives

- To distinguish between the vowel pair **ow**—pronounced long **o** as in **crow**—and the diphthong **ow**—pronounced **ow** as in **town**

- To recognize that the diphthong **ou** may be pronounced in three ways: as in **loud, couple,** or **thought**

- To decode, pronounce, and write words with the vowel pair **ow** and the diphthongs **ow** and **ou**

Warming Up

- Write these sentences on the board and read them aloud with students.

  The archery champion showed us her **bow** and took a **bow.**

  The farmer fed the **sow** and went to **sow** some grain.

  I **thought** I saw a **couple** of **trout** in the stream.

- Have a volunteer underline the two words that are spelled alike in the first sentence, pronounce each word, and circle the letters that make the vowel sound. Have another volunteer do the same activities for the second sentence. Invite a third volunteer to underline all **ou** words in the third sentence, circle the letters **ou,** and pronounce each word.

Teaching the Lesson

- Point to the third sentence in the *Warming Up* activity and ask students what they can conclude about the letters **ou.** (They can be pronounced three different ways.)

- Have a student read aloud the Helpful Hints. Then ask: *How do you know which way to pronounce the words* **bow** *and* **bow?** (context clues)

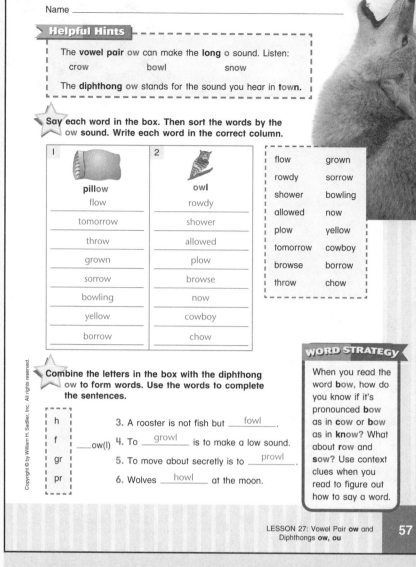

Name _____

Helpful Hints

The **vowel pair** ow can make the **long o** sound. Listen:

crow   bowl   snow

The **diphthong** ow stands for the sound you hear in **tow**n.

Say each word in the box. Then sort the words by the ow sound. Write each word in the correct column.

1 **pillow**	2 **owl**
flow	rowdy
tomorrow	shower
throw	allowed
grown	plow
sorrow	browse
bowling	now
yellow	cowboy
borrow	chow

flow	grown
rowdy	sorrow
shower	bowling
allowed	now
plow	yellow
tomorrow	cowboy
browse	borrow
throw	chow

Combine the letters in the box with the diphthong ow to form words. Use the words to complete the sentences.

| h |
| f |
| gr |
| pr |

___ow(l)

3. A rooster is not fish but ___fowl___.

4. To ___growl___ is to make a low sound.

5. To move about secretly is to ___prowl___.

6. Wolves ___howl___ at the moon.

WORD STRATEGY

When you read the word **b**ow, how do you know if it's pronounced **b**ow as in **c**ow or **b**ow as in **k**now? What about **r**ow and **s**ow? Use context clues when you read to figure out how to say a word.

LESSON 27: Vowel Pair ow and Diphthongs ow, ou   57

UNIVERSAL ACCESS
Meeting Individual Needs

Kinesthetic Learners

Invite students to have a "Vowel Pillow Case Race." Bring in two pillows and cases. Have students form two lines. The first student in each line has to put the pillow into the case while calling out a word with vowel pair **ow** (long **o** sound). The next student has to take the pillow out of the case while calling out another **ow** (long **o**) word, and so on. The first line to finish passing the pillow wins. Repeat the game using words with the diphthong **ow** (as in **town**).

Visual Learners

Have students think of four words spelled with the vowel pair **ow** and four words spelled with the dipthong **ow.** Have students create two pictures—one for each set of words—listing the words on the back of each picture. Then have students exchange work with a partner. Partners can write down each word they see illustrated and then check the back of the picture to see if they were right.

The **diphthong ou** can have the vowel sound you hear in **proud**. **Ou** can also have these three other sounds. Listen: A **couple** of doves **thought** they saw a **cougar**.

Read each group of words. Underline the word with **ou**. Then write the word in the correct column.

1. had some yummy soup
2. scored a touchdown
3. visit with some cousins
4. had enough to eat
5. joined a rock group
6. flew in rough weather
7. looked for coupons
8. drove through Utah

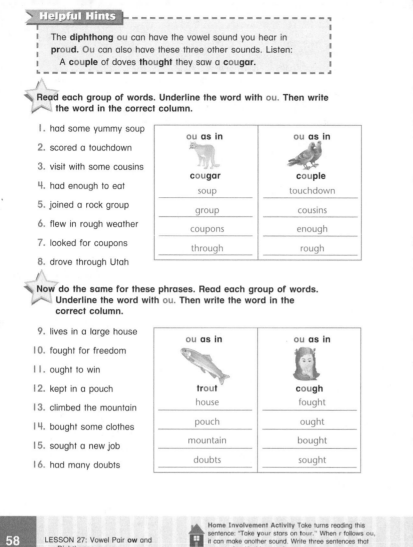

ou as in cougar	ou as in couple
soup	touchdown
group	cousins
coupons	enough
through	rough

Now do the same for these phrases. Read each group of words. Underline the word with **ou**. Then write the word in the correct column.

9. lives in a large house
10. fought for freedom
11. ought to win
12. kept in a pouch
13. climbed the mountain
14. bought some clothes
15. sought a new job
16. had many doubts

ou as in trout	ou as in cough
house	fought
pouch	ought
mountain	bought
doubts	sought

Home Involvement Activity Take turns reading this sentence: "Take your stars on tour." When r follows ou, it can make another sound. Write three sentences that use words with this sound.

Practicing the Skill

• Read aloud the direction lines on pages 57–58 and complete the first item in each exercise with students.

• Suggest that students say the words softly to themselves to be sure exactly how the **ow** or **ou** is pronounced.

Curriculum Connections

Spelling Link

Write these sentences on the board and have students fill in the blanks with correctly spelled words from the lesson.

> A freshwater fish is called a _____.
> To look through items is to _____.
> The day after today is _____.
> In bed, I put my head on a _____.
> The color of a banana is _____.
> I'd like to eat a bowl of tomato _____.
> The loud cry of a wolf is called a _____.
> I need good boots to climb a _____.
> My aunt's children are my _____.
> You can take a bath or a _____.
> The sandpaper was not smooth but _____.

(Answers: **trout, browse, tomorrow, pillow, yellow, soup, howl, mountain, cousins, shower, rough**)

Science Link

Invite students to find out more about **snow** and **snowstorms**. Then encourage them to write five sentences about **snow** using **ow** and **ou** words, such as **howling, loud, rough,** and **ground**. Students might also enjoy illustrating their sentences.

English-Language Learners/ESL

List groups of words whose diphthong or vowel pair is pronounced the same way: **pillow, crow, show, snow; town, gown, now, bow; proud, trout, ground, round, around;** and so on. Point to the words in each group one by one, saying each word with students. Show a picture of the item named by a word whenever possible.

Gifted Learners

Have students create a board game featuring words with **ow** or **ou**. For example, a player might pick a card that reads: *You get lost in the **snow**. Go back two spaces.* or *A **yellow** dragon **showers** you with rubies. Skip ahead five spaces.* Have students play their games with classmates.

Learners with Special Needs

Additional strategies for supporting learners with special needs can be found on page 31L.

Observational Assessment

*Check to see that students know all the different ways to pronounce **ow** and **ou**, and that they can use context clues to distinguish between such look-alike words as **bow/bow** and **sow/sow**.*

Syllables with Vowel Pairs, Vowel Digraphs, and Diphthongs

Objectives

- To divide into syllables words with various vowel pairs, vowel digraphs, and diphthongs

- To recognize that some vowel combinations must not be divided: long vowels, the broad o digraphs **au** or **aw**, diphthongs, or the vowel digraph **oo**

Warming Up

- Write the following paragraph on the board and read it aloud with the students, pausing at every line break.

> In 1953, Tenzing Norgay from Nepal and Sir Edmund Hillary from New Zealand—**mountaineers**—set off on a difficult **journey.** They were the first **people** to climb the highest **mountain** in the world, Mount Everest.

- Ask students to identify the places where words are divided. Have a volunteer circle each hyphen while pronouncing the syllables it divides.

Teaching the Lesson

- Ask students why hyphens are used. Help them recall that there are rules for dividing words into syllables.

- Write these words on the board.

lei-sure au-thor dou-ble fool-ish

Say the words aloud with the students. Point out where the words are divided.

- Have a volunteer read aloud the Helpful Hints as the rest of the students follow along silently.

Name _____

Helpful Hints

Here are more rules to help you divide words into syllables. Notice that these words have **vowel pairs**, **vowel digraphs**, or **diphthongs.**

- Never divide long vowels or the broad o digraphs **au** or **aw**.

   fea-ture   stee-ple   dai-sy   goat-ee   au-di-ence   draw-ing

- Never divide diphthongs or the vowel digraph **oo**.

   thou-sand   poi-son   tow-er   roy-al
   floun-der   jew-el   school-book   coop-er

⭐ Write each word. Divide it into syllables by using a hyphen (-). Check the box above to see which rule to use.

1. creature	crea-ture		15. flower	flow-er
2. faucet	fau-cet		16. doubtful	doubt-ful
3. raccoon	rac-coon		17. sawdust	saw-dust
4. bookworm	book-worm		18. teaspoon	tea-spoon
5. container	con-tain-er		19. voyage	voy-age
6. awful	aw-ful		20. naughty	naugh-ty
7. seizure	sei-zure		21. rowdy	row-dy
8. auditions	au-di-tions		22. pouncing	pounc-ing
9. groaning	groan-ing			
10. sleepwalk	sleep-walk			
11. ointment	oint-ment			
12. cheapen	cheap-en			
13. brawny	brawn-y			
14. viewpoint	view-point			

CHALLENGE

Try to divide these long words. Use a dictionary, if needed.
   cautiousness
   whereabouts
   entertainment

UNIVERSAL ACCESS
Meeting Individual Needs

Tactile Learners

Arrange students in teams and give each team the same number of cards with two-syllable words written on them. The words should contain a long vowel, the digraph **au** or **aw**, a diphthong, or the digraph **oo**. When you say, "Go!" have both teams pick a card, draw a line to divide the word into syllables, and continue until there are no cards left. The team that finishes first with the most correctly divided words wins.

Visual Learners

With the students, create a chart showing the rules for dividing words into syllables. Have students add to the chart.

Don't Divide	
Long Vowels	**Au and Aw**
chea-pen	au-dience
free-dom	aw-ful
lei-sure	saw-dust
Diphthongs	**Digraph oo**
poi-son	bloop-er
voy-age	moon-beam
jew-el	la-goon

⭐ Don't let your eyes fool you about syllables. You need to look *and* listen. Complete the chart. The first one has been done for you.

	Word	Vowels I See	Vowel Sounds I Hear	Number of Syllables
1	headache	4	2	2
2	seizure	4	2	2
3	willow	2	2	2
4	moonbeam	4	2	2
5	newspaper	3	3	3
6	toenail	4	2	2
7	treatment	3	2	2
8	houseplant	4	2	2
9	applesauce	5	3	3
10	mountain	4	2	2
11	nosebleed	4	2	2
12	embroider	4	3	3

⭐ Here are the names of some famous explorers. Divide their last names into syllables.

13. Matthew **Henson** _Hen-son_

14. John **Cabot** _Cab-ot_

15. Ferdinand **Magellan** _Ma-gel-lan_

16. Mary **Kingsley** _Kings-ley_

17. Marco **Polo** _Po-lo_

18. Leif **Ericson** _Er-ic-son_

Matthew Henson (1866–1955) reached the North Pole with Robert Peary in 1909.

60   LESSON 28: Syllables with Vowel Pairs, Vowel Digraphs, and Diphthongs

🏠 **Home Involvement Activity** Find out about one or more of the explorers above. Use the Internet, an encyclopedia, or a social studies book. Share what you learn.

Practicing the Skill

Read aloud the direction lines on pages 59–60. Remind students to say the words out loud to help them identify the sounds of long vowels, vowel pairs, digraphs, and diphthongs.

Intervention Strategy Turn to page 31K for an Intervention Strategy designed to help students who need extra support with this lesson.

Curriculum Connections

Spelling Link

Read these sentences aloud. Repeat the word in bold and have students write it, dividing it into syllables.

Is it **lawful** to turn left here?

That was a **naughty** puppy!

A **haughty** man sneered at us.

That **tower** was built years ago.

I put a red **flower** in the vase.

Then I added a white **daisy!**

It shone as brightly as a **jewel.**

I used a **teaspoon** of honey.

Was that the **cheapest** price?

The **royal** family waved to us.

Social Studies Link

Invite students to find out more about one of the explorers mentioned on page 60. Ask them to write five sentences about the explorer they choose, using five words from this lesson. Then have them divide those words into syllables.

Observational Assessment

*Check to see that students correctly divide into syllables words with long vowels, the digraphs **au** or **aw**, diphthongs, or the vowel digraph **oo.***

English-Language Learners/ESL

Write lists of words with two or more syllables on the board. The words should have long vowels, the digraphs **au** or **aw**, diphthongs, or the vowel digraph **oo.**

pea-nut	aw-ful	joy-ful	bal-loon
stee-ple	scrawn-y	saw-dust	rac-coon

Read each word aloud. Have a volunteer divide the word into syllables while the class claps once for each syllable.

Gifted Learners

Have students create a newspaper. They should write articles and draw illustrations. Then they can design the layout, arranging the illustrations and articles in columns. Remind students to use the Helpful Hints when dividing words between syllables.

Learners with Special Needs

Additional strategies for supporting learners with special needs can be found on page 31L.

Connecting Reading and Writing

Objectives

- To read a nonfiction piece and respond to it in writing
- To practice influencing decisions and synthesizing information
- To write a persuasive letter

Warming Up

Comprehension Skills

- Tell students that **making decisions** is a skill that can help them become better readers and writers. Decision-making involves higher-order thinking skills such as predicting, reasoning, and evaluating.
- Remind students that **synthesizing** is putting together the ideas within a piece of writing and making sense of them.

Teaching the Lesson

- Suggest that students reread the selection to find the answer to the first Reader's Response question.
- For the second question, brainstorm reasons why the work of marine biologists is important.
- Remind students to give at least two reasons for their answer to question three.

Practicing the Skill

- Read the direction lines on page 62. Then discuss with students reasons parents might find persuasive as well as reasons parents might find less persuasive.
- Ask volunteers to use a few words from the box in sentences to model their use.

Name _____

⭐ Read about Sylvia Earle, an underwater explorer. Then answer the questions that follow.

READ & WRITE

Meet an Underwater Explorer
by Luise Woelflein

Sylvia Earle has spent more than 6,000 hours under water. She has played around with friendly dolphins. She has gotten "personal" with animals that can be dangerous, such as sharks and moray eels. She has studied humpback whales by following them under water.

Sylvia is a *marine biologist*—a scientist who studies ocean life. She's also one of the world's best underwater divers. Being an ocean scientist and an underwater diver fit right together. Sylvia can study life in the ocean—as it's happening.

Ever since she was a little girl, Sylvia has looked for ways to get under water. Then, when she was 12, her family moved to Florida. Sylvia spent hundreds of hours playing there in the warm, clear water of the Gulf of Mexico.

When Sylvia got to college, she tried out scuba gear for the first time. (Scuba gear is equipment for breathing under water.) "It was glorious!" she says. "It was like being a fish. My professor almost had to haul me out of the water by force, I liked it so much."

It's still hard to get Sylvia out of the water. In fact, she wants lots of people to learn how to explore the ocean. Why? Because so little is known about what's there.

1. They study ocean life.
2. Yes, they unlock mysteries of the ocean that can help sea life and people.
3. Answers will vary.

Reader's Response

1. What do underwater explorers like Sylvia do?
2. Do you think their work is important? Why?
3. Would you like to be an underwater explorer someday? Give reasons for your decision.

LESSON 29: Connecting Reading and Writing
Comprehension—Make Decisions; Synthesize

61

UNIVERSAL ACCESS
Meeting Individual Needs

Visual Learners

Some students may benefit from looking at undersea pictures or a video to help them imagine specific details about underwater exploration. If students keep in mind what it might look and feel like to explore the ocean, they may be able to come up with more persuasive arguments.

Logical Learners

Remind students that both logic and emotion are useful in persuading others. Help them identify each type of reason. A logical argument appeals to the mind ("This experience will help me get into college."). An emotional argument appeals to a person's feelings ("I've always loved the ocean and I want to follow my dream."). Suggest that students use at least one argument of each type.

Learners with Special Needs

Additional strategies for supporting learners with special needs can be found on page 31L.

Imagine that you have been invited to explore the ocean with an underwater explorer. You have decided that you want to go, but you will have to get permission from your family. What will you say to persuade your family to let you go?

Write a letter to your parent or guardian. Try to persuade him or her to let you explore the ocean with a real scientist. Give three strong reasons for letting you go. Use some of these persuasive words to make your reasons more convincing.

ought	should	must	believe	think
feel	in my opinion	important	opportunity	

Answers will vary.

Writer's Tip

Words such as *ought* and *should* will help to persuade your audience.

Speaker's Challenge

Give your letter as a speech to your class. Try to persuade your listeners to agree with your point of view.

62   LESSON 29: Connecting Reading and Writing
Comprehension—Make Decisions; Synthesize

English-Language Learners/ESL

Invite students to act out what they would like to say in their letters, with a classmate in the role of the parent. Then help English learners list their three best reasons explaining why they should be allowed to go.

Gifted Learners

Encourage students to think of an undersea project and create a proposal to submit to a scientific or government foundation. The proposal should make clear what students intend to do, why they need money, and why their project is important. Students might enjoy presenting their proposals to their classmates, who can then respond as to whether they were persuaded to fund the project.

The Writing Process

Discuss the purpose of a persuasive letter—to persuade a reader to take certain actions or hold certain opinions. Ask students to identify effective and ineffective ways of persuading people. Then read aloud the directions at the top of page 62.

Prewrite Have students brainstorm a list of reasons that they might use. Then have them select the three best reasons from their lists.

Write Remind students to read the boxed words as they write and think about how including these words might help make their arguments stronger.

Revise Have volunteers read their letters aloud. Then have a student "parent" respond in character. Students can swap feedback and use it to revise their work.

Proofread Encourage students to check their work carefully for errors in grammar, punctuation, and spelling.

Publish Have students copy their final drafts onto page 62 or a separate sheet of paper.

Computer Connection Remind students who use word processors to use the spell-checking feature. In some programs, a red wavy line or other symbol appears beneath any word that the spell-checker does not recognize. In other programs, students must click on the "Spelling and Grammar" choice usually found in the menu labeled "Tools." Remind students that a word highlighted by the spell-checker may not be misspelled; it may simply not have been recognized by the computer. Computers often fail to recognize proper names, place names, and other specialized words.

Portfolio Have students add their persuasive letters to their portfolios.

Reviewing and Assessing

Short and Long Vowels, r-controlled Vowels, Vowel Pairs, Vowel Digraphs, and Diphthongs

Objective

To review and assess short and long vowels, r-controlled vowels, vowel pairs, vowel digraphs, and diphthongs

Warming Up

- Write these pairs of words on the board.

  dawn/enjoy   **jewel/doubt**

  crawl/through   **yellow/meadow**

  tiptoe/stood   **allow/train**

  farm/approach   **share/either**

- Have students read each pair and circle vowel pairs, vowel digraphs, and diphthongs. Then have them use the words together in the same sentence.

- Ask volunteers to suggest pairs of words having the same sounds, such as **peace** and **tree** or **cloud** and **town**. Compare how the words in each pair are spelled.

Teaching the Lesson

- For the first exercise on page 63, encourage students to say each word softly to themselves to help distinguish the sounds.

- For the second exercise, suggest that students use context clues. Remind them that the same letters must work for both blanks in each sentence.

Name _____

★ Say the word next to the number. Then circle the letter before the word in each row that has the same vowel sound as the letters in red.

1. feather   a. peaceful   (b.) measure   c. seasons
2. saucer   (a.) yawn   b. mouse   c. thousand
3. smooth   a. bookmark   b. crooked   (c.) raccoon
4. whirl   a. awhile   b. pear   (c.) word
5. tiptoe   (a.) approach   b. baboon   c. haunted
6. cloudy   a. shawl   b. showed   (c.) rowdy
7. stall   a. gallon   (b.) faucet   c. talent
8. avoid   a. await   (b.) annoyed   c. violin
9. book   (a.) took   b. lucky   c. harpoon
10. reins   (a.) sleigh   b. ceiling   c. diet

★ Read each sentence. Choose the letter pair from the three in each row that completes both unfinished words. Write the same letters from the chart in both spaces.

11. We __al__ways add s__al__t to our mashed potatoes.	au aw al
12. Do you agr__ee__ that this color s__ee__ms too pale?	ea ee ei
13. Matt left his j__ea__ns in a h__ea__p on the floor.	ea ee ie
14. When we saw the th__ie__f, we shr__ie__ked in fear.	ie ee ea
15. It hurts to eat t__oa__st when you have a sore thr__oa__t.	au oa oe
16. Dad's old sw__ea__ter has l__ea__ther buttons.	au oa ea
17. Karla thr__ew__ some peanuts into the st__ew__.	ew ow oo
18. She likes to embr__oi__der with turqu__oi__se thread.	oy oa oi
19. The t__ou__r of West Africa included y__ou__r village.	ea ou au

Copyright © by William H. Sadlier, Inc. All rights reserved.

UNIVERSAL ACCESS
Meeting Individual Needs

Visual Learners

Have students work in groups of three or four. Give each group a set of letter cards or tiles. Have students take turns spelling words that contain vowel pairs, vowel digraphs, and diphthongs, linking their words crossword-style. For example, the first student might spell **faucet**. The second student might then use the **f** in **faucet** to spell **fought**.

Kinesthetic Learners

Have students make hidden-word puzzles on a sheet of graph paper. Tell them first to print the letters of 15 words horizontally, vertically, or diagonally. Specify that each word must contain at least one vowel pair, digraph, or diphthong. Then have them fill in all remaining spaces with random letters. Have students trade papers and do one another's puzzles.

Learners with Special Needs

Additional strategies for supporting students with special needs can be found on page 31L.

⭐ Read about a courageous woman explorer. For each numbered blank, there is a choice of words below. Circle the letter before the word that best completes the sentence.

Do you think that all explorers are men? Well, think again. Some women took scary **1**, too. They had **2** adventures that still thrill us. One of these women was Mary Kingsley. Mary explored Africa in the 1890s. And she did it in a dress!

As a child, Mary read her father's travel books. She **3** said that his books opened up new worlds to her. Mary's father <u>loved the bright eyes of danger</u>. Maybe she had **4** because of the words he wrote about all his adventures.

Some explorers try to <u>conquer</u> the people they meet—but not Mary Kingsley. She went to parts of western and central Africa where Europeans had never been before. She lived with the local people. She **5** respect for their ways. Today, people still read about Mary Kingsley's **6** to adventure.

1. a. views (b.)voyages c. voices
2. (a.)awesome b. dawn c. crooked
3. a. never b. rarely (c.)always
4. a. bounce (b.)courage c. cougar
5. (a.)showed b. groaned c. shouted
6. a. flow b. boast (c.)road

⭐ Read the passage again to answer these questions. Circle the letter of the correct answer.

7. As an explorer, Mary Kinglsey
   a. was cautious
   b. visited schools
   (c.)lived with the local people
   d. fought dangerous animals

8. In the third paragraph, the word **conquer** means—
   a. imitate
   (b.)defeat
   c. yield to
   d. hunt

Extend & Apply

What could it mean to love "the bright eyes of danger"? Explain how it may have led Mary Kingsley to become an explorer.

AFRICA

Reteaching Activities

Linking Letters

List these digraphs, vowel pairs, and diphthongs on the board: **au, aw, al, oo, oa, oe, oi, oy, ew, ow, ou, ea.** Have a volunteer suggest a word that contains **au.** Then have another student use a different digraph, vowel pair, or diphthong in a word beginning with the last letter of the first student's word. For example, if the first student said *l**au**nch,* the second student might say *h**aw**k.* Students should say their words aloud and write them on the board.

Trading Fill-ins

Have students work in pairs. Direct them to review the first exercise on page 56. Then have them choose three different diphthongs, digraphs, or vowel pairs from the unit and create a parallel set of fill-in exercises. Encourage students to make their fill-in clues clear and specific. Then have partners exchange papers and complete each other's exercises.

Assessing the Skill

Check Up The exercises on page 63 are discussed in *Teaching the Lesson.* Assign them now, if you have not yet done so.

The assessment on page 64 asks students to demonstrate their ability to read and understand words containing vowel pairs, vowel digraphs, and diphthongs. Go over the directions for the exercises and have students complete the page. Remind students to use context clues to help them choose the correct answers.

Observational Assessment As students complete the exercises, watch for hesitation or other signs of difficulty or confusion. Observe which exercises appear to pose the greatest challenge for students. Review observational notes you made during previous lessons in the unit.

Student Skills Assessment Keep track of each student's progress in understanding vowels, vowel pairs, vowel digraphs, and diphthongs using the checklist on page 31H.

Writing Conference Meet informally with each student to discuss his or her written work. Point out the strengths in each student's writing and suggest specific ways in which the student can continue to improve. Encourage students to continue adding to both their school and home portfolios.

Group together students who need further instruction in vowels, vowel pairs, vowel digraphs, and diphthongs and have them complete the *Reteaching Activities.* Turn to page 31C for alternative assessment methods.

Word Endings, Contractions, and Compound Words

Theme: Artists and Composers

STANDARDS

- Read expository text with grade-appropriate fluency and understand its content
- Develop and strengthen vocabulary by reading words in context
- Use regular plurals, irregular plurals, and apostrophes correctly
- Divide compound words into syllables

OBJECTIVES

- ▶ To appreciate nonfiction works about artists and composers
- ▶ To identify inflectional endings, plurals, contractions, and compound words
- ▶ To identify and distinguish between singular and plural possessives
- ▶ To write plurals, possessives, contractions, and compound words

LESSONS

Assessment Strategies

An overview of assessment strategies appears on page **65C.** It offers suggestions for using unit-specific assessment tools, including **Pretests** and **Post Tests** (pages **65D–65G**), the **Activity Master** (page **65M**), and the **Assessment Checklist** (page **65H**).

Thematic Teaching

In Unit 3, students will learn about inflectional endings, plural nouns, singular and plural possessives, contractions, and compound words. Students encounter words that contain these elements in the context of nonfiction selections and exercises related to the theme *Artists and Composers.*

Students begin their investigation of *Artists and Composers* by creating a "Wall of Talent" that displays and labels the various categories of artists, including painters, composers, singers, dancers, and so on. The resource list below provides titles of books, videos, and other materials that can help students learn more about the lives of artists and composers. Many lessons in this unit open with poems, riddles, or tongue twisters related to *Artists and Composers.* These "hooks" can spark students' interest both in the theme and in the play of words.

Curriculum Integration

Science
Students research animals on page **80,** list animals on page **88,** and list compound words related to nature on page **92.**

Art
Students describe Jacob Lawrence's artwork on page **70** and draw pictures on page **94.**

Social Studies
Students make a map on page **76,** write about a person from history on page **86,** and list names of places on page **94.**

Drama
Students create a dialogue on page **72.**

Math
Students create word problems on page **78.**

Music
Students research instruments on page **92.**

Optional Learning Activities

Meeting Individual Needs
Most Teacher's Edition lessons offer activities for students with distinct learning styles or particular intellectual or sensory strengths. These activities are labeled for learners with the following "styles": **Visual, Kinesthetic, Auditory, Tactile, Musical,** and **Logical.**

Multicultural Connections
Students create original folk art on page **66** and explore traditional music and instruments from cultures around the world on page **68.**

Word Study Strategies
Pages **65I–65J** offer an array of activities that give students practice using strategies such as word sorting and word building.

Universal Access
Exercises tailored to meet the needs of **English-Language Learners** and **Gifted Learners** can be found in almost every Teacher's Edition lesson. Strategies designed to help **Learners with Special Needs,** such as students with Memory Deficits, can be found on page **65L.**

Intervention
Page **65K** offers **Intervention Strategies** designed to help those students performing below grade level understand the concepts taught in **Lessons 33, 36,** and **42.**

Reteaching
On page **84** students identify base words, and on page **98** students form singular and plural possessives of nouns.

Technology
Page **65N** offers activities for students who enjoy working with computers or audio/video equipment. In addition, **Computer Connections**—tips designed to support students who use a word processor—can be found on pages **74, 82, 90,** and **96.**

RESOURCES

Books
Krull, Kathleen. *Lives of the Artists: Masterpieces, Messes (And What the Neighbors Thought),* San Diego, CA: Harcourt Brace, 1995.
Pinkney, Andrea Davis. *Duke Ellington: The Piano Prince and His Orchestra,* NY: Hyperion, 1998.

Videos
Alexander Calder (American Masters Series), Winstar
Norman Rockwell: Painting America, Winstar

CDs
A Child's Celebration of Rock 'n' Roll; Music for Little People, Warner Brothers.

In Unit 3, students study inflectional word endings, contractions, plurals, possessives, and compound words. To evaluate students' mastery of these skills, use any or all of these assessment methods:

Pretests and Post Tests

The tests on pages **65D–65G** objectively assess how well students understand inflectional word endings, contractions, plurals, possessives, and compound words. These tests may be used at the beginning of the unit as diagnostic tools or at the end of the unit to measure students' progress.

Observational Assessment

Opportunities to observe students are suggested throughout the unit. Recommendations are included for assessing students' work. Check students' writing regularly to see whether they are applying the word study skills they are learning.

Using Technology

The Technology activities on page **65N** may also be used to evaluate students' progress.

Performance Assessment

Have students copy and complete the chart below by adding **s** or **es**, **ed**, and **ing** to each base word. Remind students to make spelling changes as needed. Finally, ask students to add two new base words to the chart and form the new words.

Base Word	s or es	ing	ed
use	_____	_____	_____
reach	_____	_____	_____
clap	_____	_____	_____
study	_____	_____	_____

Portfolio Assessment

The portfolio icon in the lesson plans indicates an opportunity for students to add to the growing body of work in their portfolios. Each student's portfolio should contain pieces that the student feels represent his or her best work. You may wish to give students additional opportunities to add to their portfolios.

Rubric for Writing

	Always	Sometimes	Never
Uses capitalization, punctuation, spelling, and grammar appropriately			
Creates a variety of sentences containing words with inflectional endings, contractions, plural nouns, possessive nouns, and compound words			
Uses time order words appropriately to explain a process			
Uses persuasive words to convey meaning through writing			

Answer Key

Page 65D
1. Let's
2. can't
3. don't
4. It's
5. we'll
6. perform
7. practices
8. memorize
9. Learning
10. studies
11. notebook
12. director's
13. teacher's
14. designing
15. Everyone
16. wives
17. sheriffs
18. geese
19. glasses
20. parties
21. matches
22. halves
23. zeroes
24. sheep
25. pianos

Page 65E
1. should not
2. you are
3. I would
4. we have
5. he is

6. princesses
7. elves
8. taxes
9. mice
10. trout
11. candies
12. clapping
13. dried
14. brushes
15. dancing
16. man's
17. puppies'
18. James's
19. boy's
20. tourists'

Page 65F
1. Who's
2. don't
3. they're
4. it'll
5. I'm
6. likes
7. sketched
8. bedroom
9. paintbrushes
10. draws
11. Monet's
12. Tim's
13. water lilies
14. haystacks
15. hopes
16. children

17. knives
18. ashes
19. people
20. classes
21. echoes
22. calves
23. moose
24. horses
25. cellos

Page 65G
1. did not
2. they will
3. I have
4. she will
5. is not
6. shadows
7. potatoes
8. cliffs
9. geese
10. foxes
11. studying
12. describes
13. played
14. carries
15. permitting
16. coach's
17. cities'
18. children's
19. singer's
20. animal's

Name _____

Read the sentence. Fill in the circle next to the contraction for the underlined words.

1. <u>Let us</u> get ready to go.	○ Lett's ○ Let's
2. We <u>cannot</u> be late for the bus.	○ can't ○ cann't
3. I <u>do not</u> want to walk to school.	○ don'nt ○ don't
4. <u>It is</u> a long walk.	○ It's ○ Its
5. Hurry, or <u>we will</u> miss the bus!	○ we'll ○ we'ill

Fill in the circle next to the word that completes the sentence.

6. Laine will _____ in the school play.	○ performed ○ perform
7. She _____ every day after school.	○ practice ○ practices
8. Laine must _____ her lines.	○ memorized ○ memorize
9. _____ lines is hard work!	○ Learning ○ Learn
10. Laine _____ with her friends.	○ study ○ studies
11. She keeps the script in her _____.	○ booknote ○ notebook
12. That was the _____ idea.	○ director's ○ directors'
13. The director is our _____ brother.	○ teachers' ○ teacher's
14. He is _____ the scenery, too.	○ designed ○ designing
15. _____ is looking forward to the play.	○ Everyone ○ Everything

Write the plural form of each word.

16. wife _____	17. sheriff _____
18. goose _____	19. glass _____
20. party _____	21. match _____
22. half _____	23. zero _____
24. sheep _____	25. piano _____

Possible score on Unit 3 Pretest 1 is 25. Score _____

Pretest 2

Name _____

Fill in the circle next to the words that form each contraction.

1. shouldn't	○ should no	○ should not	○ should will
2. you're	○ you will	○ you not	○ you are
3. I'd	○ I am	○ I would	○ I will
4. we've	○ we are	○ we will	○ we have
5. he's	○ he is	○ he will	○ he had

Fill in the circle next to the correct plural form of each word.

6. princess	○ princeses	○ princesses	○ princessez
7. elf	○ elfs	○ elvs	○ elves
8. tax	○ taxs	○ taxies	○ taxes
9. mouse	○ mouses	○ mous	○ mice
10. trout	○ trout	○ trouts	○ troutes

Fill in the circle next to the correct form of each word.

11. candy (add **s**)	○ candys	○ candies	○ candyes
12. clap (add **ing**)	○ claping	○ clapeing	○ clapping
13. dry (add **ed**)	○ dried	○ dryed	○ driied
14. brush (add **s**)	○ brushs	○ brushes	○ brushies
15. dance (add **ing**)	○ dancing	○ danceing	○ danccing

Fill in the circle next to the correct possessive form of each word.

16. man	○ man's	○ men's	○ mans'
17. puppies	○ puppie's	○ puppies'	○ puppies's
18. James	○ James'	○ James's	○ Jame's
19. boy	○ boys	○ boys'	○ boy's
20. tourists	○ tourists'	○ tourist's	○ tourists's

Possible score on Unit 3 Pretest 2 is 20. Score _____

Fill in the circle next to the contraction for the underlined words.

1. <u>Who</u> <u>is</u> coming for dinner? ○ Whose ○ Who's

2. I <u>do</u> <u>not</u> know. ○ don't ○ donn't

3. Mom said <u>they</u> <u>are</u> coming at seven. ○ they'r ○ they're

4. Maybe <u>it</u> <u>will</u> be the Martins? ○ it'll ○ it'ill

5. <u>I</u> <u>am</u> hoping they bring dessert! ○ Im' ○ I'm

Fill in the circle next to the word that completes the sentence.

6. Tim _____ to draw. ○ liking ○ likes

7. He has _____ all kinds of things. ○ sketch ○ sketched

8. He has a new easel in his _____. ○ bedroom ○ bedspread

9. The easel has a large tray for _____. ○ paintbrushs ○ paintbrushes

10. First he _____. Then he paints. ○ draws ○ drawing

11. Tim is trying to paint _____ garden. ○ Monets ○ Monet's

12. Monet is _____ favorite artist. ○ Tim's ○ Tims

13. Monet is famous for painting _____. ○ water lily's ○ water lilies

14. He also painted _____. ○ haystacks ○ haystackes

15. Tim _____ to be a famous painter. ○ hops ○ hopes

Write the plural form of each word.

16. child _____

17. knife _____

18. ash _____

19. person _____

20. class _____

21. echo _____

22. calf _____

23. moose _____

24. horse _____

25. cello _____

Possible score on Unit 3 Post Test 1 is 25. Score _____

Post Test 2

Name _____

Fill in the circle next to the words that form each contraction.

1. didn't	○ do not	○ did not	○ did are
2. they'll	○ they have	○ they are	○ they will
3. I've	○ I are	○ I have	○ I will
4. she'll	○ she have	○ she would	○ she will
5. isn't	○ is not	○ is will	○ is are

Fill in the circle next to the correct plural form of each word.

6. shadow	○ shadowes	○ shadowies	○ shadows
7. potato	○ potatos	○ potatoes	○ potatoez
8. cliff	○ cliffes	○ clifes	○ cliffs
9. goose	○ gooses	○ geese	○ geeses
10. fox	○ foxs	○ foxese	○ foxes

Fill in the circle next to the correct form of each word.

11. study (add **ing**)	○ studing	○ studying	○ studiing
12. describe (add **s**)	○ describes	○ describs	○ describbes
13. play (add **ed**)	○ playd	○ plaied	○ played
14. carry (add **s**)	○ carrys	○ carries	○ carryies
15. permit (add **ing**)	○ permiting	○ permitting	○ permiteing

Fill in the circle next to the correct possessive form of each word.

16. coach	○ coach's	○ coachs'	○ coache's
17. cities	○ cities's	○ cities'	○ city's
18. children	○ childrens'	○ children's	○ childrens's
19. singer	○ singer's	○ singers'	○ singers's
20. animals	○ animal's	○ animals'	○ animales'

Possible score on Unit 3 Post Test 2 is 20. Score _____

UNIT 3 STUDENT PROGRESS CHECKLIST

Student Name ______________________________

UNIT THREE STUDENT SKILLS ASSESSMENT CHECKLIST

☐ Assessed ☒ Retaught ■ Mastered

- ☐ Inflectional Endings
- ☐ Contractions
- ☐ Plurals **s, es, ies**
- ☐ Plurals with **f, lf, fe, ff,** and **o**
- ☐ Irregular Plurals
- ☐ Singular Possessives
- ☐ Plural Possessives
- ☐ Compound Words
- ☐ Compound Words and Syllables

TEACHER COMMENTS

In Unit 3, students study inflectional endings, contractions, plurals, possessives, and compound words. To give students opportunities to master word study strategies, use any or all of the activities suggested below.

Word Endings

Add **s, es, ed,** or **ing** to the word in parentheses to complete each sentence. Write the new words on the lines.

1. The painter is known for _____ blue paint. (use)
2. Watch as she _____ the paint. (mix)
3. Now she is _____ the sky in her picture. (color)
4. Yesterday, she _____ the picture over to the window. (carry)
5. Then the wet paint _____ overnight. (dry)
6. See how she has _____ the different shades of blue. (blend)

Contraction Match-Up

Choose from the box a contraction that is formed by each pair of underlined words in the sentence. Write the contraction on the line.

I'll	It's	didn't
doesn't	wasn't	We've

1. <u>It is</u> a great day for a parade. _____
2. It <u>does not</u> look like rain. _____
3. <u>I will</u> march in the school band. _____
4. <u>We have</u> practiced all year. _____
5. Alex <u>did not</u> march last year. _____
6. He <u>was not</u> a musician then. _____

Word Sort

Write the plural form of each word. Then sort the plural forms using the headings below.

dress _____   shelf _____

radio _____   echo _____

piano _____   brush _____

city _____   stage _____

match _____   cliff _____

potato _____   monkey _____

penny _____   leaf _____

Add **s**	Add **es**	Change **y** to **i**, add **es**
_____	_____	_____
_____	_____	_____
		Change f to v, add es
_____	_____	_____
_____	_____	_____

Singular or Plural

Write the singular or plural form of each word in parentheses.

1. one (men) _____
2. two (child) _____
3. many (goose) _____
4. some (cattle) _____
5. several (tooth) _____

Show Possession

Circle the word that correctly completes each sentence. Write the word on the line. Then use the possessive forms to complete the chart.

1. Where are the _____ invitations?

   parents'   **parents**   **parent's**

2. Many _____ parents will come to the show.

   classmates's   **classmates'**   **classmates**

3. _____ song is the most popular.

   Chris's   **Chriss'**   **Chris**

4. Those _____ voices are the loudest.

   singers   **singer's**   **singers'**

5. Did you return the _____ book?

   library's   **libraries**   **libraries'**

6. Yes, I returned it to the _____ section.

   childrens   **childrens'**   **children's**

Singular Possessive	Plural Possessive
_____	_____
_____	_____
_____	_____

Building Words

Replace the underlined word in each compound with a word from the box to make a new word. Write the new word on the line. Then write another compound word using one of the words that make up the original compound word.

rain	note	dog	any
end	proof	class	set
stone	light	head	back

1. <u>some</u>thing _____ _____
2. <u>wind</u>storm _____ _____
3. key<u>board</u> _____ _____
4. under<u>cover</u> _____ _____
5. moon<u>beam</u> _____ _____
6. <u>tooth</u>ache _____ _____
7. water<u>color</u> _____ _____
8. week<u>day</u> _____ _____
9. <u>room</u>mate _____ _____
10. birth<u>day</u> _____ _____
11. sun<u>flower</u> _____ _____
12. <u>barn</u>yard _____ _____

LESSONS	**33** More Inflectional Endings	**36** Plurals	**42** Plural Possessives
Problem	Student does not adjust the spelling as needed when adding inflectional endings **-ed** and **-ing**.	Student has difficulty remembering when to add **-es** or **-ies** to base words.	Student misplaces the apostrophe in plural possessives.
Intervention Strategies	• Remind student of the rules for pronouncing vowel pairs **ee** and **ei**. • Then ask how **danceed** and **danceing** would be pronounced according to these rules. • Tell them that the only way to keep the usual pronunciation of **dance** is to drop the silent **e** before adding **-ed** or **-ing**. • Explain how doubling the final consonant of base words with short vowels preserves their pronunciation.	• Explain that adding an **e** before the inflectional ending **s** makes it easier to pronounce and read plural words that end in **s, ss, ch, sh, x, z,** or **zz.** Write on the board **princesss** and **princesses.** Ask which word is easier to say, and which word is more clearly plural. • Suggest that the student use the words **key** and **try** as examples of the rule for changing **y** to **i** when adding **-es.** Have them write **key/keys** and **try/tries** in their word-study notebooks and refer back to them when forming plurals.	• Explain that the placement of the apostrophe in a possessive noun shows whether the noun is singular or plural. • Write on the board: **the teacher's room.** Explain that **teacher** is a singular noun. Ask student to write teacher in its plural form **(teachers)**, and then show that many teachers own the room by changing the position of the apostrophe. • Remind the student that when the plural noun does not end in **s**, the apostrophe goes before the **s** to indicate possession.

The following activities offer strategies for helping students with special needs to participate in selected exercises in Unit 3.

Memory Deficits

Adding s, ed, or ing to Base Words

Students with memory deficits may have trouble remembering and/or understanding the reasons for adding inflectional endings to verbs.

A simple cartoon strip can help show how adding inflectional endings affects the verb's meaning. The following frames could be used to show how different endings change the meaning of the verb **paint:**

- Frame #1 shows a boy in front of an easel holding a paintbrush, smiling broadly. The caption reads: **Joseph loves <u>painting</u>.**

- Frame #2 shows the same boy in front of the same easel, now painting. A clock shows that it is 4:00 p.m. The caption reads: **Joseph <u>paints</u> every day after school.**

- Frame #3 shows the same boy next to the easel, on which is a finished painting. The caption reads: **Joseph <u>painted</u> a picture**.

- Have students circle the inflectional endings in each caption and write them on the board. Encourage students to create their own cartoon strips that illustrate a verb using the inflectional endings **s, ed,** and **ing.**

- When doing this activity, be sure to give students a choice of verbs whose base words do not change when endings are added. The verbs should also be easy to illustrate with a simple drawing.

Visual/Perceptual Deficits

Contractions

Students with visual/perceptual deficits may have difficulty recognizing a contraction in print even if they can understand and use contractions orally.

The following activity may help students learn to recognize and read a contraction.

- On the board write phrases such as: **I will, you have, he is, let us, could not.** Then say the contracted form of each phrase **(I'll, you've, he's, let's, couldn't)**. Have students suggest the phrase each contraction stands for. Then write the contraction beside the phrase, using colored chalk for the apostrophe.

- Have students use the same color chalk to circle the letters in each phrase on the board that were left out of the contraction. Erase the phrases and then ask students to say the phrases represented by each contraction. Write their answers next to their corresponding contractions. Have students copy the contractions and phrases in their notebooks, using a different color ink for the apostrophes.

Spatial Relationships Deficits

Giving Instructions

Students with spatial relationships deficits have trouble differentiating between left and right and may need help with the maze activity on page 96.

- Give students a photocopy of the maze, labeled with the following directional words: **right, left, upper,** and **lower.** Below the picture of the maze, list the following time-order words: **first, next, then,** and **finally.**

- As the students trace a path through the maze with a pencil, have them explain to you what they are doing. Remind them to use the directional and time-order words on their mazes.

- Then ask the students to write directions for navigating the maze using the directional and time-order words.

Match words from the sketch pads to make compound words. Write the new words on the easel. The first one has been done for you.

sail	color
brain	boat
light	storm
water	flake
snow	house
sea	field
paint	time
summer	pack
back	port
corn	brush

sailboat

Meet the Artist

 Invite students to research an artist of their choice. The students will then present the findings of their research by impersonating the artist on videotape.

- Allow students time in class to research the artists using books from the library and articles on the Internet. Encourage them to use verbs with the inflectional endings **s, ed, ing** when writing about the artists' lives and works.

- Students should also obtain samples of the artists' works to display when presenting the information. The samples could be in the form of posters, books, or a student-made copy. Encourage students to consult with the school's art teacher for assistance.

- Encourage students to use classroom items or things from home to use as props in their presentations. Give them time to work on the project. You may have partners work together to videotape each other's presentations.

- Invite another class to view the finished product.

Create a Class Poetry Book

 Have students use a word-processing program on the computer to create a collection of original poems.

- Set aside time at the end of each month for students to write a poem about something they have experienced or discovered during that period of time.

- For example, they may have made new friends, discovered something in nature, or solved some type of a problem.

- Have students check their poems to see if they have used contractions. Ask them to experiment with changing contractions into phrases with complete words and changing phrases with complete words into contractions. Encourage them to discuss how each change affects their poems.

- Encourage students to use computer graphics to illustrate their poems. At the end of the year, have them compile the poems to create a poetry book and make copies for students in other classes.

Tape-Record a Fantasy Tale

Tell students that creative people often get ideas for stories, pictures, and music by trying to see familiar things or ideas in a new way. Invite students to use some familiar compound words as a basis for a fantasy tale.

- For example, they might substitute **shadow** for **thunder** in the compound word **thunderstorm** and write a story about a town that disappeared from sight because a **shadowstorm** flooded it with darkness.

- Have students brainstorm ways to change such words as **nightmare, jellyfish, snowflake,** and **butterfly** into something strange and fun. Then ask students to write stories about their new concepts.

- Encourage students to take turns operating the tape recorder as the others read their stories aloud.

- Play the tape for the class.

Introduction to
Word Endings, Contractions, and Compound Words

Objectives

- **To enjoy a piece of nonfiction related to the theme *Artists and Composers***
- **To identify word endings, compound words, and contractions**

Starting with Literature

- Ask a student to read "An American Artist" aloud for the class.

- Point out the **'s** that follows the name **Moses** in the last three paragraphs. Ask students what the apostrophe indicates.

Critical Thinking

- Urge students to review the article for details to support their answer to item 1.

- Remind them to look carefully at the painting (in the upper right-hand corner of the page) before suggesting caption ideas.

Introducing the Skill

Have students reread "An American Artist" to find words ending in **s.** Write these words on the board. Have a volunteer circle the words in this list that are not plurals. **(has, famous, Moses, was, Moses's, that's)** Explain that **famous** is an adjective, **Moses** is a proper name, **has** and **was** are verbs, **Moses's** is a possessive, and **that's** is a contraction.

Practicing the Skill

Have students work in pairs to create their own singular/plural flash cards using words they find themselves. They can write the singular form of the word on one side of the card and its plural form on the other.

An American Artist

The United States has produced many great artists and composers. Read about one American artist who became famous at the age of 100!

Do you know the saying "better late than never"? These words fit the life of Grandma Moses. Like some well-known artists and composers, Grandma Moses did not become famous until late in her life. However, she did not begin painting until she was in her seventies. Imagine that!

Grandma Moses's real name was Anna Mary Robertson Moses. She was born in upstate New York in 1860. Grandma Moses had no real art training. Yet once she began painting, nothing could stop her. Her subject was the small-town life she knew and loved. She was still painting at the age of 100! By then, Grandma Moses was a household name.

Grandma Moses's fame began to grow in 1940. That's when she had her first art show in New York City. She was 80 years old! Her paintings delighted art lovers. They were amazed by the many details. People liked her happy, colorful scenes.

Grandma Moses's fame made people notice the joy of American art. Today, Americans can thank her for being a true American artist.

Critical Thinking

1. Why are the paintings of Grandma Moses so popular?

2. What do you like about Grandma Moses's painting at the top of the page?

3. If you were to give this painting a caption, what would you write?

1. Her happy, colorful scenes of American life delight people.
2. Answers will vary.
3. Answers will vary.

Theme Activity

WALL OF TALENT Ask students to look through magazines for pictures related to the theme *Artists and Composers*. Have students work together to cut out the images and sort them according to categories such as Painters, Composers, Singers, Dancers, and so on.

Suggest that students create colorful labels for each category and mount them along the top of a blank bulletin board. Then students can arrange each group of pictures in an attractive way underneath the appropriate label.

Ask students to write and post "Unit 3" words for each category. "Unit 3" words would include any of the kinds of words taught in Unit 3: words that have inflectional endings, possessives, compound words, and contractions. Students may wish to add words to the "Wall of Talent" as they work through the unit.

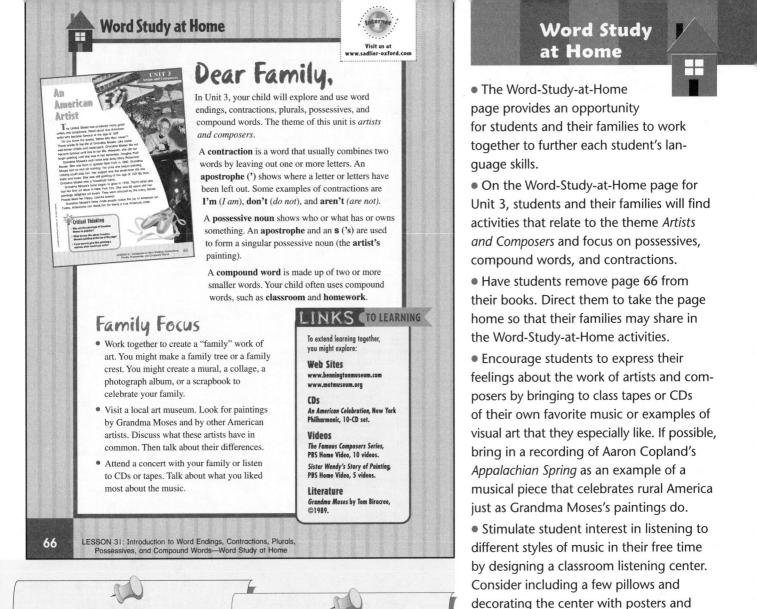

Dear Family,

In Unit 3, your child will explore and use word endings, contractions, plurals, possessives, and compound words. The theme of this unit is *artists and composers*.

A **contraction** is a word that usually combines two words by leaving out one or more letters. An **apostrophe (')** shows where a letter or letters have been left out. Some examples of contractions are **I'm** (*I am*), **don't** (*do not*), and **aren't** (*are not*).

A **possessive noun** shows who or what has or owns something. An **apostrophe** and an **s ('s)** are used to form a singular possessive noun (the **artist's** painting).

A **compound word** is made up of two or more smaller words. Your child often uses compound words, such as **classroom** and **homework**.

Family Focus

- Work together to create a "family" work of art. You might make a family tree or a family crest. You might create a mural, a collage, a photograph album, or a scrapbook to celebrate your family.

- Visit a local art museum. Look for paintings by Grandma Moses and by other American artists. Discuss what these artists have in common. Then talk about their differences.

- Attend a concert with your family or listen to CDs or tapes. Talk about what you liked most about the music.

LINKS TO LEARNING

To extend learning together, you might explore:

Web Sites
www.benningtonmuseum.com
www.metmuseum.org

CDs
An American Celebration, New York Philharmonic, 10-CD set.

Videos
The Famous Composers Series, PBS Home Video, 10 videos.
Sister Wendy's Story of Painting, PBS Home Video, 5 videos.

Literature
Grandma Moses by Tom Biracree, ©1989.

- The Word-Study-at-Home page provides an opportunity for students and their families to work together to further each student's language skills.

- On the Word-Study-at-Home page for Unit 3, students and their families will find activities that relate to the theme *Artists and Composers* and focus on possessives, compound words, and contractions.

- Have students remove page 66 from their books. Direct them to take the page home so that their families may share in the Word-Study-at-Home activities.

- Encourage students to express their feelings about the work of artists and composers by bringing to class tapes or CDs of their own favorite music or examples of visual art that they especially like. If possible, bring in a recording of Aaron Copland's *Appalachian Spring* as an example of a musical piece that celebrates rural America just as Grandma Moses's paintings do.

- Stimulate student interest in listening to different styles of music in their free time by designing a classroom listening center. Consider including a few pillows and decorating the center with posters and other examples of visual art that students bring in themselves. Make sure students realize that they can check out music from the listening center to enjoy at home.

Multicultural Connection

Have students create their own works of "folk art" depicting life in their town or community. Students can either work independently to create individual drawings or work together to create a mural.

To help students get started, show them examples of Grandma Moses's art or other folk art. Remind them that Grandma Moses had no formal training and learned by doing.

Art Link

Have students discuss the significance of the fact that Grandma Moses created her art in America. Ask: *In what ways does it matter that Grandma Moses was American? It what ways does it not matter what country an artist is from?*

Theme-Related Resources

CDs

Aaron Copland's Greatest Hits, New York Philharmonic, Leonard Bernstein

Antonín Dvořák: Symphony No. 9 in E minor, Op. 95 "From the New World," Czech Philharmonic Orchestra, Vaclav Talich

Books

Grandma Moses: Painter of Rural America by Zibby Oneal. New York: Penguin Books USA, 1986.

Student Pages 67-68

Inflectional Endings

Objectives

- To write words with the inflectional endings **s, es, ed,** and **ing**
- To form plurals by adding **s** or **es**
- To form plurals of words ending in **y**

Warming Up

- Write the following tongue twisters on the board and read them aloud with students. Emphasize the inflectional endings shown in bold type.

Shauna stud**ies** sing**ing** on Saturday.

Fran fix**es** frame**s** on famous photo**s**.

Tom tr**ied** toot**ing** tune**s** on trumpet**s**.

Paulo paint**ed** polka dot**s** on bus**es**.

- List these base words in a column on the board: **study, fix, frame, photo, tune, trumpet, dot, bus, sing, toot, paint,** and **try**. Have volunteers locate their inflected forms in the sentences, circle the endings, and write the whole word to the right of the base word.

Teaching the Lesson

- Have students look at each word in the right-hand column on the board. Ask a volunteer to describe how the spelling of the base word changed. Help students identify other words that follow the pattern and list them. **(study/dry, fix/wish, bus/pass, try/dry)** Ask students to use these words in sentences.

- Have a student read the Helpful Hints aloud as others follow along silently.

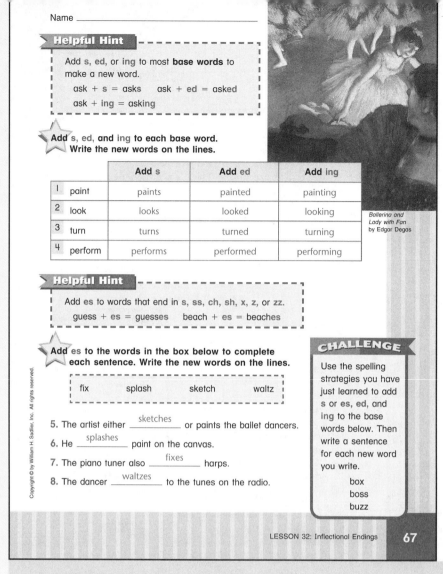

Name _____

> **Helpful Hint**
>
> Add **s, ed,** or **ing** to most **base words** to make a new word.
>
> ask + s = asks   ask + ed = asked
> ask + ing = asking

Add **s, ed,** and **ing** to each base word. Write the new words on the lines.

		Add **s**	Add **ed**	Add **ing**
1	paint	paints	painted	painting
2	look	looks	looked	looking
3	turn	turns	turned	turning
4	perform	performs	performed	performing

Ballerina and Lady with Fan by Edgar Degas

> **Helpful Hint**
>
> Add **es** to words that end in **s, ss, ch, sh, x, z,** or **zz.**
>
> guess + es = guesses   beach + es = beaches

Add **es** to the words in the box below to complete each sentence. Write the new words on the lines.

| fix | splash | sketch | waltz |

5. The artist either ___sketches___ or paints the ballet dancers.

6. He ___splashes___ paint on the canvas.

7. The piano tuner also ___fixes___ harps.

8. The dancer ___waltzes___ to the tunes on the radio.

CHALLENGE

Use the spelling strategies you have just learned to add **s** or **es**, **ed**, and **ing** to the base words below. Then write a sentence for each new word you write.

box
boss
buzz

LESSON 32: Inflectional Endings **67**

UNIVERSAL ACCESS
Meeting Individual Needs

Visual Learners

Have groups of students make two sets of cards: one with base words from the warm-up exercise and the lesson, the other with the requests **add s**, **add es**, **add ing**, **add ed**, **change the y to i and add ed or es**. Players draw a card from each set and decide if the pair can make a correctly spelled new word. Have students write the new words on the board.

Auditory Learners

Have students listen for the the rhyming words as you read each sentence below. Say the sentence, emphasizing the words that rhyme. Have students write the rhyming words on the board.

They like **yams, clams,** and all **jams.**

Grapes by the **bunches** were packed in their **lunches.**

He **sneezes** when **breezes** blow cold.

She **flies** a kite in blue **skies.**

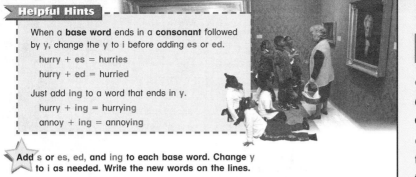

When a **base word** ends in a **consonant** followed by y, change the y to i before adding es or ed.

hurry + es = hurries

hurry + ed = hurried

Just add **ing** to a word that ends in y.

hurry + ing = hurrying

annoy + ing = annoying

⭐ **Add s or es, ed, and ing to each base word. Change y to i as needed. Write the new words on the lines.**

		Add s or es	Add ed	Add ing
1	dry	dries	dried	drying
2	carry	carries	carried	carrying
3	deny	denies	denied	denying
4	study	studies	studied	studying
5	play	plays	played	playing

⭐ **Add s or es, ed, or ing to each word in bold print so that the sentence makes sense. Write the new words on the lines.**

6. Danny **visit** the art museum earlier today.   visited

7. Right now, a guide is **try** to explain oil painting.   trying

8. The class was **listen** closely to her.   listening

9. At this moment, Danny **want** to be an artist.   wants

10. After he **finish** his homework, he will create his first painting.   finishes

11. He is **think** of a circus scene.   thinking

12. Danny **study** some drawings about an hour ago.   studied

🏠 **Home Involvement Activity Cut** and **put** are words that are the same in the present and the past tense. Work together to write a brief list of words that do not change from the present to the past.

English-Language Learners/ESL

On the board, list the following: **add s, add es, add ies, add ed, add ing.** Help students find words from the lesson that follow these spelling patterns. Then distribute a magazine. Have students look for words with inflectional endings and circle them. Help students read the words aloud and write them next to the appropriate spelling pattern on the board.

Gifted Learners

Suggest that students write a poem. Encourage them to create as many rhymes as possible using words with inflected endings. Ask volunteers to read their poems aloud to the class.

Learners with Special Needs

Additional strategies for supporting learners with special needs can be found on page 65L.

Practicing the Skill

● Read aloud the direction lines on pages 67–68 and complete the first item in each exercise with students.

● As students work on page 68, remind them to look at the letter that precedes the **y** before they add an ending.

● Encourage students to say each new word softly to themselves before they write it.

Curriculum Connections

Spelling Link

Read each word and its context sentence aloud. Emphasize the boldfaced word. Ask volunteers to spell the words. Have other students write the words on the board.

studied	She **studied** music history.
asking	Cam is **asking** about jazz.
denied	Ed **denied** hitting a wrong note.
buzzes	Rehearsal ends when the timer **buzzes.**
wants	Jane **wants** to be a conductor.
played	They **played** to a big audience.
hurries	Laura **hurries** to her seat.
fixed	Cyd **fixed** her violin string.

Multicultural Link

Share some of the unique rhythms and melodies of traditional music from cultures around the world. Play selections from folk recordings. Show pictures of musicians or the actual instruments when possible. If you have students who play instruments, invite them to play a piece for the class.

Observational Assessment

Check to see that students can properly determine when to add es to base words and when to change y to i at the end of a base word before adding an inflectional ending.

More Inflectional Endings

Objectives

- To add the inflectional endings **s, ed,** and **ing** to base words ending in silent **e**

- To determine when to double the last consonant in a base word before adding **s, ed,** or **ing**

- To write words with the inflectional endings **s, ed,** and **ing**

Warming Up

- Write this rhyme on the board and read it aloud with students. Emphasize the inflectional endings shown in bold.

  They've danc**ed** and pranc**ed** and gone through their pac**es.**

  They're humm**ing** and drumm**ing** in wide-open spac**es.**

  He slid**es**; she glid**es**, tapp**ing** and wrapp**ing**.

  They haven't slipp**ed** yet, or dropp**ed,** — (*pause*) PLOP!

- Ask volunteers to underline each word that ends in **s, ed,** or **ing**. Have them say the word and circle its ending.

Teaching the Lesson

- Have students identify the underlined words on the board that kept the silent **e** before adding **s**. (**paces, spaces, slides, glides**)

- Have students identify underlined words that dropped the final **e** before adding **ed** or **ing**. (**danced, pranced**)

- Ask volunteers to identify the remaining underlined words. (**humming, drumming, tapping, wrapping, slipped, dropped**) Discuss how they are alike. (They all have doubled consonants that come before the **ing** or **ed** endings.)

69

Name _____

Helpful Hints

When a **base word** ends in **silent e**, drop the **final** e before adding ed or ing.

dance + ed = danced   dance + ing = dancing

For most words ending in silent e, keep the e when adding s.

dance + s = dances

Add **s, ed,** and **ing** to each base word below. Write the new words in the chart.

		Add s	Add ed	Add ing
1	wave	waves	waved	waving
2	skate	skates	skated	skating
3	trace	traces	traced	tracing
4	erase	erases	erased	erasing
5	practice	practices	practiced	practicing
6	glide	glides	glided	gliding
7	exercise	exercises	exercised	exercising
8	describe	describes	described	describing
9	bake	bakes	baked	baking
10	divide	divides	divided	dividing

Write the base word for each word below.

11. moves ___move___   12. tuned ___tune___

13. writing ___write___   14. pronounced ___pronounce___

15. traded ___trade___   16. losing ___lose___

CHALLENGE

Change the headlines in a newspaper so that the verbs end in s or es, ed, or ing. Make needed spelling changes.

LESSON 33: More Inflectional Endings   **69**

UNIVERSAL ACCESS
Meeting Individual Needs

Kinesthetic Learners

At opposite ends of the board, write **Drop Silent e** and **Double Final Consonant.** Have students line up. On the board, write a base word that requires dropping the silent **e** or doubling the final consonant before adding an inflectional ending. The first student says the word aloud, goes to the correct side of the board, and writes the word with the ending added.

Auditory Learners

Encourage students to make lists of rhyming words that double their final consonants before adding **ed** or **ing**.

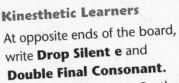

tap nap rap clap snap wrap
hop drop pop top flop mop
grin spin win begin pin
admit fit flit permit quit

Students might enjoy using inflected forms of these words in original rhymes that they can share with the class.

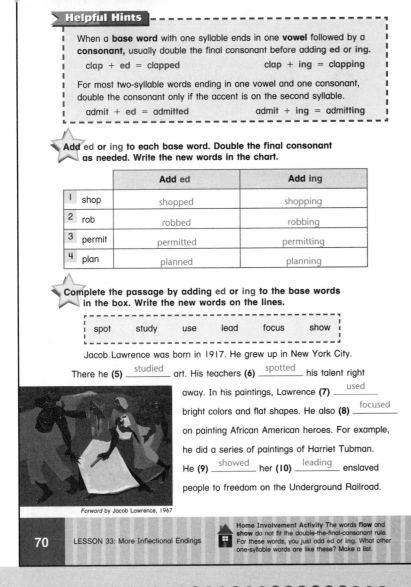

Add ed or ing to each base word. Double the final consonant as needed. Write the new words in the chart.

		Add ed	**Add ing**
1	shop	shopped	shopping
2	rob	robbed	robbing
3	permit	permitted	permitting
4	plan	planned	planning

Complete the passage by adding ed or ing to the base words in the box. Write the new words on the lines.

| spot | study | use | lead | focus | show |

Jacob Lawrence was born in 1917. He grew up in New York City.

There he **(5)** _studied_ art. His teachers **(6)** _spotted_ his talent right

away. In his paintings, Lawrence **(7)** _used_

bright colors and flat shapes. He also **(8)** _focused_

on painting African American heroes. For example,

he did a series of paintings of Harriet Tubman.

He **(9)** _showed_ her **(10)** _leading_ enslaved

people to freedom on the Underground Railroad.

Forward by Jacob Lawrence, 1967

70   LESSON 33: More Inflectional Endings

Home Involvement Activity The words **flow** and **show** do not fit the double-the-final-consonant rule. For these words, you just add ed or ing. What other one-syllable words are like these? Make a list.

Read aloud the direction lines on pages 69–70 and complete the first item in each exercise with students.

Turn to page 65K for an Intervention Strategy designed to help students who need extra support with this lesson.

Curriculum Connections

Spelling Link

Read the following words and sentences aloud. Ask volunteers to spell the words. Have others write them on the board.

writes	My father **writes** music.
skating	Jenna loves **skating** in Central Park.
bakes	Hallie **bakes** cookies for her piano teacher
glided	The swans **glided** by.
waves	The **waves** pounded the cliffs.
clapping	Franz's speech had the whole audience **clapping.**

Art Link

Invite students to look at additional examples of Jacob Lawrence's artwork and choose a favorite painting. Have students write about what they see in the painting, using at least three words whose spellings change when **s**, **ed**, or **ing** is added.

Observational Assessment

*Check to see that students know when to drop a silent **e** and when to double a final consonant before adding **s**, **ed**, or **ing**.*

English-Language Learners/ESL

Write **clap, snap,** and **tap** on the board in white chalk. Say each word aloud with students as you all perform each action. Beneath each word, write the base word two more times in white chalk. Then say **clapped** and **clapping** and write the extra **p** and the ending in colored chalk. Repeat the process with the other two words, helping students to identify the pattern. Use other examples as needed.

Gifted Learners

Encourage students to write a story about a mixed-up character who always uses the wrong endings, such as saying "stopping" when he or she means "stopped." The character might mix up other words as well, such as saying "go" instead of "stop." Have students share their stories with the class.

Learners with Special Needs

Additional strategies for supporting learners with special needs can be found on page 65L.

70

Contractions

Objectives

- **To identify contractions**
- **To identify the two words represented by a contraction**
- **To write contractions**

Warming Up

- Write this rhyme on the board and say it with students:

    We'd like to play the song we wrote.

    It's fresh and fun. **You'll** see.

    You **haven't** heard one quite like this.

    We're sure that **you'll** agree.

- Ask volunteers to underline and say each word that has an apostrophe in it.

Teaching the Lesson

- Write these sentences on the board and read them to the class:

    It's fresh and fun.

    It is fresh and fun.

Ask students to identify the words that make the sentences different. Explain that **it's** is a contraction—a way of writing two words as one. In a contraction, one or more letters is left out. An apostrophe (') shows where the letter or letters were.

- Begin the following list on the board and have students complete the pattern.

    we'd = we + would

    you'll = you + will

    you've = you + have

    it's = it + is

    haven't = have + not

    we're = we + are

- Ask volunteers to identify the letter(s) that the apostrophe replaces.

- Have a student read the Helpful Hint aloud as others follow along.

Name _____

▶ Helpful Hint

A **contraction** usually combines two words into one. In a contraction, one or more letters have been left out. An **apostrophe** (') shows where the missing letter or letters were.

does + not = doesn't   it + is = it's   would + not = wouldn't
I + have = I've   she + would = she'd   he + will = he'll

Write the contraction for each pair of words. Use the contractions from the box. Then write the letter or letters that have been left out of each contraction.

can't	we'll	let's	aren't	you've

		Contraction	Letter(s) Left Out
1	we will	we'll	wi
2	are not	aren't	o
3	let us	let's	u
4	you have	you've	ha
5	cannot	can't	no

Underline the contraction in each sentence. Then write the two words it stands for.

6. Georgia O'Keeffe always knew she'd be

    a painter. _____she_____ _____would_____

7. She wouldn't let anything stop her.

    _____would_____ _____not_____

8. You'll love her colorful paintings

    of flowers. _____you_____ _____will_____

Red Canna
by Georgia O'Keeffe,
1924

WORK TOGETHER

Work with a group to write a different contraction on each of ten index cards. Take turns picking cards. Tell your group the two words that make up the contraction on each card you pick.

UNIVERSAL ACCESS
Meeting Individual Needs

Tactile Learners

Use magnetic letters or create letter cards that students can manipulate to form words. Have students form a contraction from the words **should not** by removing the **o** in **not**, replacing it with an apostrophe magnet or letter card, and pushing **should** and **n't** together. Have students repeat the process with other contractions from the lesson.

Kinesthetic Learners

Write contractions from the lesson on separate cards. Have the class form teams and line up in front of the board. Give each team the same number of cards. When you say, "Go!" the first player on each team picks a card, writes the words that make up the contraction on the board, and passes the chalk to the next player. The team that identifies the most words correctly in the least amount of time wins.

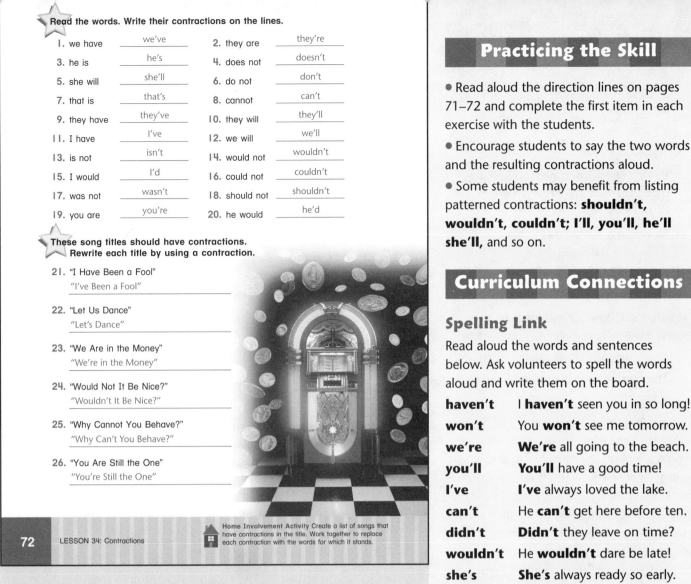

⭐ **Read the words. Write their contractions on the lines.**

1.	we have	we've	2.	they are	they're
3.	he is	he's	4.	does not	doesn't
5.	she will	she'll	6.	do not	don't
7.	that is	that's	8.	cannot	can't
9.	they have	they've	10.	they will	they'll
11.	I have	I've	12.	we will	we'll
13.	is not	isn't	14.	would not	wouldn't
15.	I would	I'd	16.	could not	couldn't
17.	was not	wasn't	18.	should not	shouldn't
19.	you are	you're	20.	he would	he'd

⭐ **These song titles should have contractions. Rewrite each title by using a contraction.**

21. "I Have Been a Fool"
"I've Been a Fool"

22. "Let Us Dance"
"Let's Dance"

23. "We Are in the Money"
"We're in the Money"

24. "Would Not It Be Nice?"
"Wouldn't It Be Nice?"

25. "Why Cannot You Behave?"
"Why Can't You Behave?"

26. "You Are Still the One"
"You're Still the One"

72   LESSON 34: Contractions

🏠 **Home Involvement Activity** Create a list of songs that have contractions in the title. Work together to replace each contraction with the words for which it stands.

English-Language Learners/ESL

Use photos to review some basic feeling words with students, such as **happy, excited, sad,** etc. Then write the following on the board: **I am, I'm, you are, you're, he is, he's, she is, she's.** Say: *I am happy. I'm happy* as you act out the feeling. Continue the activity with the remaining words and contractions.

Gifted Learners

Have students find dialogue from a story in which the main character uses contractions often. Have them compare it with dialogue from another story in which the characters do not use contractions. Have students tell which they prefer and why.

Learners with Special Needs

Additional strategies for supporting learners with special needs can be found on page 65L.

Practicing the Skill

● Read aloud the direction lines on pages 71–72 and complete the first item in each exercise with the students.

● Encourage students to say the two words and the resulting contractions aloud.

● Some students may benefit from listing patterned contractions: **shouldn't, wouldn't, couldn't; I'll, you'll, he'll she'll,** and so on.

Curriculum Connections

Spelling Link

Read aloud the words and sentences below. Ask volunteers to spell the words aloud and write them on the board.

haven't	I **haven't** seen you in so long!
won't	You **won't** see me tomorrow.
we're	**We're** all going to the beach.
you'll	**You'll** have a good time!
I've	**I've** always loved the lake.
can't	He **can't** get here before ten.
didn't	**Didn't** they leave on time?
wouldn't	He **wouldn't** dare be late!
she's	**She's** always ready so early.

Drama Link

Have students work in pairs to create a dialogue in which the characters use a contraction at least once each time they speak. The topic might be an interview with a popular artist or singer. Suggest that students write their dialogues, practice them, and present them to the class.

Observational Assessment

Check to see that students know which letters to replace with apostrophes when forming contractions.

Connecting Spelling and Writing

Objectives

● **To say, spell, sort, and write contractions and words with inflectional endings**

● **To write a list of steps**

Warming Up

● Write the following sentences on the board. Have a volunteer read them aloud.

The artist is <u>painting</u> a work of art.

The composer is <u>planning</u> to write a symphony.

The dancers are <u>moving</u> gracefully.

● Ask students how the three underlined words are alike. (all consist of a base word + **ing**) Then ask how the three words differ. Explain that to form the word **painting** you simply add **ing** to the base word **paint**. To form the word **planning**, you double the consonant before adding **ing** to the base word **plan**. To form the word **moving**, you drop the **e** before adding **ing** to the base word **move**.

Teaching the Lesson

● List the following words on the board: **race, burn, cry, finish, hurry, taste, prefer, guess, slam, slide.** Have volunteers add the ending **s, es, ed,** or **ing** to each word to form a new word.

● Review with students what a contraction is. Then have volunteers use several examples in sentences.

Practicing the Skill

Go over the directions for page 73. Ask students to read each phrase aloud. Then have students complete the page.

Name _____

⭐ Read each group of words. Say and spell each word in bold print. Repeat the word. Then sort the words. Write the words correctly in the boxes below.

- **doesn't** have a partner
- **practicing** the piano
- heard the **buzzing**
- **chatting** all day
- never **tried** tap dancing
- began **showing** the pictures
- on the **planning** committee
- **listens** to the orchestra

- **reaches** for the brush
- **isn't** in the band
- **carries** a violin case
- **played** the harp
- **scrubbed** the chalkboard
- **describing** the photograph
- **shouldn't** talk during the concert
- **danced** to the music

Drop Final e
practicing
describing
danced

Change y to i
carries
tried

Double Final Consonant
chatting
scrubbed
planning

No Base Changes
reaches
buzzing
played
showing
listens

Has a Contraction
doesn't
isn't
shouldn't

LESSON 35: Connecting Spelling and Writing   **73**

UNIVERSAL ACCESS
Meeting Individual Needs

Tactile Learners

Give each student a page from a newspaper or a magazine. Tell students to find as many examples as they can of verbs ending in **s, es,** or **ing.** Have students list the words on a sheet of paper. Next to each word, students should write the base word. Extend the activity by having the class create a master list of all the words students find.

Visual Learners

List the following words on the board. Have volunteers draw a line connecting each phrase with its contraction. Then have students explain what the apostrophe replaces.

they will	**it's**
is not	**doesn't**
let us	**hasn't**
she is	**they'll**
could not	**we're**
it is	**isn't**
has not	**couldn't**
does not	**she's**
we are	**let's**

Learners with Special Needs

Additional strategies for supporting learners with special needs can be found on page 65L.

Choose a song that you know and like. Imagine that you are going to teach it to a friend. Think about the best way to teach your friend the song.

⭐ **Write a list of the steps you would follow to teach a song to your friend. Put the steps in the order that makes the most sense. Use at least three of these spelling words.**

doesn't	practicing	buzzing	chatting	tried	showing
planning	listens	reaches	isn't	carries
played	scrubbed	describing	shouldn't	danced

Answers will vary.

Writer's Tips

First, list all the steps on a separate sheet of paper. Next, arrange the steps in order by numbering them. If you've left anything out, now is the time to add it. Finally, write your steps on this page.

Writer's Challenge

Think about a game or a sport that you know how to play. How would you teach this game to someone who had never played it? First, list the steps of the game in order. Then write a paragraph explaining how to play the game.

English-Language Learners/ESL

On the board, write words naming activities that can be easily identified by visual cues, such as **singing** or **dancing.** For each word, have students say the base word and the **ing** ending. Then ask the student to use the word in a simple sentence and demonstrate its meaning through pantomime.

Gifted Learners

Challenge students to write a poem about an activity they are interested in. Ask them to include at least one contraction in each line. Have students share their poems with the class.

The Writing Process

Tell students that on page 74 they will write a list of steps for teaching someone a song. Go over the directions and spelling words at the top of the page.

Prewrite Discuss with students how they would go about learning the words to a song. For example, would they write down the words and memorize them? Would they play a recording of the song over and over? Would they learn one verse at a time? Guide students in using their responses to formulate a plan.

Write Direct students' attention to the Writer's Tips on page 74. Suggest that students consider which spelling words might be most appropriate to include.

Revise Have students compare their sequence of steps with those of a partner and exchange feedback. Then have them make whatever revisions they think will improve their work.

Proofread Tell students to check for errors in spelling, grammar, and punctuation.

Publish Have students copy their final drafts onto page 74 or a separate sheet of paper. Then ask volunteers to try out their list of steps.

Computer Connection

Share the following tip with students who use a word processor to do their writing.

● Word-processing programs allow you to display text in various ways. You can make letters **bold** or *italic.* You can underline words, double underline them, or even underline them with a wavy line.

● Your program may also let you display text in colors. If you have a color printer, you can print documents that show words in two or more colors.

Portfolio Have students add their lists of instructional steps to their portfolios.

Plurals **s, es, ies**

Objectives

- **To form plurals by adding *s* or *es***
- **To form plurals of words ending in *y* by adding *s* or *ies***

Warming Up

- Write the following tongue twister on the board and say it with students:

  Sally sews shirt**s**, sketch**es** scene**s**, and sells stor**ies** in sixty-six cit**ies**, sixteen state**s**, and six countr**ies**.

- List these base words in a column on the board: **shirt, sketch, scene, story, city, state, country**. Have volunteers locate their plural forms in the sentences, circle the plural endings, and write the plural word to the right of the base word.

Teaching the Lesson

- Have students look at each word in the right-hand column on the board. Ask a volunteer to describe how the spelling of the base word changed when the plural was formed. Help students come up with other words that follow each pattern; list the words. Examples include **color, song; glass, kiss, brush, beach, wish; lady, sky, baby, hobby.** Ask students to use those words in sentences.

- Have a student read the Helpful Hints aloud as others follow along silently. Remind students that saying the plural word aloud can help them remember how to write it.

Name _____

> **Helpful Hint**
>
> **Plural** means "more than one." To make most **base words** plural, add s.
>
> | band + s = bands | stage + s = stages |
>
> Add es to words that end in s, ss, ch, sh, x, z, or zz.
>
> dress + es = dresses   inch + es = inches
> brush + es = brushes   box + es = boxes

CHALLENGE

Make a list of ten songs, stories, books, or movies that have plural words in their titles. Here are some ideas:

101 Dalmations
The Three Wishes

Circle each plural word on your list.

⭐ **Add *s* or *es* to form the plural of each word. Write the plural word on the line.**

1. song	songs	2. concert	concerts
3. tax	taxes	4. violin	violins
5. flute	flutes	6. porch	porches
7. waltz	waltzes	8. fizz	fizzes
9. genius	geniuses	10. mix	mixes
11. princess	princesses	12. bush	bushes

⭐ **Add *s* or *es* to each word in bold print so that the sentence makes sense. Write the new word on the line.**

13. Darla is one of the **sculptor** in my art class.
    sculptors

14. Most of her sculptures are of **athlete**.
    athletes

15. Two of them show **coach** working with students. coaches

16. Wayne's **sketch** are the best in the class.
    sketches

UNIVERSAL ACCESS
Meeting Individual Needs

Visual Learners

Create this chart on the board and have students copy it. Ask them to add words that follow each spelling pattern.

SINGULAR	PLURAL
most words	add s
trumpet	trumpets
note	notes
words ending in s	add es
genius	geniuses
words ending in ss	add es
kiss	kisses
words ending in ch	add es
bench	benches

Musical Learners

Ask students to write a song or jingle about the rules for forming plurals with different endings, like the one below. Students can present the song or jingle for classmates to use as a mnemonic device.

If you've got a double **s**,
Don't stress! Just add **es**.

If you've got a **ch** or **x**,
Cheer up! And add **es**.

75

☆ Write the plural of each of these base words.

1. monkey   monkeys   2. melody   melodies
3. county   counties   4. diary   diaries
5. berry   berries   6. journey   journeys

☆ Use a word from the box for each clue. Write one letter in each space. Read down the shaded column to answer the question.

coins	medleys	adventures	buddies
bunches	plays	couches	tubas

7. performances in a theater   p l a y s
8. large wind instruments   t u b a s
9. exciting experiences   a d v e n t u r e s
10. pennies, nickels, dimes, quarters   c o i n s
11. music made from different songs   m e d l e y s
12. groups of similar things   b u n c h e s
13. sofas   c o u c h e s
14. good friends   b u d d i e s

Question: What do you call the people who come to a concert?

Answer: the _____ audience _____

🏠 **Home Involvement Activity** Play a game. One person says, "One [any **A** word]." The next player says, "Two [plural of that word]." (*One ax, two axes*) Continue with a **B** word, then a **C** word, and so on, through the alphabet.

Practicing the Skill

● Read aloud the direction lines on pages 75–76. Tell students to say each plural word aloud to help them decide whether to add **s** or **es**. Have them listen, for example, to the difference between **dish** and the plural **dishes.**

● Invite students to create their own tips for remembering when to change the letter **y** to **i**. Here is an example:

Look at the letter before the **y.**

If it's a vowel, leave the **y** alone.

If it's a consonant, change the **y** to **i.**

Then add **es.**

Turn to page 65K for an Intervention Strategy designed to help students who need extra help with this lesson.

Curriculum Connections

Spelling Link

Ask pairs of students to make a set of twenty flash cards with plurals from the lesson. Students can write a base word on one side and its plural form on the other side. Have students shuffle the cards and sort the plural forms according to the spelling patterns they share.

Social Studies Link

Invite students to make an imaginary map. Ask them to suggest common nouns that name places and list them on the board. **(city, country, state, highway, lake, beach)** Then invite students to say and spell the plural of each noun. Finally, have students write a brief paragraph about an imaginary country, using the plural form of five nouns on the list.

Observational Assessment

Check to see that students can determine when to add **s,** *add* **es,** *or change* **y** *to* **i** *and add* **es** *when forming a plural.*

English-Language Learners/ESL

Using magazine cutouts and large index cards, make some simple picture cards for words and their plurals. **(boxes, foxes, couches, brushes, cities)** Show two of the same item on one side of each card; show only one item on the other side. Display the cards and help students label them, encouraging students to say the words with you.

Gifted Learners

Show students pictures of two sculptures. Have them compare the two works of art in a composition. Ask students to include as many plurals as they can in their writing.

Learners with Special Needs

Additional strategies for supporting learners with special needs can be found on page 65L.

Plurals with
f, lf, fe, ff, and o

Objectives

● **To identify the plurals of words ending in f, lf, fe, ff, or o**

● **To write the plurals of words ending in f, lf, fe, ff, or o**

Warming Up

● Write the following rhyme on the board and say it with students:

> You make **leaves** from **leaf**,
> **Halves** from **half**,
> **Lives** from **life**,
> And **loaves** from **loaf**.
>
> **Roofs, chiefs,** and **cliffs**
> Don't work that way;
> And **radios** and **heroes**
> Is what we say.

● List the singular forms of the boldfaced words in a column on the board. Ask volunteers to locate their plural forms in the rhyme. Have students say each word and write it next to its singular form.

⭐ Teaching the Lesson

● Ask students to look again at the list of singular forms of words. Encourage students to describe how the spelling changed when the plural was formed. Help students suggest other words they know that follow similar spelling patterns. List the words. (Examples include **calves, shelves; loaves, knives; videos; potatoes.**)

● Have a student read the Helpful Hints aloud as others follow along silently.

Name _____

> **Helpful Hints**
>
> For most words ending in f, lf, or fe, form the plural by changing the f to v and adding es.
>
> | | | |
> |---|---|---|
> | leaf = leaves | calf = calves | life = lives |
>
> There are some exceptions to this rule. Form the plural of some words that end in f and all words ending in ff by adding s.
>
> | | | |
> |---|---|---|
> | roof = roofs | chief = chiefs | cliff = cliffs |

⭐ Write the plural form of each word. Look in a dictionary if you need help.

1. chef	chefs		2. thief	thieves	
3. half	halves		4. knife	knives	
5. elf	elves		6. clef	clefs	
7. cuff	cuffs		8. shelf	shelves	
9. wife	wives		10. muff	muffs	

CHALLENGE

Work backward. Write the singular form of the plural words below. Then write a sentence for each word in its singular form.

scarves
wharves
hooves

⭐ Complete each sentence with a word from the box below. Use the plural form of each word.

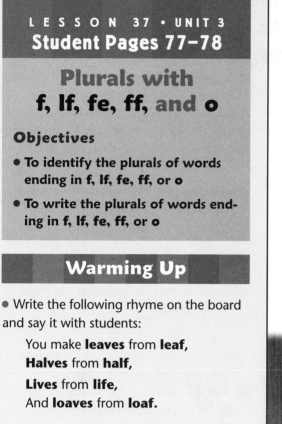

> wolf   belief   life   loaf

11. There are two ___loaves___ of bread in the basket.

12. In "Little Red Riding Hood" ___wolves___ are villains.

13. Many children's ___beliefs___ are formed at a young age.

14. Do you believe that a cat has nine ___lives___?

LESSON 37: Plurals with **f, lf, fe, ff,** and **o.**   **77**

UNIVERSAL ACCESS
Meeting Individual Needs

📌 Kinesthetic Learners

Divide the class into teams. Have each team create cards with base words ending in **f, lf, fe, ff,** or **o** and put them in a box. Ask the teams to switch boxes. When the game starts, the first player from each team chooses a card and writes the correct plural form of the word on the board. Have students continue until the box is empty. The team with the most correct answers in the least amount of time wins.

📌 Logical Learners

Have small groups of students create cards for the following words: **leaf, chief, loaf, life self, shelf, half, chef, belief, hero, echo, potato, piano, stereo, rodeo.** Write the singular form on one side, and the plural on the other. Ask students to shuffle the cards and place them singular side up. Have students take turns selecting a card, saying the plural, and spelling it. Ask students to sort the cards according to the words' spelling patterns.

⭐ Write the plural form of each word. If you aren't sure whether to add s or es, check a dictionary.

1. tomato __tomatoes__   2. igloo __ingloos__
3. stereo __stereos__   4. studio __studios__
5. oboe __oboes__   6. soprano __sopranos__
7. echo __echoes__   8. trio __trios__

⭐ Write the plural form of each of the eight words below. Then find and circle these eight plural words in the puzzle. The words can go across, on a slant, or up and down.

9. wife __wives__
10. loaf __loaves__
11. shelf __shelves__
12. thief __thieves__
13. knife __knives__
14. solo __solos__
15. rodeo __rodeos__
16. piano __pianos__

s	o	l	o	s	t	w	s	e
t	a	r	e	w	p	e	a	v
h	i	v	k	n	i	v	e	s
i	l	e	l	o	a	v	e	s
e	a	r	s	a	n	v	e	t
v	r	o	d	e	o	s	p	s
e	a	h	g	o	s	t	u	e
s	o	s	h	e	l	v	e	s

LESSON 37: Plurals with f, lf, fe, ff, and o

Home Involvement Activity The following plural music words are scrambled. Unscramble the words. Then place them on a word map, with the word *music* in the center.
inaspo tosal ospnrsoa sleoci sloos

Practicing the Skill

• Read aloud the direction lines on pages 77–78 and complete the first item in each exercise with students.

• Remind students that the exceptions to the spelling patterns have to be memorized. Invite students to suggest various ways of remembering these words, for example:

1) Make up a silly sentence with a few spelling exceptions in it: *The **chiefs** sat on the **roofs** and looked at the **cliffs**.*

2) Use rhythm and repetition: ***Piano**, no **e**, **cello**, no **e**, **solo**, no **e**, **soprano** no **e**.*

Curriculum Connections

Spelling Link

Have students work in pairs to unscramble the following plurals and write them correctly.

oesters	**boseo**	**dustios**
gloois	**posranos**	**ritos**
topatoes	**motatoes**	**evidos**
veslah	**veslac**	**vesnik**
leves	**evwis**	**velshs**

(Answers: **stereos, oboes, studios, igloos, sopranos, trios, potatoes, tomatoes, videos, halves, calves, knives, elves, wives, shelves**)

Math Link

Have students work in small groups to create word problems for other groups to solve, using plurals made from words ending in **f, lf, fe,** or **o**. For example: *If two **chefs** each add two **halves** of an orange to the fruit salad, how many oranges did they add?*

Observational Assessment

Check to see that students know how to form each type of plural correctly.

English-Language Learners/ESL

Display objects whose names end in **f, lf, fe** or **o**, such as **tomato, potato, knife, scarf, video,** and **radio.** Have more than one of each item available. On the board, write either the singular or the plural form of the word. Have students respond by saying the word and holding up the correct number of objects.

Gifted Learners

Invite students to write silly sentences including as many words ending in **f** or **o** and their plural forms as they can. Have students read their sentences aloud to the class.

Learners with Special Needs

Additional strategies for supporting learners with special needs can be found on page 65L.

Irregular Plurals

Objectives

- To identify irregular plurals of words
- To write the irregular plurals of words

Warming Up

- Write the following riddle on the board and give students time to answer it.

  What goes on four **feet** in the morning, two **feet** in the afternoon, and three **feet** in the evening?

- Write the answer on the board: a person. **Children** crawl on all fours when they're young; adults walk on two legs; and elderly **men** and **women** often use a cane, the third leg.

- List the irregular plurals from the riddle and ask students to supply the singular forms. Encourage students to identify what is unusual about these plurals. (They aren't formed by adding **s** or **es**.)

★ Teaching the Lesson

- Write the following headings on the board: *Plurals without **s** or **es**, Stay the same.* Have students list the plurals in the riddle under the appropriate heading.

- Ask students to listen carefully as you use each of the words below in a sentence. Say the word and ask a volunteer to write it under the proper heading on the board. **(mice, teeth, women, fish, geese, moose, children, series)**

- Invite a student to read the Helpful Hints aloud as others follow along silently.

Name _____

► Helpful Hints

The **plurals** of some words do not have s or es at the end. These words become plural in irregular ways.

mouse → **mice**   child → **children**   tooth → **teeth**   goose → **geese**

Some words stay the same when singular or plural.

sheep   deer   elk   salmon   moose   series   cattle

★ Look at the plural forms in the box below. Write each plural next to its singular form.

moose	men	oxen	geese	women
oases	feet	mice	bison	children

1. woman _____women_____   2. foot _____feet_____
3. child _____children_____   4. man _____men_____
5. oasis _____oases_____   6. mouse _____mice_____
7. moose _____moose_____   8. ox _____oxen_____
9. bison _____bison_____   10. goose _____geese_____

★ Complete each sentence by using the plural form of the word in the box.

trout	tooth	Child	deer	series

11. Dogs have sharp canine _____teeth_____.

12. _____Children_____ can get into the movies for half price.

13. We caught several _____trout_____ in Lake Ward.

14. There are twelve new TV comedy _____series_____.

15. The _____deer_____ darted across the country road.

WORD STRATEGY

Some words, such as **deer** and **sheep**, have the *same* singular and plural form. Use context clues when reading to figure out whether the word means "one" or "more than one" in a sentence.

UNIVERSAL ACCESS
Meeting Individual Needs

Auditory Learners

Have students work in groups to tell a story using the plural words listed on the board. Ask students to take turns continuing the story with sentences containing an irregular plural that has not been used before. For example: *Once upon a time, some **children** were walking by the river. They saw a beautiful flock of **geese**. One goose said, "I can grant you a **series** of wishes."*

Kinesthetic Learners

Invite students to play "plural charades." Have a volunteer act out a word with an irregular plural while the rest of the class guesses. Students who are performing can make sounds—squeaking like mice or honking like geese—but they can't use words.

Each clue for this crossword puzzle is given in singular form.
Write the plural form in the boxes to solve the crossword puzzle.

Across

1. series	15. ox	26. melody
4. crowd	16. spray	27. oasis
5. cattle	17. chance	28. igloo
6. waltz	18. deer	29. inch
9. knife	19. hen	30. solo
12. piano	23. elk	

Down

1. self	8. wish	21. zero
2. donkey	10. video	22. wife
3. bean	11. story	24. key
5. canvas	13. studio	25. dog
6. woman	14. echo	
7. tax	20. bison	

80   LESSON 38: Irregular Plurals

Home Involvement Activity Make up small word-search puzzles that include irregular plurals, such as **teeth** and **feet.** Write your words across, on a slant, or up and down. Then exchange and solve each other's puzzles.

Practicing the Skill

- Read aloud the direction lines on pages 79–80 and complete the first item in each exercise with students.
- Encourage students to search for patterns among irregular plurals:

man–men	foot–feet
woman–women	tooth–teeth

- Explain to students that the crossword puzzle includes words whose plurals are formed by adding **s, es,** or **ies.**

Curriculum Connections

Spelling Link

Read each of the following words and its context sentence aloud. Ask students to write down the word in its singular form. Then write the plural form beside it. Have students exchange papers and go over each other's work.

moose	I saw a **moose** in the woods.
trout	We were fishing for **trout.**
man	A **man** asked for directions.
woman	The **woman** knew the way.
bison	Is a **bison** like a buffalo?
foot	Jo was standing on one **foot.**
tooth	A dentist will fix that **tooth!**
ox	The **ox** pulled the plow.

Science Link

Have students make a list of animals and fish mentioned on page 79: **sheep, deer, elk, salmon, moose, oxen, bison, mice, trout, geese, deer.** Invite students to research one of them and write a few sentences giving interesting facts about it.

Observational Assessment

Check to see that students know how to form irregular plurals of words.

Connecting Reading and Writing

Objectives

- **To read a nonfiction piece and respond to it in writing**
- **To practice comparing, contrasting, and synthesizing information**
- **To write original song lyrics using pairs of rhyming words**

Warming Up

Comprehension Skills

- Have students choose two performers to **compare and contrast**. Ask: *In what ways are these two people alike? In what ways are they different?*

- Remind students that **synthesizing** is putting together the ideas within a piece of writing and making sense of them.

Teaching the Lesson

- To help students answer the first Reader's Response question, have them reread the article to find details that support the main idea and opening sentence: "Aaron Copland was a great American composer."

- Tell students who need help with the second question to reread the first paragraph of the article carefully.

- Suggest that students include details from the article to support their answers to the third question.

Practicing the Skill

Read aloud the directions on page 82. Have students look over the pairs of rhyming words. Ask: *What makes these words particularly good for a lullaby?* Then have students create their lullabies.

81

Name _____

⭐ **Read about a famous American composer. Then answer the questions that follow.**

An American Composer

Aaron Copland was a great American composer. You may not know his name, but you probably have heard his music. Copland was born in 1900 in New York City. Like Grandma Moses, he lived a very long life. Yet unlike her, Copland began studying what he loved at a young age. His music teachers heard his talent right away.

Like many children of immigrants, Copland loved the adventure stories of the American West. In fact, many of his best ideas came from the Wild West or from American folk music. His music for the ballets, *Billy the Kid*, *Rodeo*, and *Appalachian Spring*, are filled with the spirit of the West.

Throughout his career, Copland wrote music for large and small orchestras. He even wrote music for the movies. Copland would find popular tunes that he liked. Then he would use them to build works of great music. For example, he once started with an old Southern lullaby. He then arranged the music for a small orchestra and a solo voice. Today, people still like to pick out popular tunes that they hear in Copland's classical music.

📖 Reader's Response

1. What makes Aaron Copland a great American composer?

2. How are Aaron Copland and Grandma Moses alike? How are they different?

3. Would you like to hear some of Aaron Copland's music? Explain your reasons.

1. He used American folk music and popular tunes to write classical music.
2. Both lived a long life and were American "artists." Copland began studying what he loved at a young age.
3. Answers will vary.

LESSON 39: Connecting Reading and Writing
Comprehension—Compare and Contrast; Synthesize

81

UNIVERSAL ACCESS
Meeting Individual Needs

Auditory Learners

If you have a recording of Aaron Copland's ballet *Appalachian Spring* available, play it for the class. Help students identify the melody of the traditional Shaker hymn "Simple Gifts" within Copland's piece. After students have listened to the recording for a while, ask them to compare and contrast Copland's work with the hymn that inspired it.

Learners with Special Needs

Additional strategies for supporting learners with special needs can be found on page 65L.

Visual Learners

Find a book of American art that includes, if possible, paintings by Grandma Moses. Have students listen to some folk-inspired works of Copland or other composers. Then ask students to flip through the book and find a painting that they feel goes well with the music. Suggested recordings include Copland's *Rodeo* and Dvořák's *Symphony from the New World*.

Aaron Copland once used a Southern lullaby to build a piece of great music. You may know the lullaby. It begins:

Hush-a-bye, don't you cry,
Go to sleep, you little baby.

⭐ **Now it's your turn.** Imagine singing a baby to sleep. Write words to your own lullaby. Use at least one pair of the rhymes below to help you write your song.

close	head	sleep	eyes	night	hush	smooth
doze	bed	sheep	rise	light	rush	soothe

Answers will vary.

_____

_____

_____

_____

_____

_____

_____

_____

_____

Writer's Tips
Use rhyming pairs to write your lullaby.
Also, think about the soothing music that would put a baby to sleep.

Speaker's Challenge
Tell how you wrote your lullaby. Then sing your lullaby to a small group of classmates. Did anybody get sleepy?

The Writing Process

Discuss the purpose of a lullaby—to lull a baby to sleep—and the qualities an effective lullaby might have.

Prewrite Have students begin by choosing a tune for their lullaby. Remind them that restful and soothing melodies make the best lullabies. To help students get started, suggest these tunes: "Rock-a-Bye, Baby," "Twinkle, Twinkle, Little Star," "Hush, Little Baby," and "Brahms's Lullaby."

Write Suggest that students think of sounds and sights associated with sleep. Point out that many lullaby lyrics are simply commands such as "go to sleep" or "rest your head."

Revise Direct students to sing or recite their lullaby to a partner. Remind them to listen carefully to each other and to give positive feedback as well as negative.

Proofread Suggest that students read their work slowly and carefully to check for errors in grammar, punctuation, and spelling.

Publish Have students copy their final drafts onto page 82. Invite volunteers to sing or recite their lullabies aloud.

Computer Connection
When writing song lyrics or poetry on a word processor, it is important to know how to set and clear tabs. First highlight your poem or song. Then click on "Format" at the top of the screen, drag the cursor down to "Tabs," and release the mouse button. To clear any previously set tabs, hit "Clear." To set a tab, type a number (representing inches) in the box marked "Tab stop position," and hit "Set."

Portfolio Suggest that students add their finished lullabies to their portfolios.

English-Language Learners/ESL

Display pictures that show dancers, musicians, painters, and other artists. (You may have already created a collage of artists for the *Theme Activity* at the beginning of the unit.) Have English learners work in pairs with fluent speakers to write the singular, plural, possessive, and plural possessive forms of the word that names each artist pictured.

Gifted Learners

Ask students in your class who sing or play a musical instrument to take a simple, well-known tune and elaborate on it. They may wish to use the tune as the basis for "jazzy" improvisation or a repetitive round. Perhaps they can invent a harmony for the tune. You may wish to request the assistance of a music teacher or other professional at your school to give students guidance in creating their compositions.

Reviewing and Assessing

Word Endings, Contractions, and Plurals

Objective

To review and assess word endings, contractions, and plurals

Warming Up

● List the following pairs of words on the board in two columns as shown:

Column A	Column B
paint/paints	**dry/dries**
turn/turned	**trace/traced**
perform/performed	**rob/robbed**
song/songs	**city/cities**
play/playing	**wave/waving**
coin/coins	**elf/elves**
duck/ducks	**moose/moose**
mix/mixing	**put/putting**

● Have volunteers read aloud one pair from each column. Ask them how the Column B pair differs from the Column A pair. For example, **dry/dries** differs from **paint/paints** because **paint** is made plural by adding **s.** But **dry** is a base word ending in a consonant followed by **y**, and the **y** changes to **i** before adding **es.**

Teaching the Lesson

● Lessons 32–38 (pages 67–80) present more than a dozen Helpful Hints. Have volunteers choose one Helpful Hint from these lessons and explain it to the class in their own words. Continue until all Helpful Hints have been covered. Encourage students to ask questions if anything is unclear.

● As students review each Helpful Hint, have the class provide examples that illustrate the particular rule.

Name _____

⭐ Add **s** or **es, ed,** or **ing** to each base word. Write the new words in the chart. Remember to make spelling changes as needed.

		Add **s** or **es**	Add **ed**	Add **ing**
1	dress	dresses	dressed	dressing
2	attach	attaches	attached	attaching
3	mix	mixes	mixed	mixing
4	buzz	buzzes	buzzed	buzzing
5	splash	splashes	splashed	splashing
6	dry	dries	dried	drying
7	play	plays	played	playing
8	dance	dances	danced	dancing
9	clap	claps	clapped	clapping
10	admit	admits	admitted	admitting

⭐ Write the base word for each word below.

11. brushes ___brush___
12. planning ___plan___
13. waved ___wave___
14. sketching ___sketch___
15. diaries ___diary___
16. tracing ___trace___

⭐ Add **ed** or **ing** to the base word in the box to complete each sentence.

hope	17. My chorus is ___putting___ on a concert tomorrow.
put	18. We have been ___practicing___ for three months.
have	19. We are ___hoping___ to sing a Russian song.
practice	20. We look forward to ___having___ you in the audience.

UNIVERSAL ACCESS
Meeting Individual Needs

Visual Learners

Write these contractions on the board, but scramble the letters and omit the apostrophe. Ask students to unscramble the words, add the apostrophes, and tell what letters the apostrophe replaces.

he's	**I'll**	**wasn't**
she'd	**can't**	**you'll**
I'd	**they'll**	**you're**
don't	**we've**	**they're**

Auditory Learners

Say each of the following sentences aloud. Have students repeat the sentence and then change the verb to past tense and the noun to plural. For example: **They perform in a city.** becomes **They performed in cities.**

Anne buys a dress.
They dance to a tune.
Hal fixes the shelf.
They deny the charge.

Ask volunteers to write their sentences on the board. Then have students make up other sentences to change.

Learners with Special Needs

Additional strategies for supporting students with special needs can be found on page 65L.

Write the correct plural form of the words below.

1. tax — taxes
2. salmon — salmon
3. wife — wives
4. stereo — stereos
5. woman — women
6. shelf — shelves
7. foot — feet
8. tooth — teeth

Choose the pair of words that make up each contraction in the sentence. Fill in the circle of your answer.

9. I shouldn't be late. ○ should have ● should not ○ shall not
10. He could've called. ○ could not ○ should have ● could have
11. You're a great singer. ○ You will ○ You were ● You are
12. She doesn't dance. ● does not ○ do not ○ did not
13. It's time to start. ○ It has ● It is ○ It was

Read the sentences. Fill in the circle of the word that correctly completes each sentence. Then write the word on the line.

14. One of the world's oldest flutes still ___plays___ music.
    ○ play ● plays ○ playing

15. There are similar instruments, but ___they're___ too fragile to use.
    ● they're ○ their ○ there

16. This ancient flute has been around for ___centuries___.
    ○ century ○ centurys ● centuries

17. Such flutes were made from the bones of ___animals___.
    ● animals ○ animal ○ animal's

18. The flute is about nine ___inches___ long and has a few small holes.
    ○ inchs ○ inch ● inches

Extend & Apply

How do you think the ancient flute might have been played? Write your answer in a short "how-to" paragraph. Use two plural words.

An ancient flute

Reteaching Activities

Touching Base

List the words below on the board. Next to each, have students write the corresponding base word. Then have students make up a sentence for each word. Finally, ask students to suggest other words that follow the same base word + ending patterns.

studied	waltzes
princesses	melodies
exercising	practiced
monkeys	thieves
spotted	chatting
describing	buzzed
igloos	echoes

Contraction Challenge

Have students copy these charts and fill in the contractions. Then have students use each contraction in a sentence.

	have	will	would
I			
she			
we			
you			

	not
are	
do	
is	
could	

Check Up The exercises on pages 83–84 will help students review word endings, contractions, and plurals and help you evaluate students' progress toward mastery.

Encourage students to use context clues to help them complete items 17–20 on page 83 and 14–18 on page 84.

Observational Assessment As students do the exercises, watch to see whether they correctly make spelling changes when adding endings. Review and compare your observational notes from earlier lessons to gain a clearer perspective on individual student's progress.

Student Skills Assessment Keep track of each student's progress with word endings, contractions, and plurals using the checklist on page 65H.

Writing Conference Meet with students to talk over the writing they have done in this unit, such as the list of instructional steps on page 74 and the lullaby on page 82. Compare these samples with earlier works from the student's portfolio. Point out areas of progress and make suggestions for further improvement.

Group together students who need further instruction in word endings, contractions, and plurals and have them complete the *Reteaching Activities.* Turn to page 65C for alternative assessment methods.

Singular Possessives

Objectives

- **To identify singular possessives**
- **To write singular possessives**

Warming Up

- Write the following tongue twisters on the board and say them with students:

  Sula's songs sure sound savvy.

  This painting's proportions pose possible problems.

  Fred's friends flip flapjacks fast.

- Have students repeat each line and ask volunteers to identify who or what has or owns something in each of the lines. **(Sula, painting, Fred)** Ask students to explain how the spelling of the words **Sula's, painting's,** and **Fred's** indicates ownership.

Teaching the Lesson

- Point to various things in the classroom and model statements using possessives: *The **room's** color is blue. The **book's** cover is yellow. This **author's** name is Natalie Babbit.* Have students continue the process. As students supply statements, list the possessives on the board with the apostrophe and **s** lining up vertically, showing the pattern.

- Explain that words that show possession (having or owning something) are called possessives. To show who or what has or owns something, add **'s**.

- Have a student read the Helpful Hints as the class follows along silently.

Name _____

> **Helpful Hint**

Add an **apostrophe** and an s ('s) to the end of a singular noun to show who or what has or owns something.

the tool that Scott owns = Scott's tool
the thoughts of one student = one student's thoughts
the guitar that Chris has = Chris's guitar

★ Rewrite each phrase. Add **'s** to the word in bold print to show who or what has or owns something.

1. the easel that belongs to **Juan**	Juan's easel
2. the music book that **Emily** has	Emily's book
3. the hands of a **conductor**	conductor's hands
4. the piano of **Charles**	Charles's piano
5. the trumpet of the **orchestra**	orchestra's trumpet
6. the ideas of this **composer**	composer's ideas
7. the studio that the **artist** owns	artist's studio
8. the statue of that **sculptor**	sculptor's statue

★ Write the possessive form of each word.

9. friend	friend's	10. painter	painter's
11. teacher	teacher's	12. man	man's
13. coach	coach's	14. Mr. Lee	Mr. Lee's
15. doctor	doctor's	16. woman	woman's
17. dancer	dancer's	18. city	city's
19. child	child's	20. mayor	mayor's
21. musician	musician's	22. James	James's

> **WORK TOGETHER**
>
> Many place names are named for their owners or settlers. Sutter's Mill in California, once owned by Mr. Sutter, is one example. With a partner, list place names that use the possessive form. Use a map to help.

UNIVERSAL ACCESS
Meeting Individual Needs

Auditory Learners

Have a student sit in a circle and play an alphabet game, with each student contributing a pair of sentences like the following: *Annie had an apple. That was **Annie's** apple.* or *Betty has a book. That is **Betty's** book.* Have students say their sentences and write the possessive phrases **(Annie's apple, Betty's book)** on the board.

Visual Learners

Suggest that students create an original painting or sculpture. Have them present it to the class. Encourage students to use singular possessives in each sentence of their presentation. Record the phrases on the board (for example, *the **balloon's** color, the **arm's** position,* and so on).

Greg's music book	two harps	the band's music
the writer's play	the girl's crayons	pieces of music
the artist's paintings	the actors	Kevin's paints
the singer's performance	sheets of music	the city's theaters

1. Sentences will vary.

2.

3.

4.

5.

6.

7.

8.

The Migration of the Negro, Panel No. 1, by Jacob Lawrence 1940–1941

86 LESSON 41: Singular Possessives

Home Involvement Activity Choose one of these creative people. Discuss how the person used art or music to show what was meaningful to him or her.
Grandma Moses   Jacob Lawrence   Aaron Copland

Practicing the Skill

● Read aloud the direction lines on pages 85–86 and complete the first item in each exercise with students.

● Ask students to create their own tips for doing the exercise on page 86. Here is an example:

To know which words are possessives:

✓ Look for an apostrophe plus **s.**

✓ Be careful! An **s** by itself, with no apostrophe, is a plural.

✓ Watch out for the word **of**. It sounds like it's making a possessive but it might not be—for example: **pieces of music.**

Curriculum Connections

Spelling Link

● Have students work in groups of three or four. Ask them to create a list of nouns from the lesson, each student contributing one word.

● Students then work independently to write one possessive phrase for each word on their group's list. For example, for the word **piano,** they might write **the teacher's piano** or **the school's piano.**

● Have students exchange papers with a partner and check each other's work.

Social Studies Link

Invite students to choose someone from history whom they admire. Ask students to write five sentences about that person, telling about his or her life, education, work, and accomplishments.

Observational Assessment

Check to see that students know how to form a singular possessive by using an apostrophe plus **s.**

English-Language Learners/ESL

Provide sentence pairs that follow this pattern: *The **button of the jacket** is blue. The **jacket's button** is blue.* Mask the second sentence in each pair. Have students read the first sentence aloud. Help them rephrase the sentence using the possessive form. Then unmask the second sentence and read it with students.

Gifted Learners

Suggest that students write a review about a concert, play, or movie they went to recently. Encourage them to use as many possessives as possible as they discuss the work.

Learners with Special Needs

Additional strategies for supporting learners with special needs can be found on page 65L.

Plural Possessives

Objectives

- **To identify plural possessives**
- **To distinguish between singular possessives, plural possessives, and plurals**
- **To write plural possessives, singular possessives, and plurals**

Warming Up

Write this dialogue on the board. Have the boys read José and the girls read Josie.

José: My **cousins'** band is really cool.

Josie: Wow! Your cousin is in a band?

José: Not just one cousin—all three **cousins!** My **aunt's children** all play in the band.

Josie: I thought you had only one aunt.

José: That's right. She's the **children's** mother.

Josie: But you just said, "My **aunts' children**..."

José: Not my *aunts'* **children**—my *aunt's* **children**.

Josie: Now I'm really confused!

Teaching the Lesson

- Write these words on the board:

aunt	**aunts**	**children**
aunt's	**aunts'**	**children's**

- Ask students to identify the plural words. **(aunts, children)** Then have students identify the words that show possession. **(aunt's, aunts', children's)** Tell students that **aunt's** refers to one person, whereas **aunts'** and **children's** refer to more than one person.

- Have a student read the Helpful Hints aloud as others follow along silently.

Name _____

▶ Helpful Hints

Add only an **apostrophe** (') to form the **possessive** of a plural noun that ends in s.

the cameras that belong to the students = the student**s'** cameras

Add an **apostrophe** and an s (**'s**) to form the possessive of a plural noun that does not end in s.

the chorus of the women = the women**'s** chorus
the voices of the men = the men**'s** voices
the band of the children = the children**'s** band

Rewrite each phrase. Add an apostrophe (') or an apostrophe and an s ('s) to the word in bold print to show who has or owns something.

1. the pictures that belong to my **friends**	my friends' cameras
2. the books that my **classmates** have	my classmates' books
3. the games of the **children**	the children's games
4. the classes of the **teachers**	the teachers' classes
5. the room of my **brothers**	my brothers' room
6. the sketches of the **artists**	the artists' sketches
7. the chorus of the **men**	the men's chorus

Write the possessive form of these plural words.

8. women	women's	9. girls	girls'
10. doctors	doctors'	11. singers	singers'
12. cities	cities'	13. animals	animals'
14. sisters	sisters'	15. boys	boys'
16. babies	babies'	17. tourists	tourists'

◀ CHALLENGE

Change each of these words to its plural form. Then write the possessive form of each plural word.

country
parent
wife

UNIVERSAL ACCESS
Meeting Individual Needs

Kinesthetic Learners

Have students play "plural possessives relay." The first player finds something in the classroom that belongs to more than one person, goes to it, touches it, says: *the **students'** books*, and spells **students'**. The player then writes the word on the board and hands the chalk to the next player. Continue playing until all students have had a turn.

Visual Learners

Draw the chart below on the board for students to copy. Have them add words to each list of examples.

singular	singular possessive
aunt	aunt's
child	child's
drums	drum's
plural	**plural possessive**
aunts	aunts'
children	children's
drums	drums'

⭐ **Read each phrase. If the words show that one person has or owns something, write the word *one*. If the words show that more than one person has or owns something, write the words *more than one*.**

1. the dancers' performance ___more than one___
2. the comic's jokes ___one___
3. the singer's solo ___one___
4. the actors' play ___more than one___
5. the owners' theater ___more than one___
6. the pianist's fingers ___one___
7. the writer's books ___one___
8. the painters' mural ___more than one___

⭐ **Read the sentences about the artist Winslow Homer. Fill in the circle of the word that completes each sentence correctly. Then write the word on the line.**

9. Winslow Homer was one of the ___country's___ greatest painters.
   ● country's   ○ countries   ○ countries'

10. His many Civil War ___drawings___ made him famous.
    ● drawings   ○ drawing's   ○ drawings'

11. Homer made sketches of ___soldiers'___ lives.
    ○ soldiers   ○ soldier's   ● soldiers'

12. These sketches were true ___works___ of art.
    ● works   ○ work's   ○ works'

13. The artist was moved by the young ___men's___ shyness.
    ○ man   ○ mens   ● men's

14. His ___pictures___ of the sea are also famous.
    ○ picture's   ● pictures   ○ pictures'

15. Homer made large ___paintings___ from some of his sketches.
    ● paintings   ○ painting's   ○ paintings'

Drum and Bugle Corps, Civil War Encampment by Winslow Homer, 1865

🏠 **Home Involvement Activity** Use each pair of words in the same sentence. Make sure your sentences make sense. Remember not to confuse plurals and possessives.
painters/painters'   friends/friends'

Practicing the Skill

● Read aloud the direction lines on pages 87–88 with students.

● Invite students to create tips to help them remember how to form plurals, singular possessives, and plural possessives. Here is an example:

plural: just add **s**

singular possessive: apostrophe+**s**

plural possessive: **s**+apostrophe

Intervention Strategy Turn to page 65K for an Intervention Strategy designed to help students who need extra support with this lesson.

Curriculum Connections

Spelling Link

Read the following words and sentences aloud and have students write the words.

children's The **children's** theater is upstairs.

doctors' Six **doctors'** offices were open.

doctor's My **doctor's** name is Dr. Chen.

apples How many **apples** are there in a pie?

apple's That **apple's** skin is shiny red.

women's The **women's** chorus is here.

sisters' My **sisters'** room has two beds and two desks.

animal's That **animal's** paw is hurt.

Science Link

Ask students to make a list of animals from a particular region, such as the desert, the Arctic, or the rainforest. Then ask them to write five sentences about an animal, using at least three singular or plural possessives.

Observational Assessment

Check to see that students know how to form plural possessives.

English-Language Learners/ESL

Show students magazine photos and illustrations and talk about plural and singular possessive nouns. Ask questions such as: *Whose hats are these? What's another way of saying the **legs of the chairs?*** Model a response orally and in writing: *The **boys'** hats, the **chairs'** legs.*

Gifted Learners

Suggest that students write a humorous dialogue, tongue-twister, poem, or short story whose humor is based on the mix-ups that can happen when someone confuses plurals, singular possessives, and plural possessives. Have students read or perform their work for the class.

Learners with Special Needs

Additional strategies for supporting learners with special needs can be found on page 65L.

Connecting Spelling and Writing

Objectives

- **To say, spell, sort, and write plurals and posessives**
- **To write a letter using plurals and possessives in context**

Warming Up

- Write the following riddle on the board and read it aloud with students.

  I'm as quiet as a mouse
  While sleeping **children** dream.
  But when the **birds** begin to rouse,
  I make a **banshee's** scream
  What am I? (an alarm clock)

- Have a volunteer underline the plurals and circle the possessive. Point out that **children** is an irregular plural, while the plural **birds** is formed by adding **s**.

Teaching the Lesson

- On the board, write **mouse, cliff, store, leaf, house, knife, kite, sky, cow,** and **dancer.** Have students write the plural forms next to each word.

- Then ask the students to write the (singular) possessives of each word.

- Finally, have students form the plural possessives. Remind them to add only an apostrophe to plurals than end in **s** (**knives'**) and an apostrophe and **s** to plurals that do not end in **s** (**mice's**).

Practicing the Skill

Read aloud the directions on page 89. Call on students to read aloud each bulleted phrase. Ask students to write on the board the words that are possessives. Have them identify the plural possessives. Then have students complete the page.

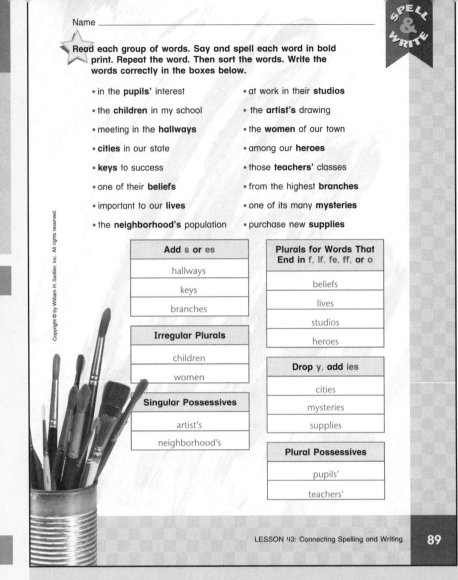

Name _____

Read each group of words. Say and spell each word in bold print. Repeat the word. Then sort the words. Write the words correctly in the boxes below.

- in the **pupils'** interest
- the **children** in my school
- meeting in the **hallways**
- **cities** in our state
- **keys** to success
- one of their **beliefs**
- important to our **lives**
- the **neighborhood's** population
- at work in their **studios**
- the **artist's** drawing
- the **women** of our town
- among our **heroes**
- those **teachers'** classes
- from the highest **branches**
- one of its many **mysteries**
- purchase new **supplies**

Add s or es
hallways
keys
branches

Irregular Plurals
children
women

Singular Possessives
artist's
neighborhood's

Plurals for Words That End in f, lf, fe, ff, **or** o
beliefs
lives
studios
heroes

Drop y, **add** ies
cities
mysteries
supplies

Plural Possessives
pupils'
teachers'

LESSON 43: Connecting Spelling and Writing **89**

UNIVERSAL ACCESS
Meeting Individual Needs

Visual Learners

To help students see how a base word can change forms as it becomes a plural, a possessive, and a plural possessive, have them complete the following chart. Suggest that students add base words to the chart.

Singular	city	life	hero	key
Plural	cities			
Possessive	city's			
Plural Possessive	cities'			

Learners with Special Needs

Additional strategies for supporting learners with special needs can be found on page 65L.

Kinesthetic Learners

Write the following sentences on the board, underlining the words in bold.

I gave my **kite's** string three sharp **tugs.**

The **sculptor's tools** were on the **shelves.**

The **painters' smocks** were hung on **hooks.**

Point to each underlined word and have students do one of the following actions: clap for plurals, raise their arms straight up for singular possessives, and stamp their feet for plural possessives.

How would you feel if the music and art programs at your school were canceled? What would you do about it? You could write a letter to the editor of your local newspaper. What would you say? How would you persuade people to save these programs at your school?

⭐ Write a letter to the editor of your local newspaper. Give three strong reasons for keeping the art and music programs open at your school. Try to convince your audience that these programs are important. Use two or more of these spelling words.

pupils'	children	hallways	cities	keys	beliefs
lives	neighborhood's	studios	artist's	women
heroes	teachers'	branches	mysteries	supplies

Dear Editor: _Answers will vary._

_____

_____

_____

_____

_____

_____

_____

Writer's Tips

State the main idea of your letter right away. Then support it with strong reasons or details. Persuade your readers to agree with you.

Speaker's Challenge

Give your letter as a speech. Use persuasive words, a strong tone of voice, and eye contact to get your audience to agree with your point of view.

English-Language Learners/ESL

Review the spelling changes made to base words when forming plurals. Say **pencil** and write it on the board. Next, display several pencils. Say **pencils,** emphasizing the letter **s,** and write it on the board. Repeat the activity with items such as a paintbrush, leaf, penny, book, foot etc. Then have students label each item with the singular and plural form of the word that names it.

Gifted Learners

Invite a group of students to plan a debate. Propose that the debate will be about cutting funding for school programs: Will the school cut the music program or sports? Have the debaters pick from a hat to join a team. Emphasize that debaters must use reason in their arguments and leave personal opinions aside. Have each team present its arguments, giving the other side a chance to refute them briefly. Then give each team an opportunity to sum up and let the class vote.

The Writing Process

Tell students that on page 90 they will write a letter to the editor of a local newspaper. Go over the directions and spelling words at the top of the page.

Prewrite Have students talk about situations in which they tried to persuade an audience by communicating clearly, logically, and tactfully. Students may also wish to brainstorm specific reasons for saving the art and music programs.

Write Explain that students should write a draft of their arguments without referring to the spelling words. They can figure out how to include the spelling words at a later stage.

Revise Direct students to read their letters with a partner and exchange feedback. Then have partners revise accordingly.

Proofread Have students review their work carefully for errors in punctuation, grammar, and spelling.

Publish Students can copy their final drafts onto page 90 or a separate sheet of paper. Ask volunteers to read their letters aloud for their classmates.

Computer Connection

Give the following tip to students who use a word-processor to do their writing:

● Many word-processing programs allow you to create a manuscript in letter format. Access the "Format" bar at the top of the screen and pull the menu down and click on "AutoFormat."

● Within the AutoFormat feature you can select the type of document you wish to create—in this case, "Letter."

Portfolio Have students add their completed letters-to-the-editor to their portfolios.

Compound Words

Objectives

- **To identify compound words**
- **To identify the words within compound words**
- **To write sentences using compound words**

Warming Up

- Write the following poem on the board and read it aloud with students.

  Sing a song of summer nights,

  When **fireflies** flash their lovely lights,

  And **bullfrogs** chant with voices deep,

  And crickets lull us all to sleep.

- Have a volunteer go to the board and underline the words shown in bold. Ask students how the words are similar. (Both are made up of two words.)

- Draw a line dividing the words that make up **fireflies** and **bullfrogs**. Explain that words can be joined to form a new word called a compound word.

Teaching the Lesson

- Write these clues on the board:

  a box for mail

  a bird that is blue

  a gold-colored fish

  a house for dogs

- Then have students use the clues to create words that answer the question "What is it?" (**mailbox, bluebird, goldfish, doghouse**)

- Write this "equation" on the board:

  mail + box = mailbox

Have volunteers write the answers to the other clues in the form of an equation.

- Point out that the answers to all the clues are made up of two separate words and are, therefore, compound words.

Name _____

> **Helpful Hint**
>
> A **compound word** is made up of two or more smaller words.
> key + board = **keyboard**   paint + brush = **paintbrush**

Read each clue. The clue describes a compound word. Then write the compound word on the line.

1. Name an ache in your tooth. _____ toothache
2. Name a field of corn. _____ cornfield
3. Name flakes of snow. _____ snowflakes
4. Name a fish that looks like jelly. _____ jellyfish
5. Name a storm of thunder. _____ thunderstorm
6. Name shelves for books. _____ bookshelves
7. Name a boat driven by steam. _____ steamboat

Circle the compound word in each phrase. Then draw a line between the two parts of the compound word.

8. through the (water way)   9. in the (summer time)
10. dancing on a (show boat)   11. guided by (torch light)

> **WORD STRATEGY**
>
> When you read, divide an unfamiliar **compound word** into two smaller words. This will help you figure out the pronunciation and meaning of the word. Use this strategy to divide these compound words:
>
> concertgoer
> painstaking

Through the Bayou by Torchlight by Currier & Ives

UNIVERSAL ACCESS
Meeting Individual Needs

Visual Learners

Display the words below. Have teams join pairs of words to make compound words. The first team to make all seven words wins.

boat	shelf	tooth
tug	book	jelly
ball	light	home
ache	flash	base
fish	work	

(Answers: **tugboat, bookshelf, toothache, jellyfish, baseball, flashlight, homework**)

Kinesthetic Learners

Write compounds words on sets of cards. Divide the class into teams and give each team a set of cards. When you say, "Go!" have the first player on each team pick a card, go to the board, and write the two words that make up the compound word on his or her card. The player then passes the chalk to the next team member, who does the same. Play continues until any team uses all its cards. The team with the most correct answers at that time wins the game.

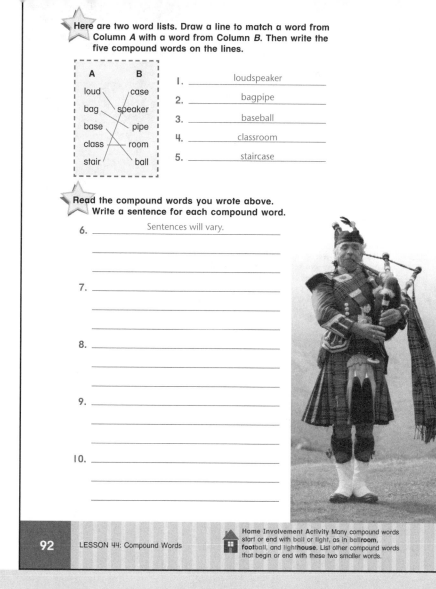

☆ Here are two word lists. Draw a line to match a word from Column *A* with a word from Column *B*. Then write the five compound words on the lines.

A	B
loud	case
bag	speaker
base	pipe
class	room
stair	ball

1. _____ loudspeaker _____
2. _____ bagpipe _____
3. _____ baseball _____
4. _____ classroom _____
5. _____ staircase _____

☆ Read the compound words you wrote above. Write a sentence for each compound word.

6. _____ Sentences will vary. _____
_____
_____

7. _____
_____
_____

8. _____
_____
_____

9. _____
_____
_____

10. _____
_____
_____

92   LESSON 44: Compound Words

Home Involvement Activity Many compound words start or end with ball or light, as in ball**room**, **foot**ball, and light**house**. List other compound words that begin or end with these two smaller words.

92

Compound Words and Syllables

Objectives

- To read compound words with more than two syllables
- To identify the number of syllables in compound words with more than two syllables
- To write compound words with more than two syllables

Warming Up

- Write the following on the board:

  When is **applesauce** blue?

  When is **watermelon** purple?

  When is a **grasshopper** red?

  Answer: When I use **watercolors.**

- Have a student underline the compound words (in bold) and draw a line between the words that make up each one.
- Read each compound word aloud, pausing between syllables. Have students identify the syllables. (**ap/ple/sauce, wa/ter/mel/on, grass/hop/per, wa/ter/col/ors**)

Teaching the Lesson

- Write the following words on the board and read them aloud:

breakfast	**lunchtime**
coffeepot	**gentleman**
television	**supermarket**

- Ask students what all the words have in common. (all compound words) Then ask them what the words in the first row have in common. (two syllables) Repeat the question with the second and third rows, which contain three- and four-syllable words, respectively. Then read the words aloud and have students clap with each syllable.

Name _____

Helpful Hints

Some **compound words** have more than two syllables. Look at the compound word **watercolor.** How many syllables does it have? Here's how you can figure it out.

- First, break apart the compound word.

  watercolor = water + color

- Then count the number of syllables.

  Water has 2 syllables.

  Color has 2 syllables.

  2 + 2 = 4

The compound word **watercolor** has 4 syllables.

Separate each compound word into two smaller words. Write the two words. Count the number of syllables in each smaller word. Then add the number of syllables. The first one has been done for you.

Compound Word	Smaller Words	Syllables
1. applesauce	apple + sauce	2 + 1 = 3
2. watermelon	water + melon	2 + 2 = 4
3. motorcycle	motor + cycle	2 + 2 = 4
4. bookkeeper	book + keeper	1 + 2 = 3
5. supermarket	super + market	2 + 2 = 4
6. Thanksgiving	Thanks + giving	1 + 2 = 3
7. ballplayer	ball + player	1 + 2 = 3
8. gentlemen	gentle + men	2 + 1 = 3
9. paperweight	paper + weight	2 + 1 = 3
10. handkerchief	hand + kerchief	1 + 2 = 3

CHALLENGE

Separate each of these long compound words into two smaller words. Then write a sentence for each compound word.

newscaster
checkerboard
broncobuster

UNIVERSAL ACCESS
Meeting Individual Needs

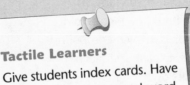

Tactile Learners

Give students index cards. Have them write a compound word from the lesson on a card, cut it apart between syllables, mix up the card parts, and exchange them with a partner. Students then put the syllables in the correct order, tape them together to make the compound word, and draw a line between the words that make up the compound word.

Musical Learners

Have students write and perform raps or chants that include compound words with more than two syllables. Ask them to identify each compound word and the number of syllables it has. Remind students that saying a word aloud, particularly within the rhythm of a chant or rap, can help them become more aware of syllables.

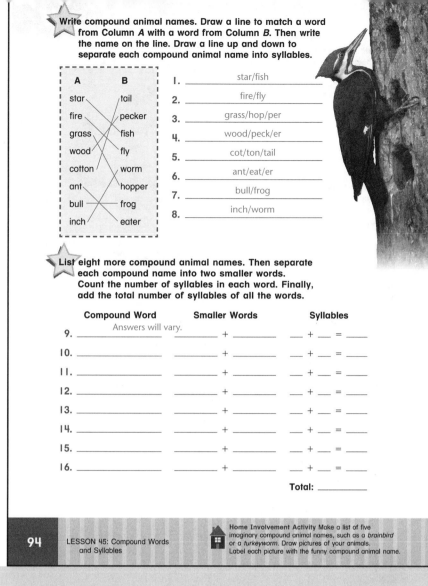

Write compound animal names. Draw a line to match a word from Column **A** with a word from Column **B**. Then write the name on the line. Draw a line up and down to separate each compound animal name into syllables.

A	B
star	tail
fire	pecker
grass	fish
wood	fly
cotton	worm
ant	hopper
bull	frog
inch	eater

1. star/fish
2. fire/fly
3. grass/hop/per
4. wood/peck/er
5. cot/ton/tail
6. ant/eat/er
7. bull/frog
8. inch/worm

List eight more compound animal names. Then separate each compound name into two smaller words. Count the number of syllables in each word. Finally, add the total number of syllables of all the words.

Compound Word	Smaller Words	Syllables
Answers will vary.		

9. _____   _____ + _____   ___ + ___ = ___
10. _____   _____ + _____   ___ + ___ = ___
11. _____   _____ + _____   ___ + ___ = ___
12. _____   _____ + _____   ___ + ___ = ___
13. _____   _____ + _____   ___ + ___ = ___
14. _____   _____ + _____   ___ + ___ = ___
15. _____   _____ + _____   ___ + ___ = ___
16. _____   _____ + _____   ___ + ___ = ___

Total: _____

LESSON 45: Compound Words and Syllables

Home Involvement Activity Make a list of five imaginary compound animal names, such as a *brainbird* or a *turkeyworm*. Draw pictures of your animals. Label each picture with the funny compound animal name.

Practicing the Skill

● Read aloud the direction lines on pages 93–94. Complete the first item in each exercise on page 94 with students.

● With students, brainstorm compound animal names for use in items 9–16 on page 94. (Examples include **jellyfish, dragonfly, rattlesnake, mockingbird.**)

Curriculum Connections

Spelling Link

applemarket	**supersauce**
newsboard	**checkercaster**
watercycle	**motorcolor**
bookweight	**paperkeeper**

Have students recombine the separate words in each mismatched pair to make real compound words. Then ask students to divide the words into syllables. (**ap/ple/sauce, su/per/mar/ket; news/cast/er, check/er/board; wa/ter/col/or, mo/tor/cy/cle; book/keep/er, pa/per/weight**)

Art Link

● Have students choose a compound animal name, separate its component words, and draw a picture that illustrates the literal meaning of the word pair. For example, the words **jelly** and **fish** might be represented by a drawing of a fish made of grape jelly.

● Invite students to display their pictures and challenge classmates to identify the compound animal name it illustrates.

Observational Assessment

Check to see that students recognize multisyllabic compound words and correctly identify the number of syllables they have.

English-Language Learners/ESL

On the board, write multisyllable compound words that can be illustrated. (Examples include **butterfly** and **newspaper**.) Say each word with students and show a picture that conveys its meaning. Model dividing a compound into smaller words and into syllables. Use one color to divide words and another to divide syllables. Point to each syllable and say it. Help students practice with other words.

Gifted Learners

Have students create word-search puzzles with multisyllabic compound words. Suggest that students write clues that hint at each word's meaning and tell how many syllables it has. Have partners swap and solve each others puzzles.

Learners with Special Needs

Additional strategies for supporting learners with special needs can be found on page 65L.

Connecting Reading and Writing

Objectives

- **To read a nonfiction piece and respond to it in writing**
- **To practice recognizing sequence and synthesizing information**
- **To write a list of directions**

Warming Up

Comprehension Skills

- Have students think about times in which they have followed a list of written directions to make something or use something. Ask them to explain why the order, or **sequence**, of the steps is so important.
- Remind students that to **synthesize** ideas in a piece of writing is to put the ideas together and make sense of them.

Teaching the Lesson

- Suggest that students look carefully at the selection's first paragraph to help them answer the first Reader's Response question.
- To answer the second question, students might want to make a numbered list of steps as they reread the selection.
- For the third question, ask students to give specific reasons for their feelings.

Practicing the Skill

- Together, read the directions on page 96. Have a student read aloud the words in the box. Then ask: *How might these words be useful in giving directions?*
- Ask students what might happen if someone were not clear about the order in which directions should be followed.

95

Name _____

READ & WRITE

⭐ **Read about a different kind of artist. Then answer the questions that follow.**

Twisted Trails

A nonfiction article from Time for Kids magazine

Adrian Fisher is A-MAZE-ING! Mr. Fisher, who lives in England, designs mazes for a living. He makes walk-through mazes that people must solve by finding a clear path from entrance to exit.

A good maze requires careful planning and a real understanding of math. Adrian Fisher's job requires him to be part scientist and part artist. "I studied math in school, and I always loved gardening," he says. "Building mazes is a way to combine these two loves."

In 1996, Fisher broke a record by making the largest maze up to that time. This Michigan corn maze was in the shape of a car. At least 2,000 people could try to find their way through it at once.

Mr. Fisher takes pleasure in watching people walk through his mazes. "Eleven- and 12-year-old children are often better than their parents at making their way through mazes," Fisher says. "I especially like to watch adults go through them. They get lost right away, and it forces them to act like children for half an hour."

Do grown-ups take a professional puzzlemaker seriously? You bet. A museum in Florida has shown Fisher's mazes in a special show. That makes sense to Fisher. "Maze design is very much like art," says the maze master. "There's a story behind each one."

"Turtle" maze by Adrian Fisher, Edinburgh Zoo

⭐ **Reader's Response**

1. What does Adrian Fisher do?
2. What might Adrian Fisher do first to design a maze? What might he do last?
3. Would you like to go through one of Adrian Fisher's mazes? Why or why not?

1. He designs mazes.
2. First, he might get an idea for the shape of a maze. Last, he might build a model.
3. Answers will vary.

UNIVERSAL ACCESS
Meeting Individual Needs

Kinesthetic Learners

Students may want to recreate the maze using blocks or some other material, with toys or other items from the classroom representing the various features in the maze. Students can then actually move an object through the maze, rather than completing the exercise on paper.

Visual Learners

Encourage students to use an erasable colored pencil to trace a path through the maze. After the maze is completed, some students may wish to use different colored markers to highlight each leg of the journey, so that they can easily identify which step comes "first," "next," and so on.

Learners with Special Needs

Additional strategies for supporting learners with special needs can be found on page 65L.

Imagine having to walk through this maze. Where would you begin? Where would you end?

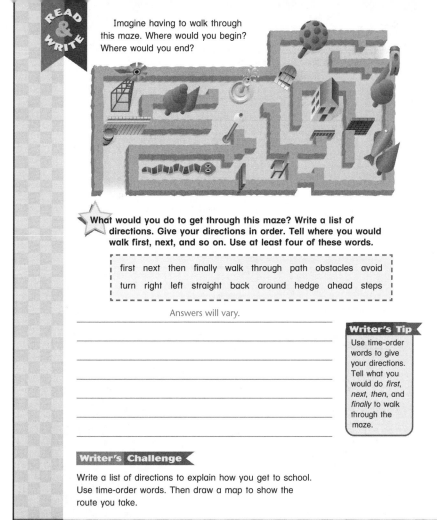

What would you do to get through this maze? Write a list of directions. Give your directions in order. Tell where you would walk first, next, and so on. Use at least four of these words.

| first | next | then | finally | walk | through | path | obstacles | avoid |
| turn | right | left | straight | back | around | hedge | ahead | steps |

Answers will vary.

_____

_____

_____

_____

_____

_____

_____

Writer's Tip

Use time-order words to give your directions. Tell what you would do *first*, *next*, *then*, and *finally* to walk through the maze.

Writer's Challenge

Write a list of directions to explain how you get to school. Use time-order words. Then draw a map to show the route you take.

LESSON 46: Connecting Reading and Writing
Comprehension—Sequence; Synthesize

The Writing Process

Discuss the purpose of giving directions—to let another person know how to do something. Ask students to identify what characteristics make directions easier to understand and follow.

Prewrite Have students begin by completing the maze. Suggest that students find a way to mark each step that must be followed: highlighting steps, numbering steps, and so on.

Write Remind students that the main goal of writing directions is to be clear and precise. Make sure students are specific about each step of their directions.

Revise Have students read their directions aloud to a partner. Invite the partner to follow the directions and see what happens.

Proofread Encourage students to read their work slowly and carefully to check for errors in grammar, punctuation, usage, and spelling.

Publish Have students copy their final drafts onto page 96 or a separate sheet of paper. Invite volunteers to read their directions aloud.

 Computer Connection Suggest that students who write on word processors explore ways of deleting text as they write or revise their work. Various programs have different ways of deleting a word, the remainder of a line, a sentence, or an entire paragraph. Suggest that students experiment with these methods in a "practice" document so that they do not accidentally delete live copy.

Portfolio Have students add their lists of directions and their completed mazes to their portfolios.

English-Language Learners/ESL

Model how to give directions for going through a maze. Then have students show you, step by step, how to get through the same maze. As students give you instructions, write them down. Help students see the relationship between the written directions and the pathway through the maze.

Gifted Learners

Encourage students to create a different set of directions such as, how to live a happy life, how to become successful in a chosen field, or how to reach a goal. Invite students to convey their directions in a poem, song, cartoon, or picture. Suggest that they share their work with the class.

Reviewing and Assessing

Word Endings, Plurals, Possessives, and Compound Words

Objective

To review and assess word endings, plurals, possessives, and compound words

Warming Up

● Draw seven circles on the board. Label the circles as follows:

*Plurals made by adding **s** or **es***

*Plurals of words ending in **f, ff, fe,** or **o***

*Plurals made by dropping **y** and adding **ies***

Irregular plurals

Singular possessives

Plural possessives

Compound words

● Say the following words as you write them on the board. Have students write each word in the correct circle.

knives	firefly	teeth
baseball	child's	buddies
oxen	studios	monkeys
sisters'	ranches	counties
James's	brother's	classmates'

Teaching the Lesson

● Review the rules for forming plurals and possessives. Encourage students to ask questions if they feel uncertain about anything.

● Have a volunteer suggest a noun. Ask another student to form the plural of the noun. Ask other students to form the singular and plural possessives of the same noun. Repeat the process, covering nouns with various endings.

Name _____

⭐ Write the plural form of each of these base words. Make spelling changes as needed.

1. tax _____taxes_____   2. child _____children_____
3. piano _____pianos_____   4. waltz _____waltzes_____
5. mouse _____mice_____   6. deer _____deer_____
7. loaf _____loaves_____   8. berry _____berries_____
9. monkey _____monkeys_____   10. man _____men_____

⭐ Rewrite each phrase. Use an apostrophe (') or an apostrophe and an s ('s) to show who or what has or owns something.

11. the paints that belong to the artists _____the artists' paints_____
12. the game of the boy _____the boy's game_____
13. the classroom of those teachers _____those teachers' classroom_____
14. the clay that belongs to the children _____the children's clay_____
15. the blankets of those babies _____those babies' blankets_____
16. the owners of the animals _____the animals' owners_____

⭐ Read each sentence. Circle the word that correctly completes it. Then write the word on the line.

17. *The Sound of Music* is _____Mom's_____ favorite movie.
    Moms   Mom's   (Moms')

18. Many of this _____movie's_____ songs are still popular.
    (movie's)   movies   movies'

19. Do you know the _____words_____ to "My Favorite Things"?
    word's   words'   (words)

From the movie
The Sound of Music, 1965

UNIVERSAL ACCESS
Meeting Individual Needs

Kinesthetic Learners

Write twenty compound words on index cards. Then cut the cards in half, breaking up each compound into its component words. Distribute twenty card halves to students. Display the remaining halves on the board. Have students come up to the board and match their word half with its mate.

Learners with Special Needs

Additional strategies for supporting students with special needs can be found on page 65L.

Logical Learners

Write the following phrases on the board.

the music of Mr. Kim

the paintings of the artists

the brushes that belong to Lee

the shouts of the audience

the smiles of the performers

Have students rewrite each phrase on a card, using 's or s' to form the possessive. Then have students sort the cards according to whether the possessives are singular or plural.

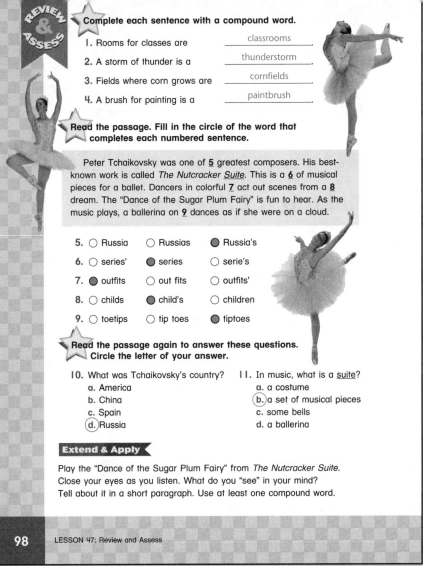

REVIEW & ASSESS

Complete each sentence with a compound word.

1. Rooms for classes are _____ — classrooms
2. A storm of thunder is a _____ — thunderstorm
3. Fields where corn grows are _____ — cornfields
4. A brush for painting is a _____ — paintbrush

Read the passage. Fill in the circle of the word that completes each numbered sentence.

Peter Tchaikovsky was one of **5** greatest composers. His best-known work is called *The Nutcracker Suite*. This is a **6** of musical pieces for a ballet. Dancers in colorful **7** act out scenes from a **8** dream. The "Dance of the Sugar Plum Fairy" is fun to hear. As the music plays, a ballerina on **9** dances as if she were on a cloud.

5. ○ Russia   ○ Russias   ● Russia's
6. ○ series'   ● series   ○ serie's
7. ● outfits   ○ out fits   ○ outfits'
8. ○ childs   ● child's   ○ children
9. ○ toetips   ○ tip toes   ● tiptoes

Read the passage again to answer these questions. Circle the letter of your answer.

10. What was Tchaikovsky's country?
    a. America
    b. China
    c. Spain
    d. Russia ⟵

11. In music, what is a <u>suite</u>?
    a. a costume
    b. a set of musical pieces ⟵
    c. some bells
    d. a ballerina

Extend & Apply

Play the "Dance of the Sugar Plum Fairy" from *The Nutcracker Suite*. Close your eyes as you listen. What do you "see" in your mind? Tell about it in a short paragraph. Use at least one compound word.

98 LESSON 47: Review and Assess

Reteaching Activities

Column Fill-in

Have students work in small groups. Have the first student write a word in the first column below—for example, **cat.** The next student must then fill in one of the remaining spaces (for example, **cat's**), and so on. The student who fills in the last open space then writes a new word in the next column.

Singular:	cat
Singular Possessive:	cat's
Plural:	cats
Plural Possessive:	cats'

Rephrase the Phrase

Write these phrases on the board.

the eyes of the baby
the fur of the monkey
the clothes of the child
the hands of the man
the feathers of the goose

Have students change each phrase first to a singular possessive, and then to a plural possessive. Have students use both singular and plural possessives in sentences.

Assessing the Skill

Check Up The exercises on pages 97–98 will help students review word endings, plurals, possessives, and compound words. The exercises will also help you assess the progress students have made in applying these skills.

Make sure students understand what they have to do for each set of exercises on page 97. Then have them complete the page. Next, go over the directions for page 98, and have students do the exercises.

Observational Assessment As students work with plurals and possessives, be alert for signs of uncertainty. Note, for example, whether students hesitate when changing a **y** to **i** before adding **es**.

Student Skills Assessment Keep track of each student's progress with word endings, plurals, possessives, and compound words using the checklist on page 65H.

Writing Conference As you complete Unit Three, meet with students individually to discuss their writing. Review their portfolio samples and other written work. Offer students encouragement and constructive suggestions. Recommend that they share with the class a favorite piece of writing from their Home Portfolios.

Group together students who need further instruction in word endings, plurals, possessives, and compound words and have them complete the *Reteaching Activities*. Turn to page 65C for alternative assessment methods.

Prefixes, Roots, and Syllables

Theme: Making a Difference

STANDARDS

- ✪ Read grade-appropriate expository text and understand its content
- ✪ Develop and strengthen vocabulary by reading words in context
- ✪ Use knowledge of common prefixes, roots, and base words to determine the meanings of new words
- ✪ Divide words into syllables

OBJECTIVES

- ▶ To appreciate nonfiction works about people who make a difference
- ▶ To determine the meanings of words with prefixes
- ▶ To use clues in roots and base words to figure out word meanings
- ▶ To write words with prefixes
- ▶ To separate words into syllables

LESSONS

Assessment Strategies

An overview of assessment strategies appears on page **99C.** It offers suggestions for a variety of unit-specific assessment tools, including **Pretests** and **Post Tests** (pages **99D–99G**), the **Activity Master** (page **99M**), and the **Assessment Checklist** (page **99H**).

Thematic Teaching

In Unit 4, students will learn about prefixes and roots. Students encounter words containing prefixes in the context of nonfiction selections and exercises related to the theme *Making a Difference.*

Students begin their study of the *Making a Difference* theme by creating a collage, using pictures from newspapers and magazines along with their own drawings and writings. The resource list on this page provides titles of books, videos, and CDs that celebrate the "making a difference" theme. Many of the lessons in this unit open with poems, riddles, or tongue twisters related to the theme. These "hooks" can spark students' interest both in the theme and in the play of words.

Curriculum Integration

Social Studies

Students research women's rights on page **104,** write biographies on page **110,** discuss the Underground Railroad on page **120,** research the world's petroleum on page **128,** and research the census on page **132.**

Writing

Students will write about the idea of change on page **116** and write a poem on page **126.**

Science

Students will look for communities that have reversed pollution on page **100,** research the effects of water pollution on page **102,** and research the word **contract** on page **130.**

Math

Students will describe triangles on page **118.**

Optional Learning Activities

Meeting Individual Needs

Most of the Teacher's Edition lessons offer activities for students with distinct learning styles or particular intellectual or sensory strengths. The activities included are: **Visual, Kinesthetic, Auditory, Logical, Musical** and **Tactile.**

Multicultural Connections

Students will discuss working together for a common cause on page **100** and research the fight for self-government on page **112.**

Word Study Strategies

Pages **99I–99J** offer an array of activities that give students practice using strategies such as word sorting, word building, and dividing words into syllables.

Universal Access

Exercises tailored to meet the needs of **English-Language Learners** and **Gifted Learners** can be found in almost every Teacher's Edition lesson. Strategies designed to help **Learners with Special Needs,** such as students with Visual/Perceptual Deficits, can be found on page **99L.**

Intervention

Page **99K** offers **Intervention Strategies** designed to help students performing below grade level understand the concepts taught in **Lessons 62, 64,** and **66.**

Reteaching

On page **108** students will write words with prefixes, on page **124** students will hunt for prefixes and make a presentation, and on page **136** students match prefixes and make a word chain.

Technology

Page **99N** offers activities for students who enjoy working with computers, video cameras, or audio equipment. In addition, **Computer Connections**—tips designed to support students who use a word processor—can be found on pages **106, 114, 122,** and **134.**

RESOURCES

Books
Hallinan, P.K. *For the Love of Our Earth,* Ideals Children's Books, 2000.
VanCleave, Janice Pratt. *Ecology for Every Kid: Easy Activities that Make Learning Science Fun,* NY: John Wiley & Sons, 1996.

Videos
Biography: Benjamin Franklin, A&E Home Video.

The Magic Schoolbus–In the Rainforest, Scholastic.
Schoolhouse Rock: Science Rock, Walt Disney Video.

CDs
Birds, Beasts, Bugs & Fishes Little & Big: Animal Folk Songs, Pete Seeger, Smithsonian Folkways.
Mother Earth, Tom Chapin, Sony/Wonder.

In Unit 4, students study word parts: prefixes, roots, and syllables. To evaluate students' mastery of these skills, use any or all of the assessment methods suggested below.

Pretests and Post Tests

The tests on pages **99D–99G** objectively assess how well students understand prefixes, base words, roots, and syllables. These tests may be used at the beginning of the unit as an informal diagnostic tool or at the end of the unit as a more formal measure of students' progress.

Observational Assessment

Opportunities for observing students as they work are suggested throughout the unit. Lesson-specific recommendations are included for assessing students' work. Check students' written work on a regular basis to see whether they are applying what they learn to their own writing.

Using Technology

The activities on page **99N** may be used to evaluate students whose language skills are best shown when using computers or audio/video equipment.

Performance Assessment

Assign each student five words from the lesson to "dissect." Have students write the words in large letters on a sheet of paper, underlining the base word or root and circling the prefix in each word. Then have them draw lines to divide the syllables in each word. Finally, students should change one word part of each word to form five new words.

Portfolio Assessment

The portfolio icon in the lesson plans indicates an opportunity for students to add to the growing body of work in their portfolios.

Each student's portfolio will be different and should contain pieces that the student feels represent his or her best work. You may wish to give students additional opportunities to add to their portfolios.

Rubric for Writing

	Always	Sometimes	Never
Uses capitalization, punctuation, spelling, and grammar appropriately			
Creates a variety of sentences containing words with prefixes			
Creates a clear, well developed explanation with a beginning, middle, and end			
Conveys a purpose and meaning through writing			

Answer Key

Page 99D
1. un
2. co
3. under
4. pre
5. il
6. pro
7. in
8. mis
9. mid
10. reduce
11. spectators
12. bicycle
13. four
14. three
15. explain
16. prescription
17. nonstop
18. subtract
19. two
20. impossible

Page 99E
1. semi
2. mid
3. in
4. ir
5. un
6. con
7. re
8. mis
9. pre

10. tract
11. pel
12. port
13. pos
14. ject
15. script
16. scrib
17. duc
18. spect
19. 3
20. 2
21. 2
22. 3
23. 2
24. 4

Page 99F
1. non
2. over
3. sub
4. ex
5. pre
6. under
7. tri
8. com
9. re
10. reporter
11. subjects
12. posture
13. educate
14. three
15. inscription

16. discovered
17. inspected
18. prehistoric
19. misunderstood
20. two

Page 99G
1. mis
2. uni
3. il
4. im
5. dis
6. pro
7. com
8. under
9. un
10. tract
11. scrib
12. spect
13. pel
14. port
15. script
16. pos
17. ject
18. tract
19. 2
20. 3
21. 3
22. 3
23. 2
24. 3

Name _____

Fill in the circle next to the prefix that can be added to each base word.

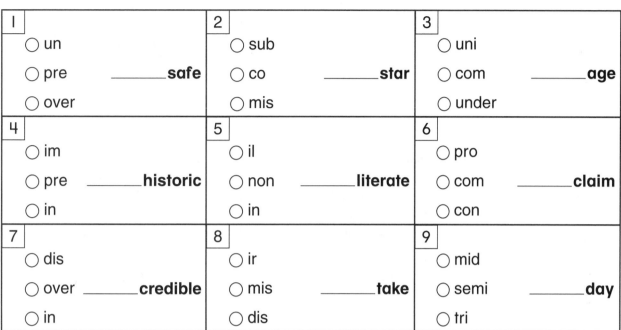

1	2	3
○ un ○ pre _____**safe** ○ over	○ sub ○ co _____**star** ○ mis	○ uni ○ com _____**age** ○ under
4	**5**	**6**
○ im ○ pre _____**historic** ○ in	○ il ○ non _____**literate** ○ in	○ pro ○ com _____**claim** ○ con
7	**8**	**9**
○ dis ○ over _____**credible** ○ in	○ ir ○ mis _____**take** ○ dis	○ mid ○ semi _____**day** ○ tri

Underline the word that correctly completes each sentence.

10. Removing two items will **(duce, reduce)** the weight of the package.

11. The **(spectators, spectacles)** watched the baseball game.

12. There are only two wheels on a **(tricycle, bicycle)**.

13. The word **transportation** has **(four, five)** syllables.

14. The word **uniform** has **(three, four)** syllables.

15. Can you **(explain, complain)** the assignment?

16. The doctor wrote a **(prescription, subscription)** for cough medicine.

17. Is the flight **(unstop, nonstop)** from Miami to Boston?

18. If you **(distract, subtract)** seven, you will have the answer.

19. The word **subject** has **(two, three)** syllables.

20. The word **(impossible, possible)** has four syllables.

Possible score on Unit 4 Pretest 1 is 20. Score _____

Underline the prefix in each word.

1. semicircle	2. midnight	3. inactive
4. irregular	5. unhappy	6. confirm
7. review	8. misspell	9. prehistoric

Circle the root in each word.

10. contract	11. expel	12. export
13. posture	14. subject	15. description
16. scribe	17. produce	18. inspector

Circle the number of syllables in each word.

19. educate	20. distract	21. unhappy
3 4 5	1 2 3	1 2 3
22. illegal	23. cosign	24. superhero
1 2 3	1 2 3	3 4 5

Possible score on Unit 4 Pretest 2 is 24. Score _____

Fill in the circle next to the prefix that can be added to each base word.

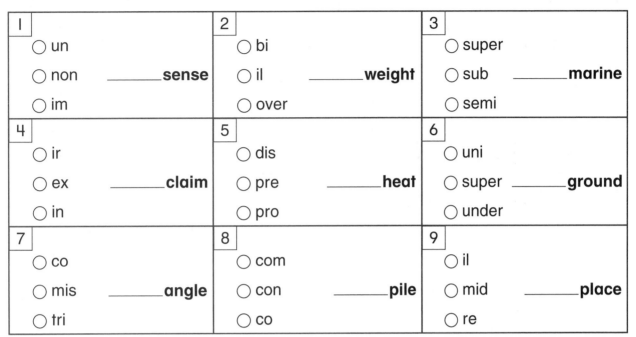

1		2		3	
○ un		○ bi		○ super	
○ non	_____ **sense**	○ il	_____ **weight**	○ sub	_____ **marine**
○ im		○ over		○ semi	
4		**5**		**6**	
○ ir		○ dis		○ uni	
○ ex	_____ **claim**	○ pre	_____ **heat**	○ super	_____ **ground**
○ in		○ pro		○ under	
7		**8**		**9**	
○ co		○ com		○ il	
○ mis	_____ **angle**	○ con	_____ **pile**	○ mid	_____ **place**
○ tri		○ co		○ re	

Underline the word that correctly completes the sentence.

10. Jennifer is a newspaper **(preporter, reporter)**.

11. She gathers information on a variety of **(subjects, rejects)**.

12. Once, she wrote about the proper **(propeller, posture)** used in golf.

13. Her articles **(educators, educate)** her readers.

14. The word **unpleasant** has **(two, three)** syllables.

15. There is an **(prescription, inscription)** on the bracelet.

16. It was **(discovered, excovered)** by accident.

17. Scientists **(respected, inspected)** the writing very carefully.

18. They think it is from **(prehistoric, subhistoric)** times.

19. The word **(mistake, misunderstand)** has four syllables.

20. The word **extract** has **(two, three)** syllables.

Possible score on Unit 4 Post Test 1 is 20. Score _____

Name _____

Underline the prefix in each word.

1. misprounce	2. unicycle	3. illogical
4. immature	5. displease	6. prolong
7. composition	8. underachieve	9. uneasy

Circle the root in each word.

10. subtract	11. scribble	12. inspection
13. repel	14. report	15. prescription
16. expose	17. projector	18. extract

Circle the number of syllables in each word.

19. **complain**	20. **bifocal**	21. **semisweet**
2 3 4	3 4 5	1 2 3
22. **incomplete**	23. **prescribe**	24. **overview**
3 4 5	1 2 3	3 4 5

Possible score on Unit 4 Post Test 2 is 24. Score _____

Student Name _____

UNIT FOUR
STUDENT SKILLS ASSESSMENT
CHECKLIST

☑ Assessed ☒ Retaught ▣ Mastered

- ❑ Prefixes **un-**, **re-**, **dis-**
- ❑ Prefixes **pre-**, **in-**, **im-**, **over-**, **super-**
- ❑ Prefixes **sub-**, **co-**, **ex-**
- ❑ Prefixes **il-**, **ir-**, **non-**, **mis-**
- ❑ Prefixes **pro-**, **com-**, **con-**, **under-**
- ❑ Prefixes **uni-**, **bi-**, **tri-**, **mid-**, **semi-**
- ❑ Prefixes with Syllables
- ❑ Base Words
- ❑ Roots **-pos-**, **-pel-**, **-port-**, **-ject-**, **-spect-**, **-scrib-/-script-**
- ❑ Roots **-duc-/-duct-** and **-tract-**
- ❑ Syllables with Prefixes and Roots

TEACHER COMMENTS

WORD STUDY STRATEGIES

In Unit 4, students study word parts: prefixes, roots, and syllables. To give students practice using word study strategies, have them do any or all of the activities suggested below. Dictate selected activities to students or write them on the board for students to copy.

Word-Part Match-Up

Combine the prefix with each of the three base words that follow it. Write the new words on the lines. Then write an additional word that includes the prefix.

1. un-   safe   kind   happy

    _____   _____   _____

    additional word: _____

2. re-   store   fill   place

    _____   _____   _____

    additional word: _____

3. dis-   agree   appear   like

    _____   _____   _____

    additional word: _____

4. ex-   press   claim   port

    _____   _____   _____

    additional word: _____

Word-Part Search

Circle the prefix in each word. Determine whether the word contains a base word or a root and underline that word part. If you underlined a base word, write **BW** on the line. If you underlined a root, write **R** on the line.

nonsense _____   dislike _____
export _____   propel _____
costar _____   reject _____
subtract _____   overflow _____
irregular _____   mistake _____

Build on Word Roots

Think of two prefixes that can be added to each root to form two new words. Write the prefixes and the new words on the lines provided.

	Prefixes	Roots	New Words
1.	_____	-port-	_____
	_____		_____
2.	_____	-spect-	_____
	_____		_____
3.	_____	-pel-	_____
	_____		_____
4.	_____	-ject-	_____
	_____		_____
5.	_____	-tract-	_____
	_____		_____
6.	_____	-duc-	_____
	_____		_____

Consider the Context

Choose the word in bold type that best fits the context of the sentence. Circle the word. Then write a sentence using the word you did not choose.

1. Because we **(returned/overturned)** the books late, we paid a fine.

   _____

   _____

2. A magnet will **(attract/distract)** metal clips.

   _____

   _____

3. Artists often **(describe/inscribe)** their names on their works.

   _____

   _____

4. The principal will **(propel/expel)** students who break school rules.

   _____

   _____

5. The United States will **(export/import)** many products from Canada this year.

   _____

   _____

6. The clown rode a **(recycle/unicycle)** in the parade.

   _____

   _____

Divide Words into Parts

Divide each word between the prefix and the base word. Then use what you know about the prefix to write the meaning of the word.

overeat _____

unsatisfied _____

review _____

disappear _____

incorrect _____

impossible _____

cooperate _____

illiterate _____

semiannual _____

superhero _____

Word Sort

Sort these words according to how many syllables they have. Write each word under the correct heading below.

nonprofit   semifinal   exchange
irregular   preview   supermarket
uniform   costar   bicycle
illegal   underline   prehistoric
unpleasant   repose   subdivided

Two Syllables	Three Syllables	Four Syllables
_____	_____	_____
_____	_____	_____
_____	_____	_____
_____	_____	_____
_____	_____	_____

LESSONS	**62** Roots	**64** Syllables with Prefixes and Roots	**66** Reviewing Word Parts
Problem	Student has trouble identifying roots in words with suffixes or with unfamiliar prefixes; student confuses roots with base words.	Student confuses the number of word parts with the number of syllables.	Student has trouble understanding and using the word-part chart and its code.
Intervention Strategies	• Have students approach finding roots as a simple task of matching letters. Is the root spelled anywhere within the word? Point out that a root can come at the beginning of a word as in **portable** or the end as in **report**. • Remind students that base words are words, such as **happy, like,** or **turn.** Roots are only parts of words. All base words can stand alone, whereas most roots cannot. Point out that in Lesson 62, the only root that can stand alone is -**port**-.	• Remind students that syllables are not the same as word parts. A syllable always contains one vowel sound. Prefixes such as **under-, super-,** and **over-** contain two vowel sounds, thus they each contain two syllables. Advise students to identify the number of syllables in the base word, then the number of syllables in the prefix before totaling.	• Create a simpler version of the chart with only two columns and three rows of word parts. • Choose word parts that form familiar words such as **report** and **project.** • Demonstrate for students how to use the code's letters and numbers to locate word parts in the chart. You may also wish to show students maps that use similar codes to help locate places.

The following activities offer strategies for helping students with special needs to participate in selected exercises in Unit 4.

Visual/Perceptual Deficits
Prefixes

When reading a word whose meaning is changed by a prefix, some students may respond only to the familiar part of the word—for example, in a word such as **disagree,** they may notice only **agree.** The exercise on page **101** will be helpful to these students, because it directs attention to the unfamiliar element.

- Reinforce the benefit of these exercises by providing students with a tactile experience. Give them three jigsaw puzzle pieces, each labeled with the prefixes **un-, re-,** and **dis-.**

- Then give them other jigsaw pieces, each labeled with one of the base words in the lesson. These pieces should link to the appropriate prefix jigsaw pieces to form words.

- Have students put the prefix and base-word jigsaw pieces together to form words. Ask them to write each correct word in the blanks provided. To extend the activity, have students use each word in a sentence.

Visual/Perceptual Deficits
Unscrambling Words

The unscrambling exercise on page **109** may be difficult for students who reverse letters when reading. You may wish to give these students an alternative activity.

- Replace the list of scrambled words on the left with the prefixes listed out of order. Instead of the blank on the right side of the page, provide the correct base word.

- Have students find the prefix that makes the base word fit the given definition and write the complete word on the line.

Conceptual Deficits
Roots

Some students may need props or specific actions as references when learning the concept of word roots. A student may have learned the prefix **ex-** and still be confused when it precedes the root **-pel-.**

- Using the list of common roots on top of page **127,** illustrate the root **-pel-** by pushing a chair across the room. Ask students the meaning of the prefix **ex-** and the meaning of the root **-pel-.** Have them see that **expel** means to push or drive out.

- Review the meanings of the prefixes and the roots for the words in the list. Then ask students to illustrate the meaning of the complete word by pantomiming.

Spatial Discrimination Deficits
Coding

Children who have difficulty understanding spatial relationships may become confused by tasks such as the one on page **135.** To help these students scan the columns correctly, try the following strategy.

- Highlight the column number and the word parts in that column with the same color. It may also help them if you underline the horizontal rows and reduce the number of items in the activity.

- If students continue to experience difficulty with the exercise, give them cardboard squares labeled with the letter indicating its horizontal row, the number indicating its vertical row, and the syllable. Tell students to use the labeled cardboard squares to make three syllable words. They can then write the codes for the words they made on a separate piece of paper using only the letter and number from the squares that they used to make their words.

Name _____

**Write the words that contain the same root on the
lines below.**

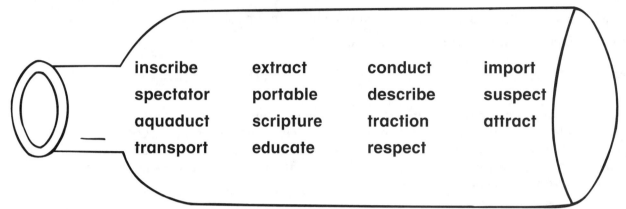

inscribe   extract   conduct   import

spectator   portable   describe   suspect

aquaduct   scripture   traction   attract

transport   educate   respect

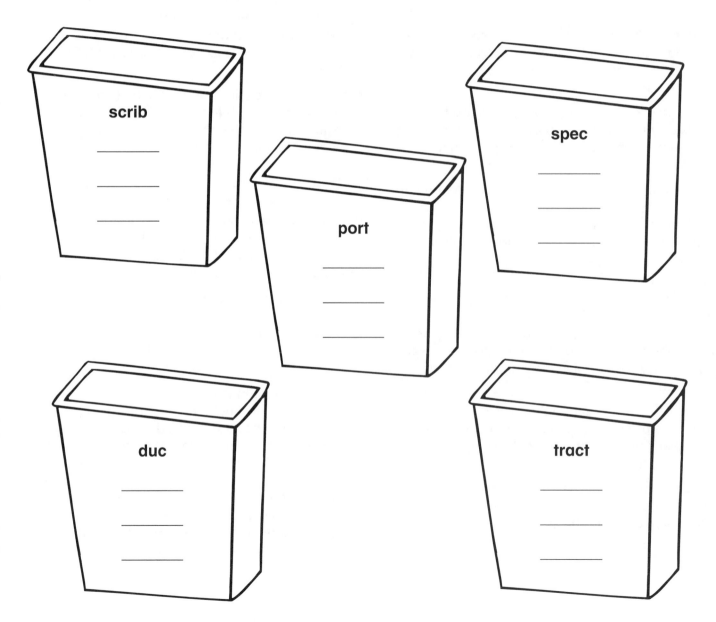

scrib

port

spec

duc

tract

Create a Documentary

Invite students to create a documentary video about someone in their community who has made a difference in their lives. If a video camera is not available, students can use an ordinary camera and present the "documentary" as a photo essay.

- Once students have chosen a topic, they should decide what has to be done (such as researching the topic, writing the script or the text, operating the camera, and so on) and then agree on who should do which task.

- You may wish to give students examples of biographical documentaries or photo essays to use as models. Be sure to set aside time for students to work on the project and to present the final product to their class.

- To give students extra practice with prefixes and roots, photocopy the script or text for the class. Have students read it and highlight words that contain one or more prefixes. Then have them review the highlighted words and circle any roots they find.

Play Build-a-Word

To prepare for this game, write each of the nine roots taught in the lesson **(-pos-, -pel-, -port-, -ject-, -spect-, -scrib-, -script-, -duc-/-duct-,** and **-tract-)** on slips of paper and place them in a box. Bring the box and a small group of students to the computer lab or to a place where they can use a word processor. Have students play the game as described below.

- The first player chooses three roots from the box and types them across the top of a blank document, separated by tabs. He or she then uses the copy feature to copy the line of type and the paste feature to paste it five times—so that the screen shows six rows of the same three roots.

- A volunteer sets a timer for one minute and tells the player to begin. The player must make as many words as possible out of the roots. He or she can add prefixes, word endings, or both, but the words must be actual words.

- Have the other players use the same three roots until all students have participated. The student who creates the most words in the timed period wins the round. Then have a different student choose three roots and continue playing until all the roots have been used.

dis**tract**	re**port**	sub**scribe**
tractor	**port**able	pre**scribe**
ex**tract**	ex**port**	-**scrib**-
-**tract**-	-**port**-	-**scrib**-
-**tract**-	-**port**-	-**scrib**-
-**tract**-	-**port**-	-**scrib**-

Make a Difference on Tape

Have students tape-record an interview with a friend or family member about something important they did to help another person.

- Encourage students to plan their interview as much as possible by thinking of interesting questions and writing them down beforehand. Explain that students may have to change some of the questions at the time of the interview, depending on the information they learn during the process.

- Suggest that students also prepare by listening to a radio show. Ask them to notice how the interviewer elicits information from his or her subject.

- Ask volunteers to play their tapes for the class. Give students practice with dividing words into syllables by having them listen for words with three or more syllables. They can jot these words down as they listen. Later, have students draw lines between the syllables of each word.

Introduction to
Prefixes, Roots, and Syllables

Objectives

- **To enjoy a piece of nonfiction related to the theme** *Making a Difference*
- **To study prefixes, base words, roots, and syllables**

Starting with Literature

Ask a student to read "Bringing Back the Salmon" aloud for the class. On the board, write these words from the story: **returned, released.** Mask the base words and tell students that the letters **re** make up a word part called a prefix. Ask them to suggest other words with the prefix **re-**. (**rewrite, redo, replay**)

Critical Thinking

- Suggest that students reread the selection to answer the first two questions.

- Invite students to brainstorm and then discuss responses to the third question.

Introducing the Skill

Write the word **recycle** on the board. Have a volunteer circle the prefix. Ask: *What word is left when you take away the prefix?* (**cycle**) Tell students that **cycle**, like any word to which a prefix is added, is called a base word.

Practicing the Skill

- Tell students that two common prefixes are **dis-** and **in-**. Give a few examples of words with these prefixes.

- Have students play "Prefix Beat-the-Clock" by giving them a fixed amount of time to list as many words as they can beginning with the prefixes **re-, dis-,** and **in-**.

Bringing Back the Salmon

People can make a difference to their community and to the environment. Here's an example.

Pigeon Creek flows from the small city of Everett, Washington, into Puget Sound. In its last half-mile, the stream runs past Jackson Elementary School. Once, it was a clear stream, full of salmon. Fish were born there, grew there, and then swam to the sound and out to the Pacific Ocean. They always returned to their home stream to spawn. As the city grew around it, Pigeon Creek turned muddy. The salmon stayed away. Instead, all kinds of trash filled the stream. The water became polluted. The students at Jackson Elementary School decided to do something about the problem.

First, the students cleaned up the stream. They called on their neighbors to help. Then, the students cared for young salmon in tanks in their school. When the salmon were ready, the students released them into Pigeon Creek.

All the hard work paid off. Two years later, the salmon came back! The students had a right to be proud. They had solved a local problem and had really made a difference.

Critical Thinking

1. How did Pigeon Creek become polluted?

2. What did the students do to solve the problem?

3. What can you learn from the Jackson Elementary School students?

---

1. As the city grew, Pigeon Creek became muddy and fulled with all kinds of trash.
2. First, the students cleaned up the stream. Then, they cared for young salmon in their school. Finally, they released the salmon into Pigeon Creek.
3. Answers will vary.

Theme Activity

MAKING A DIFFERENCE COLLAGE Invite students to create a collage about the theme *Making a Difference*. They can use pictures they find or draw, articles and headlines from newspapers and magazines, and words describing people who work hard to make important changes in our lives.

Before students begin making the collage, have a class discussion about what it means to make a difference. Ask students to identify some of the ways in which people—especially children—can make a difference in their communities.

Ask students to identify the words in their collage that have prefixes. Give them highlighters of two different colors. Have them highlight the prefixes in one color and the base words in another. As you continue to work on the lessons in Unit 4, invite students to add words with prefixes to the collage.

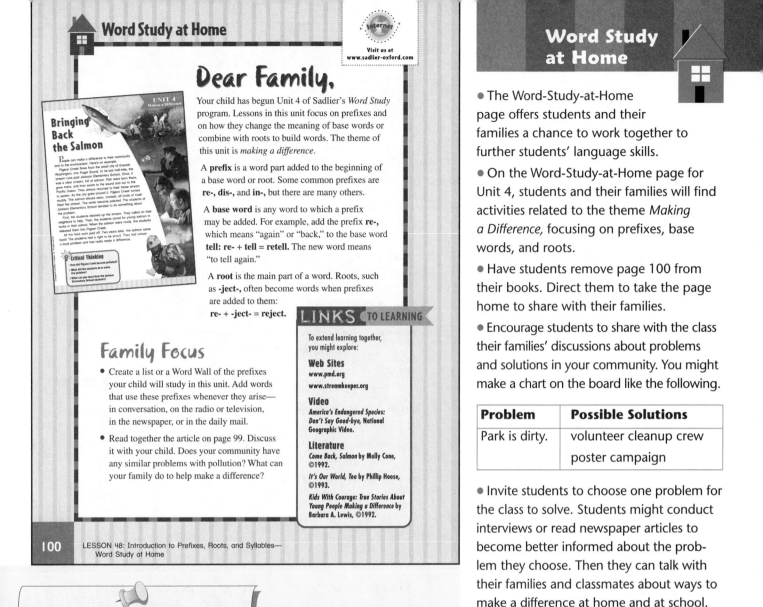

Dear Family,

Your child has begun Unit 4 of Sadlier's *Word Study* program. Lessons in this unit focus on prefixes and on how they change the meaning of base words or combine with roots to build words. The theme of this unit is *making a difference*.

A **prefix** is a word part added to the beginning of a base word or root. Some common prefixes are **re-**, **dis-**, and **in-**, but there are many others.

A **base word** is any word to which a prefix may be added. For example, add the prefix **re-**, which means "again" or "back," to the base word **tell: re- + tell = retell.** The new word means "to tell again."

A **root** is the main part of a word. Roots, such as **-ject-**, often become words when prefixes are added to them:

re- + -ject- = reject.

Family Focus

- Create a list or a Word Wall of the prefixes your child will study in this unit. Add words that use these prefixes whenever they arise—in conversation, on the radio or television, in the newspaper, or in the daily mail.

- Read together the article on page 99. Discuss it with your child. Does your community have any similar problems with pollution? What can your family do to help make a difference?

LINKS TO LEARNING

To extend learning together, you might explore:

Web Sites
www.pmd.org
www.streamkeeper.org

Video
America's Endangered Species: Don't Say Good-bye, National Geographic Video.

Literature
Come Back, Salmon by Molly Cone, ©1992.

It's Our World, Too by Phillip Hoose, ©1993.

Kids With Courage: True Stories About Young People Making a Difference by Barbara A. Lewis, ©1992.

Multicultural Connection

Discuss this idea with students: In times of crisis, people forget cultural and racial differences and work together to fight for a common cause. Have students find articles in newspapers and magazines that support this statement. Invite them to share their findings with the class.

Science Link

Encourage students to find examples of communities that have reversed the effects of pollution. Some students may enjoy contacting environmental groups and learning about how they are helping the air, water, animal, or plant life.

Word Study at Home

- The Word-Study-at-Home page offers students and their families a chance to work together to further students' language skills.

- On the Word-Study-at-Home page for Unit 4, students and their families will find activities related to the theme *Making a Difference,* focusing on prefixes, base words, and roots.

- Have students remove page 100 from their books. Direct them to take the page home to share with their families.

- Encourage students to share with the class their families' discussions about problems and solutions in your community. You might make a chart on the board like the following.

Problem	Possible Solutions
Park is dirty.	volunteer cleanup crew poster campaign

- Invite students to choose one problem for the class to solve. Students might conduct interviews or read newspaper articles to become better informed about the problem they choose. Then they can talk with their families and classmates about ways to make a difference at home and at school.

Theme-Related Resources

Videos

John Denver: Let This Be a Voice, 1999

Jane Goodall: My Life With the Chimpanzees, National Geographic, 1995

Books

The Kid's Guide to Service Projects: Over 500 Service Ideas for Young People Who Want to Make a Difference, by Barbara Lewis and Pamela Espeland, Free Spirit Pub., 1995

Prefixes
un-, re-, dis-

Objectives

- To identify prefixes **un-**, **re-**, and **dis-**
- To identify the meanings of words with these prefixes
- To write words with these prefixes

Warming Up

- Write this rhyme on the board.

  Suppose you were a word,

  And a prefix came along,

  It would change your very meaning.

  All you know might now be wrong.

  Would you feel glad or **unhappy?**

  Would you smile or feel **unkind?**

  Would you make it feel **unwelcome?**

  Would you mind?

- Read the rhyme aloud with students. Have a volunteer underline the words that contain a prefix (shown in bold type). Ask students to define these words.

- Ask students what these words have in common. (They begin with the letters **un**, and they mean the opposite of the word that follows the letters **un**.)

Teaching the Lesson

- Explain that many words begin with letter combinations called prefixes. Tell students that prefixes are not words by themselves, but they do have meaning. Point out that adding a prefix changes the meaning of the word they are added to.

- Read aloud the Helpful Hints on page 101 as students follow silently.

Name _____

Helpful Hints

A **prefix** is a word part added to the **beginning** of a **base word**.
Adding a prefix to a word can change the meaning of the word.
It can also make a new word.

The prefix **un** means "not," as in un**afraid**.
The prefix **dis** means "not" or "opposite of," as in dis**like**.
The prefix **re** means "again," as in **rewrite**, or "back," as in **return**.

Watch out for words that seem to have prefixes but really do not.
When you remove the un from **uncle**, no base word remains.

Add **un**, **re**, or **dis** to each of these base words. Write the new word on the line.

1. not **kind**

   unkind

2. **pay** back

   repay

3. the opposite of **agree**

   disagree

4. **fill** again

   refill

5. not **known**

   unknown

6. not **important**

   unimportant

Read the base word at the left of each sentence. Add the prefix **un**, **re**, or **dis** to the base word. Write the new word on the line.

welcome   7. The members of the cleanup crew were greeted by a(n) _unwelcome_ sight.

safe   8. The amount of trash left over from the parade made the street _unsafe_.

appear   9. The volunteers quickly went to work to make the garbage _disappear_.

store   10. They worked long and hard to _restore_ the street to its original condition.

pleasant   11. We are sorry their task was so _unpleasant_.

CHALLENGE

Some words have *two* prefixes. Underline the two prefixes in each of these words. Then tell what each word means.

unresolved

rediscovered

LESSON 49: Prefixes **un-**, **re-**, **dis-**   101

UNIVERSAL ACCESS
Meeting Individual Needs

Visual Learners

Write these base words and definitions on the board.

_____ **lucky** (not lucky)

_____ **obey** (not obey)

_____ **pay** (pay back)

_____ **view** (view again)

_____ **cover** (cover again)

_____ **agree** (not agree)

Have students use a different color chalk to write the prefix **un-**, **re-**, or **dis-** before each base word to make a new word.

Kinesthetic Learners

Write these words on index cards: **use, place, fill, comfort, obey, attach, new, healthy, fold, clog,** and **paid.** Place the cards around the classroom. Make another set of cards with the words **reuse, replace, refill, discomfort, disobey, reattach, renew, unhealthy, unfold, unclog,** and **unpaid.** Place these cards in a pile. Have students select a card from the pile and find its "match." Have students make up a sentence for each word.

⭐ **Add the prefixes in red to the base words in the box. Write the new words on the lines.**

1	un	2	re	3	dis
familiar	unfamiliar	place	replace	connect	disconnect
opened	unopened	turn	return	honest	dishonest
able	unable	view	review	color	discolor
happy	unhappy	solve	resolve	loyal	disloyal
checked	unchecked	think	rethink	like	dislike
tie	untie	live	relive	approve	disapprove

⭐ **Use the best word from above to complete each sentence correctly.**

4. Some people feel they are _____unable_____ to solve community problems.

5. If people are _____unfamiliar_____ with the problems in their community, they can do nothing to help solve them.

6. A community must _____resolve_____ its problems by finding solutions.

7. If pollution goes _____unchecked_____, it can make people and animals sick.

8. Waste in rivers and streams can _____discolor_____ the water, turning it from blue to muddy gray.

9. Yet rivers and streams can _____return_____ to their original state with just a little help.

10. Scientists must _____review_____ all the facts before choosing a plan of action.

11. Sometimes, scientists must _____rethink_____ their solutions to problems.

12. Their solutions must not make people sad or _____unhappy_____.

102   LESSON 49: Prefixes un-, re-, dis-

Home Involvement Activity *Return of the Jedi* is a movie with a prefix in its title. Underline the prefix in the title of these videos your whole family can enjoy: *Egypt Uncovered   Discovering Canada by Rail*

102

Prefixes
pre-, in-, im-, over-, super-

Objectives

- **To identify the prefixes pre-, in-, im-, over-, and super- in words**
- **To identify the meanings of words with these prefixes**
- **To write words with these prefixes**

Warming Up

- Write this paragraph on the board:

  What does it take to make 700 paper bags? Wood from one 15-year-old tree. Where are 700 bags used every hour? In a **supermarket**. That's an **incredible** number of trees! It's **impossible** to save them all. But you can make a difference. When you shop, bring your own bag. Help save a tree.

- Read the paragraph aloud. Tell students to look and listen for three new prefixes.

- Have a student go to the board, and circle the prefixes in the words **supermarket, incredible,** and **impossible.**

Teaching the Lesson

- Write these words on the board: **overact, incomplete, superhuman, imperfect, preteen.** Ask students to define each word and use it in a sentence. Define each prefix and show how it changed the meaning of the base word.

- Then write the following words on the board with the prefixes underlined:

  immigrate, immodest, immoral; impersonal, impolite, impractical.

  Explain that when the prefix **im-** is added to a word, the word usually begins with the letters **m** or **p.**

Name _____

> **Helpful Hints**
>
> The **prefix** pre means "before." To **pre**pay means "to pay before."
> The **prefixes** in and im mean "not" or "into."
> **In**active means "not active." **Im**press means "press into."
>
> The **prefixes** over and super mean "beyond," "extra," or "too much."
> To **over**eat means "to eat too much."
> A **super**star is more talented than other stars.

Underline the prefix in each word. Then use what you know about the prefix to write the meaning of the word.

1. overjoyed _____ too much joy
2. superhero _____ a hero greater than other heroes
3. impatient _____ not patient
4. prehistoric _____ before history
5. impressed _____ pressed into
6. incredible _____ not credible

CHALLENGE

Pre- can be used to describe a period in time. Use a dictionary to write the meaning of these words:

Precambrian
pre-Columbian

Complete each sentence about Elizabeth Cady Stanton. Choose the best word from the activity above.

7. It seems _____ incredible _____ now, but before 1920, women in the United States were not allowed to vote.

8. Elizabeth Cady Stanton disagreed with that idea and _____ impressed _____ people with her speeches about women's rights.

9. Sometimes, she was _____ impatient _____ with the slow progress women were making.

10. She would be _____ overjoyed _____ to see the rights that women have gained today.

UNIVERSAL ACCESS
Meeting Individual Needs

Logical Learners

Write these prefixes on the board: **im-, in-, over-, pre-, super-.** Have groups of students choose words from the lesson that start with one of the prefixes. Group members then take turns writing down "What am I?" riddles that can be answered with one of the chosen words. The rest of the group reads the riddle and tries to figure out the answer. For example: *I am in the sea because I fell off a boat. What am I?* **(overboard)**

Kinesthetic Learners

Make a pair of cards for ten words with the prefixes **pre-, in-, im-, over-, super-.** Print each prefix on one card and each base word on the other. Give the prefix cards to one group, the base word cards to another. Have group members hold up their cards and circulate to find matches that make new words combining the correct prefix and base. "Matching partners" can tape their cards together and write their new word in a sentence.

⭐ **Choose a word from the box to answer each question correctly. Write the word on the line.**

supermarket	impure	incorrect	overcast	imprison	inexact	superhero
overseas	indirect	overweight	immature	preview	overflow	

1. Which word means "not direct"?   *indirect*

2. Which word means "to view ahead of time"?   *preview*

3. Which word means "not mature"?   *immature*

4. Which word means "weighing too much"?   *overweight*

5. Which word means "a market greater than other food stores"?   *supermarket*

6. Which word means "beyond the sea"?   *overseas*

7. Which word means "clouded over"?   *overcast*

8. Which word means "not correct"?   *incorrect*

9. Which word means "to flow over"?   *overflow*

10. Which word means "a hero greater than other heroes"?   *superhero*

11. Which word means "not pure"?   *impure*

12. Which word means "to put in prison"?   *imprison*

13. Which word means "not exact"?   *inexact*

⭐ **Choose five words from the box above. Write a sentence for each word.**

14. _____ Sentences will vary. _____

15. _____

16. _____

17. _____

18. _____

104   LESSON 50: Prefixes **pre-, in-, im-, over-, super-**

🏠 **Home Involvement Activity** Write an index card for each of the five prefixes from this lesson. Then take turns picking a card. Say a word that starts with the prefix on the card you pick. Then use the word in a sentence.

English-Language Learners/ESL

Write these prefixes and base words in two columns on the board: **over-, in-, super-, im-; active, possible, sleep, man.** Have volunteers draw lines connecting prefixes with bases to make new words. Then write the new words on the board and use them in sentences.

Gifted Learners

Ask students to write a newspaper article about an environmental issue in their community. Recommend that they include suggestions for how people can make a difference. Have students use words that contain some of the lesson prefixes.

Learners with Special Needs

Additional strategies for supporting learners with special needs can be found on page 99L.

Practicing the Skill

● Read aloud the direction lines on pages 103–104 and complete the first item in each exercise with students.

● Remind students to use the process of elimination to narrow down their choices in items 1–13 on page 104.

Curriculum Connections

Spelling Link

● Write these scrambled words on the board:

**ehrgvteoiw   irhceitposr   eitcridn
turpsesra   aurmtiem   tieaincv**

● Have students work in groups to unscramble the words and underline the prefixes.

● Ask the group that finishes first to write their answers on the board. (Answers: **overweight, prehistoric, indirect, superstar, immature, inactive**)

Social Studies Link

● Write the following names on the board: *Elizabeth Cady Stanton, Lucretia Mott, Frederick Douglass.* Explain that these people all spoke at the first women's rights convention in the United States, which took place at Seneca Falls, New York, in 1848.

● Have students work in groups to research these people. Then have them role-play giving speeches expressing their opinion's about women's rights.

● The speeches should include the prefixes **pre-, in-, im-, over-,** and **super-.**

Observational Assessment

*Check to see that students correctly use the lesson prefixes. Be sure that students recognize prefixes with more than one meaning (**in-, im-; over-, super**) and use them correctly.*

Connecting Reading and Writing

Objectives

- **To read a nonfiction piece and respond to it in writing**
- **To practice making inferences and interpreting information**
- **To write a letter or an e-mail message**

Warming Up

Comprehension Skills

- Tell students that **making inferences** is to form ideas or guesses based on facts, clues, or evidence. Making inferences as you read can help you understand and enjoy what you read more fully, whether it is an article, novel, poem, or textbook.

- **Interpreting** is another skill that can help students as they read. To interpret an article, story, or poem is to make sense of it or to give it meaning.

Teaching the Lesson

- Suggest that students recall what they have read in the selection as they think about the answer to the first Reader's Response question. They might find additional clues in the illustration and the selection's last sentence.

- Encourage students to give specific reasons for their answer to the second question.

- Help students answer the third question by asking them to define the word **treasure.**

Practicing the Skill

- Read the directions on page 106. Have volunteers read the words in the box.

- As a class, brainstorm questions that would be interesting to ask a pen pal.

Name _____

⭐ **Read about a great musician who has spent a lifetime making a difference. Then answer the questions that follow.**

A Musical Treasure

Isaac Stern was born in Russia in 1920. When he was ten months old, his family came to the United States. They settled in San Francisco. At the age of eight, Isaac began playing the violin. He has been playing ever since!

Isaac Stern is one of the world's "musical treasures." He is also a treasure for the kind of person he is. Stern has helped hundreds of students with their musical careers.

One of the highlights of Isaac Stern's career came in 1979. That year, he went to China. Few Americans could visit that country at that time. Yet Stern brought his violin with him as well as his desire to share his talent. This amazing trip was made into a movie. The movie is called *From Mao to Mozart: Isaac Stern in China.*

This wonderful film thrilled audiences. It even won an Academy Award. In the movie you can see Isaac Stern enjoying a concert of Chinese music. You can also see him explaining to Chinese music students that it is not enough just to play the right notes. True musicians must express their feelings as they play.

From Mao to Mozart shows Isaac Stern sharing his talent with young musicians. It also shows him using his music to change the world.

🏛 Reader's Response

1. Why is Isaac Stern famous?

2. Why might a famous person want to share his or her talent with young people?

3. Which of your talents could you share with someone? Explain.

1. Isaac Stern is one of the world's "musical treasures."
2. Answers will vary.
3. Answers will vary.

LESSON 51: Connecting Reading and Writing
Comprehension—Make Inferences; Interpret

105

UNIVERSAL ACCESS
Meeting Individual Needs

Auditory Learners

Some students may have an easier time speaking their letters, either quietly to themselves or in a role-play with another student playing a pen-pal. Encourage these students to make notes as they speak, or right after, so that they can capture in written form what they began by doing orally.

Musical Learners

Some students may find it easier to imagine the world in which their pen pal lives if they listen to some music from his or her country or region. They may also find it easier to express themselves in writing while listening to music. Create a quiet corner of the classroom for these students to listen to some music, or allow them to use headphones.

Learners with Special Needs

Additional strategies for supporting learners with special needs can be found on page 99.

Isaac Stern visited China in 1979. There, he learned about Chinese music and culture. You, too, can learn about another culture—but without leaving home. How? You can become a pen pal.

⭐ Write a letter or send an e-mail to a pen pal. Your librarian or teacher can help you find a list of pen-pal names. Tell your pen pal about yourself, your family, your best friend, your school, and your community. Ask questions that you would like your pen pal to answer. Use at least two of these words.

hobbies	discover	unusual	important	typical	subjects
incredible	dislike	unfamiliar	background	culture	interests

Answers will vary.

Writer's Tip

Use clear details. Remember that a pen pal lives far away. He or she may not know the same things that you do.

Writer's Challenge

Write a letter persuading your family to let you visit your pen pal. Explain how your visit would make a difference not only to you and your pen pal but also to the world. Save your strongest reason for last.

106 LESSON 51: Connecting Reading and Writing Comprehension—Make Inferences; Interpret

The Writing Process

Discuss the purpose of writing to a pen pal—to share information about oneself and to find out more about the pen pal.

Prewrite Encourage students to brainstorm a list of things about themselves that might be fun to write about. Suggest that they create several column heads: *self, family, best friend, school, community, questions.* Invite students to brainstorm as many details as they like under each head. Then they select the ones they like best.

Write Remind students that their pen pals have never seen them or their community. Encourage students to use words that will help pen pals picture an unfamiliar person and place.

Revise Have students read their letters aloud to a partner playing the role of the pen pal. Then have writing partners share feedback.

Proofread Encourage students to read their work carefully to check for errors in grammar, punctuation, and spelling.

Publish Ask students to copy their final drafts onto page 106 or a computer. Invite volunteers to read their letters aloud.

Computer Connection Suggest that students using computers explore different sizes and types of fonts. Remind students that people usually do not mix fonts in a single letter. However, choosing a font that expresses the student's mood or personality can make a letter more fun to read.

Portfolio Have students add the completed pen-pal letters to their portfolios.

English-Language Learners/ESL

Encourage students to share with the class their experience of receiving letters, either from places they haven't visited or from relatives who have received their letters. Then have students say whether they would rather write letters to old friends and relatives or to new pen pals.

Gifted Learners

Invite students to create a short story in the form of letters between two pen pals. Students may wish to dramatize their stories by reading them aloud with a partner. Encourage students to add simple props and costumes to enhance their presentations.

Reviewing and Assessing

Prefixes
(un-, re-, dis-, pre-, in-, im-, over-, super-)

Objective

To review and assess prefixes un-, re-, dis-, pre-, in-, im-, over-, and super-

Warming Up

● Ask students what a prefix is. (a word part added to the beginning of a base word) Then ask how a prefix affects a base word. (changes its meaning or makes a new word)

● Have students explain how the prefix affects the base word in the following examples: **unwelcome, remake, incorrect, overflow.**

Teaching the Lesson

● Review the meanings of the prefixes studied so far in this unit: **un-, re-, dis-, pre-, in-, im-, over-,** and **super-.** Have students give examples of words that include these prefixes and use each word in a sentence.

● Remind students that often they need to think beyond the literal meaning of a prefix to figure out a word's meaning. For example, **super-** and **over-** mean "beyond," "extra," or "too much." Discuss how these meanings help to define such words as **supermarket** and **overdo.**

● Remind students that some words may look as though they have prefixes, but really don't. For example, when you take away the **re** from **region** or the **un** from **uncle,** there is no base word left.

107

Name _____

⭐ Add the prefix **un** to two of the following base words. Add the prefix **re** to the two other words. Write the meaning of each new word.

Base Word	Word with Prefix	Meaning of New Word
1. afraid	unafraid	not afraid
2. turn	return	turn again
3. write	rewrite	write again
4. known	unknown	not known

⭐ Add the prefix **dis** to two of the base words. Add the prefix **pre** to the two other words. Write the meaning of each new word.

Base Word	Word with Prefix	Meaning of New Word
5. agree	disagree	not agree
6. view	preview	view before
7. honest	dishonest	not honest
8. historic	prehistoric	before history

⭐ Add the prefix **in** to one of the base words. Add the prefix **over** to the other base word. Write the meaning of each new word.

Base Word	Word with Prefix	Meaning of New Word
9. direct	indirect	not direct
10. weight	overweight	too much weight

⭐ Add the prefix **im** to one of the base words. Add the prefix **super** to the other base word. Write the meaning of each new word.

Base Word	Word with Prefix	Meaning of New Word
11. patient	impatient	not patient
12. market	supermarket	market that is greater than others

LESSON 52: Review and Assess 107

UNIVERSAL ACCESS
Meeting Individual Needs

Auditory Learners

Challenge students to write a group story using words with prefixes. Give students this story starter:

Delta 7 was a most **unusual superhero. Unlike** others . . .

Have a volunteer finish the sentence. Then ask each student to add a sentence. Write the words that contain prefixes on the board and discuss their meanings.

Learners with Special Needs

Additional strategies for supporting students with special needs can be found on page 99L.

Visual Learners

On the board, write the prefixes **un-, re-, dis-, pre-, in-, im-, over-,** and **super-.** Ask a volunteer to think of a word that begins with one of these prefixes. Have the student write the prefix on the board and add blank spaces after it to indicate the rest of the word's letters. Have the other students raise their hands to guess what letters go in the blanks. The first student to guess the correct word writes the prefix for the next mystery word.

Fill in the circle of the word that completes each sentence. Then write the word on the line.

1. Once you ____discover____ how you can make a difference, lending a hand can be easy.
   - ● discover   ○ recover   ○ overcover

2. You don't have to be a ____superhero____ to help.
   - ○ disloyal   ○ unknown   ● superhero

3. A simple act of kindness can make you feel ____incredibly____ proud.
   - ● incredibly   ○ incredible   ○ overjoyed

4. Most people will be ____impressed____ with how helpful you are.
   - ● impressed   ○ unpressed   ○ overpressed

Read this story about a helpful friend. Complete each sentence by combining the prefix with the base word in the box. Write the new word on the line.

Prefixes
un
re
in
over
Base Words
active
ate
tie
live

Amy (5)____overate____ at the pizza party. "Five pieces of pizza?" I exclaimed. Amy groaned and said she felt awful. I thought I might be able to help. "Loosen your belt and (6)____untie____ your scarf," I said. "Now let's take a little walk. You'll feel better if you move around."

Amy wanted to stay (7)____inactive____, but I insisted that she walk. We went out into the cool air. We slowly walked down the street. After a little while, Amy smiled weakly. "I'm still too full, but I feel a bit better. Thanks."

"Great!" I said. "Now let's go back inside and have some more lemonade."

"No!" Amy moaned. "I'm in no rush to (8)____relive____ this feeling anytime soon!"

Extend & Apply

Write a paragraph about a time when you helped a friend, a relative, or a neighbor. Use at least two words with prefixes.

108   LESSON 52: Review and Assess

Reteaching Activities

What's the Word?

Write the following sentences on the board.

The magician was [not able] to make the rabbit [opposite of appear]. (unable, disappear)

If you do not [pay back] the money, he will be [not happy]. (repay, unhappy)

I felt [beyond joy] with my [not believable] grade on the test. (overjoyed, unbelievable)

Have students replace the clues in brackets with words that have prefixes.

Prefixes in Print

Have students look through their textbooks to find words with the prefixes **un-, re-, dis-, pre-, in-, im-, over-,** and **super-.** Tell students to use their knowledge of prefixes in combination with context clues to figure out the meaning of each word. If they get stuck, have them look up the word's meaning in a dictionary. Have students share their list of words and definitions with the rest of the class.

Assessing the Skill

Check Up Assign the exercises on pages 107–108 to help students review the prefixes they have studied. These exercises will also help you evaluate students' ability to combine prefixes with base words and determine the meaning of words that contain prefixes.

Make sure students understand the directions for each set of exercises. Remind students to use context clues and encourage them to try various prefix/base word combinations until they identify the correct words.

Observational Assessment As students do the exercises, observe whether they have difficulty determining word meaning or filling in the blanks. Review your observations from previous lessons and use them to help you assess individual and class progress with prefixes.

Student Skills Assessment Keep track of each student's progress in understanding prefixes using the checklist on page 99H.

Writing Conference Meet with students to talk about their writing progress. Discuss the letter or e-mail they wrote on page 106 and compare it with earlier writing. Help students identify their strengths and weaknesses as writers. Discuss how word-study strategies can improve students' writing.

Group together students who need further instruction in prefixes and have them complete the *Reteaching Activities.* Turn to page 99C for alternative assessment methods.

Prefixes
sub-, co-, ex-

Objectives

- **To identify the prefixes sub-, co-, and ex- in words**
- **To identify the meanings of words with these prefixes**
- **To write words with these prefixes**

Warming Up

- Write the following poem on the board:

If fish could talk, what would they say
about **submarines** that get in their way?

"The ocean is big," they might
explain,

"With room for ships as well as fish.
If we could simply **coexist,**
The problem could be quickly fixed."

- Read the poem aloud. Have volunteers circle the prefixes in the words (**submarines, explain, coexist**)

Teaching the Lesson

- Write the words **cocaptain, exterminate, subplot** on the board. Have volunteers circle the prefixes and underline the base words. Then read these sentences aloud:

This book has a good plot, but I am more interested in the **subplot.**

The coach appointed a captain and a **cocaptain** for each team.

My dad had to **exterminate** the termites in the wood shed.

- Have students use the prefix and base word to define each word. Then challenge them to write sentences using each word.

- Ask a volunteer to read the Helpful Hints aloud as others follow along silently.

Name _____

Helpful Hints

Sub is a **prefix** meaning "under" or "less than."
A **sub**way runs under the street.

Co means "together" or "jointly."
A **co**pilot works with a pilot to fly an airplane.

Ex means "out of," "from," or "beyond."
I'd like to **ex**change this shirt for that one.

Underline the prefix in each word.

1. explain	2. subtopic	3. express
4. exclaim	5. cosign	6. suburban
7. coexist	8. subdivide	9. coauthor
10. subtitle	11. costar	12. submarine

Unscramble the letters at the left to form a word that fits each clue. Write the word on the line. All the words appear in the list above.

spxsere	13. to put into words	express
tosrca	14. to star with someone else	costar
videudisb	15. to divide into more parts	subdivide
busicopt	16. a second, or less important, topic	subtropic
bmesnurai	17. a ship that can travel underwater	submarine
rothcuao	18. to write a book together	coauthor

CHALLENGE

The words **un**like and **dis**like have different prefixes, but they share the same base word. Which prefixes that you have studied can you add to these base words?

_____press

_____solve

_____claim

LESSON 53: Prefixes **sub-, co-, ex-** 109

UNIVERSAL ACCESS
Meeting Individual Needs

Visual Learners

Draw three circles on the board, and label them with the prefixes **ex-, sub-,** and **co-**. Have students suggest base words that can be added to each prefix. Write each new word in the appropriate circle. When the activity is finished, have students define each word and use it in a sentence.

Auditory Learners

Write the words from the lesson with the prefixes **ex-, co-,** and **sub-** each on a slip of paper to play a game of Bingo. Have students choose four words from the lesson and write them on a sheet of paper. Then select slips of paper at random and read aloud the words written on them. When students hear one of their words, they circle it. The first student to circle all four words calls out "Bingo" and wins the game.

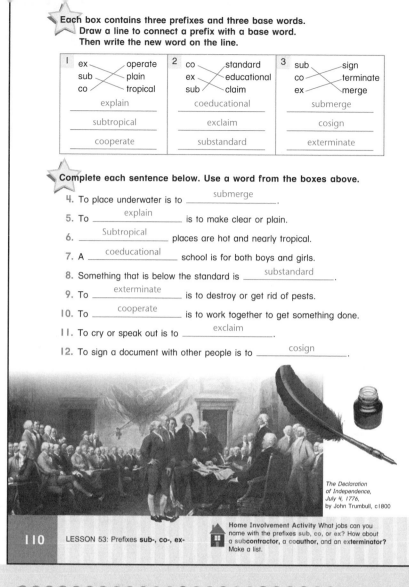

⭐ Each box contains three prefixes and three base words.
Draw a line to connect a prefix with a base word.
Then write the new word on the line.

1
ex — operate
sub — plain
co — tropical

explain
subtropical
cooperate

2
co — standard
ex — educational
sub — claim

coeducational
exclaim
substandard

3
sub — sign
co — terminate
ex — merge

submerge
cosign
exterminate

⭐ Complete each sentence below. Use a word from the boxes above.

4. To place underwater is to _____submerge_____.

5. To _____explain_____ is to make clear or plain.

6. _____Subtropical_____ places are hot and nearly tropical.

7. A _____coeducational_____ school is for both boys and girls.

8. Something that is below the standard is _____substandard_____.

9. To _____exterminate_____ is to destroy or get rid of pests.

10. To _____cooperate_____ is to work together to get something done.

11. To cry or speak out is to _____exclaim_____.

12. To sign a document with other people is to _____cosign_____.

The Declaration of Independence, July 4, 1776, by John Trumbull, c1800

110   LESSON 53: Prefixes **sub-, co-, ex-**

Home Involvement Activity What jobs can you name with the prefixes sub, co, or ex? How about a sub**contractor**, a co**author**, and an **exterminator**? Make a list.

Prefixes
il-, ir-, non-, mis-

Objectives
- To identify the prefixes **il-, ir-, non-,** and **mis-** in words
- To identify the meanings of words with these prefixes
- To write words with these prefixes

Warming Up

- Write the following paragraph on the board and read it aloud.

  In our town, it is **illegal** to combine newspapers, glass, plastic, and cans with other trash. The town council appointed a **nonprofit** committee to make sure the law is obeyed. If people make a **mistake,** they get a warning. If they are still **irresponsible,** they pay a fine. The money is used to keep our town clean.

- Have volunteers underline the words that contain prefixes and circle the prefixes.

Teaching the Lesson

- Write these prefixes on the board: **non-, mis-, ir-.** Have students add the correct prefix to each boldface word in the paragraph.

  Natural resources like oil, iron, and sand are _____**replaceable.** For that reason, we should be careful not to _____**handle** them. We do not want to waste our resources on _____**essential** things. (**irreplaceable, mishandle, nonessential**)

- Have students explain the reason for their choice of prefix, think of other words that contain each prefix, and write sentences using their words in context.

Name _____

Helpful Hints

The **prefixes il, ir, non,** and **mis** mean "not."

illegal = not legal	irregular = not regular
nonstop = not stopping	mistrust = not trusting

The **prefix mis** can also mean "wrong" or "wrongly" or "bad" or "badly."

misguided = wrongly guided
misconduct = bad conduct

Underline the prefix in each word.

1. mistake	2. irresistible	3. misspelled
4. nonsense	5. misuse	6. nonprofit
7. irresponsible	8. illogical	9. nonfiction
10. misplace	11. nonworking	12. illiterate

Answer each question. Use a word from the list above.

13. Which word means "not able to read or write"? _____ illiterate
14. Which word means "not responsible"? _____ irresponsible
15. Which word means "to put in the wrong place"? _____ misplace
16. Which word means "not making sense"? _____ nonsense
17. Which word means "to use badly"? _____ misuse
18. Which word means "wrongly spelled"? _____ misspelled
19. Which word means "not logical"? _____ illogical
20. Which word means "not fiction"? _____ nonfiction

WORD STRATEGY

To figure out the meaning of an unfamiliar word with a prefix, cover the prefix and read the rest of the word.

Try that strategy with these words. Then write the meaning of each of the words.

mislead
nonviolent

LESSON 54: Prefixes **il-, ir-, non-, mis-**

111

UNIVERSAL ACCESS
Meeting Individual Needs

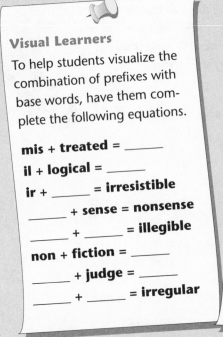

Visual Learners

To help students visualize the combination of prefixes with base words, have them complete the following equations.

mis + treated = _____
il + logical = _____
ir + _____ = irresistible
_____ + sense = nonsense
_____ + _____ = illegible
non + fiction = _____
_____ + judge = _____
_____ + _____ = irregular

Logical Learners

Write these words on the board: **misstep, illegal, nonprofit, irreversible, misspent, nonpayment, irresponsible, illogical, irregular, illiterate, misspelled, nonworking.** Have students sort the words by prefix and write them on the board in four separate boxes. Then point out the words in which the prefix ends with the same letter that begins the base word. Remind students to retain both letters in such cases.

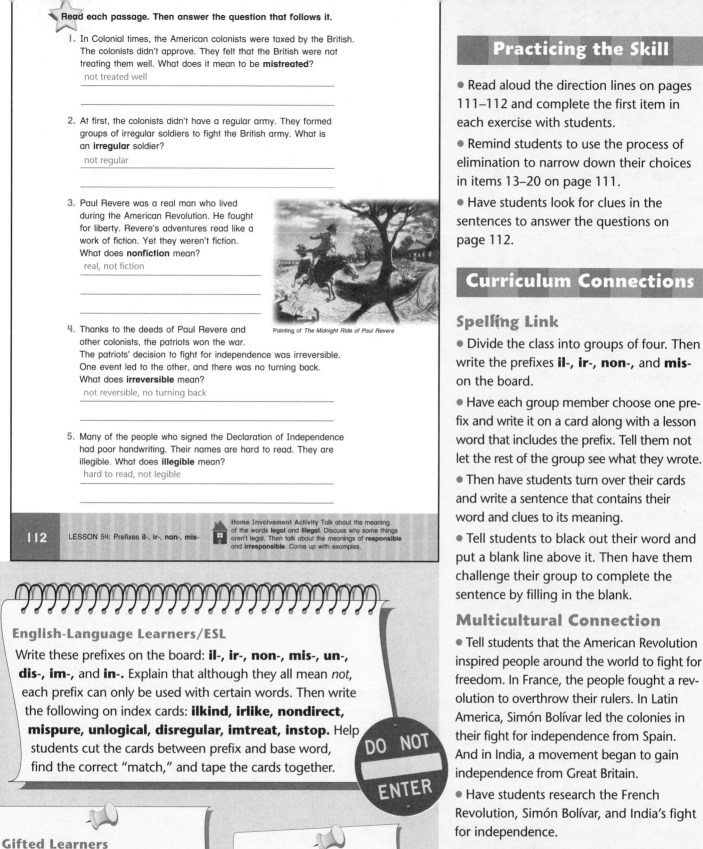

Read each passage. Then answer the question that follows it.

1. In Colonial times, the American colonists were taxed by the British. The colonists didn't approve. They felt that the British were not treating them well. What does it mean to be **mistreated**?

   not treated well

2. At first, the colonists didn't have a regular army. They formed groups of irregular soldiers to fight the British army. What is an **irregular** soldier?

   not regular

3. Paul Revere was a real man who lived during the American Revolution. He fought for liberty. Revere's adventures read like a work of fiction. Yet they weren't fiction. What does **nonfiction** mean?

   real, not fiction

   Painting of The Midnight Ride of Paul Revere

4. Thanks to the deeds of Paul Revere and other colonists, the patriots won the war. The patriots' decision to fight for independence was irreversible. One event led to the other, and there was no turning back. What does **irreversible** mean?

   not reversible, no turning back

5. Many of the people who signed the Declaration of Independence had poor handwriting. Their names are hard to read. They are illegible. What does **illegible** mean?

   hard to read, not legible

112   LESSON 54: Prefixes **il-, ir-, non-, mis-**

Home Involvement Activity Talk about the meaning of the words **legal** and **illegal**. Discuss why some things aren't legal. Then talk about the meanings of **responsible** and **irresponsible**. Come up with examples.

English-Language Learners/ESL

Write these prefixes on the board: **il-, ir-, non-, mis-, un-, dis-, im-,** and **in-**. Explain that although they all mean *not*, each prefix can only be used with certain words. Then write the following on index cards: **ilkind, irlike, nondirect, mispure, unlogical, disregular, imtreat, instop.** Help students cut the cards between prefix and base word, find the correct "match," and tape the cards together.

Gifted Learners

Challenge students to make crossword puzzles using words from the lesson. Remind them to make sure their puzzles are numbered correctly and that the clues are clear. Then have students exchange puzzles and solve them.

Learners with Special Needs

Additional strategies for supporting learners with special needs can be found on page 99L.

Practicing the Skill

● Read aloud the direction lines on pages 111–112 and complete the first item in each exercise with students.

● Remind students to use the process of elimination to narrow down their choices in items 13–20 on page 111.

● Have students look for clues in the sentences to answer the questions on page 112.

Curriculum Connections

Spelling Link

● Divide the class into groups of four. Then write the prefixes **il-, ir-, non-,** and **mis-** on the board.

● Have each group member choose one prefix and write it on a card along with a lesson word that includes the prefix. Tell them not let the rest of the group see what they wrote.

● Then have students turn over their cards and write a sentence that contains their word and clues to its meaning.

● Tell students to black out their word and put a blank line above it. Then have them challenge their group to complete the sentence by filling in the blank.

Multicultural Connection

● Tell students that the American Revolution inspired people around the world to fight for freedom. In France, the people fought a revolution to overthrow their rulers. In Latin America, Simón Bolívar led the colonies in their fight for independence from Spain. And in India, a movement began to gain independence from Great Britain.

● Have students research the French Revolution, Simón Bolívar, and India's fight for independence.

Observational Assessment

*Check that students correctly use the prefixes **il-, ir-, non-,** and **mis-** in context.*

112

Connecting Reading and Writing

Objectives

- **To read a nonfiction piece and respond to it in writing**
- **To practice making judgments and decisions and synthesizing information**
- **To write a description of someone the students admire**

Warming Up

Comprehension Skills

- Tell students about a person that you admire, someone who has made a difference in your life. Then inform students that you have made a **judgment** about this person. Ask them to identify what that judgment is and what you have based it on.
- Remind students that **synthesizing** is putting together the ideas within a piece of writing and making sense of them.

Teaching the Lesson

- Remind students that the first Reader's Response question has two parts: the reason black students weren't allowed to attend a white school, a factual question; and their own opinions about this fact.
- To help students with the second question, ask them to define what a hero is. Then ask whether Daisy Bates fits the definition.
- Encourage students to give examples as they answer the third question.

Practicing the Skill

- Invite volunteers to read the directions and the words in the box on page 114.
- Ask why details are important in a description of a person.

113

Name _____

★ Read about a brave woman who made a difference to our nation. Then answer the questions that follow.

Deciding What's Right

Daisy Bates was born and raised in a small town in Arkansas. She went to a school for black students only. White students went to other schools. Many people knew these separate schools were unequal. Daisy Bates was one of these people.

In 1954, the United States Supreme Court decided that it was unfair and illegal to allow separate schools for black and white students. However, many people in Arkansas and other Southern states disagreed. Despite the new law, many people refused to allow black children into white schools or white children into black schools. Some people, like Daisy Bates, wanted to test the new law. They did so by trying to register black children in white schools.

In 1957, Daisy Bates and her husband ran a newspaper. Through Daisy's words and acts, she succeeded in getting nine black students admitted to Central High School in Little Rock, Arkansas.

Daisy's efforts led to a big victory for civil rights. When she died in 1999, President Clinton called her a hero. Daisy *had* made a difference.

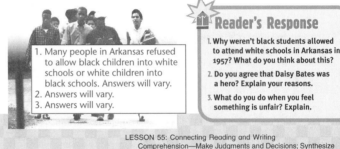

1. Many people in Arkansas refused to allow black children into white schools or white children into black schools. Answers will vary.
2. Answers will vary.
3. Answers will vary.

★ Reader's Response

1. Why weren't black students allowed to attend white schools in Arkansas in 1957? What do you think about this?

2. Do you agree that Daisy Bates was a hero? Explain your reasons.

3. What do you do when you feel something is unfair? Explain.

LESSON 55: Connecting Reading and Writing
Comprehension—Make Judgments and Decisions; Synthesize

113

UNIVERSAL ACCESS
Meeting Individual Needs

Auditory Learners

Students might prefer describing their special person to a writing partner or small group. Have them use vivid details that can help bring their person to life for their listeners. Encourage partners or group members to help students recall their stories and details so that they can go on to express their oral work in written form.

Logical Learners

Students might make a list of reasons why the person they choose to write about is special and then arrange their reasons in order of importance. Suggest that students visualize a reader who must be persuaded that this person is special. The writer's job would then be to make effective arguments showing how this person has affected other people's lives.

Learners with Special Needs

Additional strategies for supporting learners with special needs can be found on page 99L.

The true story of Daisy Bates shows that she was a hero. In fact, many people, including a President, admired her. Which person in your life do you admire? What are your reasons?

Write about someone special. Tell why you admire this person. Explain how this person has made a difference in your life or in the lives of other people. Use at least two of these words to describe your special person.

unafraid respect superhero discourage impress injustice
overjoyed mistake cooperate misunderstand unfair nonstop

Sentences will vary.

_____

_____

_____

_____

_____

_____

_____

_____

_____

_____

Writer's Tip
Include strong details in your description so that your audience can see why this person is so special.

Speaker's Challenge

Work with a partner. Role-play an event that you wrote about in your description. Act out your event for the class. Use appropriate gestures. Will you play yourself or your special person? Why?

114

LESSON 55: Connecting Reading and Writing
Comprehension—Make Judgments and Decisions; Synthesize

English-Language Learners/ESL

Invite English-language learners to retell the Daisy Bates story in their own words and to discuss in a small group what made her special. You might allow them to simply make a list of qualities that describe their own special person, rather than writing a complete description.

Gifted Learners

Invite students to create a "Hall of Heroes," using writing, poetry, music, drama, art, photographs, and any other media they can think of to convey information about four or five heroes chosen from widely different times and places. Have students share their "Hall of Heroes" with the class.

The Writing Process

Discuss the purpose of a description—to bring a person (or a topic) to life for your readers. Ask students to identify what makes a description fun and interesting to read. Review the words in the box and make sure students know what they mean.

Prewrite Have students begin by brainstorming a list of qualities that make their person special. Students might draw pictures of their person or create a word web with the person's name in the center. Encourage students to choose the most vivid and significant details.

Write Suggest that students look over the words in the box and select two or more to include as they develop their first drafts.

Revise Have students read their descriptions to a writing partner. Then have them ask: *Tell me why you think this person is special.* If the listener leaves out important details, the writer knows that more work is needed.

Proofread Remind students to read their work slowly and carefully to check for errors in grammar, punctuation, and spelling.

Publish Have students copy their final drafts onto page 114 and invite volunteers to read their descriptions aloud.

Computer Connection Suggest that students working on word processors might want to use the Thesaurus feature, usually found in the menu under "Tools." Tell students that a thesaurus provides synonyms—words with the same or nearly the same meanings. Place the cursor on a word you wish to replace. The thesaurus may offer a more vivid or unusual synonym to use instead.

Portfolio Have students add their descriptions of a special person to their portfolios.

Prefixes
pro-, com-
con-, under-

Objectives

- To identify the prefixes **pro-, com-, con-,** and **under-** in words
- To identify the meanings of words with the prefixes **pro-, com-, con-,** and **under-**
- To write words with the prefixes **pro-, com-, con-,** and **under-**

Warming Up

- Write the the poem on the board and read it aloud.

  Pollution exists everywhere,

  On land, at sea, and in the air.

  We simply cannot rest,

  Until we all **protest.**

  Confront the issue now,

  By speaking out aloud.

  For if we sit and wait,

  It just may be too late.

- Have a volunteer underline the two words with prefixes. Then have students identify each base word and suggest the meaning of each word.

Teaching the Lesson

- Write these words on the board: **pile, go, firm, long.** Have students add the words to the boldface prefixes to form new words in the paragraph below.

People who get sick often **under**_____ tests. Sometimes the tests **con**_____ that the cause is air, land, or water pollution. Scientists **com**_____ the results of these tests. Doctors have learned how to **pro**_____ people's lives. But fighting pollution is something everyone must learn. (undergo, confirm, compile, prolong)

115

Name _____

> **Helpful Hints**
>
> The **prefix** pro means "forward," "before," "in favor of," or "for."
>
> promotion = moving someone forward in a job
> prologue = words before a poem or a play
> prodemocracy = in favor of democracy
>
> The **prefixes** com and con mean "with" or "together."
>
> compile = to gather and put together
> confront = to bring face to face with
>
> The **prefix** under means "below," "less than," or "not enough."
>
> underground = below the ground
> undercharge = to charge too little or not enough

Underline the prefix in each word. Then write the meaning of the word on the line.

1. pro-American — in favor of American
2. underage — below the age
3. confirm — to make firm
4. undercover — below cover
5. prolong — to make longer
6. underweight — below weight
7. composition — to gather and put in place
8. underpass — below the pass
9. proclaim — to make clear
10. underpaid — paid too little

> **CHALLENGE**
>
> The prefix pro can mean "for." What part of speech does a **pronoun** stand in *for*?

UNIVERSAL ACCESS
Meeting Individual Needs

Kinesthetic Learners

Label cards with the following: **pro-, under-, com-, con-;** **foot, test, position, firm.** Tape an eight-box grid on the floor and place one card in each box. Then have students pair up to play Hopscotch. When you call out a completed word (**protest, underfoot, composition, confirm**), one partner jumps to the prefix box the other to the base word box. Continue until all words are completed.

Visual Learners

Use grid paper to make a word-search puzzle. Students circle words from the lesson that contain prefixes.

G	O	C	O	M	P	I	L	E	U	R
G	A	C	O	N	F	R	O	N	T	N
A	O	U	N	D	E	R	P	A	I	M
O	R	J	F	I	L	I	D	B	E	F
R	H	I	P	R	T	L	L	C	R	Z
H	E	P	R	O	F	I	L	E	L	A
B	R	M	T	D	A	G	P	R	I	O
U	N	D	E	R	A	G	E	L	N	R
U	D	F	S	L	O	P	R	I	E	A
C	P	O	T	F	J	K	O	R	T	V

Use a word from the box for each clue. Write one letter in each space. Then read down the shaded column to answer the question below.

composition promote underage protest underhand underline compile
profile underpass confirm undercooked underfoot proportion undershirt

1. another word for an essay — c o m **p** o s i t i o n
2. thrown with the hand kept below — u n d e r **h** a n d
3. to make firm or strengthen with the truth — c o n f **i** r m
4. a side view of the face — p r o f **i** l e
5. below the legal age — u n d e r **a** g e
6. not cooked enough — u n d e r c o o k e d
7. to be in the way — u n d e r f o o **t**
8. a shirt worn under a shirt — u n d e r s **h** i r t
9. relation of one part to another — p **r** o p o r t i o n
10. to gather and put together — c **o** m p i l e
11. a passageway under a highway — u n d e r **p** a s s
12. to mark with a line under — u n d e r **l** i n e
13. to speak up for or against — p r o t e **s** t
14. to move to a higher job — p r o m o **t** e

Question: In *The Wizard of Oz*, this kind of person is called a "good-deed doer." What is another word for someone who gives money to worthy causes?

Answer: _____philanthropist_____

From the movie
The Wizard of Oz, 1939

116   LESSON 56: Prefixes **pro-, com-, con-, under-**

Home Involvement Activity Pretend that your family has $1 million to donate to a few worthy causes. Which causes would you want to help? Why? How much would you give to each?

English-Language Learners/ESL

Display or draw pictures of an undershirt, a side view of someone's face, a student-written composition, and two people standing face to face as if arguing. Then write the following words on the board: **undershirt, profile, composition, confront.** Have students take turns matching the picture to the word from the board that best describes it.

Gifted Learners

Have students write sentences with words from the lesson. Tell them to separate the prefixes from the base words and scramble the words in the sentence. Then have students exchange sentences and unscramble them.

Learners with Special Needs

Additional strategies for supporting learners with special needs can be found on page 99L.

Practicing the Skill

● Read aloud the direction lines on pages 115–116 and complete the first item in each exercise with students.

● Point to item 1 on page 115 and explain that when a prefix is added to a capitalized word, a hypen is used.

Curriculum Connections

Spelling Link

● Divide the class into groups with each group sitting in a separate row. Then play "Prefix Relay."

● Write the prefix **pro-** on the board along with its meanings. When you say "GO," the first person in each row writes a word from the lesson that uses the prefix and passes the paper to the next person, who writes another word. This continues until the last person in the row has written a word or until all the lesson words have been used. The first group to complete a correct list wins the round.

● Repeat the procedure with the prefixes **under-, com-,** and **con-.**

Writing Link

In the *Wizard of Oz,* the Tin Man wants a heart, the Cowardly Lion wants courage, the Scarecrow wants brains, and Dorothy wants to go home. Have students think of changes they would like to make in themselves or their lives. Suggest that they write their ideas in a journal, which they can review periodically.

Observational Assessment

*Check that students do not mix up **n** and **m** when writing words with the prefixes **con-** and **com-.***

Prefixes
uni-, bi-, tri-, mid-, semi-

Objectives

- To identify the prefixes **uni-, bi-, tri-, mid-,** and **semi-**
- To identify the meanings of words with these prefixes
- To write words with these prefixes

Warming Up

- Put these items in a box: a picture of a bicycle, a picture of a tricycle, a round tinfoil pie plate bent in half, and a soda can. Label the box "Buried Treasures." Have volunteers open the box and hold up each item. Explain that the items are all made from the same natural resource. Challenge students to figure out what that resource is. (aluminum)

- Explain that aluminum is a "buried treasure" because it is found under the ground in limited supplies. Like other natural resources, we cannot afford to waste it.

- Tell students that in this lesson, they will work with the prefixes **uni-, bi-, tri-, mid-,** and **semi-.** Have them use words with these prefixes to identify two of the "buried treasures." **(bicycle, tricycle)**

Teaching the Lesson

- Write these words on the board: **biplane, tricolored, midstream, semi-annual.** Have students define each word. Elicit responses that convey the meaning of each prefix.

- Explain that the prefixes **uni-, bi-, tri-, mid-,** and **semi-** often refer to a time, a location, or an amount.

- Read aloud the Helpful Hints as students follow along silently.

117

Name _____

Helpful Hints

The **prefix uni** means "one."	A **uni**cycle has only one wheel.
The **prefix bi** means "two."	A **bi**cycle has two wheels.
The **prefix tri** means "three."	A **tri**cycle has three wheels.

Underline the prefix in each word in the box. Then use the words to complete the sentences. Use a word only once.

    bicolored   tristate   unicorn   triangle   biweekly   uniform

1. Which word means "having two colors"? _____ bicolored
2. What figure has three sides and three angles? _____ triangle
3. Which word means "twice a week"? _____ biweekly
4. Which word describes something worn by members of a certain group? _____ uniform
5. Which word describes a make-believe animal with one horn on its forehead? _____ unicorn
6. What is the word for a three-state area? _____ tristate

Complete each sentence. Use a word from the box above.

7. Our class chose a hospital in the ____tristate____ area.
8. On Mondays and Wednesdays, we made ____biweekly____ visits to patients.
9. The ____bicolored____ hospital rooms were blue and yellow.
10. Each room had a picture of a horselike ____unicorn____.
11. The nurses' caps were shaped like a ____triangle____.
12. Each nurse's ____uniform____ was white.

CHALLENGE

Benjamin Franklin invented a pair of eyeglasses that helped him read a book and also see at a distance. Unscramble this word to "see" what Franklin invented:

facilbos

UNIVERSAL ACCESS
Meeting Individual Needs

Visual Learners

Have four volunteers come to the board and draw a picture illustrating one of the following phrases. Then have four other volunteers come to the board, label each picture with words from the lesson having prefixes, and circle each prefix.

a **tri**colored **tri**angle;

a **bi**colored **semi**circle;

a **uni**corn on a **uni**cycle;

midnight on a **bi**cycle clock

Logical Learners

Write these words in random order on the board: **uni**corn, **uni**cycle, **bi**cycle, **bi**weekly, **bi**colored, **tri**cycle, **tri**state, **mid**day, **mid**air, **Mid**west, **mid**way, **mid**night, **semi**circle, **semi**annual. Have students sort the words by prefix. Then have them group the words under these headings: Time, Location, Amount. (**Time: biweekly, semiannual, midday, midnight; Location: midair, Midwest, midway; Amount: bicycle, bicolored, unicycle, unicorn, tricycle, tristate, semicircle**)

The **prefix semi** means "half," "partly," or "happening twice."
A **semi**circle is half a circle. **Semi**annually is twice a year.

The **prefix mid** means "in the middle of."
Midweek is the middle of the week.

★ **Underline the prefix in each word in the box. Then use the words to complete the sentences. Use a word only once.**

midair	semiannual	midnight	Midwestern	semifinal
semisweet	midway	semitropical	semiretired	midday

1. In some countries, people take a __midday__ nap.

2. Kansas City is a __midwestern__ city on the Missouri River.

3. The climate of southern Florida is __semitropical__.

4. Our family takes a __semiannual__ trip in the fall and the spring.

5. That horror movie will be on TV at __midnight__.

6. New York City is __midway__ between Boston and Washington, DC.

7. The dog leaped up to catch the ball in __midair__.

8. I prefer milk chocolate, but my sister likes the __semisweet__ kind.

9. Our team lost in the __semifinal__ game of the tournament.

10. Grandma is now __semiretired__ and works only part-time.

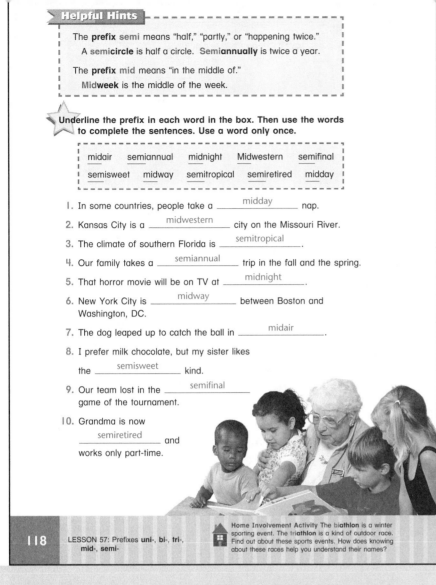

118   LESSON 57: Prefixes **uni-, bi-, tri-, mid-, semi-**

🏠 **Home Involvement Activity** The bi**athlon** is a winter sporting event. The tri**athlon** is a kind of outdoor race. Find out about these sports events. How does knowing about these races help you understand their names?

English-Language Learners/ESL

Ask volunteers to pantomime the following words after writing them on the board: riding a bike **(bicycle)**, circling Wednesday on a calendar **(midweek)**, splitting a pie and pointing to half **(semicircle)**, drawing a picture with three different-colored crayons **(tricolored)**, standing up with a finger extended outward from the middle of the forehead **(unicorn)**. Have students call out the word that relates to the activity.

Gifted Learners

Pair students for this research activity. One partner finds information about bifocals, the other about trifocals. Then both partners share their findings with the class, comparing bifocals with trifocals and explaining how each pair of eyeglasses got its name.

Learners with Special Needs

Additional strategies for supporting learners with special needs can be found on page 99L.

Practicing the Skill

● Read aloud the direction lines on pages 117–118 and complete the first item in each exercise with students.

● Remind students to look for clues in the sentences as they complete items 7–12 on page 117 and items 1–10 on page 118.

Curriculum Connections

Spelling Link

● Divide the class into groups of five. Give each group five cards, each with one of these prefixes: **uni-, bi-, tri-, semi-, mid-.**

● Have the members of each group select one card and list words from the lesson with the prefix. Then have group members work together to choose one word and write a sentence using it in context.

● When you call "Time," have groups trade sentences. Have them check to make sure that the words are correct and that the sentences clearly illustrate the meanings of the chosen words.

● Groups can call "Challenge" if they find a mistake, but they must back up the challenge by correcting the error.

Math Link

Draw three triangles on the board: one with all sides of equal length (equilateral), one with two sides of equal length (isosceles), and one with all sides of different lengths (scalene). Point out that while all triangles have three sides and three angles, the sides of a triangle can be equal or different in length. Then invite students to draw a triangle of their own, measure the sides, and describe it.

Observational Assessment

Check to see that students understand the meanings of the lesson prefixes and can use them to decode unfamiliar words.

Prefixes with Syllables

Objectives

- **To identify words with prefixes**
- **To identify the number of syllables in words with prefixes**

Warming Up

- Write the following rhyme on the board and read it aloud:

  Incredible as it seems,
  Sometimes I actually dream
  Of **prehistoric** times,
  With no pollution and no crime.
  When the only thing to fear
  Was a dinosaur quite near.
  A very **unpleasant** sight,
  Since it just might take a bite.

- Using the rhyme, ask volunteers to underline the words that contain prefixes. Have students read the words aloud and clap to determine the number of syllables in each word.

Teaching the Lesson

- Write these words on the board: *preteach, unarmed, invisible, improper, subcommittee, semicircle, overact, superwoman, underseas.*

- Have volunteers read each word aloud, identify the number of syllables, name each prefix, and explain how it changed the number of syllables in each base word. (**pre**/teach, **un**/armed, **in**/vis/i/ble, **im**/prop/er, **sub**/com/mit/tee, **se**/**mi**/cir/cle, **over**/act, **su**/**per**/wom/an, **un**/**der**/seas. Each prefix added one or more syllables.)

- Challenge students to identify the two prefixes in the word **overreact (over-, re-)** and then divide the whole word into syllables. (**o/ver/re/act**)

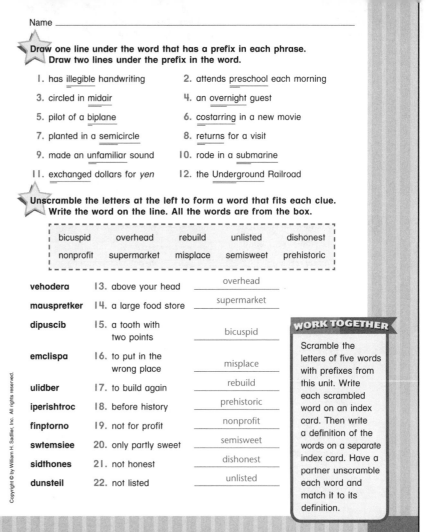

Name _____

⭐ Draw one line under the word that has a prefix in each phrase. Draw two lines under the prefix in the word.

1. has illegible handwriting
2. attends preschool each morning
3. circled in midair
4. an overnight guest
5. pilot of a biplane
6. costarring in a new movie
7. planted in a semicircle
8. returns for a visit
9. made an unfamiliar sound
10. rode in a submarine
11. exchanged dollars for *yen*
12. the Underground Railroad

⭐ Unscramble the letters at the left to form a word that fits each clue. Write the word on the line. All the words are from the box.

| bicuspid | overhead | rebuild | unlisted | dishonest |
| nonprofit | supermarket | misplace | semisweet | prehistoric |

vehodera	13.	above your head	overhead
mauspretker	14.	a large food store	supermarket
dipuscib	15.	a tooth with two points	bicuspid
emclispa	16.	to put in the wrong place	misplace
ulidber	17.	to build again	rebuild
iperishtroc	18.	before history	prehistoric
finptorno	19.	not for profit	nonprofit
swtemsiee	20.	only partly sweet	semisweet
sidthones	21.	not honest	dishonest
dunsteil	22.	not listed	unlisted

WORK TOGETHER

Scramble the letters of five words with prefixes from this unit. Write each scrambled word on an index card. Then write a definition of the words on a separate index card. Have a partner unscramble each word and match it to its definition.

UNIVERSAL ACCESS
Meeting Individual Needs

Auditory Learners

Say the following words, stressing each syllable: *mid/air, dis/hon/est, ex/change, su/per/mar/ket, im/pos/si/ble, re/u/nite.* As you say each word, have students clap for each syllable. Then have students determine the number of syllables, pronounce each syllable and name each prefix, and identify the prefix.

Kinesthetic Learners

Write these words on index cards: **misplace, midwinter, nonsense, illegible, overjoyed, cooperate.** Have students cut each word card by syllables and display the parts in random order. Then have students tape the syllables together to form the original word. (**mis/place, mid/win/ter, non/sense, il/leg/i/ble, o/ver/joyed, co/op/er/ate**)

Underline the prefix in each word in the box. Then sort the words according to how many syllables they have. Write each word correctly in the chart below.

compass	subdivided	unpleasant	proclaim	midwinter
impossible	reunite	tricycle	overjoyed	cooperate
nonsense	explain	unicycle	incredible	preheat

1 Has Two Syllables	2 Has Three Syllables	3 Has Four Syllables
compass	reunite	impossible
nonsense	unpleasant	subdivided
explain	tricycle	unicycle
proclaim	overjoyed	incredible
preheat	midwinter	cooperate

Answer each question. Use a word from the chart above. Write the word on the line.

4. Which four-syllable word means "not possible"? _impossible_

5. Which two-syllable word means "to make clear or plain"? _explain_

6. Which four-syllable word means "to work together"? _cooperate_

7. Which two-syllable word describes something that makes no sense? _nonsense_

8. Which three-syllable word describes a three-wheeled vehicle? _tricycle_

9. Which four-syllable word means "hard to believe"? _incredible_

10. Which three-syllable word means "not pleasant"? _unpleasant_

120 LESSON 58: Prefixes with Syllables

Home Involvement Activity Many vehicles include prefixes in their names. What are **tri**marans, **tri**remes, and super**tankers?** Find out together.

English-Language Learners/ESL

Choose two prefixes, and words that contain them, from each preceding lesson in Unit 4. Select multi-syllabic words that contain the prefixes. Write each word on an index card. Place the cards in random order. Have students sort the words by prefix and then by number of syllables.

Gifted Learners

Have students write about one person making a difference in the life of another. Challenge students to use words beginning with the prefixes in this unit and to include some that have five or more syllables (examples: **un/der**/es/ti/mate, **o/ver**/sim/pli/fy)

Learners with Special Needs

Additional strategies for supporting learners with special needs can be found on page 99L.

- Read aloud the direction lines on pages 119–120 and complete the first item in each exercise with students.

- Suggest that students use the process of elimination to answer items on page 119.

- Remind students to check off each word as they use it on page 120.

Curriculum Connections

Spelling Link

- On separate cards, list the prefixes taught in each lesson of Unit 4. Write each prefix on an index card. Divide the class into pairs and give each pair one card.

- Have each partner write a word that contains the prefix on the index card. Collect the word-cards, put them in a bag, and shake it.

- Have pairs choose a card from the bag. Partners work together to underline the prefixes, divide the words into syllables, define the words, and write contextual sentences.

Social Studies Link

- Have students complete the paragraph about the Underground Railroad (page 119, item 12) by filling in each blank with one of these prefixes: **in-, co-, Under-, un-, over-.**

The term __ground Railroad was first used in 1830 to describe an __formal system that helped thousands of slaves in the South escape. They traveled by night, using the stars __head to guide them to freedom in the North. The people who helped were willing to __operate because they believed that slavery was __just.

- Discuss how the Underground Railroad made a difference in people's lives.

Observational Assessment

Check to see that students can identify the number of syllables in words with prefixes.

Connecting Spelling and Writing

Objectives

- **To say, spell, sort, and write multi-syllabic words with prefixes**
- **To write a paragraph using spelling words**

Warming Up

- Write the following paragraph on the board. Ask a student to read it aloud.

  Some people see an <u>unpleasant</u> situation and say, "We are <u>unable</u> to change it." Others <u>disagree</u>. They <u>exclaim</u>, "Nothing is <u>impossible</u>! We can make a difference if we all <u>cooperate</u>."

- For each underlined word, have a volunteer identify the prefix, give the definition, and tell how many syllables the word has.

Teaching the Lesson

- Ask the following two questions and have students write their answers on the board. *What two-syllable word means "to build again"?* **(rebuild)** *What three-syllable word means "not patient"?* **(impatient)**
- Then have volunteers use the same question format to ask their classmates similar questions. Encourage students to use words from Lessons 53–58.

Practicing the Skill

- Read aloud the directions for the exercise on page 121.
- Have students complete the page. Encourage them to say the words softly to themselves to help them count the number of syllables.

Name _____

Read each group of words. Say and spell each word in bold print. Repeat the word. Then sort the words. Write the words in the correct column below.

- painted her **profile**
- farm animals as a **subtopic**
- gave an **illogical** reason
- **coauthor** of the book
- in the **midday** sun
- a 10-speed **bicycle**
- drew a **semicircle**
- going **nonstop**

- kept **irregular** hours
- wearing a **uniform**
- **misunderstand** the point
- ride a **tricycle**
- use a **compass** for direction
- leave out the **unimportant** details
- **underline** the answer
- **exchange** a library book

Words with Two Syllables	Words with Three Syllables	Words with Four Syllables
profile	uniform	irregular
subtopic	coauthor	illogical
midday	tricycle	misunderstand
compass	bicycle	unimportant
nonstop	underline	semicircle
exchange		

LESSON 59: Connecting Spelling and Writing   121

UNIVERSAL ACCESS
Meeting Individual Needs

Auditory Learners

Have students draw three circles on paper and label them *2 syllables, 3 syllables,* and *4 syllables.* Say each word aloud. Tell them to write each word in the correct circle.

misplace	**superhero**	**unicorn**
semifinal	**dishonest**	**midweek**
undergo	**misplace**	**exhale**
irregular	**complain**	**rebuild**

Tactile Learners

Write these words on cards: **explain, subway, copilot, subtopic, illegal, midair, exterminate, subtropical, nonfiction, underweight, promotion, supermarket, tristate, prehistoric.** Shuffle the cards and place them face down, Concentration-style. The first player turns over two cards to see whether their words have the same number of syllables. If so, the player goes again. If not, the next player goes. Continue until all cards are matched.

Learners with Special Needs

Additional strategies for supporting learners with special needs can be found on page 99L.

How often do you go to the library? Libraries can make a big difference in how well you do in school. Thanks to Andrew Carnegie, more than 2,500 public libraries were built in the United States.

Carnegie was a poor boy when he came to the United States from Scotland. In time, he made a fortune in the steel business. Although Carnegie had very little schooling, he loved books. He gave money so that cities and towns could build their own libraries. Is there a Carnegie library in your town?

Andrew Carnegie (1835–1919)

⭐ In a paragraph, explain how public libraries can make a difference. Use two or more of these spelling words.

profile	subtopic	illogical	coauthor	midday	bicycle
semicircle	nonstop	irregular	uniform	misunderstand
tricycle	compass	unimportant	underline	exchange

Sentences will vary.

_____

_____

_____

_____

_____

_____

_____

_____

Writer's Tip

Start with a clear main idea of your topic. Add strong supporting details.

Writer's Challenge

Use ideas from your paragraph to create a "library" poster for your school or community library. Write a slogan and illustrate it. Get across the idea that libraries can make a difference.

The Writing Process

Tell students that on page 122 they will write a paragraph about public libraries. Go over the directions and the spelling words at the top of the page.

Prewrite Have the class discuss the many different activities that people, young and old, can do at a library. Encourage students to think about the library's range of media and services as well as its importance as a community center and cultural resource.

Write Encourage students to plan before they write by jotting down a main idea and supporting details and examples. Suggest that they look over the spelling words and think about which ones they might be able to use.

Revise Have students reread their paragraphs and revise as needed. Ask: *Have you clearly explained "how public libraries can make a difference"? Have you included specific details and examples? Have you used two or more spelling words?*

Proofread Have students check their work for errors in spelling, grammar, and punctuation.

Publish Tell students to copy their final drafts onto page 122 or onto separate paper.

Computer Connection

Share the following tip with students who use a word processor to do their writing.

● The "Find and Replace" feature allows you to search for and change text quickly and easily.

● You can replace words one at a time or all at once. Be careful. If you give the command to replace all instances of **car** with **automobile**, **carpet** will become **automobilepet**.

Portfolio Suggest that students add their finished paragraphs to their portfolios.

English-Language Learners/ESL

Display pictures of items named by multisyllabic words with prefixes, such as: **supermarket, superhero, subway, copilot, submarine, uniform, unicorn, bicycle, tricycle, underpass, undershirt, triangle, semicircle, biplane, compass, unicycle.** Have students name each item, write the word, and use the word in a sentence.

Gifted Learners

Challenge students to expand the paragraph they wrote on page 122 into a three-paragraph essay, with each paragraph focusing on another way in which libraries can make a difference.

Reviewing and Assessing
Prefixes

Objective

To review and assess prefixes

Warming Up

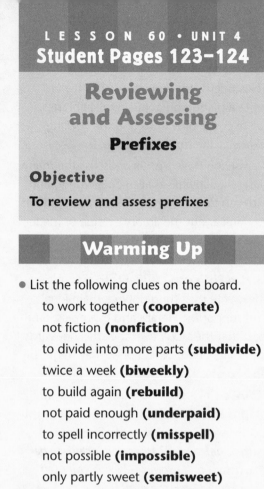

- List the following clues on the board.

  to work together (**cooperate**)

  not fiction (**nonfiction**)

  to divide into more parts (**subdivide**)

  twice a week (**biweekly**)

  to build again (**rebuild**)

  not paid enough (**underpaid**)

  to spell incorrectly (**misspell**)

  not possible (**impossible**)

  only partly sweet (**semisweet**)

- Next to each clue, have students write the corresponding word that begins with a prefix. Then have students draw a line between the prefix and the base word.

Teaching the Lesson

- Use the chalkboard or chart paper to create a review chart of all the prefixes studied so far in this unit. Use the following three-column format:

  Prefix   Meaning   Example Words

- List the prefixes in the first column. Then have students complete the chart, on their own. Have students provide at least two example words for each prefix and use the words in sentences.

- Review the fact that prefixes do not always make word meaning clear. But they usually provide helpful clues. Discuss some examples, such as **subway, undercover,** and **prehistoric.** Ask students how the prefixes of such words help to suggest what the word means.

Name _____

⭐ Add the prefix **sub** to two of the following base words. Add the prefix **ex** to the two other words. Write the meaning of each new word.

Base Word	Word with Prefix	Meaning of New Word
1. urban	suburban	beyond urban
2. change	exchange	to give and receive
3. press	express	to put into words
4. standard	substandard	below standard

⭐ Add the prefix **ir** to two of the base words. Add the prefix **il** to the two other words. Write the meaning of each new word.

Base Word	Word with Prefix	Meaning of New Word
5. regular	irregular	not regular
6. legal	illegal	not legal
7. responsible	irresponsible	not responsible
8. legible	illegible	not legible

⭐ Add the prefix **mis** to one of the base words. Add the prefix **pro** to the other base word. Write the meaning of each new word.

Base Word	Word with Prefix	Meaning of New Word
9. place	misplace	to put in the wrong place
10. long	prolong	to make longer

⭐ Add the prefix **under** to one of the base words. Add the prefix **bi** to the other base word. Write the meaning of each new word.

Base Word	Word with Prefix	Meaning of New Word
11. cycle	bicycle	has two wheels
12. ground	underground	below the ground

LESSON 60: Review and Assess   **123**

UNIVERSAL ACCESS
Meeting Individual Needs

Visual Learners

Cut out thought-provoking pictures from magazines and display them in the classroom. Challenge students to write captions for each picture, using words with prefixes. Encourage students to use their imaginations. For example, for a picture of cars on a highway, a student might write: *Driving over the speed limit is **illegal** and **irresponsible.***

Auditory Learners

Read the following words aloud. Have volunteers spell the words orally as they write them on the board.

biweekly	**incredible**	**costar**
illogical	**submarine**	**confirm**
submerge	**cooperate**	**protest**
mistake	**undershirt**	**exclaim**
uniform	**nonworking**	**midair**
dishonest	**unpleasant**	**explain**

Challenge pairs of students to write a story using as many of the words as they can. Have students share their stories with the class.

Learners with Special Needs

Additional strategies for supporting students with special needs can be found on page 99L.

Read the sentences. Fill in the circle of the word that completes each sentence. Then write the word on the line.

1. In 1981, _____coworkers_____ in El Salvador got an idea to help people who were physically challenged.
   ● coworkers ○ preworkers ○ biworkers

2. They opened a _____nonprofit_____ pottery workshop called ACOGIPRI.
   ○ biprofit ○ uniprofit ● nonprofit

3. ACOGIPRI helps make life better for people with _____disabilities_____.
   ○ exabilities ● disabilities ○ unabilities

4. Members make things to sell over the Internet to people who _____prepay_____ for the items.
   ○ repay ○ tripay ● prepay

Complete each sentence by combining the prefix with the correct base word in the box. Write the new word on the line.

Prefixes
re
non
il
pro
Base Words
legal
claimed
turned
working

After eating breakfast at Dan's Diner, I (5) _____returned_____ there for lunch. The sign on the door said "NO DOGS ALLOWED." Yet I could see that a big brown dog was lying near my favorite booth. I thought it was

(6) _____illegal_____ to let dogs into restaurants. So I asked Dan why someone would ignore the sign.

"Oh, that's Corky," Dan (7) _____proclaimed_____. Her owner, Jake, is blind. Then I saw the dog's gentle face and the special leather harness that Corky wore. Dan said that the law permits service dogs to enter places where

(8) _____nonworking_____ dogs would be kept out. Maybe it would help if Dan changed the sign to say, "NO DOGS ALLOWED UNLESS WORKING."

Extend & Apply

A dog is a **quadruped**—it has four (quadru) feet (ped). What would you call a person?
_____biped_____

Check Up Have students complete pages 123–124 to help them review the prefixes presented in this unit. The exercises on these pages will also help you assess students' ability to combine prefixes with base words to make new words. Review the directions for each set of exercises. For the second exercise on page 124 (items 5–8), remind students to use context clues and to try different prefix/base word combinations until they determine the correct words.

Observational Assessment As students are working on the exercises, watch for signs of difficulty with particular prefixes. Review observational notes taken during earlier lessons and use them to help you gauge students' overall progress in understanding prefixes.

Student Skills Assessment Keep track of each student's progress in understanding prefixes using the checklist on page 99H.

Writing Conference Meet with students individually to talk over written work they have completed in this unit, such as the composition about someone special on page 114 and the paragraph about libraries on page 122. Discuss how understanding prefixes can help students build their vocabulary and become better readers and writers.

Group together students who need further instruction in prefixes, and have them complete the *Reteaching Activities*. Turn to page 99C for alternative assessment methods.

Reteaching Activities

Prefix Hunt

Write the following sentences on the board.

Midway through the show, the actress **pro**claimed: "I am **under**paid!"

"I made a **mis**take," the driver **ex**plained, "when I took the **over**pass."

"It is **in**credible," Tony thought, "that I can ride a **uni**cycle in a **semi**circle!"

Ask volunteers to read the sentences aloud. Then have students find the words with prefixes, identify the prefixes, and explain their meanings.

Prefix Presentations

Tell students to choose the two prefixes from this unit that they find most challenging. Have each student make a mini-presentation to the class, offering tips for understanding and using the two prefixes. Ask presenters to include as many examples of words that have these prefixes as they can. Encourage listeners to ask questions about and/or add to the tips that each student presents.

Base Words

Objectives

- **To combine prefixes and base words to form new words**
- **To identify the meanings of words formed by combining prefixes and base words**

Warming Up

- Write this riddle on the board, and call on a volunteer to read it aloud.

  Q: What did one fruit tree say to the other fruit tree when spring arrived?

  A: Prepare to **"repear."**

- Have a student underline the prefixes **pre** and **re.** Point out that **"repear"** is not an actual word. Ask students which part of this imaginary word would be the base word. (**pear**)

- Have students discuss what **"repear"** might mean in this riddle. Then ask them to name an actual word that sounds the same. (**repair**)

Teaching the Lesson

- Review with students that they have learned many prefixes. Have students find the prefixes in the boxes on pages 125 and 126.

- Point out the base words. Review that when a prefix is added to a base word, a new word with a different meaning is formed.

- Explain that different prefixes can be added to the same base word. Have students experiment with the prefixes and base words on page 125.

- Read aloud the Helpful Hint. Ask students why there is a plus sign connecting the prefix to the base word and an equal sign before the new word. (You add a prefix to a base word to make a new word.)

Name _____

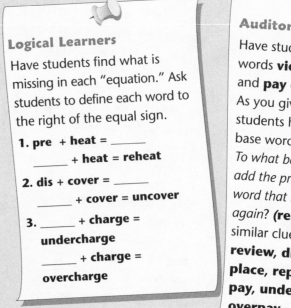

Helpful Hint

You can form a new word by adding a **prefix** to a **base word.**

un + lucky = unlucky = not lucky
re + start = restart = start again
re + cycle = recycle = cycle again

Read the clues. Combine the prefixes and the base words in the box to form words that will answer the clues. Write the new words on the lines. You can use a prefix and a base word more than once.

Prefixes	
un	pre
over	dis
under	re

Base Words

turn	pay
heat	cycle
used	cover

1. To knock over is to _____ overturn _____.
2. To come back is to _____ return _____.
3. To pay ahead of time is to _____ prepay _____.
4. To pay too much is to _____ overpay _____.
5. To heat ahead of time is to _____ preheat _____.
6. To heat too much is to _____ overheat _____.
7. To heat again is to _____ reheat _____.
8. Something not used is _____ unused _____.
9. Something used too much is _____ overused _____.
10. Something used too little is _____ underused _____.
11. Something used again is _____ reused _____.
12. To be the first to find out is to _____ discover _____.
13. To get well again is to _____ recover _____.
14. To be a spy is to work _____ undercover _____.
15. To pass through a cycle again is to _____ recycle _____.

CHALLENGE

Not all words with a prefix have base words that can stand alone. Underline the words below that do have base words.

recycle
disturb
reject
undercurrent

U N I V E R S A L   A C C E S S
Meeting Individual Needs

Logical Learners

Have students find what is missing in each "equation." Ask students to define each word to the right of the equal sign.

1. pre + heat = _____
_____ **+ heat = reheat**

2. dis + cover = _____
_____ **+ cover = uncover**

3. _____ **+ charge =**
undercharge
_____ **+ charge =**
overcharge

Auditory Learners

Have students write the base words **view, appear, place,** and **pay** on four index cards. As you give verbal clues, have students hold up the correct base word. Say:
To what base word would you add the prefix **re** *to make a word that means appear again?* **(reappear)** Provide similar clues for **preview, review, disappear, misplace, replace, repay, prepay, underpay,** and **overpay.**

Combine prefixes and base words to make as many words as you can. Write the words on the lines. If you are not sure about a word, look it up in the dictionary. Then use your words to answer the questions that follow.

Prefixes			
un	re	dis	under
pre	in	im	over
co	ex	il	ir
non	pro	semi	tri

Base Words			
circle	angle	cycle	claim
poisonous	charge	legal	star
cook	turn	possible	complete
view	write	responsible	kind

unkind	incomplete	illegal	return
recycle	impossible	irresponsible	overturn
review	rewrite	nonpoisonous	underwrite
discharge	overview	proclaim	reclaim
undercharge	costar	semicircle	tricycle
preview	exclaim	triangle	overcook

1. Which word means "not responsible"? _irresponsible_

2. Which word means "not poisonous"? _nonpoisonous_

3. Which word means "a half-circle"? _semicircle_

4. Which word means "not legal"? _illegal_

5. Which word means "to write over" or "revise"? _rewrite_

6. Which word means "to star with another person"? _costar_

7. Which word means "to view ahead of time"? _preview_

8. Which word means "a figure with three sides and three angles"? _triangle_

9. Which word means "not complete"? _incomplete_

10. Which word means "not kind"? _unkind_

LESSON 61: Base Words

Home Involvement Activity Some words that are spelled the same have a different sound and a different meaning. **Invalid** and **invalid** are examples. How do you pronounce each word? What does each word mean?

English-Language Learners/ESL

Write **overturn, return, triangle, unkind,** and **rewrite** on index cards and place them in a hat. Have a student choose a card, and pantomime the word for classmates to guess. Whoever guesses the word writes it on the board and identifies the prefix and the base word. That student selects the next card. Continue until all cards have been used.

Gifted Learners

Have students look for words with prefixes that relate to the theme, *Making a Difference.* Have them identify the prefix and the base word. Have students write new sentences with the words.

Learners With Special Needs

Additional strategies for supporting learners with special needs can be found on page 99L.

Practicing the Skill

● Read aloud the direction lines on pages 125–126. Work through the first item in each exercise as a group.

● On page 125, encourage students to look for clues. For example, in item 7, "to heat again," the word **again** suggests the prefix **re**.

● On page 126, encourage students to use the dictionary. Point out that students may find more words than they can write on the lines.

● For new or difficult words, such as **underwrite** or **discharge,** discuss how the prefix and base word offer clues to meaning.

Curriculum Connections

Spelling Link

● Make a pair of index cards for these words. Write the prefix on one card, and the base word on the other.

costar	**illegal**	**recover**
semicircle	**preview**	**exclaim**
triangle	**misplace**	**undercover**

● Mix the prefix cards and place them facedown in a row. Do the same with the base word cards.

● Have students turn over one card from each row. If the cards make an actual word, the student writes it on the board.

● Students may check their words in a dictionary.

Writing Link

● Have students write a poem about a personal acquaintance or someone mentioned in the unit lesson who has made a difference.

● The poem should contain words with prefixes.

● Have students exchange papers and circle the base words in the poem.

Observational Assessment

Check that students are able to form actual words by adding prefixes to base words.

Roots
-pos-, -pel-, -port-, -ject-, -spect-, -scrib-/-script-

Objectives

- **To recognize and identify the root of a word**
- **To understand that prefixes or suffixes can be added to roots**
- **To recognize the meanings of words made up of roots and prefixes or suffixes**

Warming Up

- Write the following sentence on the board.

  As **spectators** gathered nearby, the **inspector** peered through his **spectacles** and contemplated the **prospect** of solving the mystery.

- Have students find the part of each bold word that is the same. (**-spect-**) Then have them identify the prefixes and suffixes that are attached to this word part. Explain that **-spect-** is a root. Like prefixes and other word parts, roots have meaning; **-spect-** means "to see, look at, or examine."

- Ask students to find the bold words in a dictionary and discuss their meanings.

Teaching the Lesson

- Point out the difference between base words and roots. Explain that base words are words, but most roots are not words without a prefix or a suffix. A base word is like a root in that the same base word or root can be found in many different words.

- Sketch a tree on the board. Write **-spect-** on the trunk. On each branch, write a word from the *Warming Up* activity. Suggest that students look in the dictionary to find other words with the root **-spect-** and add them to the tree.

127

Name _____

Helpful Hints

A **root** is the main part of a word. Roots have meaning, but few roots can stand alone. Roots often become words when **prefixes** or **suffixes** are added to them. When you know the meaning of a root, you can often figure out the meaning of a word.

Root	Word	Definition
pos means "put" or "place"	deposit	= to put money in a bank
pel means "push" or "drive"	expel	= to push or drive out
port means "carry"	import	= to carry goods from one country into another
ject means "throw" or "force"	inject	= to force into

Read each word in the box. Place it correctly in the chart.

expel	porter	posture	transport	reject	subject
report	expose	propellor	composition	repel	project

1 Words with **pos**	2 Words with **pel**	3 Words with **port**	4 Words with **ject**
posture	expel	porter	reject
expose	propellor	transport	subject
composition	repel	report	project

Write the word from the chart that fits the definition.

5. to carry people or goods — transport

6. to force out of school — expel

7. to make known or reveal — expose

8. to refuse to accept — reject

WORK TOGETHER

With group members, browse through books or newspapers to find words formed from the roots in this lesson. List the words you find.

LESSON 62: Roots -pos-, -pel-, -port-, -ject-, -spect-, -scrib-/-script-   **127**

UNIVERSAL ACCESS
Meeting Individual Needs

Visual Learners

Have students complete the following "equations." Then have students write a sentence that illustrates the meaning of each new word. Students may wish to review earlier lessons about prefixes.

Prefix		Root		New Word
re	+	pel	=	_____
dis	+	pel	=	_____
im	+	port	=	_____
re	+	port	=	_____
pro	+	ject	=	_____
sub	+	ject	=	_____

Logical Learners

Encourage students to use their knowledge of prefixes and roots to determine the meaning of words such as **depose, impel, inscribe,** and **propose.** For example, the prefix **de-** means "take away" and the root **-pos-** means "put" or "place." By trying out different combinations, students can determine that **de-** + **-pos(e)** = "take away from a place," as in **depose** a king.

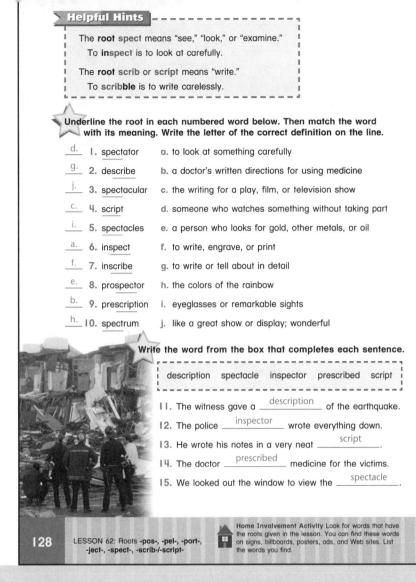

Underline the root in each numbered word below. Then match the word with its meaning. Write the letter of the correct definition on the line.

d. 1. spectator   a. to look at something carefully

g. 2. describe   b. a doctor's written directions for using medicine

j. 3. spectacular   c. the writing for a play, film, or television show

c. 4. script   d. someone who watches something without taking part

i. 5. spectacles   e. a person who looks for gold, other metals, or oil

a. 6. inspect   f. to write, engrave, or print

f. 7. inscribe   g. to write or tell about in detail

e. 8. prospector   h. the colors of the rainbow

b. 9. prescription   i. eyeglasses or remarkable sights

h. 10. spectrum   j. like a great show or display; wonderful

Write the word from the box that completes each sentence.

> description   spectacle   inspector   prescribed   script

11. The witness gave a _description_ of the earthquake.

12. The police _inspector_ wrote everything down.

13. He wrote his notes in a very neat _script_.

14. The doctor _prescribed_ medicine for the victims.

15. We looked out the window to view the _spectacle_.

128   LESSON 62: Roots -pos-, -pel-, -port-, -ject-, -spect-, -scrib-/-script-

Home Involvement Activity Look for words that have the roots given in the lesson. You can find these words on signs, billboards, posters, ads, and Web sites. List the words you find.

Practicing the Skill

- Review the meanings of the prefixes **ex-, re-, sub-, pro-,** and **com-.**
- Read aloud the directions on page 127 and 128. Do the first items in each exercise with the class. Then have students complete the exercises independently.

Intervention strategy

Turn to page 99K for an Intervention strategy designed to help students who need extra support with this lesson.

Curriculum Connections

Spelling Link

Read aloud the sentences below. Repeat the words in bold and have students write them in their notebooks. Ask students to check their spelling in a dictionary.

> The United States **exports** some food products and **imports** others.
>
> The doctor **scribbled** a **prescription**.
>
> The referee had to **expel** two noisy **spectators** from the gym.

Social Studies Link

Saudi Arabia is one of many nations that has large deposits of petroleum. They **export** it, or sell it and ship it away. Countries that do not produce enough petroleum **import** it, or have it shipped in. Tell students to find out which nations export most of the world's petroleum and which nations import it. Have students list the uses of petroleum in industry as well as in everyday life.

Observational Assessment

Note whether students are able to distinguish roots from base words.

English-Language Learners/ESL

Students who speak a Latin-based language may recognize common roots, such as **-port-** and **-pos-**. Have students share words from their language that have these roots and explain their meaning. Extend the activity by having the rest of the class learn these words.

Gifted Learners

Have students use the dictionary to find additional words with the roots from the lesson. Ask students to look for information about the meanings of the words, the etymology of the roots, and the relationships among different words with the same root. Students should post their findings in the classroom.

Learners with Special Needs

Additional strategies for supporting learners with special needs can be found on page 99L.

Roots
-duc-/-duct- and -tract-

Objectives

- To identify words with the roots -duc-/-duct- and -tract-
- To use words that have the roots -duc-/-duct- and -tract- correctly

Warming Up

- Write this rhyme on the board and read it aloud to students.

    A secret **contract** once was made—
    A railroad under ground was laid,
    With **conductors** brave and free
    Who led slaves north to liberty.

- Have a volunteer come to the board and underline the two words with the prefix **con-**. (**contract** and **conductors**)

- Ask: *What would be left of these words if the prefix **con-** were taken away?* (**tract** and **ductors**) Point out that if the ending -ors were taken away from **ductors**, what would be left is **duct**. Explain that the word parts -**duct**- (also -**duc**-) and -**tract**- are roots.

Teaching the Lesson

- In this lesson students will work with the roots -**duc**-/-**duct**- and -**tract**-. Have them read the words in the box on page 129. Point out that all of the words contain either the root -**duc**-/-**duct**- or the root -**tract**-.

- Ask students to name the prefixes that were added to these roots.

- Have a student read aloud the Helpful Hints on page 129. Discuss examples of how /-**duc**-/ may also mean "bring" (as in the word **produce**) and **tract** may also mean "drag" or "draw away" (**tractor, distract**).

129

Name _____

Helpful Hints

Here are more **roots** that appear in many English words. The **root** duc or duct means "lead" or "bring."

 reduce = to bring down in size or amount
 conduct = to lead

The **root** tract means "pull," "drag," or "draw back."

 tractor = a vehicle used for pulling farm machinery

Read each definition. Then find the verb in the box that matches it. Write the word on the line. Circle its root.

conduct	attract	reduce	subtract
extract	produce	distract	educate

1. to draw someone's attention away from something ___dis(tract)___

2. to lead an orchestra ___con(duct)___

3. to take away one number from another ___sub(tract)___

4. to create or bring forth ___pro(duc)e___

5. to pull toward oneself ___at(tract)___

6. to pull out a tooth ___ex(tract)___

7. to bring down in size or amount ___re(duc)e___

8. to lead to knowledge ___e(duc)ate___

Choose three words from above. Write a sentence for each word.

9. Sentences will vary. _____

10. _____

11. _____

CHALLENGE

The Latin roots duc/duct and tract mean "bring" and "pull." Use what you know about prefixes and these roots to write a sentence for each of these verbs:

 induct
 retract

UNIVERSAL ACCESS
Meeting Individual Needs

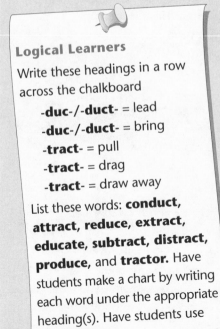

Logical Learners

Write these headings in a row across the chalkboard

- -**duc**-/-**duct**- = lead
- -**duc**-/-**duct**- = bring
- -**tract**- = pull
- -**tract**- = drag
- -**tract**- = draw away

List these words: **conduct, attract, reduce, extract, educate, subtract, distract, produce,** and **tractor.** Have students make a chart by writing each word under the appropriate heading(s). Have students use a dictionary.

Visual Learners

Write these sentences on the board:

To <u>bring down</u> costs, the club <u>took away</u> $75 from the planned budget. (**reduce, subtracted**)

The filmmaker signed a <u>written agreement</u> to <u>make</u> three movies. (**contract, produce**)

As volunteers read each sentence aloud, they should substitute a word with the root -**duc**-/-**duct**- or -**tract**- for each underlined word or phrase.

Use a word from the box to solve each clue. Write one letter in each space. Then copy all the letters that appear in the shaded boxes. Unscramble these letters to answer the question at the bottom of the page.

attract	retracts	deposit	distract	inspect
inscribe	spectator	produce	propel	respects

1. looks at someone with high regard

   r e s p e [c] t s

2. to pull toward oneself

   a t t [r] a c t

3. to create or bring forth

   p [r] o d u c e

4. to draw someone's attention away from something

   d i [s] t r a c t

5. to push or drive forward

   p r [o] p e l

6. to write, engrave, or print

   i [n] s c r i b e

7. pulls back or withdraws

   r e t r [a] c t s

8. to put money in a bank

   d e p [o] s i t

9. to look at something carefully

   i n s p e [c] t

10. someone who watches something without taking part

    s p e c [t] a t o r

Scrambled letters from boxes: crrtonaoct

Simon volunteers his time for a good cause. He helps a group to build houses for the homeless. He plans and organizes the building. He makes sure that people have the tools they need and that each task gets done.

Question: What is the name of Simon's job?

Answer: contractor

130

LESSON 63: Roots -duc-/-duct- and -tract-

Home Involvement Activity The word **produce** has different pronunciations and different meanings, depending on which syllable you accent. Pronounce this word and discuss its different meanings.

Practicing the Skill

● Read aloud the directions on page 129, and complete the first item together. Then have students finish exercises 2–8 independently. Call on volunteers to read sentences for items 9–11.

● Discuss the directions for page 130 and complete the first item together. Point out that there will be one boxed letter for each answer.

● Explain that students will have to unscramble these letters to answer the question next to the photograph.

● If the word **contractor** is unfamiliar to students, discuss its meaning. Point out that the suffix **-or** means "someone or something that performs an action." Also, point out that **contractor** contains the word **contract**, which in turn contains the root /-**tract**-/.

Curriculum Connections

Spelling Link

Hold a spelling bee. Have students spell one of the words below and then have them use the word in a sentence. To stay in the bee, they must be able to spell the word *and* use it correctly in a sentence.

conduct	tractor	educate
attract	reduce	extract
produce	distract	subtract

Science Link

● The verb **contract**—pronounced differently from the noun—has several meanings relating to science. For example, muscles **contract**. People **contract** diseases.

● Have students research the meanings of **contract** and share what they learn with the class. Discuss how the combined meanings of the prefix **con-** and the root -**tract**- apply to each meaning of **contract.**

Observational Assessment

Note whether students are able to use their knowledge of roots and prefixes to identify word meanings.

Syllables with Prefixes and Roots

Objectives

- To identify the number of syllables in words with prefixes
- To use words with prefixes correctly

Warming Up

- Write this rhyme on the board and read it aloud.

  Add a prefix, maybe two.
  It changes words around—
  The syllables, the meaning,
  Or even the whole sound.

- Review the idea that a prefix changes the meaning of a root or a base word.

- To illustrate the message of the rhyme, write the words **cook** and **overcook** on the board. Have a volunteer read the words and explain how the prefix changes the meaning of the word **cook**.

★ Teaching the Lesson

- Remind students that words can be divided into parts called **syllables** and that every syllable has one vowel sound.

- Return to the words **cook** and **overcook** to identify them as words with one and three syllables. Use a hyphen to show how **overcook** can be divided into syllables between the prefix and the base word (**over-cook**). Show that the prefix **over** has two syllables too, and that there are three syllables in the word **overcook**.

- Have students read aloud the Helpful Hint on page 131 as their classmates follow along silently.

Name _____

> **Helpful Hint**
>
> To separate words with prefixes into syllables, divide between the prefix and the root.
>
> ex-tract con-duct com-pose pro-ject re-in-spect

Read each word. Draw one line under the prefix. Draw two lines under the root. Then write the number of syllables in the word.

Word	Syllables	Word	Syllables
1. report	2	2. propellor	3
3. subject	2	4. subtraction	3
5. inspection	3	6. conductor	3
7. producer	3	8. disposal	3
9. composition	4	10. reject	2
11. contract	2	12. injection	3
13. prescription	3	14. subscribe	2
15. propose	3	16. export	2

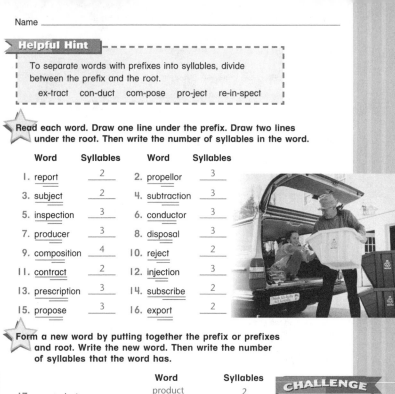

Form a new word by putting together the prefix or prefixes and root. Write the new word. Then write the number of syllables that the word has.

	Word	Syllables
17. pro + duct	product	2
18. super + scribe	superscribe	3
19. over + pro + duce	overproduce	4
20. dis + re + spect	disrespect	3
21. under + re + port	underreport	4
22. super + im + pose	superimpose	4

> **CHALLENGE**
>
> Circle the prefixes in the words below. Underline the roots. How many syllables does each word have? What does each word mean?
>
> underproduce
> oversubscribe

UNIVERSAL ACCESS
Meeting Individual Needs

Auditory Learners

Read the list of words below. After each word, have students hold up 1, 2, 3, or 4 fingers to show the number of syllables in the word. Then have a volunteer say the prefix, tell what the word means, and use the word in a sentence.

contract   **reject**

reduce   **composition**

inscribe   **overproduce**

disrespect   **compel**

subtract   **import**

Tactile Learners

Have partners use letter cards or tiles to spell words with prefixes and roots. Refer students to pages 127–131 for examples. Have them leave a space between syllables. Encourage students to use words with three and four syllables.

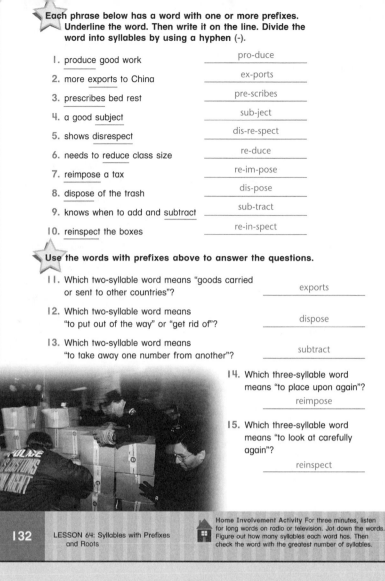

Each phrase below has a word with one or more prefixes. Underline the word. Then write it on the line. Divide the word into syllables by using a hyphen (-).

1. produce good work   pro-duce
2. more exports to China   ex-ports
3. prescribes bed rest   pre-scribes
4. a good subject   sub-ject
5. shows disrespect   dis-re-spect
6. needs to reduce class size   re-duce
7. reimpose a tax   re-im-pose
8. dispose of the trash   dis-pose
9. knows when to add and subtract   sub-tract
10. reinspect the boxes   re-in-spect

Use the words with prefixes above to answer the questions.

11. Which two-syllable word means "goods carried or sent to other countries"?   exports

12. Which two-syllable word means "to put out of the way" or "get rid of"?   dispose

13. Which two-syllable word means "to take away one number from another"?   subtract

14. Which three-syllable word means "to place upon again"?   reimpose

15. Which three-syllable word means "to look at carefully again"?   reinspect

Home Involvement Activity For three minutes, listen for long words on radio or television. Jot down the words. Figure out how many syllables each word has. Then check the word with the greatest number of syllables.

132   LESSON 64: Syllables with Prefixes and Roots

Practicing the Skill

● Read aloud the directions for the exercises on pages 131–132. Work together to complete the first item in the first three exercises.

● Have students find words in a dictionary which may be unfamiliar, such as **superscribe, disrespect, superimpose,** and **oversubscribe.**

Intervention Strategy

Turn to page 99K for an Intervention strategy designed to help students who need extra support with this lesson.

Curriculum Connections

Spelling Link
● Read each word aloud.

conduct	**export**	**project**
reinspect	**prescribe**	**propose**
subtract	**propellor**	**overproduce**

● Have a student say a word and spell it. Have another student write the word and divide it into syllables. Continue with remaining words.

Social Studies Link
● The amount of funding a government program gives to a community can be based on how many people require that program. Officials need an accurate count of the people in that community. If the population is **underreported,** they may receive less money than they are entitled to.

● Have students analyze the word **underreport**. First have them find the prefix and base word. Have students speculate about the word's meaning. (to report fewer than the true number)

● Have students research how an accurate count of people in a community is taken.

Observational Assessment

Note whether students can divide a word with a prefix into syllables.

English-Language Learners/ESL
Write each of the following words on index cards:

export, subscribe, injection, produce, subject, disrespect, reinspect, reduce, subtract

Have students pronounce each word and clap for each syllable in the word. Then have students sort the cards by the number of syllables in each word.

Gifted Learners
Challenge students to extend the second activity on page 132. Have them write five questions for the five words that were left over (**produce, prescribes, subject, reduce, disrespect.**) They should model their questions after the ones on the page.

Learners with Special Needs
Additional strategies for supporting learners with special needs can be found on page 99L.

132

Connecting Reading and Writing

Objectives

- To read a nonfiction piece and respond to it in writing
- To practice identifying a main idea and details, and synthesizing information
- To write a paragraph explaining something the students did to make a difference

Warming Up

Comprehension Skills

- Write the words *Making a Difference* on the board and ask students to make a list of people who have made a difference. They could be famous people, family members, or friends. Then ask students to sum up the main thing each person did to make a difference. Finally, ask for a few more **details** about the **main idea.**

- Remind students that **synthesizing** is putting together the ideas within a piece of writing and making sense of them.

Teaching the Lesson

- As students consider the first Reader's Response question, remind them that the main idea is the one idea that sums up the most important thing about the story.

- For the second question, remind students that details are small pieces of information.

- Encourage students to share answers to the third question.

Practicing the Skill

- Invite volunteers to read the directions and boxed words on page 134.

- Remind students to be specific when they tell what they have done.

133

Name _____

Read about a student, Dwaina Brooks, who has made a difference in the lives of the homeless. Then answer the questions that follow.

It's Our World, Too!
Stories of Young People Who Are Making a Difference
by Phillip Hoose

Each morning on her way to school, Dwaina Brooks saw the line of men and women outside a homeless shelter and soup kitchen in Dallas. At school, her fourth-grade class was doing a unit on homelessness. Once a week, students telephoned a shelter and talked with someone who was staying there. Dwaina would ask the person on the other end of the phone. "What do you need?" The answer was always "a home" or "a job." It never seemed as though she could do much. Then one afternoon, Dwaina talked with a young man who had been without a home for a long time.

"What do you need?" she asked him.

"I would love a really good meal again."

"Well, now," said Dwaina, brightening. "I *can* cook."

Dwaina tore into the house that night after school and found her mother, Gail. As usual, she was in the kitchen. "Mama," she said. "I need you to help me fix some stuff to take down to that shelter we call at school. Let's make up as much as we can. Sandwiches and chicken. Let's get everyone to do it. C'mon."

In a little more than two years, Dwaina has organized several thousand meals for unfortunate people in the Dallas area. She and her mother and the classmates who sometimes still join in have perfected the art of helping others and having fun at the same time.

Reader's Response

1. What is the main idea of this true story?
2. What details show you that Dwaina has made a difference?
3. If you could meet Dwaina, what would you ask her? Why?

Answers will vary.

LESSON 65: Connecting Reading and Writing
Comprehension—Main Idea and Details; Synthesize

133

UNIVERSAL ACCESS
Meeting Individual Needs

Musical Learners

You might give students the option of writing a ballad about the difference they made, rather than creating a straight description. You could also encourage students to look for the proper background music to play while reading aloud their description to the class.

Learners with Special Needs

Additional strategies for supporting learners with special needs can be found on pages 99L.

Kinesthetic Learners

Invite students to work in pairs. Each student takes a turn at acting out (with or without speech) the thing he or she did to make a difference. The student who is acting can use the writing partner as a role-play partner. Literally walking through the event might help students remember their experience more clearly and write about it more easily.

Dwaina Brooks has helped change the lives of thousands of homeless people. One way she did this was to make meals for the homeless. Another way was to explain to students and adults how they, too, could make a difference.

★ **Think of something you have done that has made a difference to a person, an animal, or your community. Explain in a paragraph what you did, why you did it, and how it helped. Be sure to speak in your own voice. Use at least two of these words.**

produce	important	impossible	overlook	understand	positive
report	position	object	subject	respect	attract

Answers will vary.

_____

_____

_____

_____

_____

_____

_____

_____

_____

Writer's Tips

Summarize your ideas at the end of your writing. Combine any sentences that you can. Remember to leave your audience with something to think about.

Speaker's Challenge

Give your paragraph as a speech to your class. Begin with your purpose. Speak loudly and clearly so that everyone can hear you. Make eye contact to keep your audience's interest. Leave time for questions and answers at the end of your speech.

134 LESSON 65: Connecting Reading and Writing
Comprehension—Main Idea and Details; Synthesize

English-Language Learners/ESL

Invite English-language learners to pair up with fluent English speakers and discuss the idea of making a difference. Make sure both students give plenty of examples of how fourth-graders can make a difference to others, to animals, or to the community. You might allow English-language learners to make an oral presentation on this topic.

Gifted Learners

Invite students to write a story with two endings. In the first, the main character chooses not to make a difference; in the second, the main character takes a more active role and events turn out differently. Students could also write this story in the form of a drama with two endings. Encourage them to share their work with the class.

The Writing Process

Discuss the purpose of this paragraph—to help readers understand exactly what each writer did that made a difference to a person, an animal, or a community. Ask students why people like to read about those who make a difference, and what readers gain from this type of information. Finally, ask for examples showing how some of the boxed words might be used.

Prewrite Have students begin by recalling a time when they made a difference. Students may wish to jot down notes or create an outline so that they remember all the key details about their actions.

Write Suggest that as they write, students picture an interested reader who is eager to learn how young people can make a difference.

Revise Have students read their paragraphs to a writing partner. Encourage partners to ask questions that occur to them, which writers can use for feedback.

Proofread Remind students to read their work carefully to check for errors in grammar, punctuation, and spelling.

Publish Have students copy their final drafts onto page 144 and invite volunteers to read their paragraphs aloud.

Computer Connection Suggest that students working on word processors might want to use the "Insert" mode rather than the "Typeover" mode. Make sure students understand that in "Type-over," each letter or space that is typed takes the place of any letter or space that follows it. In "Insert," however, students can add new words without automatically deleting the words that come after.

Portfolio Have students add their paragraphs about making a difference to their portfolios.

Reviewing and Assessing
Prefixes, Roots, and Syllables

Objective

To review and assess prefixes, roots, and syllables

Warming Up

● Write the following words on the board: **dishonest, recycle, impatient, expel, misplace, overseas, subtract, triangle, nonfiction,** and **conduct.**

● Have a volunteer draw a line between the prefix and the base word or root of each. Tell another student to circle the base words and underline the roots (-**pel**-, -**tract**-, and -**duc**-/-**duct**- are roots). Remind students that base words such as **honest** and **cycle** are words, whereas roots such as -**pel**- are parts of words.

Teaching the Lesson

● Before students begin, draw their attention to the word-part chart at the top of page 135. Have a volunteer identify the names of the word parts in each column. Point out that the word parts in column 3 are called suffixes and will be treated in depth in the next unit of the book.

● Explain that students will be using the chart to make up words. To illustrate, create a word using the code "H1 + F2." Show sudents how to find the H1 (**pro**) and F2 (**pel**) positions on the chart and add the word parts to create **propel.**

● For the exercise on page 136, suggest that students try each possible answer in the passage to see which word's meaning best fits the surrounding context.

Name _____

⭐ Look at the word-part chart below. You can use it to form many words. For example, you can form the word **respect** by combining B1 + G2.

	1	2	3
A	un	duct	able
B	re	tract	er
C	dis	port	ion
D	pre	pos	ing
E	in	ject	al
F	im	pel	ed
G	ex	spect	or
H	pro	scrib	less
I	sub	script	ment

⭐ Use the word-part chart to decode these words. On the lines, write the words you get from these letters and numbers.

1. I1 + B2 ___subtract___
2. E1 + G2 ___inspect___
3. G1 + F2 ___expel___
4. B2 + G3 ___tractor___
5. I1 + I2 + C3 ___subscription___
6. C1 + B2 ___distract___
7. B1 + C2 + B3 ___reporter___
8. H1 + E2 ___project___
9. H1 + D2 + E3 ___proposal___
10. B1 + A2 + C3 ___reduction___
11. B1 + E2 + F3 ___rejected___
12. D1 + I2 + C3 ___prescription___

⭐ Use the word-part chart to encode these words. Write the letters and the numbers on the lines.

13. export ___G1+C2___
14. production ___H1+A2+C3___
15. subject ___I1+E2___
16. disposable ___C1+D2+A3___
17. importing ___F1+C2+D3___
18. inscription ___E1+I2+C3___

UNIVERSAL ACCESS
Meeting Individual Needs

Visual Learners

On a transparency or on chart paper, prepare a word-part chart like the one on page 135 and display it for the class. Have students work in teams to make up as many words as possible from the word parts shown. The team that creates the most legitimate words wins the game. Nonsense words will not count toward the final totals.

Kinesthetic Learners

Write each of the prefixes taught in the unit on a slip of paper and put the slips in a box. Invite students, one at a time, to come up to the front of the room and choose a slip of paper. They should read the prefix aloud, think of a word beginning with that prefix, and act it out for the class to guess. Suggest that students choose words whose meanings can be conveyed by body movement or pantomime.

Learners with Special Needs

Additional strategies for supporting learners with special needs can be found on page 99L.

Read the passage. For each numbered blank, there is a choice of words below. Fill in the circle of the word that correctly completes the sentence. Then write the word on the line.

Oseola McCarty grew up poor. She quit school after the sixth grade to care for a sick aunt. She earned money by washing and ironing other people's clothes. It was dull work.

Yet she did it without (1) __complaint__.

When she was 87, Oseola went to visit the University of Southern Mississippi. She could not have gone there as a girl. African Americans could not go there then. Oseola gave the college $150,000 to help poor students. "I'm too old to get an education, but they can," she said.

How did Oseola get so much money? She (2) __prepared__ for the future. She made weekly (3) __deposits__ into her bank account.

Oseola might have been (4) __unknown__ to most people. However, by the time she died at age 91, the world knew she had made a difference.

1. ○ compliment ● complaint ○ comma
2. ● prepared ○ repaired ○ retired
3. ○ details ○ delays ● deposits
4. ○ unbroken ● unknown ○ uneasy

Read the passage again to answer these questions. Circle the letter of the correct answer.

5. How did Oseola McCarty make a living?
   a. She was a teacher.
   b. She worked in a bank.
   c. She did people's laundry.
   d. She worked at a college.

6. Why did she give money to the university?
   a. She had once been a student there.
   b. She wanted to help others.
   c. She disliked having so much money.
   d. She was retired.

Extend & Apply

Oseola saved money for the future. What will you save money for someday?

Reteaching Activities

Mix and Match

Give students the list of word parts shown below. Have students create as many words as they can by mixing and matching roots and prefixes. Suggest that students look in a dictionary to verify any words they are not sure about.

Prefixes	Roots
re	port
im	pos(e)
ex	tract
sub	scrib(e)
dis	pel
pro	ject
in	spect

Chain of Words

Have students sit in a circle. Ask a volunteer to say a word made up of a prefix and a base word or a root (e.g., **discover**). The player next to him or her then says a word with either the same prefix, base word, or root (e.g., **dishonest** or **uncover**). Students may wish to write the words down as they play.

Assessing the Skill

Check Up The exercises on page 135 give students practice building words by combining roots, prefixes, and suffixes. Page 136 will help you assess students' mastery of using word parts and context to determine word meaning.

Read aloud both sets of directions. Make sure students understand that they must fill in the circle of the correct word and write the word on the line provided.

> **Intervention Strategy** Turn to page 99K for an Intervention Strategy designed to help students who need extra support with this lesson.

Observational Assessment As students work, check to make sure they understand how the word-part chart is coded and how to use the code to find word parts. Review your recorded observations from the other lessons in the unit. Evaluate specific improvements as well as overall progress by comparing your earlier notes with your current observations.

Student Skills Assessment Record each student's progress in understanding word parts using the checklist on page 99H.

Writing Conference As you conclude the unit, meet with students individually. Review portfolio samples and any other written work from earlier in the unit. Have students compare early efforts, such as their letter to a pen pal on page 106, with their latest writing, such as the paragraph about making a difference on page 134. Help students identify words with prefixes and base words or roots and make sure those words are spelled correctly. Ask students to recall a favorite piece of writing in their Home Portfolios and invite them to share it with their classmates.

Group together students who need further instruction on word parts and have them complete the *Reteaching Activities*. Turn to page 99C for other assessment methods.

Suffixes and Syllables

Theme: Scientists

STANDARDS

- ✪ Read expository text with grade-appropriate fluency and understand its content
- ✪ Develop and strengthen vocabulary by reading and studying words in context
- ✪ Use knowledge of suffixes, roots, and base words to determine the meanings of new words
- ✪ Divide words with suffixes into syllables

OBJECTIVES

- ▶ To appreciate nonfiction works about scientists
- ▶ To determine the meanings of words with suffixes
- ▶ To identify suffixes in words
- ▶ To write words with suffixes
- ▶ To divide words with suffixes into syllables

LESSONS

Assessment Strategies

An overview of assessment strategies appears on page **137C.** It offers multiple suggestions for ways in which teachers can use a variety of unit-specific assessment tools, including **Pretests** and **Post Tests** (pages **137D–137G**), the **Activity Master** (page **137M**), and the **Assessment Checklist** (page **137H**).

Thematic Teaching

In Unit 5, students will learn about suffixes. Students encounter words containing suffixes in the context of nonfiction selections and exercises related to the theme *Scientists*.

Students begin their investigation of the *Scientists* theme by creating a journal of scientists. The resource list on this page provides titles of multimedia materials that celebrate the scientists and discoveries that have changed our lives. Many of the Teacher's Edition lessons in this unit open with poems, riddles, or tongue twisters related to *Scientists*. These "hooks" can spark students' interest both in the theme and in the play of words.

Curriculum Integration

Social Studies

Students research scientific discoveries on page **138,** look for features of our planet on page **140,** research cats in history on page **146,** identify languages on page **154,** list places to find ancient artifacts on page **160,** read newspapers on page **162,** research a country on page **164,** and research inventions on page **170**.

Science

Students write a description of a place as seen through the eyes of a scientist on page **168.**

Math

Students make up arithmetic problems on page **148.**

Optional Learning Activities

Meeting Individual Needs

Most of the Teacher's Edition lessons offer activities for students with distinct learning styles or particular intellectual or sensory strengths. The activities are labeled for learners with the following "styles": **Visual, Kinesthetic, Auditory, Logical, Musical,** and **Tactile.**

Multicultural Connections

Students will research discoveries in the field of astronomy on page **138,** write travelogues on page **142,** research their own heritage on page **144,** identify nationalities of scientists on page **156,** and discuss foods from different countries on page **172.**

Word Study Strategies

Pages **137I–137J** offer an array of activities that give students practice using strategies such as word sorting, word building, and dividing words into syllables.

Universal Access

Exercises tailored to meet the needs of **English-Language Learners** and **Gifted Learners** can be found in almost every Teacher's Edition lesson. Strategies designed to help **Learners with Special Needs,** such as students with Attention Deficit Disorder, can be found on page **137L.**

Intervention

Page **137K** offers **Intervention Strategies** designed to help students understand the concepts taught in **Lessons 69, 72,** and **83.**

Reteaching

Students hunt for suffixes and complete equations on page **152,** sort words and make a word chain on page **166,** and use suffixes to make connections on page **176.**

Technology

Page **137N** offers activities for students who enjoy working with computers or audio/video equipment. In addition, **Computer Connections**—tips designed to support students who use a word processor—can be found on pages **150, 158,** and **174.**

RESOURCES

Books
Pinkney, Andrea Davis. *Dear Benjamin Banneker,* Voyager Picture Book, 1998.
Sobol, Donald J. *Wright Brothers at Kitty Hawk,* NY: Scholastic, 1986.

Videos
From the Earth to the Moon, HBO Home Video.

This Is America, Charlie Brown: The Great Inventors, Paramount.

CDs
Muppets from Space: The Ultimate Muppet Trip, Sony/Wonder.
One Light One Sun, Uni/Rounder

In Unit 5, students study word parts: suffixes and syllables. To evaluate students' mastery of these skills, use any or all of the assessment methods suggested below.

Pretests and Post Tests

The tests on pages **137D–137G** objectively assess how well students understand suffixes, base words, and syllables. These tests may be used at the beginning of the unit as an informal diagnostic tool or at the end of the unit as a more formal measure of students' progress.

Observational Assessment

Opportunities for observing students as they work are suggested throughout the unit. Lesson-specific recommendations are included for assessing students' work. Check students' written work on a regular basis to see whether they are applying what they learn to their own writing.

Using Technology

The Technology activities on page **137N** may also help to evaluate students whose language skills are best shown when using computers or audio/video equipment.

Performance Assessment

Have students divide their papers into three columns with the headings: **2 Syllables, 3 Syllables,** and **4 Syllables.** Have them write the following words in the correct columns: **wisdom, comfortable, earliest, neighborhood, ability, kindness, careful, seriously,** and **importance.** Then have them circle the base word and underline the suffix in each word.

Portfolio Assessment

The portfolio icon in the lesson plans indicates an opportunity for students to add to the growing body of work in their portfolios.

Each student's portfolio will be different and should contain pieces that the student feels represent his or her best work. You may wish to give students additional opportunities to add to their portfolios.

Rubric for Writing

	Always	Sometimes	Never
Uses capitalization, punctuation, spelling, and grammar appropriately			
Creates a variety of sentences containing words with suffixes and multisyllabic words with prefixes and suffixes			
Creates a clear, well-developed explanation with a beginning, middle, and end			
Conveys purpose and meaning through writing			

Answer Key

Page 137D
1. ment
2. ful
3. ness
4. ive
5. ly
6. age
7. ish
8. able
9. ion
10. taller
11. eastern
12. springlike
13. division
14. attendance
15. humidity
16. 4
17. 4
18. 3
19. 2
20. 4
21. 2
22. 3
23. 2
24. 4
25. 2

Page 137E
1. y 2
2. er 2
3. ment 3
4. ful 3
5. able 4
6. age 2
7. ly 3
8. en 2
9. y 2
10. est 2
11. tion 3
12. ive 3
13. ness 2
14. age 2
15. y 2
16. ity 5
17. ship 2
18. ish 2
19. or 2
20. ance 3
21. ish 2
22. ern 2
23. ship 3
24. ward 2
25. ist 3
26. er 3
27. dom 2
28. ism 4
29. ance 2
30. less 2

Page 137F
1. y
2. ly
3. less
4. able
5. en
6. ion
7. ish
8. ward
9. dom
10. hotter
11. astronomer
12. rotation
13. powerful
14. remarkable
15. luggage
16. 4
17. 2
18. 4

19. 3
20. 2
21. 3
22. 2
23. 4
24. 2
25. 2

Page 137G
1. er 2
2. ism 4
3. dom 2
4. ance 3
5. ship 4
6. less 2
7. ion 3
8. ly 2
9. ward 2
10. ly 3
11. est 2
12. ion 3
13. en 2
14. ern 2
15. tion 3
16. sion 3
17. er 2
18. y 2
19. able 3
20. ly 2
21. age 3
22. ish 2
23. ment 2
24. est 2
25. ist 3
26. or 4
27. dom 2
28. ful 2
29. ish 2
30. en 2

Fill in the circle next to the suffix that can be added to each base word.

1 argue____	◯ ment ◯ ful ◯ less	2 beauty____	◯ ment ◯ ful ◯ less	3 aware____	◯ ment ◯ less ◯ ness
4 create____	◯ y ◯ ive ◯ age	5 quick____	◯ y ◯ ly ◯ age	6 post____	◯ y ◯ ly ◯ age
7 child____	◯ able ◯ sion ◯ ish	8 profit____	◯ able ◯ sion ◯ ish	9 rotate____	◯ ion ◯ sion ◯ ish

Underline the word that correctly completes the sentence.

10. A tree is tall, but a mountain is **(taller, tallest)**.

11. John lives in the **(easten, eastern)** part of Colorado.

12. The warm sun made the winter day feel **(springy, springlike)**.

13. My brother helps me with long **(division, divition)**.

14. Listen for your name when the teacher takes **(attendant, attendance)**.

15. Today the weather contained high levels of **(humidity, humidy)**.

Say each word. Write the number of syllables in each word.

16. available _____   **17.** development _____

18. thirstiest _____   **19.** friendship _____

20. fascination _____   **21.** lengthen _____

22. parenthood _____   **23.** backward _____

24. violinist _____   **25.** actor _____

Possible score on Unit 5 Pretest 1 is 25. Score _____

Pretest 2   Name _____

Underline the suffix and write the number of syllables next to each word.

1. wavy _____   2. faster _____

3. measurement _____   4. wonderful _____

5. enjoyable _____   6. marriage _____

7. happily _____   8. straighten _____

9. funny _____   10. youngest _____

11. election _____   12. negative _____

13. vastness _____   14. baggage _____

15. noisy _____   16. electricity _____

17. hardship _____   18. boyish _____

19. sailor _____   20. performance _____

21. Polish _____   22. northern _____

23. scholarship _____ 24. outward _____

25. scientist _____   26. producer _____

27. freedom _____   28. criticism _____

29. guidance _____   30. painless _____

Possible score on Unit 5 Pretest 2 is 30. Score _____

Fill in the circle next to the suffix that can be added to each base word.

1 cloud_____	○ ness ○ ful ○ y	2 soft_____	○ ly ○ ful ○ less	3 hope_____	○ ment ○ less ○ ness
4 depend_____	○ y ○ able ○ age	5 short_____	○ ive ○ en ○ le	6 champ_____	○ ion ○ ly ○ age
7 England_____	○ able ○ sion ○ ish	8 west_____	○ able ○ ward ○ ish	9 king_____	○ ship ○ most ○ dom

Underline the word that correctly completes the sentence.

10. Which planet is **(hottest, hotter)** Venus or Mars?

11. Galileo was a famous **(astronomer, astronomist)**.

12. It takes twenty-four hours for Earth to make a full **(rotative, rotation)**.

13. You must use a **(powerless, powerful)** telescope to see the outer planets.

14. Myths about the constellations are quite **(remarklike, remarkable)**.

15. Ray always packs a telescope in his **(luggage, luggish)**.

Say each word. Write the number of syllables in each word.

16. observation _____

17. flutist _____

18. authority _____

19. inventive _____

20. slowly _____

21. yellowish _____

22. kinship _____

23. valuable _____

24. harmless _____

25. chatty _____

Possible score on Unit 5 Post Test I is 25. Score _____

Post Test 2

Name _____

Underline the suffix and write the number of syllables next to each word.

1. singer _____

2. socialism _____

3. wisdom _____

4. importance _____

5. citizenship _____

6. thoughtless _____

7. direction _____

8. hardly _____

9. westward _____

10. finally _____

11. biggest _____

12. attraction _____

13. darken _____

14. southern _____

15. subtraction _____

16. decision _____

17. smarter _____

18. salty _____

19. laughable _____

20. neatly _____

21. orphanage _____

22. reddish _____

23. pavement _____

24. deepest _____

25. scientist _____

26. operator _____

27. kingdom _____

28. graceful _____

29. English _____

30. widen _____

Possible score on Unit 5 Post Test 2 is 30. Score _____

Student Name _____

UNIT FIVE
STUDENT SKILLS ASSESSMENT CHECKLIST

☑ Assessed   ☒ Retaught   ☐ Mastered

- ☐ Suffixes **-er** and **-est**
- ☐ Suffixes **-ful, -ment, -ness, -ly, -y**
- ☐ Suffixes **-like, -able, -age**
- ☐ Suffixes and Syllables
- ☐ Suffixes **-ity, -ive, -ion, -sion, -tion**
- ☐ Suffixes **-en, -ern, -ish**
- ☐ Suffixes and Syllables
- ☐ Suffixes **-ward, -less, -ship**
- ☐ Suffixes **-er, -or, -ist**
- ☐ Suffixes **-ance, -dom, -ism**
- ☐ Suffixes **-some, -hood, -most**
- ☐ More Than One Prefix or Suffix
- ☐ Spelling Rules for Adding Suffixes

TEACHER COMMENTS

In Unit 5, students study word parts: suffixes, base words, and syllables. To give students opportunities to master word study strategies, use any or all of the activities suggested below.

Suffix Build-Up

Add the suffix in parentheses to each base word and write the new words on the lines. Then, use the words to complete the chart below.

1. great (-**er**) _____
2. early (-**er**) _____
3. fun (-**y**) _____
4. clear (-**ly**) _____
5. beauty (-**ful**) _____
6. like (-**ness**) _____
7. marry (-**age**) _____
8. sad (-**en**) _____
9. forget (-**able**) _____

Word Meanings

Circle the word that completes each sentence. Write the word on the line.

Double	Drop	No Change
_____	_____	_____
_____	_____	_____
_____	_____	_____

1. She is an _____ person.

   attractive   **attraction**   **attract**

2. The boat made a safe _____ in rough weather.

   passable   **passage**   **passion**

3. A glass tabletop is quite _____ .

   break   **breakable**   **breakage**

4. The driver wore a seatbelt for _____ .

   protection   **protective**   **protect**

Suffix Know-How

Circle the suffix in each word in the box. Then rewrite each sentence using a word from the box that means the same as the underlined words in each sentence.

inventor	sharpen	westward
swimmer	cartoonist	reddish

1. The <u>person who invents</u> developed a new type of engine.

   _____

2. The explorer traveled <u>toward the west</u> along the harbor.

   _____

3. I will <u>make sharp</u> my new pencil.

   _____

4. Our cheeks were <u>somewhat red</u> from the cold air.

   _____

5. The <u>person who draws cartoons</u> worked for a newspaper.

   _____

6. The <u>person who swims</u> dove into the deep end of the pool.

   _____

Word-part Match-up

Add the suffix to each base word to write three new words. Then, write a contextual sentence using one of the new words.

-dom   king   bore   free

_____ _____ _____

sentence: _____

-ance   guide   import   insure

_____ _____ _____

sentence: _____

-some   trouble   two   lone

_____ _____ _____

sentence: _____

-hood   child   neighbor   parent

_____ _____ _____

sentence: _____

-most   inner   top   outer

_____ _____ _____

sentence: _____

Word Equations

Solve each equation by writing the new word on the line.

1. south + ern + most = _____
2. re + fill + able = _____
3. co + work + er = _____
4. un + manage + able = _____
5. care + less + ness = _____
6. dis + grace + ful = _____
7. thought + less + ly = _____
8. over + achieve +ment = _____
9. boy + hood = _____
10. non + pay +ment = _____

Syllables With Suffixes

Identify the word in each sentence that contains a suffix. Write the word on the line. Then underline the base word, circle the suffix, and write the number of syllables.

1. Fresh eggs were not available.

    _____

2. He is part of a management team.

    _____

3. This typist is very fast.

    _____

4. Her green eyes are catlike.

    _____

5. That bowl of soup is the hottest.

    _____

6. Clues to a puzzle are helpful.

    _____

7. Flowers brought her happiness.

    _____

8. There are many ideas in development.

    _____

9. The class election will take place on Friday.

    _____

10. The coach said the score of the game was predictable. _____

11. We had a discussion before the game.

    _____

12. The athletes were graceful.

    _____

13. I sat on a comfortable bench.

    _____

14. There was electricity in the air.

    _____

15. It was a domelike arena.

    _____

	69 Suffixes	**72** Suffixes	**83** More Than One Prefix or Suffix
Problem	Student confuses the suffixes -**ment** and -**ness,** which share a meaning.	Student has difficulty remembering the meanings of various suffixes.	Student is confused by words with more than one prefix or suffix.
Intervention Strategies	• Help students make a Venn diagram to compare and contrast the meanings of the suffixes –**ment** and –**ness.** Then have students select words from the lesson that contain these suffixes to write contextual sentences. • Encourage students to make a section in their word-study notebook for suffixes covered in this unit. Have them write each suffix, its meaning, and words that contain the suffix from the lesson.	• Write a list of words on the board that contain the suffixes covered in this lesson. Have a student highlight the suffix in each word. Next, have a student define each suffix and then define each word using the suffix's meaning and the base word. • Tell students that learning suffixes will facilitate defining words. Write an unfamiliar word, such as **fluidity**, on the board. Tell students that **fluid** means **liquid.** Then have the students define **fluidity.** (state of being liquid)	• Give students more practice with word parts. Review definitions of the prefixes and suffixes in this lesson. Separate one of the words from the lesson into prefix, base, and suffix. Have students first define the prefix and/or the suffix and then define the whole word. Ask students to make two different words from a base word, such as **happy**, by adding a prefix and then a suffix to it. (**happiness, unhappiness**)

The following activities offer strategies for helping students with special needs to participate in selected exercises in Unit 5.

Memory Deficits

Suffixes

Some students have difficulty recalling information when exposed to new or extremely detailed material. As you begin teaching this unit, tell these students that they are going to categorize words according to the suffix it contains in their notebooks.

- At the beginning of each lesson, have students list in their notebooks the new suffixes that are introduced. **Lesson 68** introduces the suffixes **–er** and **–est.**

- Ask students to write a suffix and its meaning at the top of each page. Tell students to find words in the lesson that contain the listed suffixes and write them on the appropriately labeled page. Students should continue this activity for each new suffix that is introduced in the lessons.

- At the end of the unit, have students review the suffixes and definitions listed in their notebooks. Ask them to add an additional word (not included in the unit) to each suffix page. Have them write a sentence for the additional words.

Attention Deficit Disorder (ADD)

Suffixes

Students with ADD are often unable to finish assignments in the allotted time. Feeling rushed they may use only one element in a word as a cue to its meaning or interpret an entire sentence in terms of a few words. The exercise at the top of page **145** requires students to read carefully to determine which word in a phrase contains a suffix.

- Help students read more deliberately by encouraging them to create illustrations for phrases that describe something visual.

- After students have made their sketches, tell them to reread the phrase. As they write words that belong in the blanks, ask them to read each word softly while tapping the number of syllables in the word.

- When they complete an item, encourage them to proceed to the next item on the page.

Conceptual Deficits

Suffixes

Students who have difficulty generalizing may have trouble with suffixes that change concrete adjectives into abstract nouns, such as **-ness.** Engage students' sense of sight to teach this concept.

- Draw the outline of an apple on the board with a piece of red chalk. Use the red chalk to shade an area on the board next to the outline of the apple.

- Ask students which drawing shows an object that happens to be red and which shows **redness.** Draw several other red objects. Use the shaded area of red chalk to demonstrate that, even though it is not a solid thing, **redness** exists separately from objects as an idea.

- Discuss with students other qualities that can be possessed by the apple, such as roundness and smoothness. Ask students to suggest other words that end in **-ness.**

Visual Perceptual/Visual Motor Deficits

Syllables

Students who have poor visual acuity may not notice the difference between groups of letters that include vowels and groups that include only consonants. The following strategy may help them identify syllables

- Give students a list of all the vowels (including **y**), each printed in a different color. Then give students colored markers, and have them circle each vowel in the bold words on page **149** with the correct color from the list you gave them.

- Have students count each circled vowel as a syllable. When two vowels are adjacent, **(cre̲a̲tive)** students tap out the word to ascertain if the vowels should be divided into separate syllables or remain together as one syllable.

Name _____

Connect the puzzle pieces to make a new word. Then write the word on the line. Some words may need spelling changes.

1. easy + er _____

2. humid + ity _____

3. tense + ion _____

4. dark + ness _____

5. safe + ly _____

6. skin + y _____

7. enjoy + able _____

8. store + age _____

9. lucky + est _____

10. perform + ance _____

11. awe + some _____

12. write + er _____

13. England + ish _____

14. science + ist _____

15. marry + age _____

16. relate + ive _____

17. beauty + ful _____

18. develop + ment _____

19. educate + ion _____

20. length + en _____

21. life + like _____

22. west + ern _____

23. thought + less _____

24. wise + dom _____

25. hero + ism _____

26. citizen + ship _____

27. child + hood _____

28. up + ward _____

29. act + or _____

30. care + ful _____

Videotape Scientific Experiments

Ask students to videotape scientific experiments. If a camera is not available, have them demonstrate the experiments "live" for another class.

- Have students write on a slip of paper a brief description of an experiment that they have successfully conducted. Select the experiments to be demonstrated by putting the slips into a bag and have three volunteers each select a slip of paper.

- Organize the class into three groups. Put the three selected slips of paper into another bag. Have a representative from each group select one from the bag. Then have the members of the groups select one person to complete each of the following tasks: conduct the experiment, give an explanation, write a step-by-step description of the process, and videotape the experiment.

- Encourage students to work together to write the explanation and description of the experiment. Ask students to include words with the suffixes: **-ity, -sion, -tion, -ive** in their explanations and demonstrations. A list of these words might include: **completion, conduction, fluidity, rotation, electricity, active, negative, tension,** and **reaction.** Have students underline these words and explain the meaning of their suffixes.

Tape a Game Show

 Invite students to tape a game show entitled *Mystery Scientist.*

- Organize students into groups. Brainstorm a list of different kinds of scientists. Based on the number of groups, select from the list different types of scientists such as: physicist, geneticist, inventor, and astronomer and write them on slips of paper. Place the slips in a bag. Have a student from each group choose a slip of paper. Then have the groups research the different scientists.

- Each group should determine who will be the mystery scientist. The mystery scientist records a riddle about his or her work for the class to guess. For example, the geneticist might say, "I can turn one thing into two things." Have a student record the other members of the class while they take turns asking "yes" or "no" questions such as: "Is one of the things a living thing?" Then have the class replay the tape to determine the identity of the mystery scientist.

- Point out the suffixes **-ist, -er,** and **-or** that signify a profession or function. Ask students to make a list of jobs that end with these suffixes. (teacher, doctor, pharmacist)

Create a Science Class Newsletter

 Have groups of students write a brief article about one of their science activities. Then, have students organize the articles on a computer newsletter program and include graphics.

- Have the groups discuss the variety of activities they plan to write about. The groups can also choose the graphics that would be appropriate to each article—diagrams, graphs, photographs, and so on.

- Ask them to look through their articles for words with the suffixes they have studied in Unit 5. For example, they may have used words such as: **negative, measurement, pollution,** and **magnetism**. Tell them to list the words that contain suffixes in their articles and to write a definition of each word and its suffix.

Introduction to
Suffixes and Syllables

Objectives

- To enjoy a piece of nonfiction related to the theme *Scientists*

- To identify suffixes

Starting with Literature

Ask a student to read "The Sky Is the Limit" aloud for the class. On the board, write this word from the story: **scientist.** Mask the base word and tell students that the letters **-ist** make up a word part called a suffix. Ask them to suggest other words with the suffix **-ist. (artist, dentist)**

Critical Thinking

- Suggest that students reread the selection to answer the first two questions.

- Encourage students to share their own opinions in response to the third question and give details or reasons that support their opinions.

Introducing the Skill

Write the word **careful** on the board. Have a volunteer circle the suffix. Ask: *What word is left when you take away the suffix?* **(care)** Tell students that **care,** like any word to which a prefix or suffix is added, is called a base word.

Practicing the Skill

- Tell students that three common suffixes are **-ful, -ness,** and **-less.** Give a few examples of words with these suffixes.

- Have students play "Suffix Beat-the-Clock" by giving them a fixed amount of time to list as many words as they can that end with the suffixes **-ful, -ness,** and **-less.**

The Sky Is the Limit

Look up at the night sky on a clear evening. If you know where to look, you will see planets like Venus and Jupiter. Look again later, and you will see that these planets have moved.

For many years, people saw that stars and planets were in different parts of the sky at different times. They thought that the earth was the center of the universe. They believed that the moon, the sun, and all the planets moved around the earth.

Then along came Nicolaus Copernicus, a Polish astronomer. He did not think that the earth was the center of the universe. Instead, he believed that the sun was the center of the Solar System. Copernicus thought that the earth and the other planets revolved around the sun. He worked carefully to prove that his idea was correct. Yet even when he had it all figured out, Copernicus knew that his new ideas would make some people angry.

We know now that Copernicus was right. We know that the planets in our Solar System all move around the sun. We also know that scientists are proving new ideas all the time.

? Critical Thinking

1. What did Copernicus believe?

2. Why did he think his idea would make some people angry?

3. Would you be angry at someone for having an idea that was different from your own? Give reasons for your answer.

1. Copernicus believed that the sun was the center of the Solar System.
2. Answers will vary.
3. Answers will vary.

Theme Activity

WHO'S WHO IN SCIENCE Invite students to create a class directory of famous scientists throughout history. Have them work together to learn about men and women who have become part of history by making valuable contributions in various scientific fields. Suggest that students conduct their research using textbooks, reference books, biographies, the Internet, and other resources.

Once students have gathered the information they need, have them write entries giving the scientist's name, telling when he or she lived, and describing the scientist's most important discoveries, inventions, or contributions. Encourage students to include the suffixes taught in Unit 5 in their entries. Some may wish to illustrate their entries with pictures of the scientist, drawings, or diagrams. Help students compile their entries into a class "Who's Who in Science" for all to use.

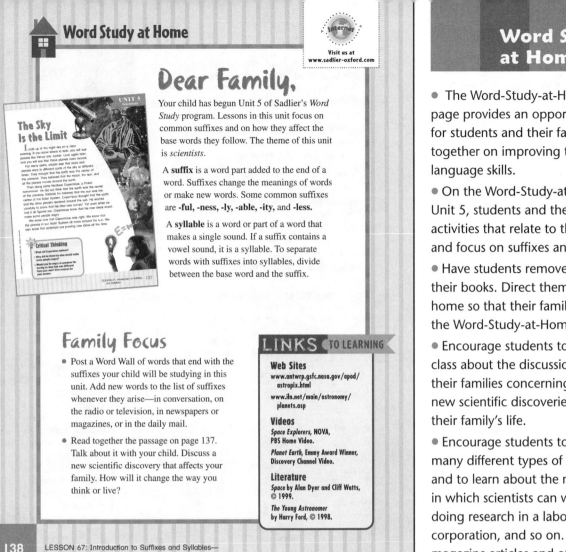

Word Study at Home

Dear Family,

Your child has begun Unit 5 of Sadlier's *Word Study* program. Lessons in this unit focus on common suffixes and on how they affect the base words they follow. The theme of this unit is *scientists*.

A **suffix** is a word part added to the end of a word. Suffixes change the meanings of words or make new words. Some common suffixes are **-ful, -ness, -ly, -able, -ity,** and **-less.**

A **syllable** is a word or part of a word that makes a single sound. If a suffix contains a vowel sound, it is a syllable. To separate words with suffixes into syllables, divide between the base word and the suffix.

Family Focus

- Post a Word Wall of words that end with the suffixes your child will be studying in this unit. Add new words to the list of suffixes whenever they arise—in conversation, on the radio or television, in newspapers or magazines, or in the daily mail.

- Read together the passage on page 137. Talk about it with your child. Discuss a new scientific discovery that affects your family. How will it change the way you think or live?

LINKS TO LEARNING

Web Sites
www.antwrp.gsfc.nasa.gov/apod/
astropix.html
www.iln.net/main/astronomy/
planets.asp

Videos
Space Explorers, NOVA,
PBS Home Video.

Planet Earth, Emmy Award Winner,
Discovery Channel Video.

Literature
Space by Alan Dyer and Cliff Watts,
© 1999.

The Young Astronomer
by Harry Ford, © 1998.

Word Study at Home

- The Word-Study-at-Home page provides an opportunity for students and their families to work together on improving the student's language skills.

- On the Word-Study-at-Home page for Unit 5, students and their families will find activities that relate to the theme *Scientists* and focus on suffixes and syllables.

- Have students remove page 138 from their books. Direct them to take the page home so that their families may share in the Word-Study-at-Home activities.

- Encourage students to report back to the class about the discussions they had with their families concerning the ways in which new scientific discoveries might change their family's life.

- Encourage students to find out about as many different types of science as possible, and to learn about the many different ways in which scientists can work: teaching, doing research in a laboratory, assisting a corporation, and so on. You might bring in magazine articles and other research materials and invite small groups of students to find out more about one type of scientist or job.

Theme-Related Resources

Books

African-American Scientists: A Proud Heritage, by Pat McKissack, Patricia McKissack, Frederick L. McKissack, Millbrook Press, 1994

Multicultural Women of Science: Three Centuries of Contributions With Hands-On Activities and Exercises for the School Year, by Leonard Bernstein, Alan Winkler, and Linda Zierdt-Warshaw, Peoples Publishing Group, 1996

Pioneers of Discovery (Profiles of Great Black Americans), edited by Richard Rennert, Chelsea House Publishers, 1994

Multicultural Connection

Tell students that people had been studying the heavens long before the 16th century, when Copernicus made his discovery. For example, evidence shows that the Chinese had enough knowledge of astronomy in the 13th century B.C. to measure the length of the lunar month as 29.53 days. This figure is very close to the 29.530879 days recorded by scientists today.

Have students do research to find out about similar discoveries in the field of astronomy made by people of different cultures.

Social Studies Link

Have students look through current newspapers and/or magazines to find out about a recent scientific study or discovery. Ask students to outline the main points covered in the article. Have volunteers share their findings in a brief oral report. Encourage listeners to ask questions.

Suffixes -er and -est

Objectives

- To write words with the suffixes -er and -est
- To distinguish between comparative and superlative forms of words
- To write comparative and superlative forms of words

Warming Up

- Write the following rhyme on the board and read it aloud:

    The **faster** of two planes,

    The **biggest** of three trains;

    An **easier** kind of software,

    The **finest** of all medical care;

    The credit for all of this,

    Belongs to scientists.

- Have a student underline the words that compare two things (**faster, easier**). Have another student circle the words that compare more than two things (**biggest, finest**). Identify the endings in each group.

Teaching the Lesson

- Tell students that a word part added to the end of a base word is called a suffix. Explain that the endings **-er** and **-est** are suffixes used to show comparison. Write the following words on the board and have students circle the suffixes:

    wet   wetter   wettest

    early   earlier   earliest

    tame   tamer   tamest

- Discuss the spelling changes made to the base words when the suffixes were added. (**t** in **wet** doubled, **y** in **early** changed to **i**, and **e** in **tame** was dropped)

- Then read the Helpful Hints aloud as students follow along silently.

Name _____

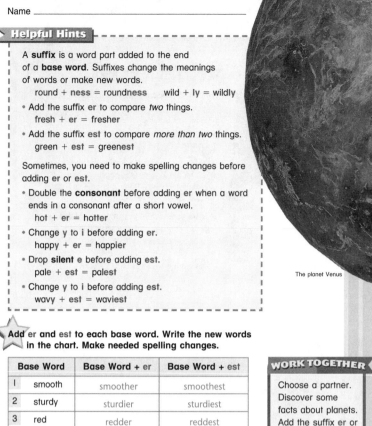

Helpful Hints

A **suffix** is a word part added to the end of a **base word**. Suffixes change the meanings of words or make new words.

round + ness = roundness   wild + ly = wildly

- Add the suffix er to compare *two* things.

    fresh + er = fresher

- Add the suffix est to compare *more than two* things.

    green + est = greenest

Sometimes, you need to make spelling changes before adding er or est.

- Double the **consonant** before adding er when a word ends in a consonant after a short vowel.

    hot + er = hotter

- Change y to i before adding er.

    happy + er = happier

- Drop **silent** e before adding est.

    pale + est = palest

- Change y to i before adding est.

    wavy + est = waviest

The planet Venus

⭐ **Add er and est to each base word. Write the new words in the chart. Make needed spelling changes.**

	Base Word	Base Word + er	Base Word + est
1	smooth	smoother	smoothest
2	sturdy	sturdier	sturdiest
3	red	redder	reddest
4	fine	finer	finest
5	flat	flatter	flattest
6	easy	easier	easiest

WORK TOGETHER

Choose a partner. Discover some facts about planets. Add the suffix er or est to base words such as **near, close, heavy, large,** and **small,** to compare facts about planets.

LESSON 68: Suffixes **-er** and **-est**   **139**

UNIVERSAL ACCESS
Meeting Individual Needs

Auditory Learners

Give groups of three students three items that are the same but that differ in some way, such as pencils of different lengths. Have each group member hold up an item and say a sentence comparing the items, using a word with the suffix **-er** or **-est**.

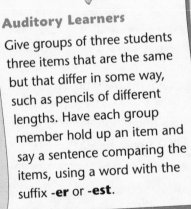

Visual Learners

The chart below shows spelling changes made to base words when **-er** and **-est** are added. Have students note the patterns and add new words to the chart.

Double consonant	Change y to i	Drop silent e
hot	pretty	pale
hotter	prettier	paler
hottest	prettiest	palest
fat	early	wide
fatter	earlier	wider
fattest	earliest	widest

Read each sentence. Draw one line under the word that compares two things. Draw two lines under the word that compares more than two things.

1. A modern telescope is a <u>finer</u> instrument than a spyglass.

2. Copernicus' telescope was <u>clumsier</u> than the telescope used by Galileo.

3. The world's largest telescope is the Keck in Hawaii.

4. The Keck is <u>sharper</u> than an ordinary telescope.

5. The Keck's mirrors are the <u><u>biggest</u></u> of all the earth's telescopes.

6. The astronauts who repaired the Hubble Space Telescope had the <u><u>hardest</u></u> job of all the astronauts.

7. Of all telescopes, the Hubble is the <u><u>farthest</u></u> from the earth.

8. The Hubble's view of the earth is the <u><u>greatest</u></u> of all telescopes.

The Hubble Space Telescope

Read the base word before each sentence. Add er or est to the base word to complete the sentence correctly. Write the new word on the line.

strong 9. The telescope built by Galileo was _____ **stronger** _____ than the telescope used by Copernicus.

dark 10. Usually, the _____ **darker** _____ the sky, the better the view with a telescope.

early 11. Observatories on mountains or on towers were the _____ **earliest** _____ ones built.

old 12. The _____ **oldest** _____ observatory still in use today is in Paris.

dense 13. Venus has a _____ **denser** _____ atmosphere than Earth has.

cloudy 14. Even on the _____ **cloudiest** _____ nights, radio telescopes with computers can work.

wide 15. Puerto Rico's large Arecibo radio receiver is much _____ **wider** _____ than a football field.

140 | LESSON 68: Suffixes **-er** and **-est**

Home Involvement Activity Discuss these questions: Which day of the year is the longest? The shortest? Why? What are these two special days called?

English-Language Learners/ESL

Many languages form comparatives and superlatives by using words that mean "more" or "most" before words. Explain that in English, **-er** or **-est** added to the ends of some words do the same job. We say **faster**, not "more fast," and **fastest** instead of "most fast." Give additional examples.

Gifted Learners

Have students discuss inventions that have changed people's lives. Ask students to choose an invention and write a paragraph describing how it improved our lives. Encourage students to use as many comparison words as possible.

Learners with Special Needs

Additional strategies for supporting learners with special needs can be found on page 137L.

Read aloud the direction lines on pages 139–140 and complete the first item in each exercise with students. Suggest that students refer to the Helpful Hints to check their work.

Practicing the Skill

Read aloud the direction lines on pages 139–140 and complete the first item in each exercise with students. Suggest that students refer to the Helpful Hints to check their work.

Curriculum Connections

Spelling Link

Have students fill in the blanks with words created by adding **-er** and **-est** to the base words **heavy, cold, large, hot**.

August is usually _____ than July. But the _____ day in U.S. history was July 10, 1913, when the temperature rose to 134° in Death Valley, California.

February is often _____ than January. But the _____ day in the U.S. was January 23, 1971, when the temperature fell to -80° in Prospect Creek, Alaska.

In the winter, snowfalls are _____ than in the spring. But the _____ snowfall in the U.S. was on April 14–15, 1921, when 76 inches fell in Silver Lake, Colorado.

Nobody ever saw a hailstone _____ than the one that fell in Coffeyville, Kansas, on September 3, 1970. At a weight of almost two pounds, it is the _____ hailstone on record. (Answers: **hotter, hottest; colder, coldest; heavier, heaviest; larger, largest**)

Social Studies Link

• Invite students to look for amazing features of our planet. They can consult an atlas, encyclopedia, almanac, or record books.

• Ask students to write at least two sentences using comparisons. For example: *Mount McKinley is **taller** than most mountains. Mount Everest is the **tallest**.*

Observational Assessment

*Check to see that students correctly use and spell words with the suffixes **-er** and **-est**.*

140

Suffixes -ful, -ment, -ness, -ly, -y

Objectives

- To identify the suffixes, **-ful, -ment, -ness, -ly,** and **-y** in words
- To identify the meanings of words with these suffixes
- To write words with these suffixes

Warming Up

- Write this limerick on the board and say it with students.

    A **lucky** researcher from Shay,

    Made a **wonderful** finding one day.

    "What **greatness**!" She shouted

    amazement about it,

    Then **happily** hurried away.

- Underline the words that appear in boldface type above. Ask volunteers to circle the suffix in each word.

Teaching the Lesson

- On the board, write the following words from the limerick, using this pattern:

    luck + y = lucky

    wonder + ful = wonderful

    great + ness = greatness

    amaze + ment = amazement

- Discuss the meaning of each suffix and base word. Remind students that a suffix changes the meaning of the base word.
- Ask students to think of other words with these suffixes. Write them beside the examples.
- Write **happy + ly = happily.** Point out the spelling change made to the base word when the suffix is added. Then read aloud the Helpful Hints on page 142.

Name _____

► Helpful Hints

The **suffix** ful means "full of."

    Joyful means "full of joy."

    Beautiful means "full of beauty."

The **suffix** ment means "result of," "act of," or "state of being."

    Improvement is the result of being improved.

    Movement is the act of moving.

    Disappointment is the state of being disappointed.

The **suffix** ness means "a state of being."

    Greatness is the state of being great.

CHALLENGE

Make three lists. Use these headings: **ful, ment,** and **ness.** Write at least three words that use each of those suffixes.

Underline the suffix in each word.

1. measur<u>ement</u>
2. pay<u>ment</u>
3. vast<u>ness</u>
4. argu<u>ment</u>
5. power<u>ful</u>
6. wonder<u>ful</u>
7. delight<u>ful</u>
8. care<u>ful</u>
9. aware<u>ness</u>
10. help<u>ful</u>
11. content<u>ment</u>
12. enjoy<u>ment</u>

Answer each question. Use the words from the list above.

13. Which word means "full of delight"?   delightful
14. Which word means "the result of being paid"?   payment
15. Which word means "the act of measuring"?   measurement
16. Which word means "being aware"?   awareness
17. Which word means "full of power"?   powerful
18. Which word means "being contented"?   contentment
19. Which word means "full of care"?   careful

LESSON 69: Suffixes -ful, -ment, -ness, -ly, -y   141

UNIVERSAL ACCESS
Meeting Individual Needs

Kinesthetic Learners

On index cards, write words from the lesson that students can act out, such as **joyful, disappointment, noisy.** Distribute cards to students, who take turns pantomiming the word for the class to guess. When students guess correctly, have a volunteer use the word in a sentence. For example: *I am **noisy** when I shout.*

Auditory Learners

Brainstorm words with the suffixes **-ful, -ment, -ness, -ly,** and **-y.** Write them on the board. Point to a word and ask half the class to say the base word. Ask the other half to say the suffix. Then have the class say the entire word. Challenge students to identify base words whose spellings changed when suffixes were added.

The **suffix** ly means "in a certain way."
 Neatly means "in a neat way."

- When you add ly to a word that ends in le, drop the le.
  humble + ly = humbly   possible + ly = possibly

- When a word ends in y, change the y to i before adding ly.
  happy + ly = happily   mighty + ly = mightily

The **suffix** y means "full of" or "having."
 Lucky means "having luck."

- When a word ends in **silent** e, usually drop the e before adding y.
  bone + y = bony   mange + y = mangy

- When a word ends in a single consonant after a short vowel, double the consonant before adding y.
  skin + y = skinny   fun + y = funny

★ **Read each phrase. Add y or ly to the word in bold print. Write the new word on the line.**

1. in a **quick** way _____ quickly
2. in an **easy** way _____ easily
3. full of **leaks** _____ leaky
4. having **salt** _____ salty
5. full of **fun** _____ funny
6. in a **safe** way _____ safely
7. full of **noise** _____ noisy
8. in a **serious** way _____ seriously
9. full of **bounce** _____ bouncy
10. in a **sad** way _____ sadly
11. full of **bubbles** _____ bubbly

142

LESSON 69: Suffixes **-ful, -ment, -ness, -ly, -y**

Home Involvement Activity Write the five suffixes, ful, ment, ness, ly, and y, each on an index card. Shuffle the cards. For each card you pick, say a word that uses the suffix. Then use the word in a sentence about science.

Practicing the Skill

- Read aloud the direction lines on pages 141–142 and complete the first item in each exercise with students.

- Suggest that students refer to the Helpful Hints on page 142 to check their spelling in items 1–11 on the same page.

Intervention Strategy Turn to page 137K for an Intervention Strategy designed to help students who need extra support with this lesson.

Curriculum Connections

Spelling Link

| easy | happy | bubble |
| care | power | argue |

On the board, write the base words above. Then have students use them to complete the sentences below.

Sadness is the opposite of _____**ness.**
I can do my homework _____**ly.**
We had an _____**ment** about movies.
Seltzer is too ____**y** for my taste.
Be _____**ful** crossing the street.
The U.S. is a _____**ful** country.

(Answers: **happiness, easily, argument, bubbly, careful, powerful**)

Multicultural Connection

- Ask students to choose a country they would like to visit. Suggest that they use guidebooks and/or encyclopedias to learn about places of interest in that country.

- Have students write travelogues describing those places. Encourage them to use words with the lesson suffixes.

Observational Assessment

*Check to see that students correctly use the suffixes **-ful, -ment, -ness, -ly,** and **-y**.*

English-Language Learners/ESL

Have students draw pictures of places they are familiar with or especially like. Help them use words with the lesson suffixes to describe their pictures. Then have students label their pictures with descriptive phrases. (Examples include **sandy** beach, **beautiful** mountains, and so on.)

Gifted Learners

Suggest that students imagine they are archaeologists who have unearthed an amazing find: for example, dinosaur bones or a relic from an ancient civilization. Have students write about their "experience," explaining what they did, how they felt, and what they found. Ask them to use words with the lesson suffixes.

Learners with Special Needs

Additional strategies for supporting learners with special needs can be found on page 137L.

Suffixes
-like, -able, -age

Objectives

- To identify the suffixes **-like, -able,** and **-age** in words
- To identify the meanings of words with these suffixes
- To write words with these suffixes

Warming Up

- On the board, write these travel tips for an imaginary trip to Mercury. Have students say them with you.

✓ Pack your **luggage** with **washable** cotton clothes. On this **desertlike** planet, you'll feel much more **comfortable**.

✓ Be sure to collect your frequent-flyer **mileage**.

✓ Make a point of bringing back film **footage**. It will be very **valuable!**

- Write **-like, -able,** and **-age** on the board. Ask students to underline words with these suffixes in the travel tips.

Teaching the Lesson

- Have a volunteer circle the suffixes in each underlined word. Challenge students to figure out the meaning of each suffix by using clues in the travel tips.

- Then read the Helpful Hints with students to find out whether their guesses were correct.

- Finally, read the following rule aloud: "If a word ends in silent **e**, drop the **e** before adding **age**." Explain that rules often have exceptions. Point out that the word **mileage** is an exception to this rule.

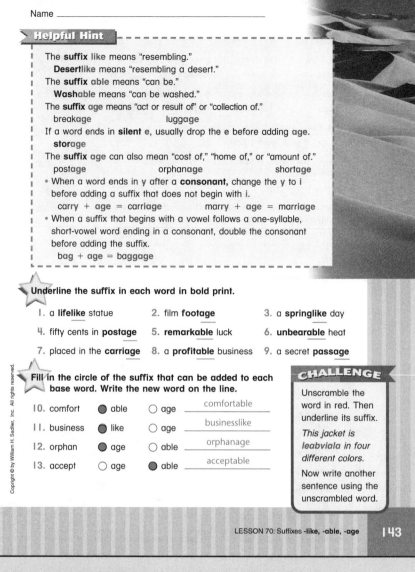

Name _____

> ### Helpful Hint
>
> The **suffix** like means "resembling."
> **Desert**like means "resembling a desert."
> The **suffix** able means "can be."
> **Wash**able means "can be washed."
> The **suffix** age means "act or result of" or "collection of."
>   breakage   luggage
> If a word ends in silent e, usually drop the e before adding age.
>   storage
> The **suffix** age can also mean "cost of," "home of," or "amount of."
>   postage   orphanage   shortage
> • When a word ends in y after a **consonant**, change the y to i before adding a suffix that does not begin with i.
>   carry + age = carriage   marry + age = marriage
> • When a suffix that begins with a vowel follows a one-syllable, short-vowel word ending in a consonant, double the consonant before adding the suffix.
>   bag + age = baggage

Underline the suffix in each word in bold print.

1. a **lifelike** statue
2. film **footage**
3. a **springlike** day
4. fifty cents in **postage**
5. **remarkable** luck
6. **unbearable** heat
7. placed in the **carriage**
8. a **profitable** business
9. a secret **passage**

Fill in the circle of the suffix that can be added to each base word. Write the new word on the line.

10. comfort ● able ○ age _comfortable_
11. business ● like ○ age _businesslike_
12. orphan ● age ○ able _orphanage_
13. accept ○ age ● able _acceptable_

CHALLENGE

Unscramble the word in red. Then underline its suffix.

This jacket is leabviala in four different colors.

Now write another sentence using the unscrambled word.

LESSON 70: Suffixes **-like, -able, -age**   143

UNIVERSAL ACCESS
Meeting Individual Needs

Musical Learners

Invite students to create songs whose lyrics include words with the suffixes taught in this lesson. Suggest that they set their lyrics to familiar tunes so that everyone can sing along. Photocopy students' songs and distribute them. Ask volunteers to act as chorus directors and lead the class in first rehearsing and then performing the songs.

Logical Learners

Draw three boxes on the board, using the suffixes **-like, -able, -age** as headings. Have students list the words taught in the lesson. Then have them write the words in the box with the appropriate suffix. Extend the activity by asking students to underline the words whose spellings change when the suffixes were added.

Each box below contains three base words and three suffixes. Draw a line to connect each base word with a suffix to form three words. Then write the words on the lines.

1		2		3	
short	like	lug	able	remark	like
profit	age	enjoy	like	post	age
web	able	desert	age	child	able

1. shortage / profitable / weblike
2. luggage / enjoyable / desertlike
3. remarkable / postage / childlike

Complete each sentence about a "dig" for dinosaur bones. Write the best word from the boxes above.

4. The scientists hoped their stay in this dry place would be _____profitable_____.

5. They knew that the dry, _____desertlike_____ landscape would be filled with dinosaur bones.

6. Unfortunately, they had to live with a _____shortage_____ of food and water.

7. Their _____luggage_____ had little room for clothing in order to make space for tools and equipment.

8. The scientists paid extra _____postage_____ to have samples sent back to the laboratory.

9. One day, they made a _____remarkable_____ discovery—a complete skeleton of a dinosaur!

10. At first, they noticed the skeleton's thick, _____weblike_____ toes.

11. A video camera captured the scientists' _____childlike_____ glee when they made their discovery.

Home Involvement Activity Make a list of the suffixes taught so far. Then have your child go through a page of his or her social studies, science, or reading book to write words that use the suffixes on the list.

• Read aloud the direction lines on pages 143–144 and complete the first item in each exercise with students.

• For items 1–3 on page 144, suggest that students check off each word and suffix as they use them.

Curriculum Connections

Spelling Link

• Divide the class into teams to play the "Suffix Game." Explain that you will say the meaning of a word from the lesson. Team members must guess the word and spell it correctly to win a point for his or her team. Play continues until all the words have been used. The team with the most points wins the game.

• Below are examples for use in the game:

"can be washed"	**washable**
"can be accepted"	**acceptable**
"cost of stamps"	**postage**
"amount of film"	**footage**
"resembling a child"	**childlike**
"as if alive"	**lifelike**

Multicultural Connection

• Have students discuss what they know about the countries and cultures of their parents, grandparents, and/or ancestors.

• Encourage students to research their heritage and write at least two paragraphs that tell what they learned. Challenge them to include words that end with the suffixes **-able**, **-age**, and **-like**.

Observational Assessment

*Check to see that students understand how the suffixes **-able**, **-age**, and **-like** affect the base words to which they are added.*

English-Language Learners/ESL

Find pictures of items that can be described with words ending in **-age**, **-able**, or **-like**. Give each student a choice of pictures and say, for example: *Point to something that is easy to break.* Provide responses such as: *Yes, the glass is **breakable**.* or *No, the rock is not **breakable**.* Ask the student to say the word and write it under the appropriate picture.

Gifted Learners

Over several days, have students listen and look for words with the lesson suffixes. Have them write the words and definitions in a notebook. Encourage students to use their notes to create a "Suffix-Word Dictionary" for the class.

Learners with Special Needs

Additional strategies for supporting learners with special needs can be found on page 137L.

Suffixes and Syllables

Objectives

- **To review the suffixes -er, -est, -ful, -ment, -ness, -ly, -y, -like, -able and -age**

- **To identify the number of syllables in words with these suffixes**

- **To write multisyllabic words with these suffixes in context**

Warming Up

- Write the following rhyme on the board and read it aloud with students.

  To say a cat is **catlike**

  Is to use the word all wrong.

  A cat is more than *like* his kin.

  He *is* kin all along.

- Have a volunteer identify and say the word that has a suffix. **(catlike)** Tell the student to go to the board and underline the suffix. Ask: *What vowel sound do you hear in the suffix?* (**-like,** the long **i** sound)

Teaching the Lesson

- Write the following words on the board: **swiftness, faithful, lightest, luggage,** and **pavement.** Ask a volunteer to read the words aloud. Have the student come to the board and draw a line between the base word and suffix of each word.

- Ask the same student to divide the words into syllables. (The student should see that having divided the words between base word and suffix served to divide them into syllables.) Explain that suffixes can add one or more syllables to base words.

- Then read the Helpful Hints aloud as students follow along silently.

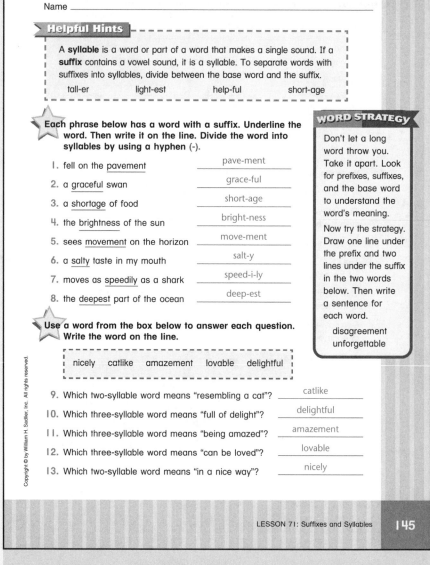

Name _____

Helpful Hints

A **syllable** is a word or part of a word that makes a single sound. If a **suffix** contains a vowel sound, it is a syllable. To separate words with suffixes into syllables, divide between the base word and the suffix.

tall-er   light-est   help-ful   short-age

★ Each phrase below has a word with a suffix. Underline the word. Then write it on the line. Divide the word into syllables by using a hyphen (-).

1. fell on the pavement ____ pave-ment
2. a graceful swan ____ grace-ful
3. a shortage of food ____ short-age
4. the brightness of the sun ____ bright-ness
5. sees movement on the horizon ____ move-ment
6. a salty taste in my mouth ____ salt-y
7. moves as speedily as a shark ____ speed-i-ly
8. the deepest part of the ocean ____ deep-est

★ Use a word from the box below to answer each question. Write the word on the line.

nicely   catlike   amazement   lovable   delightful

9. Which two-syllable word means "resembling a cat"? ____ catlike
10. Which three-syllable word means "full of delight"? ____ delightful
11. Which three-syllable word means "being amazed"? ____ amazement
12. Which three-syllable word means "can be loved"? ____ lovable
13. Which two-syllable word means "in a nice way"? ____ nicely

WORD STRATEGY

Don't let a long word throw you. Take it apart. Look for prefixes, suffixes, and the base word to understand the word's meaning.

Now try the strategy. Draw one line under the prefix and two lines under the suffix in the two words below. Then write a sentence for each word.

disagreement
unforgettable

LESSON 71: Suffixes and Syllables **145**

UNIVERSAL ACCESS
Meeting Individual Needs

Auditory Learners

Prepare a word wall with these headings: **2 syllables, 3 syllables, 4 syllables.** Then ask students to listen closely as you say words with suffixes. Invite them to repeat each word, snapping their fingers for each syllable. Then ask: *How many syllables does this word have?* Have students write the word on the word wall, under the appropriate heading.

Kinesthetic Learners

Have students sit in a circle. Explain that you will say a word with a suffix. Students should listen for the syllables. If they hear two syllables, they should pat their knees twice. If they hear three syllables, they should pat their knees twice and clap hands once. For four syllables, students should pat their knees twice and clap twice.

Word	Syllables		Word	Syllables
1. funnier	3		2. available	4
3. smoothest	2		4. birdlike	2
5. careful	2		6. tenderness	3
7. smarter	2		8. wildest	2
9. agreeable	4		10. younger	2
11. seriously	4		12. domelike	2
13. thirstiest	3		14. enjoyable	4
15. breakable	3		16. completely	3
17. shipment	2		18. darkness	2
19. windy	2		20. colorful	3
21. profitable	4		22. prettily	3
23. yardage	2		24. shortness	2
25. argument	3		26. development	4
27. usage	2		28. kindness	2

Choose six of the words from above. Write a sentence for each word.

Sentences will vary.

29. _____
30. _____
31. _____
32. _____
33. _____
34. _____

Home Involvement Activity Wattage is a measure of electric power expressed in watts. It is named after the inventor James Watt. Make a list of other words you can think of that are named after inventors or scientists.

Practicing the Skill

● Read aloud the direction lines on pages 145–146 and complete the first item in each exercise with students.

● Have students refer to the spelling rules presented in previous lessons as they work on the exercises.

Curriculum Connections

Spelling Link

Give the text below to students. Have them circle words with suffixes and divide the words into syllables. (**move/ment, break/a/ble, short/age, care/ful, se/ri/ous/ly, quick/ly, a/vail/a/ble**)

Earthquakes really shake things up. Rock **movement** during earthquakes can shatter **breakable** objects and can wreck buildings and bridges. It can also destroy water lines, causing a water **shortage.**

It's important to be **careful** and take earthquake-safety rules **seriously.** People who are outdoors when an earthquake hits should move away from tall trees and buildings as **quickly** as possible.

Scientists are working on ways to predict when and where earthquakes will occur. They make their findings **available** to the public in hopes of saving lives.

Social Studies Link

● People worldwide have had pet cats for thousands of years. The ancient Egyptians considered cats sacred and honored them in paintings and sculptures. Cats were also valued in ancient Greece and Rome, as well as in Japan and China.

● Have students research "Cats in History" and share their findings with the class.

Observational Assessment

Check to see that students can identify the number of syllables in words with suffixes.

English-Language Learners/ESL

On the board, write words from the lesson whose meanings can be illustrated. Say a word with students and display a picture that shows its meaning. Draw a line between its suffix and base word and then between syllables. Say each syllable as you point to it. Then pronounce the whole word. Repeat the process with the other words.

Gifted Learners

Have students look through printed material for long words with suffixes. Encourage students to locate at least five five-syllable words, write the definition of each, and use the words in original sentences. Invite students to demonstrate how to divide their words into syllables.

Learners with Special Needs

Additional strategies for supporting learners with special needs can be found on page 137L.

Suffixes -ity, -ive, -ion, -sion, -tion

Objectives

- To identify the suffixes -ity, -ive, -ion, -sion, and -tion in words
- To identify the meanings of words with these suffixes
- To write words with these suffixes

Warming Up

- Write the following rhyme on the board and read it aloud. Encourage students to chime in as you read it a second time.

    People who invent things

    Are **inventive,** so it seems.

    But **education** gives them wings

    To soar beyond their dreams.

- Have a volunteer underline the words with suffixes and read them aloud.

Teaching the Lesson

- Draw a line between the base word and the suffix of the underlined words on the board. (**invent/ive, educat/ion**)
- Explain that the spelling of the base word **invent** does not change when the suffix **-ive** is added.
- Point out that the base word **educate** does change in spelling when the suffix **-ion** is added. Have a volunteer explain how the spelling of **educate** changes. (The silent **e** is dropped.)
- Then have students use what they know about the words **inventive** and **education** to figure out the meanings of the suffixes that were added.
- Have students read the Helpful Hints to see whether their guesses were correct.

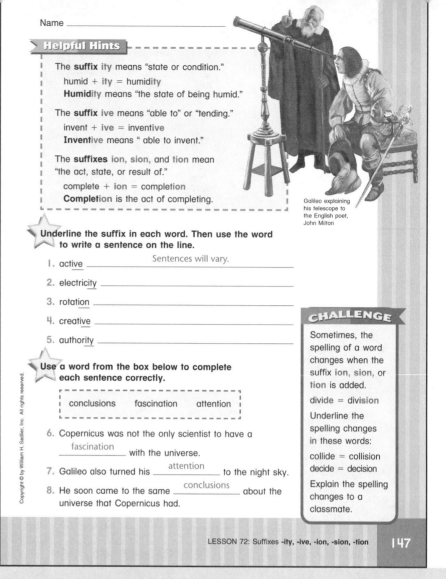

Name _____

> **Helpful Hints**

The **suffix ity** means "state or condition."

humid + ity = humidity
Humidity means "the state of being humid."

The **suffix ive** means "able to" or "tending."

invent + ive = inventive
Inventive means "able to invent."

The **suffixes ion, sion,** and **tion** mean "the act, state, or result of."

complete + ion = completion
Completion is the act of completing.

Galileo explaining his telescope to the English poet, John Milton

Underline the suffix in each word. Then use the word to write a sentence on the line.

Sentences will vary.

1. active _____
2. electricity _____
3. rotation _____
4. creative _____
5. authority _____

Use a word from the box below to complete each sentence correctly.

> conclusions   fascination   attention

6. Copernicus was not the only scientist to have a
   fascination _____ with the universe.
7. Galileo also turned his attention _____ to the night sky.
8. He soon came to the same conclusions _____ about the universe that Copernicus had.

> **CHALLENGE**
>
> Sometimes, the spelling of a word changes when the suffix ion, sion, or tion is added.
>
> divide = division
>
> Underline the spelling changes in these words:
>
> collide = collision
> decide = decision
>
> Explain the spelling changes to a classmate.

UNIVERSAL ACCESS
Meeting Individual Needs

Kinesthetic Learners

Write the lesson suffixes on cards and give a card to each student. Call out these base words, one at a time: **electric, complete, divide, tense,** and **act.** For each word, have students hold up a card with a suffix that can be added to it to make a new word. Discuss any spelling changes to be made when the suffixes are added.

Visual Learners

With students, create a chart like the following. Have them add more examples.

Drop silent e/ Add -ive	Drop silent e/ Add -ity
create/ creative	creative/ creativity
negate/ negative	active/ activity

Drop silent e/Add -ion	
tense/tension	
confuse/confusion	

147

★ **Write a word from the box to answer each question.**

operation	election	discussion	decision
subtraction	education	protection	pollution

1. Which word means "the act of operating"? _____ operation
2. Which word means "the act of discussing"? _____ discussion
3. Which word means "the act of educating"? _____ education
4. Which word means "the result of polluting"? _____ pollution
5. Which word means "the act of subtracting"? _____ subtraction
6. Which word means "the act of protecting"? _____ protection
7. Which word means "the result of electing"? _____ election
8. Which word means "the act of deciding"? _____ decision

★ **Fill in the circle of the word that completes each sentence. Then write the word on the line.**

9. Galileo's ideas got a ___ negative ___ reaction from many people.
   ○ decision   ● negative   ○ tension

10. One of Galileo's most important ___ contributions ___ to science was *the scientific method.*
    ○ education   ● contributions   ○ protections

11. Isaac Newton's ideas about gravity also took science in the right ___ direction ___.
    ● direction   ○ discussion   ○ collision

12. Albert Einstein's theory of ___ relativity ___ changed the way we think about space and time.
    ● relativity   ○ reactions   ○ relatives

148   LESSON 72: Suffixes **-ity, -ive, -ion, -sion, -tion**

🏠 **Home Involvement Activity** Work together to create one long sentence about planets and stars. Include as many suffixes from this lesson as you can.

Practicing the Skill

● Read aloud the direction lines on pages 147–148 and complete the first item in each exercise with students.

Intervention Strategy   Turn to page 137K for an Intervention strategy designed to help students who need extra support with this lesson.

Curriculum Connections

Spelling Link

● Write these suffixes on the board: **-ity, -ive, -ion, -sion,** and **-tion.** Then list these base words in one column: **create, discuss, decide, protect, electric, operate, author, act.**

● Have students add a suffix to each base to make a new word. Explain that they will use some suffixes more than once. **(creative, creation; discussion; decision, decisive; protection; protective; electricity; operation; authority; active, action)**

● Tell students that some base words can be joined with two suffixes to make two new words. Challenge them to figure out what those base words are.

● When students finish the activity, discuss any spelling changes that occurred when adding the suffixes to the base words.

Math Link

Have students make up arithmetic problems in **addition, subtraction, multiplication,** and/or **division.** Then invite students to trade problems and try to solve them.

Observational Assessment

Check that students correctly use and spell words with the suffixes **-ity, -ive, -ion, -sion,** *and* **-tion.**

English-Language Learners/ESL

On the board, write lesson words such as **active** and **electricity.** Have students copy each word on a card. Have a fluent speaker choose a card. Using pantomime, the student tries to get an English learner to point to the correct word on the board. Repeat the activity with the other words.

Gifted Learners

Encourage students to write down as many words with the suffixes **-ity, -ive, -ion, -sion,** and **-tion** as they can think of, printing each word on a separate card. Have students draw three words out of a hat and create a sentence that uses all three. They can repeat the process until they run out of words.

Learners with Special Needs

Additional strategies for supporting learners with special needs can be found on page 137L.

Connecting Spelling and Writing

Objectives

- **To say, spell, sort, and write multi-syllabic words with suffixes**
- **To write a myth**

Warming Up

- Write the following paragraph on the board. Ask a volunteer to read it aloud.

The astronomer used a <u>powerful</u> telescope to study the <u>vastness</u> of space. The view of distant stars was <u>truly</u> <u>remarkable</u>. She <u>carefully</u> recorded each <u>measurement</u> to avoid <u>confusion</u>.

- Have a volunteer identify the suffix in each underlined word and explain the meaning of the word. Ask how many syllables are in each underlined word.

Teaching the Lesson

- On the board, make the following chart of words. Have students use the clues in the first two columns to complete the third column.

Meaning	Syllables	Word
most flat	2	**(flattest)**
in a noisy way	3	**(noisily)**
can be erased	4	**(erasable)**

- Have volunteers suggest additional clues for the first two columns. Invite other students to fill in the third column.

Practicing the Skill

Review the directions for page 149. Suggest that students repeat the words softly to themselves to help them count the number of syllables.

149

Name _____

Read each group of words. Say and spell each word in bold print. Repeat the word. Then sort the words according to the number of syllables that the words have. Write the words in the correct column below.

- an **earlier** time
- **possibly** the oldest
- took it **seriously**
- **vastness** of the universe
- the **development** of radar
- **attention** to detail
- an **authority** on space travel
- write your **conclusion**
- unpack her **luggage**
- **domelike** buildings
- a **creative** mind
- **observation** deck

- the **rotation** of the earth
- a **graceful** dancer
- the **noisy** storm
- a **remarkable** shower of stars

McDonald Observatory in Texas

Words with Two Syllables	Words with Three Syllables	Words with Four Syllables
graceful	earlier	seriously
noisy	rotation	remarkable
vastness	possibly	development
luggage	attention	authority
domelike	conclusion	observation
	creative	

UNIVERSAL ACCESS
Meeting Individual Needs

Visual Learners

Have students look in books, newspapers, or magazines for examples of words containing suffixes studied in this unit. Ask students to write the words on a sheet of paper, sorting them by number of syllables. Then have students combine their words into a class list on chart paper. Discuss with students the meaning of any difficult words on the list.

Kinesthetic Learners

Write the following words on separate cards: **measurement**, **joyful**, **argument**, **payment**, **powerful**, **funny**, **noisy**, **bouncy**, **sadly**, **windy**. Distribute the cards to volunteers. Ask volunteers to act out the word or give the class verbal clues. Whenever students correctly guess a word, write it on the board. Then have students identify the word's suffix, base word, and number of syllables.

Learners with Special Needs

Additional strategies for supporting learners with special needs can be found on page 137L.

Since the beginning of time, people have made up stories about the night sky and about the changes in nature. For example, people imagined that they saw pictures in the stars. These pictures led storytellers to make up myths about the stars and constellations. People also made up stories about why thunder and lightning exist. Today, we have scientific facts to explain these natural events. Yet the old myths still entertain us.

Make up a myth that tells *why* something happens in nature. For example, you might explain why volcanoes erupt, or why Sirius (the Dog Star) is the brightest star in the sky. Use two or more of these spelling words in your myth.

earlier	possibly	seriously	vastness	development
attention	authority	conclusion	luggage	domelike	creative
observation	rotation	graceful	noisy	remarkable

Sentences will vary.

Writer's Tips

Get ideas for your myth by reading some "how" or "why" stories. You can also get ideas from the animal names and shapes of constellations. Write a strong beginning, middle, and end.

Writer's Challenge

Observe the stars on a clear night. Take a flashlight, a notebook, and a pencil with you. Describe what you see. Be creative! Then write a poem about the stars.

English-Language Learners/ESL

Display pictures of people, places, or things that can be described using words with suffixes. Here are examples: the **roundness** of a ball, the **biggest** building, a **graceful** dancer, **catlike** eyes. Describe the pictured items. Write each word with a suffix that you use on the board. Have students say the words, identify the suffixes, and count the syllables.

Gifted Learners

Have students research and write a factual explanation of a natural occurrence. If students explained a natural phenomenon in their myth, have them research that subject.

The Writing Process

Tell students that on page 150 they will write a myth explaining why something happens in nature. Read the directions and spelling words at the top of the page.

Prewrite Discuss with the class some examples of myths. Point out that myths are not based on scientific fact. Then encourage students to think about various natural occurrences that would lend themselves to mythical explanations, such as thunder and lightning.

Write Call students' attention to the Writer's Tip on page 150. Suggest that students look over the spelling words to see which ones might work best in their myth.

Revise Have students share their myths with a partner and exchange constructive, specific feedback. Then have them make revisions accordingly.

Proofread Have students check their work for errors in spelling, grammar, and punctuation.

Publish Students can copy their final drafts onto page 150 or onto a separate sheet of paper. Ask volunteers to read their myths aloud to the class.

Computer Connection

Share the following tip with students who use a word processor to do their writing.

● You can save a document on your computer and return to it at a later time. When you save the document, give it a specific file name that sets it apart from other documents.

● File names usually cannot include the following characters: / \ > < * . ? " | : ;

Portfolio Suggest that students add their finished myths to their portfolios.

Reviewing and Assessing

Suffixes

Objective

To review and assess suffixes **-er, -est, -ful, -ment, -ness, -ly, -y, -like, -able, -age, -ity, -ive, -ion, -sion,** and **-tion**

Warming Up

● Ask the class what a suffix is and how a suffix differs from a prefix. Review the fact that suffixes, like prefixes, are word parts added to a base word. They change the meaning of the word or make a new word. A prefix is added to the beginning of a word. A suffix is added to the end of a word.

● Have students first identify the base word in the following examples and then explain how the added suffix affects the base word: **greenest, powerful, acceptable, subtraction.**

Teaching the Lesson

● List on the board the suffixes studied so far in this unit: **-er, -est, -ful, -ment, -ness, -ly, -y, -like, -able, -age, -ity, -ive, -ion, -sion, -tion.** Review with students the meaning of each suffix and elicit an example of a word containing each. Discuss how the suffix contributes to the word's meaning. Have students use each word in a sentence.

● The Helpful Hints in Lessons 68, 69, 70, and 72 all contain spelling guidelines for adding suffixes to base words. Have volunteers review the guidelines aloud for the class. Encourage students to ask questions and give additional examples of words that follow the spelling patterns discussed.

151

Name _____

⭐ Add the suffix er to two of the following base words. Add the suffix est to the other two. Tell what each new word means.

Base Word	Word with Suffix	Meaning of New Word
1. happy	happier	Answers will vary.
2. funny	funniest	
3. fine	finest	
4. hot	hotter	

⭐ Add the suffix ful to two of the following base words. Add the suffix ly to the other two. Tell what each new word means.

Base Word	Word with Suffix	Meaning of New Word
5. help	helpful	full of help
6. possible	possibly	in a possible way
7. power	powerful	full of power
8. easy	easily	in an easy way

⭐ Add the suffix age to one of the following base words. Add the suffix able to the other one. Tell what each new word means.

Base Word	Word with Suffix	Meaning of New Word
9. comfort	comfortable	in the state of comfort
10. bag	baggage	collection of bags

⭐ Add the suffix ity to one of the following base words. Add the suffix ion to the other one. Tell what each new word means.

Base Word	Word with Suffix	Meaning of New Word
11. electric	electricity	the state of being electric
12. invent	invention	the act of inventing

LESSON 74: Review and Assess   **151**

UNIVERSAL ACCESS
Meeting Individual Needs

Kinesthetic Learners

Write words with the following suffixes on index cards: **-er, -est, -ful, -ment, -ness, -ly, -y, -like, -able, -age, -ity, -ive, -ion, -sion,** and **-tion.** Cut the cards so that the base words and suffixes are separated. Give the card halves to students. Have students display their card halves and find the classmate holding the one that matches theirs.

Learners with Special Needs

Additional strategies for supporting students with special needs can be found on page 137L.

Auditory Learners

Play "Mad-Libs" with the class. Have students fill in the blanks with words containing suffixes. For example, write: *My dog is _____ and walks more _____ than your dog.* Have volunteers supply a word ending in **-er** for the first blank and a word ending in **-ly** for the second. Then read the sentence aloud, inserting the students' words. (*My dog is* **bigger** *and walks more* **slowly** *than your dog.*) Have volunteers make up other "Mad-Lib" sentences to complete.

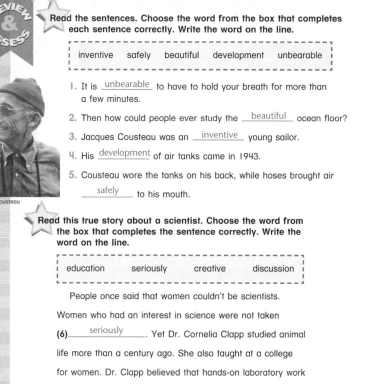

Read the sentences. Choose the word from the box that completes each sentence correctly. Write the word on the line.

| inventive | safely | beautiful | development | unbearable |

1. It is __unbearable__ to have to hold your breath for more than a few minutes.
2. Then how could people ever study the __beautiful__ ocean floor?
3. Jacques Cousteau was an __inventive__ young sailor.
4. His __development__ of air tanks came in 1943.
5. Cousteau wore the tanks on his back, while hoses brought air __safely__ to his mouth.

Jacques Cousteau

Read this true story about a scientist. Choose the word from the box that completes the sentence correctly. Write the word on the line.

| education | seriously | creative | discussion |

People once said that women couldn't be scientists. Women who had an interest in science were not taken **(6)** __seriously__. Yet Dr. Cornelia Clapp studied animal life more than a century ago. She also taught at a college for women. Dr. Clapp believed that hands-on laboratory work was important to a good science **(7)** __education__.

Back then, there were few labs for women. However, after much **(8)** __discussion__, Dr. Clapp convinced her college to add more laboratories and more science classes. Later, she helped establish the now-famous Marine Biology Lab at Woods Hole, on Cape Cod. Dr. Clapp was truly a **(9)** __creative__ thinker.

Reteaching Activities

Suffix Hunt

Have students look through short stories or novels and write down words they find that contain the suffixes **-er, -est, -ful, -ment, -ness, -ly, -y, -like, -able, -age, -ity, -ive, -ion, -sion,** and **-tion.** Tell students to figure out the meaning of each word by combining context clues with their understanding of suffixes. Have them check a dictionary if necessary. Compile a master class list. Discuss which suffixes seem most common, and why.

Completing Equations

Have students complete the following equations and explain the spelling changes that were made. Then have them suggest another word that changes in the same way when the same suffix is added.

hot + er = _____

operate + ion = _____

ugly + er = _____

dirty + est = _____

large + est = _____

easy + ly = _____

Assessing the Skill

Check Up Have students do the exercises on pages 151–152 to help them review the suffixes they have studied so far in this unit. You may use the exercises to help you gauge students' ability to form and define words with suffixes and their ability to correctly use words with suffixes.

Go over the directions for each set of exercises. For page 151, remind students to apply the spelling guidelines they have learned. For page 152, encourage students to use context clues to help them choose the correct words.

Observational Assessment Observe students as they work to determine whether they have trouble forming or spelling words with suffixes (page 151) or choosing context-appropriate words (page 152). Also check to see whether students are able to define the words they write on page 151.

Student Skills Assessment Keep track of each student's progress in understanding suffixes using the checklist on page 137H.

Writing Conference Meet with students individually to talk over their writing progress. Discuss with students examples of words with suffixes in their own writing.

Group together students who need further instruction in suffixes, and have them complete the *Reteaching Activities.* Turn to page 137C for alternative assessment methods.

Suffixes
-en, -ern, -ish

Objectives

- **To identify the suffixes -en, -ern, and -ish in words**
- **To identify the meanings of words with these suffixes**
- **To write words with these suffixes**

Warming Up

- Write these tongue twisters on the board and read them aloud with students.

  Shavonne can **shorten** skirts.

  She sews with **thickish** thread.

  Seven **Swedish** settlers succeed in **southern** states.

- Write **-en, -ern,** and **-ish** on the board. Encourage students to find and underline words from the tongue twisters with these suffixes.

Teaching the Lesson

- Have students draw a line between the suffix and base word of each underlined word in the *Warming-Up* activity.
- Then have volunteers write the words on the board using this pattern:

  short + en = shorten.

- Use the Helpful Hints on page 153 to discuss the meaning of each suffix. Call attention to occasional spelling changes made to the base word.

Name _____

Helpful Hints

The **suffix** en means "to make" or "become like."
   Pudding will **thick**en in the refrigerator.

The **suffix** ern gives a direction.
   The **south**ern part of Florida has storms.

The **suffix** ish means "belonging to a nation or people," "like," or "somewhat."
   Irish grandmother   boyish face   reddish brown

If a word ends in **silent** e, drop the e before adding ish.
   blue + ish = bluish

Underline the suffix in each word below.

1. western
2. Swedish
3. babyish
4. whitish
5. straighten
6. northeastern
7. soften
8. Spanish
9. sharpen

Complete each sentence by using one of the words from the list above. Write a word only once.

10. If you are from Sweden, you are ___Swedish___.
11. Use a ruler to ___straighten___ your lines.
12. Nail biting is a ___babyish___ habit.
13. In Spain, most people speak ___Spanish___.
14. A movie about the Old West is called a ___western___.
15. New York and New Jersey are ___northeastern___ states.
16. To make a pencil point sharper, you ___sharpen___ it.
17. A paint that is somewhat white is ___whitish___.
18. You can ___soften___ your clothes in the rinse cycle.

CHALLENGE

The great doctor William Harvey discovered that the heart pumps blood through the body. What nationality was William Harvey? Unscramble the word below to find out. Then write a sentence using the word.

sliehgn

UNIVERSAL ACCESS
Meeting Individual Needs

Musical Learners

Invite students to create songs or chants using words that contain the suffixes from this lesson. Examples include **thicken, southern, babyish, darken, western, whitish, sharpen, eastern,** and **Turkish.** Encourage students to perform their songs or chants for the class.

Kinesthetic Learners

Invite the class to play this game. On the board, list words that contain suffixes from the lesson. You say the meaning of one of the words on the board. The student you call on must go to the board and circle the correct word. Continue playing until all the words have been circled.

Underline the suffix in each word in the box. Then write the correct word from the box to answer each question. Use a word only once.

> eastern   English   straighten   southeastern   tallish
> northwestern   golden   lengthen   darkish   darken   Turkish

1. Which word means "somewhat tall"? _____ tallish
2. Which direction is to the north and west? _____ northwestern
3. Which word means "belonging to Turkey"? _____ Turkish
4. Which direction means "toward the east? _____ eastern
5. Which word means "make darker"? _____ darken
6. Which word means "somewhat dark"? _____ darkish
7. Which direction is to the south and east? _____ southeastern
8. Which word means "belonging to England"? _____ English
9. Which word means "make straighter"? _____ straighten
10. Which word means "make longer"? _____ lengthen
11. What do you call something with a gold color? _____ golden

Complete each sentence. Use a word from the box above.

12. Alabama is in the _____southeastern_____ part of the United States.
13. Buildings that are somewhat tall are _____tallish_____.
14. I love to eat _____Turkish_____ delight at fairs.
15. We need to _____darken_____ the circles on some of our tests.
16. The sun is a _____golden_____ color this morning.

154   LESSON 75: Suffixes -en, -ern, -ish

Home Involvement Activity Use a map to play *What Town Am I?* Take turns using direction words to describe the location of cities or towns on the map. Each person can ask two questions before guessing the place.

Practicing the Skill

● Read aloud the direction lines on pages 153–154 and complete the first item in each exercise with students.

● Suggest that students check their answers to items 10–18 on page 153 by saying the words softly to themselves.

Curriculum Connections

Spelling Link

On the board, write the suffixes **-en, -ern,** and **-ish** and the poem below. Read it aloud, pausing for each missing suffix. Have students repeat the poem and fill in the suffixes.

> I walked upon a **north**_____ road.
> The leaves were **red**_____ brown,
> The sky began to **dark**_____
> As I made my way towards town.
> The **east**_____ sky was **blu**_____
> And the **west**_____ sky was red,
> I **quick**_____ed my slow footsteps,
> And dreamed of my own bed!

Social Studies Link

Have students work in groups to identify countries where the following languages are spoken: English, Swedish, Danish, Turkish, and Spanish. Tell students to write five sentences about their findings. Ask them to circle words that end in the suffixes **-ish, -en,** or **-ern.**

Observational Assessment

*Check to see that students correctly use and spell words ending in the suffixes **-en, -ern,** and **-ish**.*

English-Language Learners/ESL

On the board, write color words following this pattern: **green/greenish**. Display pictures whose coloration can be described with words containing the suffix **-ish**. Say, for example: *Find a greenish item.* Ask the student to say the word **greenish** and point to something greenish in the picture.

Gifted Learners

Provide students with a passage from a familiar writer, such as Hans Christian Andersen. Challenge students to locate words with the suffixes **-en, -ern,** and **-ish** in a passage. Then invite students to create their own story using similar language, including at least two words with each suffix.

Learners with Special Needs

Additional strategies for supporting learners with special needs can be found on page 137L.

Suffixes and Syllables

Objectives

- **To identify words with suffixes**
- **To identify suffixes within words**
- **To identify the number of syllables in words with suffixes**

Warming Up

- Write the following rhyme on the board and read it with students:

  From one man's **creativity**

  Comes this bulb so bright.

  Thanks to **electricity**,

  Our nights are filled with light.

- Have a volunteer underline the words (shown in boldface type above) that end with one of the suffixes students have learned so far in this unit. Have another volunteer circle the suffixes. (Both words end in **-ity**.)

Teaching the Lesson

- Have students listen as you say and clap out each syllable of the words **creativity** and **electricity**. Then have students repeat the words and clap out their syllables. Ask: *How many syllables do these words have?* (Both words have five syllables.)

- Have students brainstorm other words that end in the syllables **-ive**, **-ish**, **-ity**, **-en**, **-ern**, **-ion**, **-sion**, or **-tion** as you list them on the board.

- Invite students to sort the words two ways: first by suffix, then by the number of syllables they have.

155

Name _____

⭐ Read each group of words below. Draw one line under the word that has a suffix. Then draw two lines under the suffix.

1. high humidity
2. will strengthen their case
3. yellowish in color
4. in an eastern county
5. won the election
6. Finnish cheese from Finland
7. a massive storm
8. waits for the clay to harden
9. a lightish color
10. wants more publicity
11. uses persuasion
12. would weaken their muscles
13. a Turkish towel
14. first city to use electricity

⭐ Underline the suffix in each of these words. Then write the number of syllables that the word has. Add the total number of syllables of all the words.

Syllables

15. invention	3
16. discussion	3
17. protective	3
18. widen	2
19. description	3
20. southwestern	3
21. British	2
22. plumpish	2
23. inferiority	6
24. babyish	3
25. education	4
Total:	34

Thomas Edison with his "light bulb" invention in 1915

WORK TOGETHER

Form a small group. One person keeps time for 2 minutes. Other group members list 2-syllable words and 3-syllable words, all with suffixes. Try to list a total of 10 words.

UNIVERSAL ACCESS
Meeting Individual Needs

Tactile Learners

Write words from the lesson on strips of oak tag and give one to each student. Have students say their word softly to themselves and tap out the syllables. Then ask students to take a pair of scissors and cut the words into syllables. Invite students to mix up their syllables and trade with a partner. Finally, partners should put the syllables back in order to form the word.

Auditory Learners

Help students hear the syllables in words with suffixes. Say the following rhyme with students, clapping for each syllable.

Length has one syllable.

Length-en has one more.

Dis-rupt has the same again.

Dis-rup-tive ups the score.

Mo-ti-vate: three syllables.

Mo-ti-va-tion: four.

★ **Underline the suffix in each word below. Then sort the words according to the number of syllables that the words have. Write each word in the correct column below.**

reddish	fascination	reality
positive	impressive	publicity
education	toughen	disruptive
northern	attraction	tension
Polish	conclusion	observation

1 Has Two Syllables	2 Has Three Syllables	3 Has Four Syllables
reddish	positive	fascination
toughen	impressive	reality
northern	disruptive	publicity
tension	attraction	education
Polish	conclusion	observation

★ **Answer each question. Write a word from the boxes above.**

4. Which four-syllable word means "the act of observing"? — observation
5. Which three-syllable word means "the act of attracting"? — attraction
6. Which two-syllable word means "belonging to Poland"? — Polish
7. Which four-syllable word means "the act of educating"? — education
8. Which two-syllable word means "to make tough"? — toughen
9. Which three-syllable word means "tending to impress"? — impressive
10. Which two-syllable word means "to the north"? — northern
11. Which two-syllable word means "somewhat red"? — reddish
12. Which three-syllable word means "tending to disrupt"? — disruptive

LESSON 76: Suffixes and Syllables

Home Involvement Activity Choose five words with suffixes. Write each word on an index card, with a scrambled version on the back. Challenge family members to unscramble the words.

Practicing the Skill

● Read aloud the direction lines on pages 155–156 and complete the first item in each exercise with students.

● Encourage students to say the words softly and tap the number of syllables.

Curriculum Connections

Spelling Link

Ask students to listen as you read each sentence aloud. Repeat the word in bold type. Have students clap the number of syllables as they say the word aloud. Then have students spell each word orally, write it, and underline its suffix.

Publicity about the first walk on the moon was worldwide.

A scientist must run many tests before drawing a **conclusion.**

The **greenish** fuzz on old cheese is mold.

Her discoveries about dinosaurs are **impressive.**

You can **strengthen** your muscles by exercising.

Multicultural Connection

● Scientists come from all over the world. Challenge students to write the words that name the nationalities of these scientists.

Newton was from England. **(English)**
Copernicus was from Poland. **(Polish)**
Celsius was from Sweden. **(Swedish)**
Watt was from Scotland. **(Scottish)**
Bohr was from Denmark. **(Danish)**

● Encourage students to count the syllables in the country and nationality.

Observational Assessment

Check to see that students can identify suffixes and count syllables correctly.

English-Language Learners/ESL

Display a map. Have students use the compass rose to identify north, south, east, and west. Say each word and have students repeat. Then point to an area on the map. Ask students to complete this sentence using the words **northern, southern, eastern,** or **western**: *This is the _____ area.* Have students say the words and count the syllables.

Gifted Learners

Give students passages from a science text that have words with suffixes. Ask students to copy the sentences that have such words. underline the word, and circle their suffixes. Then have students identify the number of syllables in each word.

Learners with Special Needs

Additional strategies for supporting learners with special needs can be found on page 137L.

Connecting Reading and Writing

Objectives

- **To read and respond to a piece of nonfiction**
- **To compare, contrast, and synthesize information**
- **To write a description**

Warming Up

Comprehension Skills

- Ask students to **compare** and **contrast** two similar items such as a wristwatch and a clock. Ask: *How are these two items alike? In what ways are they different?*

- Remind students that when you **synthesize**, you put together the ideas within a piece of writing and make sense of them. Encourage students to use the ideas they have synthesized about clocks when they write their descriptions.

Teaching the Lesson

- Suggest that students reread the article in order to answer to the first Reader's Response question.

- Remind students that the second question is asking them to compare and contrast Banneker and Copernicus.

- Invite students to make a Venn diagram to help them answer the third question.

Practicing the Skill

- Read aloud the directions and the words in the box on page 158.

- Prompt students with questions such as these: *Would your perfect clock also tell you about the weather? Where in your home would you place your perfect clock?*

Name _____

⭐ Read about a famous African American scientist and inventor. Then answer the questions that follow.

A Mind Like Clockwork

Benjamin Banneker (also spelled *Bannaker*) was born in Baltimore in 1731. Unlike most African Americans of his time, he was the son of free blacks. For a few winters, the young Banneker attended a small country school. That was all the formal education he ever had. Yet the boy had an active mind. He could understand the way things worked without being taught.

Banneker showed his genius for science by building a clock. He used only wooden parts that he invented himself. He built his clock without ever having seen a working clock. No one had told him how to do it. Banneker could teach himself whatever he wanted to learn. He was amazing.

When he was fifty-seven years old, Banneker taught himself advanced mathematics. He used this math and some instruments to learn how the planets, moon, stars, and comets move in space. He wrote a successful book about what he had learned.

Yet Banneker was more than a writer, an inventor, and a scientist. He was also an architect. In 1791, President George Washington began making plans for the nation's new capital—Washington, DC. George Washington hired Banneker to help plan the city.

By the time he died in 1806, Benjamin Banneker was famous. This great man was known for being a writer, an inventor, and a scientist. He was also famous for being the designer of a young nation's new capital.

Reader's Response

1. What was amazing about Benjamin Banneker?

2. Imagine that Banneker and Copernicus could meet. Do you think they would become friends? What would they have in common?

3. How are you like and unlike Benjamin Banneker? Do you like science? Do you teach yourself new things? Explain.

1. Benjamin Banneker could teach himself whatever he wanted to learn.
2. Answers will vary.
3. Answers will vary.

Connecting Reading and Writing
Comprehension—Compare and Contrast; Synthesize

157

UNIVERSAL ACCESS
Meeting Individual Needs

Visual Learners

Show students pictures of clocks from magazines and books. Have them draw an illustration of their clock and label the various features.

Learners with Special Needs

Additional strategies for supporting learners with special needs can be found on page 137L.

Auditory Learners

Invite students to form small groups that can offer support as writers work through the writing process. Suggest that students begin by talking about their ideas while they are still in the prewriting stage. Students can then proceed from talking about their ideas to writing them down. Students can read their first drafts to the group and incorporate the group's feedback into their revisions.

Clocks are everywhere. There are old clocks, new clocks, big clocks, and hard-to-read clocks. There are clocks on the wall, on your wrist, and on the microwave oven. There are clocks that chime, that beep, and that sing. Think about the clocks that you see every day. How are they like and unlike one another? Which clock is your favorite? Why?

⭐ **Describe your idea of the perfect clock. Tell what it looks like and what special things it can do. Use at least two of these words to write your description.**

biggest	noisiest	measurement	quickly	easily	valuable	readable
soften	colorful	fascination	ability	attractive	electricity	clearly

Sentences will vary.

_____

_____

_____

_____

_____

_____

_____

_____

Writer's Tip

Bring your ideas to life. Use vivid words and details that will help your audience see, hear, and feel your description.

▶ Writer's Challenge ◀

Imagine that one day all the clocks stopped! Describe what the day would be like for you at school and at home. How would you get by without knowing the exact time? What might go wrong? Use different kinds of sentences to make your description more interesting.

158   Lesson 77: Connecting Reading and Writing
Comprehension—Compare and Contrast; Synthesize

The Writing Process

Review the directions and Writer's Tip on page 158. Then discuss the features of a good description: vivid details that convey images that appeal to the senses. Have students explain what their clock can do and how its features make it superior.

Prewrite Suggest that students begin by freewriting about their perfect clock or by drawing an illustration of it.

Write Remind students that the goal of their descriptions is to enable their readers to visualize the clock and to understand what capacities it has.

Revise Have students read their work aloud to a partner. Suggest that students consider their partners' suggestions as they revision their descriptions.

Proofread Ask students to read their descriptions slowly to check for errors in grammar, punctuation, and spelling.

Publish Students can copy their final drafts onto page 158 or a sheet of paper.

Computer Connection This is a tip for students who use a word-processing program to do their writing:

● Most word-processing programs allow you to change fonts and type size. Changing the style and size of your type can help you direct your reader's attention to certain bits of information at certain points in your writing.

● Usually, the Format menu has a feature that enables you to select a font. Each font is available in different styles and sizes.

Portfolio Have students add their descriptions of the perfect clock to their portfolios.

English-Language Learners/ESL

Display pictures that show various types of clocks, watches, or other timepieces. Invite English-language learners to discuss these pictures with more fluent speakers, both to build vocabulary and to get ideas for their descriptions.

Gifted Learners

Encourage students to write a story about the clock they described. Perhaps their clock is placed on a spaceship or in a submarine. Maybe their clock is swallowed by a blue whale or snatched by a curious orangutan. Invite students to illustrate their stories and share them with their classmates.

Suffixes
-ward, -less, -ship

Objectives

- **To identify the suffixes -ward, -less, and -ship**
- **To identify the meaning of words with these suffixes**
- **To write words with these suffixes**

Warming Up

- Write the following riddle on the board and read it aloud with students.

   What never goes **backward**, but always goes **forward**?

   It sometimes brings **friendship**, and sometimes brings **hardship**.

   But **regardless** of everything, it's **tireless** as it marches on.

   HINT: Look **upward** at the clock! (time)

- Ask for volunteers to underline each word that has a suffix.

⭐ Teaching the Lesson

- Ask students to list the words from the riddle with the following suffixes: -**ward**, -**less**, and -**ship**.

- Have students circle the suffix in each word. Then challenge them to write a sentence using each base word. Next, have them write a sentence using each base word with its suffix.

- Discuss with students how the meaning of the base word changed when the suffix was added.

- Have a student read the Helpful Hints aloud as others follow along silently.

Name _____

Helpful Hints

The **suffix ward** means "in a certain direction."
   Eastward means "toward the east."
   Downward means "in a lower direction."

The **suffix less** means "without."
   Careless means "without care."

The **suffix ship** means "state or condition."
   Friendship is the state of being friends.

Ship may also mean "office or rank of" or "ability or skill."
   She won the **governorship** by just a few votes.
   Her **penmanship** is the best in the class.

French scientist
Louis Pasteur
(1822–1895) in
his laboratory

⭐ Read each group of words. Underline the suffix in each word in bold print.

1. pedal **backward**
2. a **harmless** prank
3. a strong **kinship**
4. a great **hardship**
5. an **upward** turn
6. a **tireless** worker
7. a **needless** expense
8. **westward** journey
9. a **hopeless** situation

⭐ Complete the sentences below. Choose from the words in bold print above.

10. The scientist Louis Pasteur led the ___tireless___ fight to discover what caused disease.

11. Years of research caused Pasteur great ___hardship___.

12. Yet one day, his research took an ___upward___ turn.

13. Pasteur's research proved a strong ___kinship___ between germs and disease.

14. This great scientist proved that germs were not ___harmless___, but harmful.

CHALLENGE

The suffixes **less** and **ful** are opposites:

helpless/helpful

painless/painful

List two other base words to which you can add the suffixes **less** and **ful**.

UNIVERSAL ACCESS
Meeting Individual Needs

Auditory Learners

Have students play "Simon's Suffixes." Make a list of words that end in -**ward, -ship,** or **-less.** Explain that you will say words with and without these suffixes. Students should clap if the word they hear has a suffix. Students who clap to a word without a suffix leave the game. Continue until one student remains.

Visual Learners

Have students write words from the lesson to complete the chart below:

Suffix	Meaning	Words
-ward	in a certain direction	upward backward westward
-less	without	harmless tireless needless

1.	name	ward	less	nameless
2.	citizen	ship	less	citizenship
3.	age	ship	less	ageless
4.	out	ship	ward	outward
5.	time	ward	less	timeless
6.	scholar	ship	ward	scholarship
7.	down	ship	ward	downward
8.	partner	ship	ward	partnership
9.	thought	ship	less	thoughtless
10.	in	ward	less	inward

★ Complete each sentence with a word from the box.
Add the suffix ward, less, or ship to each word
so that the sentence makes sense.

| citizen | count | friend | home | taste | sky |

11. Look ____skyward____ at the hot-air balloons
floating above.

12. There are ____countless____ uses for aircraft.

13. The special ____friendship____ between the gorilla
Koko and a kitten was told in an interesting book.

14. My horse seems to know when we ride in a
____homeward____ direction.

15. Babies born in the United States have American
____citizenship____.

16. Adding garlic and salt may give the ____tasteless____
soup some flavor.

160   LESSON 78: Suffixes -ward, -less, -ship

Home Involvement Activity Invite family members to
discuss the true meaning of **friend**ship. Encourage them
to use some of the words from this lesson, such as
kinship, **time**less, and **partner**ship.

Practicing the Skill

● Read aloud the direction lines on pages
159–160 and complete the first item in
each exercise with students.

● Have students work with a partner to
check their work.

Curriculum Connections

Spelling Link

● Read the following sentences aloud:

I made a new **friend** yesterday.

Our **friendship** will last forever.

It's **hard** to be on time.

It's a great **hardship** to be on time.

You don't **need** to repeat the joke.

We heard the joke; repeating it is
needless.

The compass pointed **north.**

We took the trail **northward.**

● Repeat the word in bold type. Ask a volunteer to spell the word. Have another student write the word on the board. Then
have volunteers circle the suffixes.

Social Studies Link

List places where ancient artifacts have
been found, such as: Egypt, China, Greece,
Rome, England, and Mexico. Help students
locate these places on a world map. Invite
students to pretend they are archaeologists
traveling to a new dig. Have them use
words such as **northward, southward,
westward,** and **eastward** to describe
where they will go next.

Observational Assessment

*Check to see that students can correctly
use the suffixes -ship, -ward, and -less.*

English-Language Learners/ESL

Do the following activity with students. Remind them that
the suffix **-less** means "without." Say: *without a hat.* Draw
a picture of or pantomime a person without a hat to
convey the meaning of the word **hatless.** Write it on the
board and say it with students. Continue with the other
lesson suffixes.

Gifted Learners

Invite students to write a story
using one of the following titles:
*The Backward-Forward Machine,
The Pointless Pencil,* or *Invisible Penmanship.* Encourage students to
use words with the suffixes **-ward,
-ship,** and **-less** in their stories.

Learners with Special Needs

Additional strategies for
supporting learners with
special needs can be
found on page 137L.

Student Pages 161–162

Suffixes -er, -or, -ist

Objectives

- **To identify the suffixes -er, -or, and -ist**
- **To identify the meanings of words with these suffixes**
- **To write words with these suffixes**

Warming Up

- Write the following rhyme on the board and read it aloud with students.

    A writ**er** writes,

    And an act**or** acts.

    An archaeolog**ist**

    Looks at artifacts.

- Ask volunteers to underline each word in the rhyme that names a type of person. Ask: *What suffixes do these words include?* **(-er, -or, -ist)**
- Have students talk about what these suffixes might mean.

Teaching the Lesson

- On the board, list the words from the rhyme that end in **-er, or,** and **-ist.**
- Invite students to name other words that contain these suffixes. Write students' suggestions on the board under the headings **-er, -or,** and **-ist.**
- Ask students to identify words on the board whose base word spelling changed when the suffix was added.
- Read the Helpful Hints aloud as students follow along silently.

Name _____

Helpful Hints

The **suffixes** er, or, and ist mean "someone who makes or does something."

A **teach**er is someone who teaches.

An **invent**or is someone who invents.

A **cartoon**ist is someone who draws cartoons.

If the **base word** ends in **silent** e, drop the e before adding er, or, or ist.

dance → dancer   create → creator   type → typist

If a **base word** has a short vowel sound, double the final consonant before adding a suffix.

ship → shipper   log → logger

☆ **Underline the suffix in each of these careers. Then write the meaning of the word on the blank line.**

1. art**ist** _____someone who creates art_____
2. produc**er** _____someone who produces_____
3. direct**or** _____someone who directs_____
4. report**er** _____someone who reports_____

☆ **Write a word from the box to complete each sentence.**

| chemist | inventor | journalist | painter |

5. Pablo Picasso was a modern _____painter_____.
6. A ___chemist___ in Germany made the first aspirin powder.
7. Josephine Cochrane was the ___inventor___ of the dishwasher.
8. The author of *The Wizard of Oz* began his career as a newspaper ___journalist___.

CHALLENGE

Scientists are people who practice or study science.

What areas of science do these people study? Use a dictionary to help you.

geologist
volcanologist
zoologist

LESSON 79: Suffixes **-er, -or, -ist**   161

UNIVERSAL ACCESS
Meeting Individual Needs

Kinesthetic Learners

Have students play "Suffix Charades." Whisper an activity such as "painting" to a student. Have the student pantomime the action. Ask the rest of the class to name the activity being acted out. Students should respond in a complete sentence, such as: *You are a **painter.*** Have the student confirm answers by saying: *I am a **painter.** I paint pictures.*

Visual Learners

Display pictures that show people doing specific things. Challenge students to identify the person by using a word with the suffix **-er, -or, -ist.** Then have volunteers write the word containing the appropriate suffix on a self-stick note to label the picture.

_____ the shaded column to write the answer to the question below.

1. What singers do — s i n g
2. Dial "0" to reach this person — o p e r a t o r
3. What creators do — c r e a t e
4. Where scuba divers explore — o c e a n
5. The instrument a pianist plays — p i a n o
6. Where a gardener works — g a r d e n
7. What a violinist plays — v i o l i n
8. Someone who makes art — a r t i s t
9. What swimmers do — s w i m
10. What a batter hits with — b a t

Question: What do you call people who focus on one subject or area and become experts in it?

Answer: This person is called a _____specialist_____.

⭐ **Think about people you admire. Write your answers on the lines.**

11. Name your favorite singer.
    _____Answers will vary._____

12. Name your favorite actor.
    _____

13. Name your favorite player (in any sport).
    _____

14. Name your favorite writer.
    _____

15. Name your favorite inventor.
    _____

In 1903, the Wright Brothers made the first successful flight in this motor-powered airplane, which they invented.

LESSON 79: Suffixes -er, -or, -ist

Home Involvement Activity Some English last names, such as **Baker, Cooper, Miller,** or **Singer,** came from the work people did. List other job-related names. Do you know people who have the names you have listed?

Practicing the Skill

Practicing the Skill

● Read aloud the direction lines on pages 161–162 and complete the first item in each exercise with students.

● Point out that for 1–10 on page 162, the word might not have a suffix.

Curriculum Connections

Spelling Link

Read the following sentences aloud. For each sentence, repeat the word or words shown in bold type. Have students write each word and underline the suffix.

Edison was a great **inventor**.

The U.S. **diver** won the gold medal.

This **typist** can type 100 words per minute.

The **runner** set a new world record.

The **winner** gave the **journalist** an interview.

Social Studies Link

Compile newspaper articles whose stories take place around the world. Invite students to look through the articles for words with the suffixes -**er**, -**or**, or -**ist** to refer to people who make or do something. (For example: **leader, actor, singer, pianist, senator, biologist.**) Have students circle the words and write a sentence using each one. Encourage them to share their work with the class.

Observational Assessment

Check to see that students can correctly use the suffixes **-er, -or,** and **-ist.**

English-Language Learners/ESL

Invite students to draw pictures of people doing various jobs. Then have students describe each job using one action word. Ask students to name the person in each picture by saying the action word plus the suffix -**er**, -**or**, or -**ist**. Students can label their pictures with the correct words.

Gifted Learners

Ask students to think of a person whom they admire. Students can write about that person, telling what the person does, and why he or she is admirable. Remind students to use words that end with the suffixes -**er**, -**or**, and -**ist** when describing the person.

Learners with Special Needs

Additional strategies for supporting learners with special needs can be found on page 137L.

Suffixes
-ance, -dom, -ism

Objectives

- **To identify the suffixes -ance, -dom, and -ism**
- **To identify the meanings of words with these suffixes**
- **To write words with these suffixes**

Warming Up

- Write "A Scientist's Formula" on the board and read it with students.

   Start with lots of **freedom**.

   Mix in a pound of **wisdom**.

   Add a dash of **heroism**.

   Sprinkle liberally with **guidance**.

- Ask volunteers to underline each word that has a suffix and say the word.

Teaching the Lesson

- On the board, write the words with suffixes from *Warming Up*.

- Have students say the suffixes with you. Ask students to suggest other words with the suffixes -**ance**, -**dom**, and -**ism**. List the words on the board under the headings -**ance**, -**dom**, and -**ism**.

- Ask a volunteer to read the Helpful Hints aloud as others follow along silently.

Name _____

Helpful Hints

The **suffixes** ance, dom, and ism mean "the act, state, quality, condition, or result of." The **suffix** dom may also mean "office, rank, or realm," as in king**dom**.

Assistance is the act of assisting or helping.
Freedom is the state of being free.
Heroism is the actions or qualities of a hero.

Guion S. Bluford, an example of **heroism**

Underline the suffix in each word below.

1. bore<u>dom</u>
2. inherit<u>ance</u>
3. attend<u>ance</u>
4. disturb<u>ance</u>
5. patriot<u>ism</u>
6. king<u>dom</u>
7. resembl<u>ance</u>
8. wis<u>dom</u>
9. import<u>ance</u>
10. critic<u>ism</u>
11. guid<u>ance</u>
12. terror<u>ism</u>

Read each phrase. Then unscramble the letters in bold print to form one of the words from the list above. Write the unscrambled word on the line.

13. the **dwomsi** of the elderly chief — wisdom
14. peace throughout the **modnigk** — kingdom
15. received **digceanu** from her family — guidance
16. stressed the **ipmoatrcen** of honesty — importance
17. yawning from **droombe** — boredom
18. daily **tacentaedn** taken in class — attendance
19. the **mistoirtap** of George Washington — patriotism
20. a loud **transdicube** — disturbance
21. a striking **ancesembler** — resemblance

CHALLENGE

The noun **elegance** is related to the adjective **elegant**. What adjective is each of these nouns related to?

   brilliance
   fragrance
   importance

LESSON 80: Suffixes -ance, -dom, -ism

163

UNIVERSAL ACCESS
Meeting Individual Needs

Auditory Learners

Explain that you will read words with suffixes. Ask students to stomp their feet when they hear words ending in -**ance**; snap their fingers for words ending in -**dom**; hum for words ending in -**ism**. Ask students to listen closely before responding. Write each word on the board to confirm responses.

Visual Learners

Write words with the lesson suffixes on index cards. On a bulletin board or using a pocket chart, set up a column for each suffix. Have students sort the cards and arrange them in the proper columns.

j 1. **magnetism**   a. the act of assisting or helping

i 2. **freedom**   b. the act of criticizing or making judgments

c 3. **annoyance**   c. the act of annoying; being annoyed

e 4. **hypnotism**   d. the act of destroying property

a 5. **assistance**   e. the act of putting someone into a sleeplike state

b 6. **criticism**   f. the state of being insured

g 7. **heroism**   g. the actions or qualities of a hero

d 8. **vandalism**   h. the quality of being wise

h 9. **wisdom**   i. the state of being free

f 10. **insurance**   j. the quality of being magnetic, or attracting

Use each of the words in bold print above. Write a sentence that shows the meaning of each word.

11. _____ Sentences will vary. _____

12. _____

13. _____

14. _____

15. _____

16. _____

17. _____

18. _____

19. _____

20. _____

Home Involvement Activity Discuss the meaning of the word **freedom**. Talk about the kinds of freedoms that are important to your family—and to the nation.

Practicing the Skill

● Read aloud the direction lines on pages 163–164 and complete the first item in each exercise with students.

● Remind students to use process of elimination to narrow down their choices in items 13–21 on page 163 and items 1–10 on page 164.

● Help students who have difficulty matching a word to its definition by using the word in context.

Curriculum Connections

Spelling Link

● Read the following "word equations" to students. Challenge students to spell the words correctly.

guide + ance	**bore + dom**
disturb + ance	**king + dom**
patriot + ism	**magnet + ism**
assist + ance	**free + dom**

● Ask students to circle the word that follows this spelling rule: Drop the **e** then add the suffix. (**guidance**)

Social Studies Link

Invite students to choose a country they would like to know more about. Suggest that students use nonfiction books or encyclopedias to research the country. As students read, encourage them to look for words with the suffixes: -**ance**, -**ism**, and -**dom**. Have students write a paragraph about their countries. Remind them to include words with the suffixes -**ance**, -**dom**, and -**ism**.

Observational Assessment

*Check to see that students can correctly use the suffixes -**ance**, -**dom**, and -**ism**.*

English-Language Learners/ESL

Say the words **wisdom, assistance,** and **heroism** with students. Help students understand what each word means. Then invite students to express the word in their native languages. Have students write the English word and the native language equivalent side by side. Then point to the suffix in the English word.

Gifted Learners

Ask students to imagine they are scientists who have just won an award. To accept the award, they must give a speech. Have students write their speeches using as many words as possible with the suffixes -**ance**, -**ism**, and -**dom**.

Learners with Special Needs

Additional strategies for supporting learners with special needs can be found on page 137L.

Reviewing and Assessing
Suffixes

Objective

To review and assess suffixes -en, -ern, -ish, -ward, -less, -ship, -er, -or, -ist, -ance, -dom, and -ism

Warming Up

● Write the following clues on the board: somewhat blue (**bluish**); to make sharp (**sharpen**); toward the west (**westward**); without power (**powerless**); the state of being a citizen (**citizenship**); someone who paints (**painter**); a wise attitude (**wisdom**); the qualities of a patriot (**patriotism**).

● For each clue, have students write the corresponding word that ends with a suffix (shown in bold type above). Then, have students draw a line between the base word and the suffix. Finally, have students use the word in a sentence.

★ Teaching the Lesson

● On the board or on chart paper, make a review chart for the suffixes **-en, -ern, -ish, -ward, -less, -ship, -er, -or, -ist, -ance, -dom, -ism.** Use this format:

Suffix	Meaning	Examples
-dom	the state or quality of being	**freedom** **wisdom**

● List the suffixes in the first column. Then have students fill in the meaning and give at least two example words for each suffix. Ask volunteers to use each example word in a sentence.

● The Helpful Hints on pages 153 and 161 contain spelling guidelines for adding suffixes to base words. Review these guidelines and have students give examples.

165

Name _____

★ Add the suffix **ern** to two of the following base words. Add the suffix **ance** to the other two. Then write a sentence for each word.

Base Word	Word with Suffix	Sentence
1. guide	guidance	Sentences will vary.
2. west	western	
3. disturb	disturbance	
4. northeast	northeastern	

★ Add the suffix **less** to two of the following base words. Add the suffix **dom** to the other two. Then write a sentence for each word.

Base Word	Word with Suffix	Sentence
5. free	freedom	Sentences will vary.
6. harm	harmless	
7. pain	painless	
8. wise	wisdom	

★ Add the suffix **ish** to one of the following base words. Add the suffix **ist** to the other one. Then write a sentence for each word.

Base Word	Word with Suffix	Sentence
9. tall	tallish	Sentences will vary.
10. journal	journalist	

★ Add the suffix **ism** to one of the following base words. Add the suffix **or** to the other one. Then write a sentence for each word.

Base Word	Word with Suffix	Sentence
11. invent	inventor	Sentences will vary.
12. hero	heroism	

LESSON 81: Review and Assess   **165**

UNIVERSAL ACCESS
Meeting Individual Needs

Kinesthetic Learners

Have students write these suffixes on cards: **-en, -ern, -ish, -ward, -less, -ship, -er, -or, -ist, -ance, -dom, -ism.** Then say these words: **upward, harmless, hardship, darken, eastern, magnetism, kingdom, importance, chemist, inventor, typist, partnership, boredom.** Ask students to hold up the card with the correct suffix.

Learners with Special Needs

Additional strategies for supporting students with special needs can be found on page 137L.

Auditory Learners

Write each of these suffixes on a separate sheet of paper: **-en, -ern, -ish, -ward, -less, -ship, -er, -or, -ist, -ance, -dom, -ism.** Have volunteers take turns drawing the sheets of paper from a bag. For each suffix, the student should think of a word containing that suffix and give clues to the class to help them guess the word. As each word is identified, write it on the board and underline its suffix.

Read the sentences. Choose a word from the box that completes each sentence correctly. Then write the word on the line.

kingdom	Swedish	scientists	importance

1. How do <u>scientists</u> sort living things into groups that make sense?

2. Long ago, a <u>Swedish</u> man named Linnaeus came up with a plan.

3. He saw the <u>importance</u> of finding out how living things are alike.

4. He sorted all life forms into the animal or the plant <u>kingdom</u>.

Choose a word from the box that has a different suffix from the word in bold print. Write a sentence that uses both words. An example is given below.

actor ___The **actor** played the part of the **scientist**.___

conductor	heroism	teacher	scientist	guidance

5. **dancer** _____
   Sentences will vary.
   _____

6. **sailor** _____
   _____

7. **leadership** _____
   _____

8. **wisdom** _____
   _____

Extend & Apply

Place the four terms below in an order that makes sense. All the terms belong to the animal kingdom. List them from the most general to the most exact, or specific.

Welsh terrier   mammal   dog   terrier

Reteaching Activities

Suffix Sort

Write these suffixes on separate cards: **-en**, **-ern**, **-ish**, **-ward**, **-less**, **-ship**, **-er**, **-or**, **-ist**, **-ance**, **-dom**, **-ism.** Lay the cards out, face up, in two rows. Give two blank cards to each student. Tell students to write a word containing any of these suffixes on each card. Collect all the cards, shuffle them, and place them in a pile. Have students draw a card, read the word aloud, and put the card alongside the corresponding suffix card.

Word Chain

List on the board the suffixes **-en**, **-ern**, **-ish**, **-ward**, **-less**, **-ship**, **-er**, **-or**, **-ist**, **-ance**, **-dom**, **-ism.** Have a volunteer say a word containing one of the suffixes. Then have another student use a different suffix in a word that starts with the first or the last letter of the first student's word. For example, if a student says **harmless**, the next student might say either **hardship** or **southeastern**. Continue the chain until students have used all suffixes at least once.

Assessing the Skill

Check Up Have students do the exercises on pages 165–166 to help them review the suffixes they have studied. The exercises on these pages will also help you assess students' ability to form words with suffixes and to use words with suffixes in sentences.

Go over the directions for each set of exercises. Remind students to apply the spelling guidelines they have learned. For the second exercise on page 166, make sure students understand that they are to use two words in each sentence.

Observational Assessment As students complete the exercises, check to see whether they are having difficulty forming or using words with suffixes. Do they spell the words correctly? Review your observational notes from previous lessons, and use them to evaluate both individual and class progress.

Student Skills Assessment Keep track of each student's progress in understanding suffixes using the checklist on page 137H.

Writing Conference Meet with students individually to talk over their written work. Also discuss the writing in their Home Portfolios. Help students identify words with suffixes in their writing. Discuss how these words function in sentences.

Group together students who need further instruction in suffixes, and have them complete the *Reteaching Activities.* Turn to page 137C for alternative assessment methods.

Suffixes
-some, -hood, -most

Objectives

- To identify the suffixes **-some**, **-hood**, and **-most**
- To identify the meanings of words with these suffixes
- To write words with these suffixes

Warming Up

- Write the following verse on the board.

    At a **northernmost, westernmost, outermost** tree,

    On the edge of a **fearsome** wood,

    Lived a **troublesome, lonesome, tiresome** owl,

    Who was king of his **neighborhood.**

- Read the verse aloud dramatically. Invite students to join in the second reading.

- Ask for volunteers to underline and say each word that has a suffix.

Teaching the Lesson

- Write the words with suffixes from the verse on the board.

- Ask a student to draw a line between the base word and the suffix in each word.

- Have students discuss what they think the words with suffixes mean. Then have them use each word in an original sentence.

- Ask volunteers to read the Helpful Hints aloud as others follow along silently.

167

Name _____

> **Helpful Hints**

The **suffix some** means "like" or "tending to be."
A **tiresome** buzz can make you sleepy.

The **suffix hood** means "state, quality, or condition of."
Dad spent his **boyhood** in Japan.

The **suffix most** means "greatest or closest to."
DNA is found in the **innermost** part of our cells.

Computer model of DNA

Join each base word and suffix. Write the new word on the line.

1. outer + most   outermost
2. false + hood   falsehood
3. trouble + some   troublesome
4. child + hood   childhood
5. lone + some   lonesome
6. top + most   topmost
7. fear + some   fearsome
8. neighbor + hood   neighborhood

Complete each sentence. Use a word from the list above.

9. The _____outermost_____ layer is the farthest out.

10. Six students in our class live on the same street in the same _____neighborhood_____.

11. A _____troublesome_____ problem fills you with worry.

12. A lion can be a _____fearsome_____ sight.

13. Being _____lonesome_____ is not the same thing as being alone.

> **CHALLENGE**
>
> The word **utmost** ends with the suffix **most**. Find out the meaning of **utmost**. Then describe in a sentence your utmost wish or hope.

UNIVERSAL ACCESS
Meeting Individual Needs

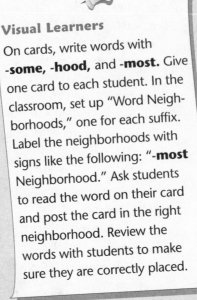

Visual Learners

On cards, write words with **-some**, **-hood**, and **-most**. Give one card to each student. In the classroom, set up "Word Neighborhoods," one for each suffix. Label the neighborhoods with signs like the following: "-**most** Neighborhood." Ask students to read the word on their card and post the card in the right neighborhood. Review the words with students to make sure they are correctly placed.

Auditory Learners

Have students sing this song to the tune of "Row, Row, Row Your Boat."

-**some, -some, -some, some,
-some**—Say the suffix -**some.
Troublesome, quarrelsome, fearsome, tiresome**—That's the suffix -**some.
-most, -most, -most, -most,
-most**—Say the suffix **most.
Uppermost, northernmost, outermost, innermost**—That's the suffix -**most.** Invite students to write a verse for -**hood.**

167

⭐ **Complete each statement. Write your answer on the line.**

Answers will vary.

1. Name a sport that can be played by a twosome. _____

2. Name a game that a threesome can play. _____

3. What game can be played by a foursome? _____

4. What sport can a foursome play? _____

⭐ **Think about good answers to the following questions. Write your answers on the lines. If you are unsure of the meaning of a word in bold print, check a dictionary.**

5. How might you deal with a **quarrelsome** person?

Sentences will vary.

_____

_____

6. What will you find at the **westernmost** border of your state?

_____

_____

7. Which is your favorite street in your **neighborhood**? Tell why.

_____

_____

8. When have you felt **lonesome?** Describe how you felt.

_____

_____

168   LESSON 82: Suffixes -some, -hood, -most

🏠 **Home Involvement Activity** Have a family discussion. Talk about the challenges and joys of **parent**hood and the challenges and joys of **child**hood. Compare and contrast these stages of life.

English Language Learners/ESL

Invite students to act out the meaning of words with the suffixes **-some, -most,** and **-hood.** For example, say the word **tiresome,** then act it out. How could they show **childhood?** **lonesome?** **westernmost?** Ask students to say the word, then demonstrate its meaning through hand, facial, and body movements.

Gifted Learners

Encourage students to imagine they are biologists exploring a natural habitat that interests them, such as the rain forest. Ask students to write a journal entry as the scientist describing the habitat. Encourage students to use words with the suffixes **-most, -some,** and **-hood.**

Learners with Special Needs

Additional strategies for supporting learners with special needs can be found on page 137L.

● Read aloud the direction lines on pages 167–168 and complete the first item in each exercise with students.

● Have students say the base words and then say the suffixes in items 1–8 on page 167 aloud.

Curriculum Connections

Spelling Link

● Write these words on the board:

mostinner	somelone
hoodneighbor	mosttop
hoodchild	sometwo
somethree	hoodfalse
somefear	mostupper

● Ask students what is wrong with the words. (The suffixes and base words are in the wrong order.) Challenge students to rewrite the words correctly.

● Encourage students to write the words again, grouping them by their suffixes.

Science Link

● Invite students to write a description of a place such as a beach, city, farm, desert, or forest, as seen through the eyes of a scientist for the first time. Encourage students to describe the animal and plant life as well as features specific to the area.

● Challenge students to include words with the suffixes **-some, -hood,** and **-most** in their descriptions.

Observational Assessment

*Check to see that students can correctly use the suffixes **-some, -hood,** and **-most.***

More Than One Prefix or Suffix

Objectives

- **To identify words with more than one suffix**
- **To identify the prefix, base word, and suffix in a word**

Warming Up

- Write the following rhyme on the board, and read it aloud with students.

  Carefully he holds the test tube.

  Fearlessly he fills it.

  He gives it to his **coworker**,

  Who **carelessly** spills it.

- Have students underline words from the rhyme that contain a prefix or a suffix (or more than one suffix).

Teaching the Lesson

- List the underlined words from the *Warming-Up* activity on the board.

- Explain that some words can have more than one suffix. To distinguish between suffixes, have students underline the first suffix using one color chalk and the second one using a different color chalk.

- Point out that one word has a prefix. Have a volunteer circle the prefix.

- Word-by-word, mask the affixes, and ask students to read aloud each base word. Remind students that they can understand the meaning of an unfamiliar word if they find the base word first, and then add the prefix and/or suffix(es).

- Have a student read the Helpful Hints aloud as others follow along silently.

Name _____

> **Helpful Hint**
>
> Some words have more than one **suffix**.
> The word **fearlessly** has the suffixes less + ly.
> The word **helpfulness** has the suffixes ful + ness.

Geologist studying a lunar rock

Each of these words has two suffixes. Draw one line under the first suffix and two lines under the second suffix.

1. skillfully   2. enjoyably   3. carelessness

4. loneliness   5. thoughtfulness   6. defensively

7. juiciness   8. wholesomeness   9. governorship

Underline the word that has more than one suffix in each sentence. Then draw two lines under each suffix. Write the base word on the line below.

10. Their inventions were filled with creativity.

    create _____

11. We spoke respectfully about their work.

    respect _____

12. Their childishness was annoying sometimes.

    child _____

13. Don't behave foolishly while working.

    fool _____

14. Scientists need to work carefully.

    care _____

15. Act thoughtlessly and you might get hurt.

    thought _____

16. That lab is in the northernmost part of the state.

    north _____

> **CHALLENGE**
>
> Write a word with more than one suffix to complete this sentence.
>
> *His* _____
> *made him a good worker.*
>
> How many different words can you think of? Make a list.

UNIVERSAL ACCESS
Meeting Individual Needs

Visual Learners

Write the suffixes, prefixes, and base words from this lesson on index cards. Then have students use the cards to form words. If they are unsure whether a word exists, suggest that they look it up in a dictionary. Have students share their words with the class. Then have students sort the cards by whether the words on them have one or two suffixes.

Tactile Learners

Students can create jigsaw puzzles using words from the lesson. Have them use scissors to cut oak tag in the form of a jigsaw puzzle. Then students can label each puzzle piece with a word part. For example, the word **disagreeable** would have three puzzle pieces, labeled **dis-**, **agree**, and **-able**. Encourage students to exchange puzzles and list each word they "put together."

Helpful Hint

Some words have both a **prefix** and a **suffix**.
The word disagreement is made up of the prefix dis,
the suffix ment, and the base word agree.

⭐ **Write the prefix, the base word, and the suffix for each word below. Use + signs to separate the three parts. You may need to change the spelling of some base words. The first one is done for you.**

1. bicyclist — bi + cycle + ist
2. refillable — re+fill+able
3. overactivity — over+active+ity
4. nonviolently — non+violent+ly
5. disgraceful — dis+grace+ful
6. coworker — co+work+er
7. unfriendly — un+friend+ly
8. mismanagement — mis+manage+ment
9. enjoyable — en+joy+able

Family on Four Position Bicycle

⭐ **Fill in the circle of the word that completes each sentence correctly. Then write the word on the line.**

10. Luckily, the new clothes we bought were ___exchangeable___.
    ○ disgraceful   ● exchangeable   ○ unfriendly

11. The company hired a ___replacement___ for the sick worker.
    ● replacement   ○ refillable   ○ returnable

12. Their ___disagreement___ was over what to wear to the dance.
    ● refreshment   ○ disagreement   ○ nonpayment

13. Our ___prepayment___ guaranteed that no one else could buy the car.
    ● prepayment   ○ refundable   ○ thoughtlessness

14. The principal disapproved of the children's ___disagreeable___ behavior.
    ○ enjoyable   ○ immaturity   ● disagreeable

170   LESSON 83: More Than One Prefix or Suffix

🏠 **Home Involvement Activity** Look through newspapers or magazines. Find as many words as you can that have two or more suffixes or a prefix and a suffix. Post the words that you find on a Word Wall.

English-Language Learners/ESL

Ask students to use a familiar word, such as **child** in an oral sentence. Add a suffix, such as **-ish**. Help the student use the word in another sentence. Then add another suffix, such as **-ly.** Help the student use the word in a third sentence. Work with students so that they understand how each suffix affects the base word in its own way.

Gifted Learners

Brainstorm with students ideas for a new machine. What will the machine do? Encourage them to draw the machine. Then have them write a description of it. Challenge students to use and identify words with a prefix and more than one suffix.

Learners with Special Needs

Additional strategies for supporting learners with special needs can be found on page 137L.

Practicing the Skill

Read aloud the direction lines on pages 169–170 and complete the first item in each exercise with students.

Intervention Strategy Turn to page 137K for an Intervention Strategy designed to help students who need extra support with this lesson.

Curriculum Connections

Spelling Link

● Write the following words on the board:

northernmost	**prepayment**
thoughtlessly	**enjoyable**
replacement	**disagreeable**

● Read the words aloud with students. Challenge volunteers to identify the base words by erasing the prefix and/or suffix(es) in each word.

● Then have students spell the words orally, adding the prefix and/or suffix(es).

● Finally, ask students to write a sentence for each word.

Social Studies Link

● Brainstorm with students inventions that have affected the world, such as satellites, vaccinations, airplanes, and so on.

● Ask students to write a paragraph describing an invention and explaining how it has brought the people of the world closer together.

● Challenge students to use words with a prefix and more than one suffix.

Observational Assessment

Check to see that students are able to identify and use words that contain a prefix and more than one suffix.

Spelling Rules for Adding Suffixes

Objectives

- To identify base words and suffixes
- To write words with suffixes
- To learn and apply rules for changing the spelling of certain base words when adding suffixes

Warming Up

- Write the following limerick on the board. Invite students to read it aloud.

  A **Scottish** inventor named Sue,

  Made plenty of **bubbly** goo.

  Far from **forgettable**,

  The end was **regrettable**—

  Goo got all over her shoe!

- Have students underline each word that has a suffix. List the words on the board.

Teaching the Lesson

- Ask for volunteers to write each base word using the words from the *Warming-Up* activity.
- Have students identify which base words changed spelling when a suffix was added by putting a star next to those words.
- Discuss how the spelling of each word changed. (The ending consonant doubled in **Scottish**; the **le** was dropped in **bubbly**; and the ending consonant was doubled in **regret** and **forget**.)
- Have a student read the Helpful Hints aloud as the others follow along silently.

Name _____

Helpful Hints

- When a word ends in **silent** e, usually drop the e before adding a **suffix** that starts with a vowel.

  nice→nicest   type→typist   inflate→inflatable

- When a word ends in le, drop the le before adding the **suffix** ly.

  reliable→reliably   humble→humbly   possible→possibly

- When a word ends in y after a consonant, change the y to i before adding a **suffix**. But *do not* change the y to i if the suffix begins with i.

  happy→happiness   thirty→thirtyish   beauty→beautiful

Scientist Marie Curie (1867–1934) working in her laboratory in 1905

Use the base word and the suffix to write a new word.

1. cute + est   cutest
2. dive + er   diver
3. foggy + er   foggier
4. baby + ish   babyish
5. store + age   storage
6. erase + able   erasable
7. plenty + ful   plentiful
8. bubble + ly   bubbly
9. steady + est   steadiest
10. adore + able   adorable

CHALLENGE

Some words may not always follow the spelling rules. How would you spell these words? Look in a dictionary to check your answers.

love + able
exchange + able
knowledge + able

Draw a line to connect each base word with a suffix to form three words. Then write the words on the lines. Spell the words correctly.

11	12	13
cure — y create — able rose — ive	bounty — able happy — ful rely — est	prank — en loose — ful care — ish
curable	bountiful	prankish
creative	happiest	loosen
rosy	reliable	careful

UNIVERSAL ACCESS
Meeting Individual Needs

Visual Learners

Have students sort the words **reliable, nicer, runner, possibly, creative, fatten, bubbly, happiest** using a chart like the one below.

Drop **e**	Change **y** to **i**
nicer creative	reliable happiest
Drop **le**	Double Final Consonant
possibly bubbly	runner fatten

Logical Learners

Have students write rules for forming words with suffixes. Below are examples.

Make a word with **happy** and **-ness**

Change **y** to **i**.

Then add **-ness**.

Make a word with **nimble** and **-ly**

Drop the **le**.

Then add **-ly**.

Make a word with **rot** and **-en**

Double the **t**.

Then add **-en**.

Use the base word and the suffix to write a new word on the line. Be sure to follow the spelling rules.

1. mad + er   madder
2. Scot + ish   Scottish
3. remit + ance   remittance
4. slim + est   slimmest
5. flop + y   floppy
6. mix + er   mixer
7. wet + est   wettest
8. run + er   runner
9. fix + er   fixer
10. box + y   boxy
11. fat + en   fatten
12. hit + er   hitter

Circle the suffix in each word in bold print. Then write the base word on the line.

13. Before 1955, polio was one of the medical world's **biggest** problems. _____ big

14. Dr. Jonas Salk discovered an **acceptable** way to fight polio. _____ accept

15. The Salk vaccine protected people from getting this **regrettable** disease. _____ regret

Dr. Jonas Salk (1914–1995) in his laboratory

Home Involvement Activity Work together to write a brief paragraph about the importance of caring for your health. Use as many suffixes as you can. Check your spelling in a dictionary or a spell-checker.

172   LESSON 84: Spelling Rules for Adding Suffixes

English-Language Learners/ESL

Display pictures of animals in nature magazines or science books. Ask students to describe the animals using base words and these suffixes: **-est, -er, -y,** and **-ish.** Have students write sentences that describe the animals. For example: *The giraffe has the **thinnest** neck.*

Gifted Learners

Invite students to write a biography about a scientist. Suggest that students write highlights from the scientist's career. Encourage students to use words whose base words change when a suffix is added.

Learners with Special Needs

Additional strategies for supporting learners with special needs can be found on page 137L.

Practicing the Skill

- Read aloud the direction lines on pages 171–172 and complete the first item in each exercise with students.

- Suggest that students say the words aloud to hear the suffixes.

- For items 13–15 on page 172, suggest that students mask the suffix before writing the base word.

Curriculum Connections

Spelling Link

Create the following chart on the board. Have students match base words and suffixes to create new words.

Base Words	Suffixes
baby	-er
bubble	-est
box	-able
store	-age
create	-ive
bounty	-ful
flop	-y
remit	-ly
adore	-ance
big	-ish

Multicultural Connection

Brainstorm a list of foods from different countries. Have students choose one and write a description of it. Ask them to use words with suffixes whose base word changes spelling when the suffix is added. Examples include words such as: **tastiest, hotter, spicier,** and **thinnest.**

Observational Assessment

Make sure that students can apply the correct spelling rule to the different combinations of base words and suffixes.

Connecting Reading and Writing

Objectives

- **To read a nonfiction piece and respond to it in writing**
- **To practice making decisions and summarizing**
- **To write a description**

Warming Up

Comprehension Skills

- To practice **making decisions** ask students to imagine that your class just received $1,000 to spend in one of two ways: taking a class trip, or buying a new computer. Make a two-column chart on the board: **Reasons to Take Trip; Reasons to Buy Computer.** Invite students to share their ideas and write them on the board. Then ask students to identify other decisions that they or someone they know must make.

- Remind students that to **summarize** means to tell only the most important ideas in a piece of writing.

Teaching the Lesson

- Suggest that students use a highlighter to identify information that can help them answer the first Reader's Response question.
- For the second question, remind students that a summary is a short statement that tells the most important ideas in a piece of writing.
- Point out that there are no "right" answers to the third question.

Practicing the Skill

Have a volunteer read aloud the directions and the boxed words on page 174. Suggest that students think about how life might be different in the future.

173

Name _____

Read what *Apollo* astronaut Alan L. Bean has to say about his career and about future careers in space. Then answer the questions that follow.

Your Future in Space

by Alan L. Bean

When John Glenn became the first American to orbit Earth on Feb. 20, 1962, I was a pilot at the Naval Air Test Center in Patuxent River, MD. I tested planes like the *F-4A Phantom Two* and *A-3J Vigilante* that flew twice the speed of sound. I thought I had the hottest job in the Navy—indeed, the world.

I listened on the radio as the *Atlas* rocket successfully boosted Glenn's *Mercury* capsule into space. Then I climbed into a *Skyhawk* for a short test hop. By the time I landed, Glenn was preparing to splash down in the Pacific after circling the planet three times. Quickly, I calculated that during the time it took me to fly 1,000 miles, Glenn went 36,000! I began to realize that somebody else might have a more interesting job.

Later that year, when the National Aeronautics and Space Administration announced plans to hire more astronauts, I applied but was not selected. I applied again one year later, and NASA accepted me. In 1969, I became the fourth man to walk on the Moon.

When I ventured into space, the only route was by learning to fly. As we explore space in the future, we will need pilots, technicians, scientists and probably people with jobs nobody has yet described. When you think about space, it's hard to dream too big a dream.

Reader's Response

1. Why did Alan L. Bean decide to become an astronaut?
2. What would you say in a summary of this article?
3. Do you think you might decide to become an astronaut or another kind of space scientist someday? Give three reasons for your answer.

1. Answers will vary but should include the fact that Bean loved to fly high-speed planes.
2. Answers will vary.
3. Answers will vary.

LESSON 85: Connecting Reading and Writing
Comprehension—Make Decisions; Summarize
173

UNIVERSAL ACCESS
Meeting Individual Needs

Auditory Learners

Have students talk through their potential jobs with a writing partner. Encourage students to be clear and specific, describing exactly what kind of work they would do. Invite partners to help each other recall what they have said, so that students can more easily translate their oral work into written form.

Logical Learners

Help students get ideas for their description by having them identify problems that must be solved—situations that require attention, dangers to be prevented, or people that require assistance. The solutions would be the creation of a new type of job. Encourage students to jot down ideas as they brainstorm.

Learners with Special Needs

Additional strategies for supporting learners with special needs can be found on page 137L.

Astronaut Alan L. Bean says that when he was growing up, his great love was airplanes. He never dreamed that one day he would have a career in space. Bean also realizes that as we continue to explore space, we will need more scientists. We will also probably need "people with jobs nobody has yet described."

⭐ **Imagine that you have applied for a job that "nobody has yet described." Write a paragraph that tells about this new job. Describe what you would do and where and how you would do it. Use at least two of these words in your job description.**

usable useless inventor scientist easily effortless protective
helpful equipment straighten ability attractive valuable clearly

Sentences will vary.

_____

_____

_____

_____

_____

_____

_____

_____

Writer's Tip
Add some simple drawings or diagrams to help your readers understand your job.

Speaker's Challenge

Write and tell a riddle that describes a real job, but don't name the job in your riddle. Challenge a partner to guess what your mystery job is. Vary your tone of voice to stress important clues.

Beyond a Young Boy's Dream, painting by Alan L. Bean

LESSON 85: Connecting Reading and Writing
Comprehension—Make Decisions;
Summarize

The Writing Process

Discuss the purpose of a job description—to let the reader know what kinds of tasks are involved in a job. Ask students to list some questions that a good job description should answer; for example: *What skills are needed for this job? What kind of training is required?*

Prewrite Suggest that students look at classified ads in a newspaper to get ideas for their job descriptions.

Write Remind students to look over the words in the box and choose at least two to include in their work.

Revise Ask students to give their job descriptions to writing partners to read aloud. Suggest that writers listen carefully to their own words. Can they picture clearly the job that is being described? Encourage them to make changes based on what they learned.

Proofread Remind students to read their work slowly and carefully to check for errors in grammar, punctuation, and spelling.

Publish Have students copy their final drafts onto page 174. Students might enjoy role-playing "job interviews" based on their job descriptions.

Computer Connection

Give the following tip to students who use a word-processing program to do their writing.

● Some word-processing programs allow you to add clip art. Perhaps the clip art available on your program will enable you to clarify or enhance your job descriptions.

● Usually, the Graphics menu has a feature that permits you to insert art.

Portfolio Suggest that students add their finished job descriptions to their portfolios.

English-Language Learners/ESL

Invite students to talk about jobs with which they are familiar. Then have them discuss a possible job of the future. You might allow students to present their descriptions to the class orally, instead of in writing. Alternately, have students work with a fluent writing partner to put their ideas in writing.

Gifted Learners

Invite students to imagine that they have already been hired to do the jobs they have described. Encourage them to choose their own format for conveying what happens on their first day at work: short story, dialogue, journal entry, scientist's log, illustration, comic strip, poem, or some other means. Suggest that students share their work with the rest of the class.

Reviewing and Assessing

Suffixes and Syllables

Objective

To review and assess suffixes and syllables

Warming Up

- List the following words on the board: **awareness, easiest, boredom, bouncy, westward, twosome, denser, orphanage, childlike, friendship, rotation, sharpen, topmost, funny.**

- Have a volunteer underline the suffix in each word and tell what base word the suffix has been added to. Have another volunteer explain what spelling change was made, if any.

- Have students suggest other words that have the same suffixes as those listed. Write them on the board.

Teaching the Lesson

- Make sure students understand that both prefixes and suffixes are word parts added to a base word or root, changing the base word's meaning and creating a new word. Prefixes are added to the beginning of a word; suffixes are added to the end.

- Call students' attention to the word-part chart on page 175. Ask what word parts each column contains. (column 1=prefixes, column 2=base words, column 3=suffixes)

- Explain that students will use the chart to make words. To illustrate, ask students what word is formed by adding A2 to A3. Show students how to locate the A2 **(help)** and A3 **(-ful)** parts on the chart, making the word **helpful.** Then tell students to add J1 **(un-)**. Ask what word J1 + A2 + A3 forms. **(unhelpful)**

175

Name _____

☆ Look at the word-part chart below. Use it to form words. You can form the word **happiness** by combining C2 + G3.

	1	2	3
A	im	help	ful
B	mid	create	ment
C	over	happy	ish
D	mis	joy	able
E	co	life	less
F	pre	name	like
G	dis	possible	ness
H	en	measure	ion
I	re	grace	ly
J	un	accept	est
K	in	friend	ive

A **volcanologist** taking measurements of the Mayon volcano in the Philippines

☆ Use the word-part chart to decode these words. Then write the words on the lines. Make spelling changes as needed.

1. H2 + B3 _____measurement_____
2. E2 + F3 _____lifelike_____
3. I2 + A3 _____graceful_____
4. I1 + F2 _____rename_____
5. A2 + E3 _____helpless_____
6. B2 + K3 _____creative_____
7. C2 + J3 _____happiest_____
8. F2 + E3 _____nameless_____
9. J1 + K2 + I3 _____unfriendly_____
10. J1 + J2 + D3 _____unacceptable_____
11. A1 + G2 + I3 _____impossibly_____
12. H1 + D2 + B3 _____enjoyment_____

☆ Use the word-part chart to encode these words. Write the letters and the numbers on the lines.

13. joyful _____D2 + A3_____
14. enjoyable _____H1 + D2 + D3_____
15. lifeless _____E2 + E3_____
16. disgraceful _____G1 + I2 + A3_____
17. overcreative _____C1 + B2 + K3_____
18. mismeasurement _____D1 + H2 + B3_____

LESSON 86: Review and Assess   175

UNIVERSAL ACCESS
Meeting Individual Needs

Visual Learners

Select words from Unit 5 that have a base word and a suffix and write them on cards. Have students draw a card and give visual clues to help classmates guess the word. The student who guesses correctly writes the word on the board, identifies its suffix and base word, tells whether any spelling change was made, and picks the next card.

Kinesthetic Learners

Have a student think of a word that ends with one (or more) of the suffixes studied in this unit. Ask him or her to write the suffix(es) on the board and add blank spaces to indicate the rest of the letters in the word. Have students raise their hands to guess what letters go in the blanks. The first student to figure out the word places the next mystery word on the board.

Learners with Special Needs

Additional strategies for supporting students with special needs can be found on page 137L.

Read the passage. For each numbered blank, there is a choice of words below. Circle the letter of the word that completes the sentence correctly.

Maria's class was studying volcanoes. The students wanted to build a model of one. They wanted their volcano to look **1**. Therefore, the class asked the art teacher for **2**.

First, she told them to make a dome-shaped frame out of wire. She helped them mount it on the **3** base they had. Then the students tore long strips of newspaper and soaked them in wheat paste. They put layers of paper onto the wire frame to make it look like a mountain.

When the model was dry, the students painted it. They hid a jar inside the mountaintop to hold **4** materials for the eruption. The jar held soap, paint, glitter, and baking soda. Then the students poured in some vinegar and—boom! The volcano came to life! It squirted a reddish liquid. The <u>lava</u> ran **5** toward the base.

1. (a) lifelike   b. lifeless   c. graceful

2. a. kindness   (b) assistance   c. baggage

3. a. happiest   (b) sturdiest   c. tiresome

4. a. childish   b. falsehood   (c) colorful

5. (a) downward   b. upward   c. northern

Read the passage again. Circle the letter of your answer.

6. Why did the students ask the art teacher for help?
   a. She liked studying about science.
   (b) She knew model-building methods.
   c. She had been to the Philippines.
   d. She was a nature photographer.

7. What does the word <u>lava</u> mean?
   a. toothpaste
   b. watery dirt
   c. rare chemicals
   (d) hot, red liquid rock

Extend & Apply

Gather information about a volcano to share with your classmates. Write a fact sheet that has at least one word with a suffix.

Reteaching Activities

Make a Connection!

On the board, list the suffixes studied in Unit 5. Suggest a word that contains one of the suffixes: for example, **colorful.** The next player must use a different suffix in a word starting with the first or the last letter of the your word. For example, the next player might say **creative** or **lifelike.** Continue until all suffixes are used at least once.

Suffix Search

Have students look through their textbooks and library books for words containing the suffixes taught in this unit. Direct students to use context clues and their knowledge of suffixes' meanings to define each word. Suggest that they consult a dictionary if they need to. Have the class compile a master list of words and definitions.

Assessing the Skill

Check Up Have students complete pages 175–176 to help them review the suffixes presented in Unit 5. Page 175 is discussed in detail in *Teaching the Lesson.*

The exercises on pages 175–176 will help you assess students' understanding of suffixes. Remind students to read the passage on page 176 carefully and to use context clues to answer the questions.

Observational Assessment As students work, watch for any signs of difficulty. Review the observational notes you made during previous lessons, and use them to help you evaluate students' progress in mastering suffixes. Note areas which may need reteaching or review.

Student Skills Assessment Keep track of each student's progress in understanding suffixes using the checklist on page 137H.

Writing Conference As you finish Unit 5, meet with students individually to talk over their portfolio samples and other written work. Ask whether students would like to share with the class any particular pieces of writing from their Home Portfolios. Call attention to words with suffixes in students' compositions. Discuss how the student's ability to use suffixes correctly can help them become better readers and writers.

Group together students who need further instruction in suffixes and have them complete the *Reteaching Activities.* Turn to page 137C for alternative assessment methods.

Dictionary and Thesaurus Skills; Vocabulary Skills

Theme: People and Government

STANDARDS

⭐ Read grade-appropriate expository text and understand its content

⭐ Develop and strengthen vocabulary

⭐ Use dictionary and thesaurus skills

⭐ Identify synonyms, antonyms, homonyms; and clipped, blended, and borrowed words

⭐ Interpret idioms and word analogies

OBJECTIVES

▶ To appreciate nonfiction works about people and government

▶ To use dictionary and thesaurus skills

▶ To distinguish between synonyms, antonyms, homonyms; and clipped, blended, and borrowed words

▶ To determine the meanings of idiomatic expressions and word analogies

LESSONS

Assessment Strategies

An overview of assessment strategies appears on page **177C**. It offers suggestions for using unit-specific assessment tools, including **Pretests** and **Post Tests** (pages **177D–177G**), the **Activity Master** (page **177M**), and the **Assessment Checklist** (page **177H**).

Thematic Teaching

In Unit 6, students learn about dictionary and thesaurus skills; synonyms, antonyms, homonyms; clipped, blended, and borrowed words; idiomatic expressions, and word analogies. Students learn these topics in the context of selections and exercises related to *People and Government.*

Students begin their investigation by creating a glossary of words related to government. The resource list on this page offers media information that celebrates the spirit of people and government. Many of the Teacher's Edition lessons in this unit open with poems, riddles, or tongue twisters that can spark student's interest both in the theme and in the play of words.

Curriculum Integration

Science
Students list technology words on page **188** and list healthy food choices on page **214.**

Music
Students write lyrics on page **190.**

Social Studies
Students create a map on page **178,** alphabetize countries on page **180,** use a map on page **186,** write a speech on page **200,** and create analogies on page **220.**

Writing
Students analyze a written passage on page **206** and write a dialogue on page **208.**

Drama
Students write a skit on page **198.**

Math
Students create word problems on page **182** and explain number expressions on page **218.**

Art
Students create a mural on page **202.**

Optional Learning Activities

Meeting Individual Needs
Most of the Teacher's Edition lessons offer activities for students with distinct learning styles. The activities are labeled for learners with these "styles": **Kinesthetic, Tactile, Auditory, Logical,** and **Visual.**

Multicultural Connections
Students research holidays on page **178,** research census data on page **184,** teach words from foreign languages on page **192,** and research Native American words on page **216.**

Word Study Strategies
Pages **177I–177J** offer an array of activities for students to practice using strategies such as word sorting, contextual usage, and word building.

Universal Access
Exercises tailored to meet the needs of **English-Language Learners** and **Gifted Learners** can be found in almost every Teacher's Edition lesson. Strategies designed to help **Learners with Special Needs** can be found on page **177L.**

Intervention
Page **177K** offers **Intervention Strategies** designed to help students performing below grade level understand the concepts taught in **Lessons 97, 101,** and **108.**

Reteaching
On page **212** students identify synonyms, antonyms, and homonyms, and on page **224** students form clipped words.

Technology
Page **177N** offers activities for students who enjoy working with multimedia. In addition, **Computer Connections**—tips designed to support students who use a word processor—can be found on pages **194, 204, 210,** and **222.**

R E S O U R C E S

Books

Fritz, Jean. *Shh! We're Writing the Constitution,* NY: Putnam Publishing, 1998.

Gutman, Dan. *Landslide: A Kid's Guide to the U.S. Elections,* NY: Simon & Schuster, 2000.

Videos

Biography: Frederick Douglass, A&E Home Video.

This Is America, Charlie Brown: The Birth of the Constitution, Paramount.

CDs

Native North American Child: An Odyssey, Buffy Sainte-Marie. Vanguard Records.

Schoolhouse Rock: America Rock, Rhino Records.

In Unit 6, students learn study skills and vocabulary skills. To evaluate students' mastery of these skills, use any or all of the assessment methods suggested below.

Pretests and Post Tests

The tests on pages **177D–177G** objectively assess students' understanding of dictionary and thesaurus skills; synonyms, antonyms, and homonyms; clipped, blended, and borrowed words; idioms and analogies. These tests may be used at the beginning of the unit as an informal diagnostic tool or at the end of the unit as a more formal measure of students' progress.

Observational Assessment

Opportunities for observing students as they work are suggested throughout the unit. Lesson-specific recommendations are included for assessing students' work. Check students' written work on a regular basis to make sure they are applying what they learn to their writing.

Using Technology

The Technology activities on page **177N** may also be used to evaluate students whose language skills are best shown when using computers or audio/video equipment.

Performance Assessment

Have students write the following pairs of words: **part/whole, plane/airplane, horse/hoarse, below/under.** Have them label each pair **S** (synonyms), **A** (antonyms), **H** (homonyms), or **CL** (clipped words). Have students find similar examples from the lesson.

Portfolio Assessment

The portfolio icon in the lesson plans indicates an opportunity for students to add to the growing body of work in their portfolios.

Each student's portfolio will be different and should contain pieces that the student feels represent his or her best work. You may wish to give students additional opportunities to add to their portfolios.

Rubric for Writing

	Always	Sometimes	Never
Uses capitalization, punctuation, spelling, and grammar appropriately			
Creates a variety of sentences containing synonyms, antonyms, homonyms, idioms; clipped, blended, and borrowed words			
Creates a clear and focused process for each step of a task			
Develops a clear dialogue to explain ideas and purpose			
Uses a dictionary and a thesaurus			
Conveys purpose and meaning through writing			

Answer Key

Page 177D
1. no
2. yes
3. crack
4. fix
5. homonyms
6. synonyms
7. homonyms
8. antonyms
9. math
10. smog
11. phone
12. brunch
13. butterflies in my stomach
14. all ears
15. (prez' ənt)
16. (kon' test)
17. foot
18. different
19. wrist
20. little

Page 177E
1. jumble/junior
2. caravan/cargo
3. attract/author
4. flawless/flicker
5. 2
6. 1
7. antonym
8. homonym
9. synonym
10. antonym
11. clipped
12. borrowed
13. blended
14. injure
15. arm

Page 177F
1. yes
2. no
3. ladder
4. blink
5. synonyms
6. synonyms
7. homonyms
8. antonyms
9. exam
10. twirl
11. pro
12. motel
13. paid an arm and a leg
14. hit the roof
15. (ad'res)
16. (prə gres')
17. odd
18. peaceful
19. song
20. drink

Page 177G
1. folio/follow
2. rascal/ravioli
3. starch/status
4. media/medley
5. 2
6. 1
7. synonym
8. homonym
9. antonym
10. synonym
11. blended
12. clipped
13. borrowed
14. paragraph
15. guilty

Name _____

Is the word list in alphabetical order? Fill in the correct answer.

1. cellar	ceiling	cello	celery	○ yes	○ no
2. torch	tornado	toss	total	○ yes	○ no

Fill in the circle next to the word that comes between the two guide words.

3. crab/cramp	○ cream	○ crack	○ crawl
4. fit/flag	○ fix	○ fig	○ flap

Fill in the circle that describes each word pair.

5. knew/new	○ synonyms	○ antonyms	○ homonyms
6. allow/permit	○ synonyms	○ antonyms	○ homonyms
7. symbol/cymbal	○ synonyms	○ antonyms	○ homonyms
8. decrease/increase	○ synonyms	○ antonyms	○ homonyms

Write the clipped or blended form of each word(s) on the line.

9. mathematics _____   **10.** smoke + fog = _____

11. telephone _____   **12.** breakfast + lunch = _____

Underline the idiom in each sentence.

13. I had butterflies in my stomach before the test.

14. Laurie was all ears when the principal gave a speech.

Fill in the circle next to the respelling that completes the sentence.

15. Are you bringing a _____ for Sam?	○ (prez′ ənt)	○ (pri zent′)
16. He won first place in the singing _____.	○ (kon′ test)	○ (kən test′)

Fill in the circle next to the word that completes each analogy.

17. Finger is to **hand** as **toe** is to _____.	○ leg	○ touch	○ foot
18. Hot is to **cold** as **same** is to _____.	○ similar	○ different	○ alike
19. Hat is to **head** as **watch** is to _____.	○ wrist	○ finger	○ neck
20. Easy is to **simple** as **small** is to _____.	○ big	○ little	○ huge

Possible score on Unit 6 Pretest 1 is 20. Score _____

Fill in the circle next to the correct guide words.

1. judge	○ job/jubilee	○ joint/judicial	○ jumble/junior
2. carbon	○ capital/caravan	○ card/carnivore	○ caravan/cargo
3. auction	○ audience/automatic	○ attract/author	○ audio/available
4. fleece	○ flawless/flicker	○ fleet/flimsy	○ flaw/flea

Write the number of the definition that is used in each sentence.

foil¹ To interfere with or stop from being successful.

foil² Metal hammered or rolled into a very thin, flexible sheet.

5. The leftovers were wrapped in **foil**. _____

6. The detective hopes his plan will **foil** the thief. _____

Fill in the circle to show whether the underlined and bold faced words are synonyms, antonyms, or homonyms.

7. rude	The class was <u>polite</u> to the guest speaker.	○ synonym	○ antonym	○ homonym
8. eight	Jamie <u>ate</u> an apple for snack.	○ synonym	○ antonym	○ homonym
9. error	I made a <u>mistake</u> on the test.	○ synonym	○ antonym	○ homonym
10. never	Maria <u>always</u> looks before she crosses the street.	○ synonym	○ antonym	○ homonym

Fill in the circle that tells whether the underlined word is a clipped, blended, or borrowed word.

11. My dog goes to the <u>vet</u> every year.	○ clipped	○ blended	○ borrowed
12. Are <u>pretzels</u> for sale at the game?	○ clipped	○ blended	○ borrowed
13. We stayed at a <u>motel</u> in Phoenix.	○ clipped	○ blended	○ borrowed

Fill in the circle next to the word that completes each analogy.

| 14. **Ancient** is to **old** as **wound** is to _____. | ○ heal | ○ recover | ○ injure |
| 15. **Knee** is to **leg** as **elbow** is to _____. | ○ arm | ○ shoulder | ○ wrist |

Possible score on Unit 6 Pretest 2 is 15. Score _____

Is the word list in alphabetical order? Fill in the correct answer.

1. treasure	treasury	treatment	treaty	○ yes	○ no
2. evening	eventually	even	every	○ yes	○ no

Fill in the circle next to the word that comes between the two guide words.

3. lace/lady	○ lark	○ ladder	○ landlord
4. blend/blister	○ blue	○ black	○ blink

Fill in the circle that describes each word pair.

5. tardy/late	○ synonyms	○ antonyms	○ homonyms
6. arid/dry	○ synonyms	○ antonyms	○ homonyms
7. knight/night	○ synonyms	○ antonyms	○ homonyms
8. wrong/right	○ synonyms	○ antonyms	○ homonyms

Write the clipped or blended form of each word(s) on the line.

9. examination _____

10. twist + whirl = _____

11. professional _____

12. motor + hotel = _____

Underline the idiom in each sentence.

13. Thomas paid an arm and a leg to get his bicycle fixed.

14. He hit the roof when I asked to borrow it.

Fill in the circle next to the respelling that completes the sentence.

15. My ____ is 112 Willow Avenue.	○ **(ad' res)**	○ **(ə dres')**
16. Matt has made much ____ in soccer.	○ **(pro' res)**	○ **(prə gres')**

Fill in the circle next to the word that completes each analogy.

17. **First** is to **last** as **even** is to ____.	○ second	○ equal	○ odd
18. **Tired** is to **weary** as **calm** is to ____.	○ peaceful	○ rough	○ stormy
19. **Step** is to **dance** as **lyric** is to ____.	○ story	○ book	○ song
20. **Fork** is to **eat** as **cup** is to ____.	○ knife	○ drink	○ liquid

Possible score on Unit 6 Post Test 1 is 20. Score _____

Name _____

Fill in the circle next to the correct guide words.

1. folk	○ fog/fold	○ folio/follow	○ fodder/foil
2. rate	○ ramp/rare	○ rally/rapport	○ rascal/ravioli
3. statue	○ starve/statement	○ stage/stardom	○ starch/status
4. medium	○ measure/medal	○ media/medley	○ meek/melt

Write the number of the definition that is used in each sentence.

rash¹ Acting with too much haste; reckless.

rash² A breaking out of spots on the skin.

5. Strawberries give me a **rash**. _____

6. Think it over, don't make a **rash** decision. _____

Fill in the circle to show whether the underlined and boldfaced words are synonyms, antonyms, or homonyms.

7. **many**	There were <u>numerous</u> calls made to the office.	○ synonym	○ antonym	○ homonym
8. **poor**	Did you <u>pour</u> the milk?	○ synonym	○ antonym	○ homonym
9. **moist**	My towel needs to <u>dry</u>.	○ synonym	○ antonym	○ homonym
10. **tardy**	Colin is never <u>late</u> to class.	○ synonym	○ antonym	○ homonym

Read each sentence. Fill in the circle that tells whether the underlined words are clipped, blended, or borrowed.

11. The <u>telethon</u> raised money for charity.	○ clipped	○ blended	○ borrowed
12. I had a severe case of the <u>flu</u>.	○ clipped	○ blended	○ borrowed
13. Be sure to take your <u>umbrella</u>.	○ clipped	○ blended	○ borrowed

Fill in the circle next to the word that completes each analogy.

14. **Page** is to **book** as **sentence** is to _____.	○ door	○ paragraph	○ sketch
15. **Lost** is to **found** as **innocent** is to _____.	○ justice	○ guilty	○ little

Possible score on Unit 6 Post Test 2 is 15. Score _____

UNIT 6 STUDENT PROGRESS CHECKLIST

Student Name ____________________

UNIT SIX
STUDENT SKILLS ASSESSMENT CHECKLIST

☐ Assessed ☒ Retaught ■ Mastered

- ☐ ABC Order
- ☐ Guide Words
- ☐ Entry Words
- ☐ Homographs—Multiple-Meaning Words
- ☐ Pronunciation Key
- ☐ Accent Marks
- ☐ Synonyms
- ☐ Antonyms
- ☐ Homonyms
- ☐ Thesaurus
- ☐ Clipped Words and Blended Words
- ☐ Borrowed Words
- ☐ Idiomatic Expressions
- ☐ Word Analogies

TEACHER COMMENTS

In Unit 6, students study dictionary and thesaurus skills; synonyms, antonyms, homonyms; clipped, blended, and borrowed words; idioms and word analogies. To give students opportunities to master these word study strategies, use any or all of the activities suggested below.

Word Order

Circle the entry words that would appear on the same dictionary page as the guide words in bold print. Then write the four entry words in ABC order on the lines.

1. **desk/dewy**

   develop   _____

   detective   _____

   dew   _____

   desert   _____

2. **fog/fool**

   folk   _____

   foot   _____

   food   _____

   follow   _____

3. **price/prison**

   prevent   _____

   prince   _____

   primary   _____

   principal   _____

4. **tea/teeth**

   technique   _____

   tear   _____

   team   _____

   telephone   _____

Word Meanings

Circle the homonyms in each row. Then choose the homonym that completes the sentence. Write the words on the lines.

male	maid	made	make
there	then	these	their
hose	horse	house	hoarse
rid	ride	rode	road
fair	fare	fire	four

1. The sculptor _____ a statue from clay.
2. The twins have bunk beds in _____ room.
3. A cowboy knows how to ride a _____ .
4. We _____ our bicycles to school yesterday.
5. The bus _____ went up twenty-five cents.
6. Many people went to the county _____ .
7. After the game, my voice sounded _____ .
8. Did you park the car on this _____?
9. No, I put the jar over _____ .
10. She hired a _____ to help with the cleaning.

Language Building

Unscramble the letters of each type of word. Write the words on the lines. Then use the words to complete the sentences below.

Clipped Words	Blended Words	Borrowed Words
gsa	chunrb	umen
_____	_____	_____
utoa	mogs	aryrlib
_____	_____	_____

1. It is a blended word of **breakfast** and **lunch**.

   _____

2. It is a clipped word for **automobile.**

   _____

3. It is a Latin word for the place where books are

   kept. _____

4. It is a blended word of **smoke** and **fog.**

   _____

5. It is a clipped word for **gasoline.**

   _____

6. It is a French word for the food list seen at a

   restaurant. _____

Meaningful Idioms

Write a word or phrase from the box that means the same as the idiom in bold print in each sentence.

unhappy	keep it a secret
free of trouble	write
become frightened	became angry

1. I get **cold feet** when I have to take a test.

   _____

2. **Drop me a line** when you move into your new home. _____

3. He was **down in the dumps** after his team lost. _____

4. The patient is **out of the woods** and will leave the hospital soon. _____

5. Mom and Dad **hit the roof** when they saw the phone bill. _____

6. When you tell me something in private, I **keep it under my hat.** _____

Word Analogies

Write a word from the box to complete each analogy. Then circle how the words in the analogy are related.

tree	low	learn	cry
thin	color	sew	car

1. Big is to small as high is to _____ .

   synonyms antonyms cause/effect

2. Shovel is to dig as crayon is to _____ .

   part/whole synonyms object/use

3. Tale is to story as slim is to _____ .

   antonyms synonyms part/whole

4. Finger is to hand as branch is to _____ .

   part/whole object/use cause/effect

5. Thirsty is to drink as study is to _____ .

   cause/effect antonyms object/use

6. Soap is to wash as needle is to _____ .

   part/whole cause/effect object/use

7. Lens is to camera as wheel is to _____ .

   synonyms part/whole object/use

8. Happy is to smile as sad is to _____ .

   synonyms antonyms cause/effect

LESSONS	**97** Synonyms	**101** Thesaurus 1	**108** Word Analogies
Problem	When writing or speaking, student exhibits difficulty in finding and using the right words.	Student has difficulty recognizing different shades of meaning in synonyms.	Student has trouble understanding the concept of analogies.
Intervention Strategies	• Write the word **tired** on the board and have students list possible synonyms, such as: **weary** and **exhausted.** Point out, while **tired** can replace these synonyms, each has a slightly different meaning. Write these sentences on the board: *I felt* **weary** *while walking up the hill. The runners were* **exhausted** *after the race.* Ask students to explain why it was better to use a different synonym in each sentence rather than repeat the word **tired.**	• If students have difficulty with the exercise on page **206,** use the synonyms listed at the top of the page in sentences that exaggerate their inappropriateness. Say: *The giant let out a booming* **giggle.** Encourage students to suggest another word that would be more appropriate for the sentence. Remind students to use the context clues when selecting appropriate synonyms to complete the exercise.	• Encourage students to break down the analogy: **Sweet** is to **sour** as **rich** is to **poor.** Ask students to tell how the words are related. (The words are opposites.) • Model the procedure with the following analogy: **Finger** is to **hand** as **minute** is to **hour.** Tell students that each word is related to the other as being part of something. Have students suggest examples of other analogies that show cause and effect, parts of a whole, and how objects are used.

The following activities offer strategies for helping students with special needs to participate in selected exercises in Unit 6.

Visual Perceptual Deficits and/or Conceptual Deficits

Alphabetical Order

Students who have difficulty identifying letters or sequencing may have to recite the alphabet while attempting the exercises in lessons 88 through 91. This may make the work tedious or more confusing to them.

- Suggest that students write the alphabet on an index card and tape it on their desks or in their dictionaries.

- Encourage them to use their knowledge of their own learning styles to devise strategies for alphabetizing quickly and correctly. For example, visual learners may be able to close their eyes and visualize an image of the alphabet in correct order. Auditory learners might be able to "hear" the alphabet song as a means of determining order.

Conceptual Deficits

Homographs

Students may fixate on one meaning of a homograph. Highlighting the context clues in the sentences on page 188 will enable students to see that the same word can be used in different ways.

- Before students answer each question, ask them to use a marker to highlight what they think the context clue might be. Then have them look at each homograph and its meanings for the word that fits the context clue. For example, *Bears sleep during the winter, and they will _____ for several months.* Ask students which homograph means something that a bear can do while it sleeps.

- Then have them make up a sentence that demonstrates the other meaning of the homograph and tell what context clues they have used.

Visual/Perceptual Deficits

Pronunciation Key

Students with visual or perceptual deficits may experience difficulty with symbols in the pronunciation key. Tell them that learning these symbols will help them pronounce not only English words but also foreign words.

- Tape-record students as they say the different sounds and words used in the pronunciation key.

- Then have them make a flash card for every symbol. Each card should contain the sound symbol on one side and a word that illustrates that sound on the other side. Underline the sound in the word to reinforce the sound symbol. For example, a card would have **ô** on one side, and **s<u>o</u>ng** on the other.

- Have students display the correct card as you say each sound.

- Encourage them to use the flash cards and sound recordings to complete the exercise on page 190.

Conceptual Deficits

Idiomatic Expressions

Mastering idiomatic expressions may help students with conceptual deficits understand other kinds of figurative language. Tell students that idiomatic expressions describe the way that certain situations feel, not the way they actually happen. Encourage students to visualize the idioms. Use the following example for page 217. Say: *Close your eyes and picture the young actor putting the stage with all the actors on it in his pocket. Is that possible? Picture the audience clapping more for one actor than the others. Is that possible? Picture the young actor sneaking backstage and taking all the scripts for the play. Is that possible?* Then tell students to choose the least silly answer. Help them identify the feelings that inspired the expressions.

Name _____

Sort the words in the box below. Then write the words on each book in alphabetical order.

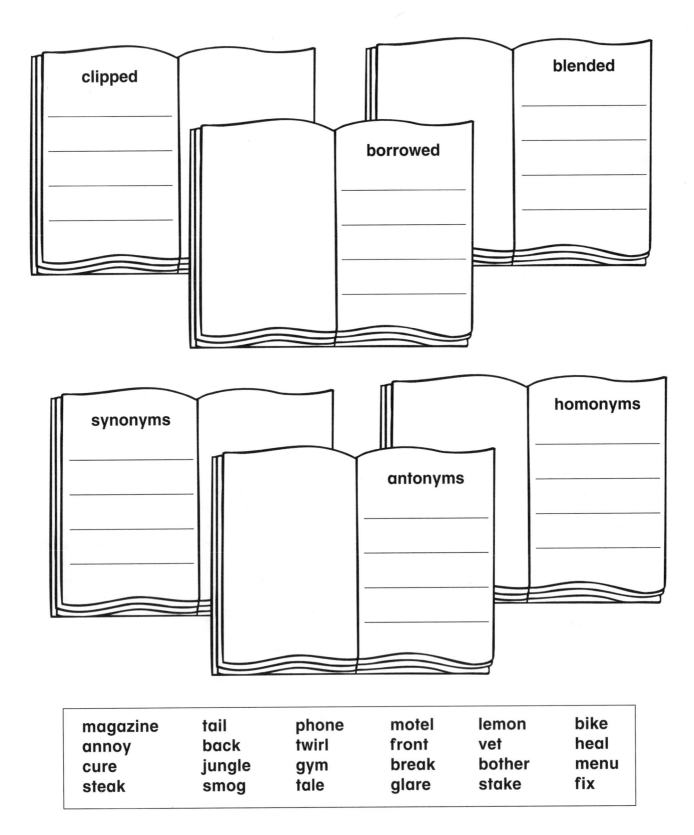

clipped
_____
_____
_____
_____

blended
_____
_____
_____
_____

borrowed
_____
_____
_____
_____

synonyms
_____
_____
_____
_____

homonyms
_____
_____
_____
_____

antonyms
_____
_____
_____
_____

magazine	tail	phone	motel	lemon	bike
annoy	back	twirl	front	vet	heal
cure	jungle	gym	break	bother	menu
steak	smog	tale	glare	stake	fix

UNIT 6 TECHNOLOGY

Create a Data Bank

Invite students to use the word processing program to create a data bank for topics in social studies. For example, they might want to compile information about several different countries.

- Create a list of information categories, such as: geographical features, government, and culture. Organize students into groups, assigning each group a category to research.

- Tell students that they need only include the most important facts in each category. Encourage them to use encyclopedias and other reference materials that are available on the Internet to gather the information.

- Encourage students to create an index of information by arranging each category with its information in alphabetical order.

Videotape an Informal Debate

Invite students to videotape a debate about a classroom rule.

- Encourage students to write a class constitution. Point out that they will need a list of rules that the teacher and the class members should follow. Then have them select a rule by voting on one that they think will make a good topic for a debate. Students can draw lots to determine whether they will be on the "pro" side or on the "con" side of the debate.

- Find or create a simple format for the debate. Set aside time for students to work on their "positions," videotape the debate, and to present the final product to another class.

- Tell students that facial expressions, body language, and verbal expression will be important to convince others to agree with their side of the argument. Urge them to use analogies to make their points clear and convincing.

Create a Handbook of Idiomatic Expressions

Ask students to use the word processing program to create a handbook of idiomatic expressions.

- Help students make a list of idiomatic expressions that are commonly used in your school. Have students note idioms that they used themselves or heard over several days and add these to the class list. When the list contains approximately fifty idiomatic expressions, divide the list among the students and ask them to write an explanation for each idiomatic expression.

- Encourage students to illustrate the expressions' literal meanings. They can use a scanner or clip art for this purpose. Print out the document and organize it into a booklet. Place a copy in the school library.

Idiom: Money burns a hole in my pocket.
Meaning: I spend money quickly.

Introduction to
Dictionary and Thesaurus Skills; Vocabulary Skills

Objectives

- **To enjoy a piece of nonfiction about *People and Government***

- **To learn how to use a dictionary and a thesaurus**

- **To learn about synonyms, antonyms, homonyms; clipped, blended, and borrowed words; idioms and analogies**

Starting with Literature

Read "Happy Birthday, U.S.A.!" aloud with the class. On the board, write words from the selection and their synonyms: **country, nation; liberty, freedom.** Have students identify what each pair of words has in common.

Critical Thinking

● Suggest that students skim the story to find answers to the first question.

● Have students explain their answers to the second and third questions.

Introducing the Skill

Point out that pairs of words such as **country/nation** and **liberty/freedom** have similar meanings. Such words are called synonyms. Tell students they will learn about synonyms in this unit. Then write the words **tall** and **hot** on the board. Ask students to suggest words with opposite meanings. **(short, cold)** Tell students that pairs of words such as **tall/short** and **hot/cold** are called antonyms and are also included in this unit.

Practicing the Skill

Have students work in groups to create their own lists of synonyms and antonyms.

177

Happy Birthday, U.S.A.!

Did you know that countries have birthdays? Every year on July 4, Americans celebrate Independence Day. On this day, we hold big parades and watch colorful fireworks displays. We sing patriotic songs and fly the American flag. Do you know what happened on July 4 to make this day our national birthday?

A daring event took place in Philadelphia on July 4, 1776. On that hot summer day, the members of the Continental Congress took a bold step. They signed a paper that called for independence from England. These 56 people signed the Declaration of Independence with pride—and some fear. John Hancock was the first to sign. He wrote his name in bold letters. Benjamin Franklin also signed. Thomas Jefferson, the author of the Declaration of Independence, signed, too.

Today, we still value this great document. We can see it on display in the National Archives building in Washington, DC. It is the place where the government keeps records of our nation's history. Just visit the National Archives building on the Fourth of July. It is open on that day for all to say, "Happy Birthday, U.S.A.!"

? Critical Thinking

1. What do we celebrate on Independence Day?

2. What could have made the signers of the Declaration of Independence feel both pride and fear?

3. Do you think it is important for a nation to keep records of its past? Why?

1. We celebrate our country's birthday, or our independence from England.
2. Answers will vary.
3. Answers will vary.

Theme Activity

GOVERNMENT GLOSSARY Have students create a bulletin-board glossary of words about government. Ask them to start by listing words from the article in this lesson, such as **countries, independence, patriotic, American,** and so on. Have them copy each word onto a sheet of paper, writing the word in the upper left-hand corner. Each sheet of paper will become a separate entry in the glossary.

As students work through the unit and learn about dictionary skills, they can add the following features to their entries: syllable breaks, phonetic respellings, word histories, definitions, and sample sentences. As they add words to the glossary, have students rearrange the words and change the guide words, as needed, to maintain alphabetical order. Suggest that students also include a pronunciation key at the bottom of their Government Glossary.

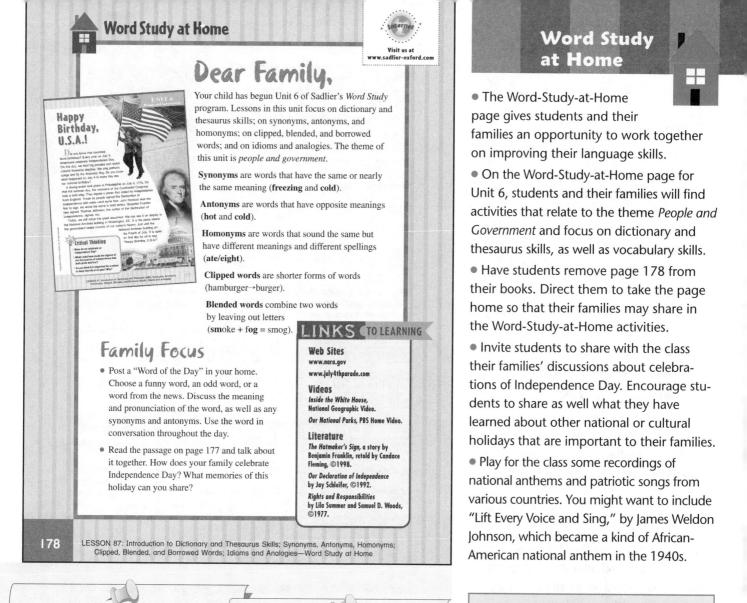

Dear Family,

Your child has begun Unit 6 of Sadlier's *Word Study* program. Lessons in this unit focus on dictionary and thesaurus skills; on synonyms, antonyms, and homonyms; on clipped, blended, and borrowed words; and on idioms and analogies. The theme of this unit is *people and government*.

Synonyms are words that have the same or nearly the same meaning (**freezing** and **cold**).

Antonyms are words that have opposite meanings (**hot** and **cold**).

Homonyms are words that sound the same but have different meanings and different spellings (**ate/eight**).

Clipped words are shorter forms of words (hamburger→burger).

Blended words combine two words by leaving out letters (**sm**oke + f**og** = smog).

Family Focus

- Post a "Word of the Day" in your home. Choose a funny word, an odd word, or a word from the news. Discuss the meaning and pronunciation of the word, as well as any synonyms and antonyms. Use the word in conversation throughout the day.

- Read the passage on page 177 and talk about it together. How does your family celebrate Independence Day? What memories of this holiday can you share?

LINKS TO LEARNING

Web Sites
www.nara.gov
www.july4thparade.com

Videos
Inside the White House, National Geographic Video.
Our National Parks, PBS Home Video.

Literature
The Hatmaker's Sign, a story by Benjamin Franklin, retold by Candace Fleming, ©1998.
Our Declaration of Independence by Jay Schleifer, ©1992.
Rights and Responsibilities by Lila Summer and Samuel D. Woods, ©1977.

LESSON 87: Introduction to Dictionary and Thesaurus Skills; Synonyms, Antonyms, Homonyms; Clipped, Blended, and Borrowed Words; Idioms and Analogies—Word Study at Home

---

Word Study at Home

- The Word-Study-at-Home page gives students and their families an opportunity to work together on improving their language skills.

- On the Word-Study-at-Home page for Unit 6, students and their families will find activities that relate to the theme *People and Government* and focus on dictionary and thesaurus skills, as well as vocabulary skills.

- Have students remove page 178 from their books. Direct them to take the page home so that their families may share in the Word-Study-at-Home activities.

- Invite students to share with the class their families' discussions about celebrations of Independence Day. Encourage students to share as well what they have learned about other national or cultural holidays that are important to their families.

- Play for the class some recordings of national anthems and patriotic songs from various countries. You might want to include "Lift Every Voice and Sing," by James Weldon Johnson, which became a kind of African-American national anthem in the 1940s.

Multicultural Connection

On the board, write **Fourth of July/Independence Day**. Then ask students to list various holidays that are important to other countries, such as Bastille Day for France or Cinco de Mayo for Mexico. You might also help students identify holidays that are important for various U.S. ethnic groups, such as St. Patrick's Day and Martin Luther King, Jr., Day. This activity might work best after students have been encouraged to ask their families about national and cultural holidays that are important to them.

Social Studies Link

As students identify different holidays, have them locate on a map or globe the places where these holidays are observed. Students might enjoy making an illustrated "worldwide holiday map," showing where and how different national holidays are celebrated.

Theme-Related Resources

Web Site

Kelly Ferjutz, "Happy Independence Days!" July 1, 1998, **suite101.com/ article.cfm/classical_music/8397** (article and links on patriotic songs and national anthems, with material from Canada, France, United States, Russia, Great Britain and the Tlingit)

CDs

National Anthems of the World, arranged by Gordon Lorenz and Mike Timoney, London Theatre Orchestra and Singers, Emporio (UK), 1997

"Lift Every Voice and Sing," included in *A Choral Tribute to Dr. Martin Luther King Jr.,* Choral Arts Society of Washington, Choral Arts (USA)

Alphabetical Order

Objectives

- **To identify words in alphabetical order**
- **To alphabetize words to the second and third letters**

Warming Up

- Display the alphabet. Write the following chant on the board. Read it aloud with the class.

  Carter, **Cl**inton, **Co**olidge, too.

  Harding, **Harr**ison, **Ho**over. Ooo!

  Garfield, **Gr**ant—who were they?

  Presidents of the U.S.A.

- Call students' attention to the names in each line and ask them what they notice about their order. (It's alphabetical.)

Teaching the Lesson

- Help students verify the alphabetical order of the names in each line. Invite students to cross out each matching letter until they come to a letter that is different.
- Help students conclude that alphabetical order in a group of words is set by the first letter that is different.
- Have a student read the Helpful Hint aloud, as others follow along silently.

Name _____

Helpful Hint

Words in a dictionary are arranged in **ABC order**, or **alphabetical order**. To put words in ABC order, look at the first letter of each word. If the first letter is the same, look at the next letter to decide the order.

The names of these cities are in ABC order.

Dayton   Denver   Detroit   Dover

Write each group of words in ABC order.

1. state   country
   country   governor
   governor   region
   region   state

2. congress   bill
   bill   congress
   vote   veto
   veto   vote

Figure out this riddle. Write the next letter of the alphabet above each letter in the box. Then write the riddle's question and answer on the lines below.

W	H	E	R	E		W	A	S		T	H	E		D	E	C	L	A	R	A	T	I	O	N
V	G	D	Q	D		V		R		S	G	D		C	D	B	K		Q		S	H	N	M

O	F		I	N	D	E	P	E	N	D	E	N	C	E		S	I	G	N	E	D	?
N	E		H	M	C	D	O	D	M	C	D	M	B	D		R	H	F	M	D	C	

A	T		T	H	E		B	O	T	T	O	M	!
S	G	D		A	N	S	S	N	L				

Question: Where was the Declaration of Independence signed?

Answer: At the bottom!

CHALLENGE

Create a sentence that uses **ABC order**, such as: Abe buys cat food. Make your sentence as long as you can.

LESSON 88: ABC Order   179

UNIVERSAL ACCESS
Meeting Individual Needs

Kinesthetic Learners

Label index cards with state capitals starting with the same first letter: **Jackson, Jefferson City, Juneau; Sacramento, Springfield, Salem, Salt Lake City; Albany, Annapolis, Atlanta, Augusta, Austin.** Have students group the cards into cities with the same beginning letter. Challenge students to alphabetize each group of names.

Auditory Learners

Say pairs of presidents' names with different beginning letters. Ask students to listen closely to the first letter of the name, and tell you which name should come first in alphabetical order. Repeat the process with names that have the same first letter, but a different second letter: **Monroe, Madison, Jackson, Jefferson, Adams, Arthur, Roosevelt, Reagan.** Have students repeat the pairs in alphabetical order.

⭐ **Write each group of words in ABC order.**

1. Capitol — capital
   captain — Capitol
   city — captain
   capital — city

2. borough — borough
   build — borrow
   borrow — build
   butter — butter

3. senator — senate
   sentence — senator
   senate — sentence
   supervisor — supervisor

4. president — pleasant
   present — presence
   pleasant — present
   presence — president

⭐ **These states begin with the letter M or N. Use the chart below to sort the states by letter. Then put the states in ABC order by numbering them from 1–8. Write the numbers on the short lines in each column.**

Maryland	Montana	North Carolina	Missouri
New York	New Mexico	Nevada	Massachusetts
Michigan	North Dakota	New Jersey	Nebraska
Maine	Minnesota	Mississippi	New Hampshire

5		M	6		N
	2	Maryland		7	North Carolina
	8	Montana		6	New York
	7	Missouri		5	New Mexico
	3	Massachusetts		2	Nevada
	4	Michigan		8	North Dakota
	1	Maine		4	New Jersey
	5	Minnesota		1	Nebraska
	6	Mississippi		3	New Hampshire

180 LESSON 88: ABC Order

🏠 **Home Involvement Activity** Eight states begin with the letter M. Eight other states begin with the letter N. Four states begin with the letter A, I, or W. Which states are they? Look at a map to see if you're right.

English-Language Learners/ESL

Invite students to list the first names of friends or people in their families. Have students circle the first letter of each name. Challenge them to rewrite the names in alphabetical order. You might also suggest that students list foods, colors, animals, or other favorite things, and arrange them in alphabetical order.

Gifted Learners

Encourage students to create a dictionary of government terms. Have them list words related to government such as **election, president, votes, Congress.** Have them write a definition for each word and then arrange the words in alphabetical order.

Learners with Special Needs

Additional strategies for supporting learners with special needs can be found on page 177L.

Practicing the Skill

● Read aloud the direction lines on pages 179–180 and complete the first item in each exercise with students.

● For words with the same beginning letters, suggest that students cross out letters that match in a sequence until they come to the different letters.

● Encourage students to say the alphabet softly to themselves if they aren't sure of a particular sequence.

Curriculum Connections

Spelling Link

● Write these tongue twisters on the board.

   Mayors mull over mighty matters.
   President poses in patch of pumpkins.
   Seth sees smart Senators smiling.

● Ask a student to underline the words in each sentence with the same beginning letters.

● Have students write the underlined words in alphabetical order.

Social Studies Link

● Display a map of the world.

● Have students list the names of six countries in South America.

● Ask students to rewrite the names in alphabetical order.

● Repeat the activity with countries in a different part of the world.

Observational Assessment

Check to see that students know alphabetical order and are able to alphabetize to the third letter.

Guide Words 1

Objectives

- **To identify words in alphabetical order**
- **To identify dictionary guide words**
- **To use guide words to locate entry words in the dictionary**

Warming Up

- Read these riddles aloud with students:

  How could you find a **cent** between a **car** and a **coat**?

  How could you find **glue** between a **garage** and a **gnu**?

  How could you find a **puppy** between a **potato** and a **pyramid**?

- Have a student tell the answer to the riddles. (a dictionary) Then ask the student to arrange the first three words in alphabetical order. **(car, cent, coat)** Call on students to alphabetize the next two sets of words and write them on the board. Remind students that dictionary entries appear in alphabetical order.

Teaching the Lesson

- Display a dictionary page. Identify the guide words on the page. Discuss with students what the guide words tell you about the other words on the page.
- Examine the first three or four entry words. Notice whether they are alphabetized to the second or third letter.
- Have a student read the Helpful Hint aloud as students follow along in their books.

Name _____

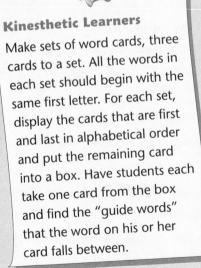

> **Helpful Hint**
>
> Two **guide words** appear at the top of each dictionary page. They show the first and last entries on that page. The other words on the dictionary page appear in alphabetical order between those two guide words.

Read the guide words in bold print. Cross out the one word that would *not* be on the same dictionary page as the guide words. Then write the three words in ABC order.

1 oat / ore	2 sense / spoon	3 diplomat / director
~~oar~~	sour	direct
opera	sister	direction
omen	~~sport~~	dipper
oh	sloppy	~~diploma~~
oh	sister	dipper
omen	sloppy	direct
opera	sour	direction

4 mass / mice	5 bread / bridle
measure	breed
mature	breath
~~marvelous~~	break
meow	~~brim~~
mature	break
measure	breath
meow	breed

> **WORK TOGETHER**
>
> Choose a partner. Ask each other riddles, such as: *I am a word found on a page with the guide words* **hectic—helpless.** *I mean "assistant." What am I?* Check your answer in a dictionary.

LESSON 89: Guide Words 1   181

UNIVERSAL ACCESS
Meeting Individual Needs

Kinesthetic Learners

Make sets of word cards, three cards to a set. All the words in each set should begin with the same first letter. For each set, display the cards that are first and last in alphabetical order and put the remaining card into a box. Have students each take one card from the box and find the "guide words" that the word on his or her card falls between.

Logical Learners

Have volunteers develop instructions that tell exactly how to use guide words to find an entry word. Suggest that students trade lists with a partner who will try to follow the steps. Partners can respond with feedback about whether or not the directions were effective so that students can revise their rules, if necessary.

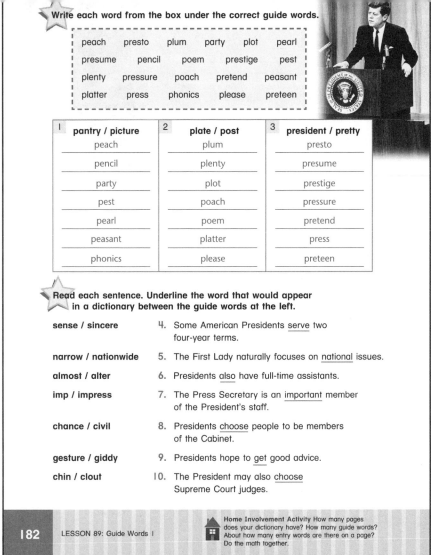

Write each word from the box under the correct guide words.

peach　presto　plum　party　plot　pearl
presume　pencil　poem　prestige　pest
plenty　pressure　poach　pretend　peasant
platter　press　phonics　please　preteen

1　pantry / picture	2　plate / post	3　president / pretty
peach	plum	presto
pencil	plenty	presume
party	plot	prestige
pest	poach	pressure
pearl	poem	pretend
peasant	platter	press
phonics	please	preteen

Read each sentence. Underline the word that would appear in a dictionary between the guide words at the left.

sense / sincere　　4. Some American Presidents <u>serve</u> two four-year terms.

narrow / nationwide　5. The First Lady naturally focuses on <u>national</u> issues.

almost / alter　　6. Presidents <u>also</u> have full-time assistants.

imp / impress　　7. The Press Secretary is an <u>important</u> member of the President's staff.

chance / civil　　8. Presidents <u>choose</u> people to be members of the Cabinet.

gesture / giddy　　9. Presidents hope to <u>get</u> good advice.

chin / clout　　10. The President may also <u>choose</u> Supreme Court judges.

182　LESSON 89: Guide Words I

Home Involvement Activity How many pages does your dictionary have? How many guide words? About how many entry words are there on a page? Do the math together.

English-Language Learners/ESL

Open an English dictionary and show students the guide words at the top of the page. Explain that the guide words tell you the first and last entry words on that page. Show students that the entry words are arranged in alphabetical order. Finally have students find the dictionary page on which their own names would be found if they were listed.

Gifted Learners

Give students some pairs of guide words in which the first three letters are the same. Have students list several entry words that might be found between the guide words you have supplied. Encourage students to check their work in the dictionary.

Learners with Special Needs

Additional strategies for supporting learners with special needs can be found on page 177L.

Practicing the Skill

● Read aloud the direction lines on pages 181–182. Help students identify the guide words in item 1 on each page.

● Allow students who have grasped the concept to work with students who are still gaining mastery.

Curriculum Connections

Spelling Link

● Tell students you will read three groups of words with four words in each group.

sour	**sister**	**sport**	**sloppy**
breed	**brim**	**breath**	**break**
platter	**peach**	**plum**	**press**

● Have students write each word as you read it aloud. Then have them look back at the group and rearrange the words in correct alphabetical order.

● When the words have been alphabetized, have students circle the two words in each group that could serve as guide words for the group.

Math Link

Have students make up math word problems involving dictionaries and guide words. Here is an example: *My dictionary has 862 pages. How many guide words does it have? (862 x 2 = 1,724)* Suggest that students give their problems to a partner to solve.

Observational Assessment

Check to see that students understand how to use guide words.

Guide Words 2

Objectives

- **To understand the idea of dividing the dictionary into three parts**

- **To determine whether an entry word would be found in the beginning, middle, or end of a dictionary**

- **To identify the guide words that can help to locate an entry word**

Warming Up

- Write this poem on the board and read it to students:

    Said **A** to **I**, "You and I are the start
    Of a dictionary divided into three
    useful parts."
    Said **J** to **Q**, "The middle are we,
    If the dictionary is divided into sections
    three."
    Said **R** to **Z**, "We close the show.
    Three dictionary parts are the way
    to go."

- Tell students that the twenty-six letters of the alphabet can be divided into the three groups **A–I, J–Q,** and **R–Z.** Thinking of the dictionary as having three parts can help you find words more quickly.

Teaching the Lesson

- Have students locate the three parts of the dictionary and separate them with bookmarks. Have ready a series of words, such as these: **astronaut, firefighter, navigator, officer, counselor.**

- When you say each word, have students first turn to the appropriate part of the dictionary. Then have them locate the page where the entry word is found.

- Have a student read the Helpful Hint aloud.

Name _____

Helpful Hint

Think of the dictionary as having three parts.

The words in the **beginning** part start with the letters A–I.
The words in the **middle** start with the letters J–Q.
The words in the **end** part start with the letters R–Z.

Turn to the beginning, the middle, or the end of the dictionary to help you quickly find words.

Sort the words according to the part of the dictionary in which you would find each word.

debate	treasury	lawyer	court
judge	voter	district	jury	tax

1 Beginning: A–I	2 Middle: J–Q	3 End: R–Z
debate	lawyer	treasury
court	judge	voter
district	jury	tax

Each sentence below has a word in bold print. Write *beginning,* *middle,* **or** *end* **to tell in which part of the dictionary you would find the word.**

4. The nation had economic **troubles** after the American Revolution. ___end___

5. The **country** had borrowed money to fight. ___beginning___

6. To raise **money**, the new government increased the property tax. ___middle___

CHALLENGE

Write the words from each sentence that would appear in the same part of the dictionary as the word in bold print.

UNIVERSAL ACCESS
Meeting Individual Needs

Tactile Learners

Have students find words about law or government in encyclopedia articles. Tell them to write the words on index cards and place each card in the beginning, middle, or end of a dictionary, depending on the first letter of the word. Then tell students to look up each word and write its definition on the card.

Logical Learners

Have volunteers develop a flow chart telling how to use the dictionary's three parts to find words more quickly.

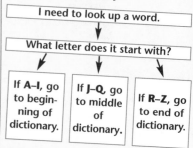

I need to look up a word.

What letter does it start with?

If A–I, go to beginning of dictionary.	If J–Q, go to middle of dictionary.	If R–Z, go to end of dictionary.

Classmates should try out the flow chart and give feedback to the student who developed it.

⭐ **Write** *Beginning,* *Middle,* or *End* to tell in which part of the dictionary you would find each numbered word. Write **A–I** for the beginning letters, **J–Q** for the middle letters, and **R–Z** for the end letters. Then circle the correct pair of *guide words* below that would appear on the same page as the numbered word.

1. sheriff _____end_____
   shift/shop   (shame/shield)   sift/silly

2. census _____beginning_____
   central/ceramic   celebrate/cell   (cement/center)

3. volunteer _____end_____
   (violet/vote)   valiant/value   valve/vanilla

4. nation _____middle_____
   narrator/nasty   (nasal/navy)   natural/neighbor

5. general _____beginning_____
   garlic/gem   geology/ginger   (geese/giant)

6. kingdom _____middle_____
   (kimono/knife)   kettle/kilogram   knob/knuckle

7. supervisor _____end_____
   support/sweatshirt   sound/sudden   (suitcase/supper)

8. brass _____beginning_____
   brave/bridge   bowl/branch   (brace/broadcast)

9. office _____middle_____
   (odor/official)   odd/offhand   often/old

10. worker _____end_____
    wood/work   workout/worldwide   (work/workshop)

⭐ **Read** the words in the box. Imagine that they are on the same page of a dictionary and that two of the words are guide words. Which would be the first guide word? Which would be the second?

conquer	coyote	connect	compete	congress
connection	content	craft	court	courtroom

11. First guide word: _____compete_____   12. Second guide word: _____craft_____

 Home Involvement Activity Do a simple dictionary test. Which letter has the greatest number of words? The fewest? First, take a guess. Then find out together.

Practicing the Skill

● Read aloud the direction lines on pages 183–184. Complete the first item in each exercise with students.

● Allow students who have difficulty with alphabetizing to work with a partner.

Curriculum Connections

Spelling Link

krowre	rsheffi	ryuj
vunoleter	yemno	waylre
raleeng	tonina	sarbs

● Have students unscramble these words and then write them correctly on a sheet of paper. **(worker, sheriff, jury, volunteer, money, lawyer, general, nation, brass)**

● When students have finished, have them say whether each word would be found at the beginning, middle, or end of the dictionary.

Multicultural Connection

● By order of the United States Constitution, the United States conducts a census, or head count, every ten years. The census finds the number of people who live here, their ethnic background, their gender, where they live, the type of home they have, their family size, and other details. Census data helps to ensure that all groups receive their rights.

● Have students work in small groups to look in an almanac for recent census data. Ask students to identify five key words about the topic. Then have them identify the part of the dictionary in which those words can be found.

Observational Assessment

Check to see that students recognize in which part of the dictionary a word can be found.

English-Language Learners/ESL

On the board, write the letters that indicate the beginning, middle, and end of the dictionary: **A–I, J–Q,** and **R–Z.** Under these headings, have a volunteer write the letters of the alphabet in that section. Work with students to find the first entry word for each letter. Then help them find the three larger section divisions. Have them label bookmarks or self-stick notes to use as the section dividers.

Gifted Learners

Have students create another way to find words quickly in a dictionary. Remind them that it should be easy to use. Have them write down their "Tips for Speedy Word Retrieval" and publish it so that classmates can try it.

Learners with Special Needs

Additional strategies for supporting learners with special needs can be found on page 177L.

Entry Words

Objectives

- To recognize when to look up a base word to find the meaning of another word
- To recognize that contractions and abbreviations may be entry words

Warming Up

- Read this rhyme aloud.

  Prefixes and **suffixes**
  Seldom get their due.
  They linger near one **entry word,**
  instead of making two.
  Contractions don't get short-changed, though;
  Abbreviations, either.
  They each get entries all their own.
  Each one happy to be shown.

- Ask students for examples of prefixes, suffixes, contractions, and abbreviations. Write them on the board. Have students name base words to go with the prefixes and suffixes. Work with students to look for some of these words in a dictionary. Tell students not to be surprised if a word is not listed.

Teaching the Lesson

- Write the prefixes **un-** and **re-**, the endings **-ed** and **-ing,** and the suffixes **-tion,** and **-ly,** on the board as column heads. Work together to create lists of words that include these prefixes, endings, and suffixes.

- Have students discuss what would happen if the dictionary included every form of the word as a separate entry. (The dictionary would be unnecessarily long, repetitive, and confusing.)

- Call on volunteers to read the Helpful Hints aloud. Then ask, *Why do you think dictionaries print separate entries for abbreviations and contractions?*

185

Name _____

Helpful Hints

Words given in a dictionary are called **entry words.** Entry words appear in bold print in **ABC order.** The information about an entry word (its syllables, pronunciation, part of speech, definition, and other information) is called the **entry.**

Many words that have **endings, prefixes,** or **suffixes** will not appear as separate entry words. You may need to figure out the **base word** to know which entry word to look up.

splitting→**split**　rapidly→**rapid**　freshness→**fresh**

The Library of Congress

Read each word. Write the entry word you would look up in the dictionary to find the word. Use a dictionary to help you.

1. connected	connect	2. discoveries	discover
3. nearest	near	4. flavorful	flavor
5. nonsense	nonsense	6. brainy	brain
7. replaster	plaster	8. terribly	terrible

Helpful Hint

Some dictionaries have entry words for **abbreviations** and **contractions.** These entry words are listed in alphabetical order as if they were entire words.

Use a dictionary to write the word or words that each abbreviation and contraction stands for.

9. ave.	avenue	10. I've	I	have
lb.	pound	it's	it	is
in.	inch	doesn't	does	not

CHALLENGE

Use a dictionary. Write two meanings for each of these abbreviations:

Mt.
DC
Dr.
Sr.

LESSON 91: Entry Words　　**185**

UNIVERSAL ACCESS
Meeting Individual Needs

Auditory Learners

Give pairs of students six words to look up in a dictionary. Have students learn the words' meanings and pronunciations. Then have them create a brief dialogue using all six words. Encourage students to perform their dialogues for the class. Invite listeners to ask questions or make comments about the dialogues.

Visual Learners

Have students write the words for exercises 1–8 on page 185 on a separate sheet of paper. Then have them underline word parts using three markers: red for a prefix, green for the base word, and blue for a suffix or an inflected ending.

Sample Dictionary Entries

chasm A deep crack or opening in the earth's surface.
chasm (kaz'əm) *noun*, *plural* **chasms**.

jubilant Feeling or showing great joy. The players were *jubilant* over their victory.
ju•bi•lant (jü'bə lənt) *adjective*.

malaria A disease that causes chills, a high fever, and sweating. Malaria is spread by the bite of a certain type of mosquito that carries the disease from infected persons.
ma•lar•i•a (mə lâr' ē ə) *noun*.

pony express A postal service in which relays of riders on horseback carried mail across the western United States. The pony express ran from 1860 to 1861.

sieve A utensil that has a bottom with many holes in it. A sieve is used for sifting or draining.
sieve (siv) *noun*, *plural* **sieves**.

From the MACMILLAN SCHOOL DICTIONARY, © 1990, reproduced with permission of The McGraw-Hill Companies.

⭐ **Read the five dictionary entries above. Then write the entry word that fits each clue.**

1. This tool is used for sifting or draining. _____ sieve _____
2. You should take care never to fall into one of these. _____ chasm _____
3. You might feel this way if you won a tough contest. _____ jubilant _____
4. Some kinds of mosquitoes can spread this sickness. _____ malaria _____
5. You could have worked for this postal service in 1860. _____ pony express _____

⭐ **Write your own sentence for each of the five entry words above.**

6. _____ Sentences will vary. _____
7. _____
8. _____
9. _____
10. _____

186 LESSON 91: Entry Words

🏠 **Home Involvement Activity** Suppose that the name of each member of your family appeared in a dictionary. What entry word would appear just before the name? Just after? Look in a dictionary to find out.

English-Language Learners/ESL

Label cards with base words such as **play** and **study** and endings such as **-s**, **-ed**, and **-ing** in different colors. Have students choose a base word card and read it aloud. Then have them choose an ending card and add the ending to the base word to form a new word. Finally, ask the student to find the word in a dictionary to check its meaning and pronunciation.

Gifted Learners

Have students look up some of the entries from page 186 in an unabridged dictionary. Show them where to find the word's etymology, and help them read it if necessary. Then have students restate the information in their own words.

Learners with Special Needs

Additional strategies for supporting learners with special needs can be found on page 177L.

- Read aloud the direction lines on pages 185–186.
- Before they do exercise 9 on page 185, tell students to reread the Helpful Hint.
- Encourage students to be creative when completing items 6–10 on page 186.

Curriculum Connections

Spelling Link

Read aloud each word and sentence and have students write the words. When students have finished, call on volunteers to name the base words.

connected	Public transportation has **connected** all parts of the city.
discoveries	NASA astronauts have made important **discoveries** about space.
nearest	Where is the **nearest** fire house?
flavorful	The health department publishes recipes for **flavorful**, healthy meals.
terribly	The National Weather Service predicts a **terribly** cold winter.
I've	**I've** just bought a book of stamps at the post office.

Social Studies Link

Have small groups of students study a road map or a local street map of their area. Tell them to list all the abbreviations they can find. Ask them what the abbreviations might stand for. Then have students check their answers by looking up the abbreviations in a dictionary.

Observational Assessment

Check to see that students can identify all the parts of a dictionary entry.

Homographs— Multiple-Meaning Words

Objectives

- **To recognize the definition of a homograph**
- **To recognize and use multiple-meaning words**

- Read the following dialogue aloud.

  Terry: I was giving my dog a bath in the tub when I heard the telephone **ring.**

  Gerry: How annoying! What did you do?

  Terry: I started to get up, but I had left my gold **ring** on the edge of the tub, and I knocked it into the water.

  Gerry: Oh, no! Then what?

  Terry: I let the water out and saw a big **ring.**

  Gerry: Your gold **ring**?

  Terry: No, a **ring** around the bathtub!

- Call on volunteers to explain why Gerry is confused. Ask students to give several different meanings of the word **ring.**

Teaching the Lesson

- Explain that in the dialogue above, students encountered a word that has more than one meaning. Point out that these words are called homographs.

- Have students look at each dictionary entry on pages 187 and 188 and explain that the words in dark type are entry words.

- For the word **elect,** draw attention to the numbers before the definitions. Ask students how many definitions of the word **elect** are given in this entry.

- Read the Helpful Hints aloud, then ask: *How can a dictionary help us figure out which meanings of a homograph to use?*

187

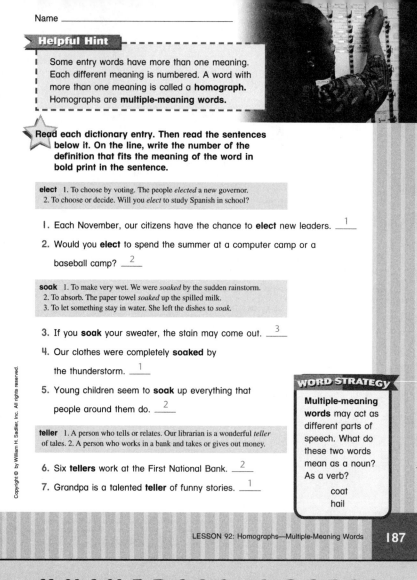

Name _____

> **Helpful Hint**
>
> Some entry words have more than one meaning. Each different meaning is numbered. A word with more than one meaning is called a **homograph.** Homographs are **multiple-meaning words.**

Read each dictionary entry. Then read the sentences below it. On the line, write the number of the definition that fits the meaning of the word in bold print in the sentence.

> **elect** 1. To choose by voting. The people *elected* a new governor.
> 2. To choose or decide. Will you *elect* to study Spanish in school?

1. Each November, our citizens have the chance to **elect** new leaders. __1__

2. Would you **elect** to spend the summer at a computer camp or a baseball camp? __2__

> **soak** 1. To make very wet. We were *soaked* by the sudden rainstorm.
> 2. To absorb. The paper towel *soaked* up the spilled milk.
> 3. To let something stay in water. She left the dishes to *soak.*

3. If you **soak** your sweater, the stain may come out. __3__

4. Our clothes were completely **soaked** by the thunderstorm. __1__

5. Young children seem to **soak** up everything that people around them do. __2__

> **teller** 1. A person who tells or relates. Our librarian is a wonderful *teller* of tales. 2. A person who works in a bank and takes or gives out money.

6. Six **tellers** work at the First National Bank. __2__

7. Grandpa is a talented **teller** of funny stories. __1__

> **WORD STRATEGY**
>
> **Multiple-meaning words** may act as different parts of speech. What do these two words mean as a noun? As a verb?
>
> coat
> hail

LESSON 92: Homographs—Multiple-Meaning Words · 187

UNIVERSAL ACCESS
Meeting Individual Needs

Visual Learners

Read aloud familiar homographs such as **wonder, column, right, clip, press, page,** or **record.** Have a student write one of the words and a brief definition of it on the board in colored chalk. Have another student write a different definition for the same word using a different color chalk. For each definition, have students use a different color chalk.

Auditory Learners

Say a word that is a homograph, such as **ring, bill, snap, light, bark, grill, fast, present, mine, school, train, lie, pupil,** and **fire.** Call on students to write sentences using different meanings of the words and read them aloud. Then have students state the definition of the word as they used it in their sentence.

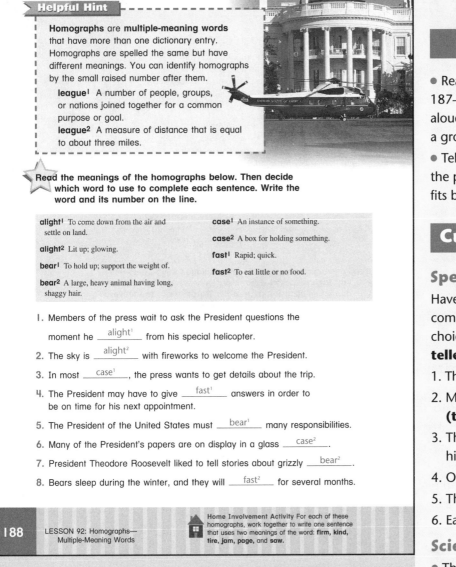

Read the meanings of the homographs below. Then decide which word to use to complete each sentence. Write the word and its number on the line.

alight¹ To come down from the air and settle on land.

alight² Lit up; glowing.

bear¹ To hold up; support the weight of.

bear² A large, heavy animal having long, shaggy hair.

case¹ An instance of something.

case² A box for holding something.

fast¹ Rapid; quick.

fast² To eat little or no food.

1. Members of the press wait to ask the President questions the moment he ___alight¹___ from his special helicopter.

2. The sky is ___alight²___ with fireworks to welcome the President.

3. In most ___case¹___, the press wants to get details about the trip.

4. The President may have to give ___fast¹___ answers in order to be on time for his next appointment.

5. The President of the United States must ___bear¹___ many responsibilities.

6. Many of the President's papers are on display in a glass ___case²___.

7. President Theodore Roosevelt liked to tell stories about grizzly ___bear²___.

8. Bears sleep during the winter, and they will ___fast²___ for several months.

Home Involvement Activity For each of these homographs, work together to write one sentence that uses two meanings of the word: **firm, kind, tire, jam, page,** and **saw.**

Practicing the Skill

● Read aloud the direction lines on pages 187–188. Read the first dictionary entry aloud and complete exercises 1 and 2 as a group.

● Tell students to match each exercise with the possible definitions to find the one that fits best.

Curriculum Connections

Spelling Link

Have students write the word that correctly completes each sentence. Read the answer choices aloud: **case, alight, fast, bear, teller, elect.**

1. The lunchroom orders juice by the **(case)**.

2. Mrs. Sanchez works in a bank. She is a **(teller)**.

3. The patient was asked to **(fast)**, before his operation.

4. Our zoo has a new **(bear)** cub.

5. The night **(alight)** with stars.

6. Each class will **(elect)** a president.

Science Link

● The word **bug** means "insect," but it also means "error in a computer program." Admiral Grace Murray Hopper, one of the first programmers, coined the term when she found a moth literally stuck in the relay of a computer that had stopped working. She removed it, taped it into her logbook, and labeled it, "first actual case of bug being found."

● Have students list as many computer terms as they can, and then see which of them are multiple-meaning words. (Possible answers: **drive, program, floppy, run, clear, enter, key, web**)

Observational Assessment

Check to see that students can use multiple-meaning words correctly in context.

English-Language Learners/ESL

Create a picture card for each definition of multiple-meaning words such as **bear, trunk, speaker, fork,** and **foot.** Use words whose meanings are easy to illustrate. Write an example sentence for each meaning of each word. Then display the cards and read aloud an example sentence. Have students identify the card that matches the word meaning used in the example sentence.

Gifted Learners

Some students may enjoy writing poems, dialogues, comic sketches, or short stories based on the confusion that can arise from multiple-meaning words. Suggest that students make a list of the homographs they might use before they begin writing. Ask them to share their finished work with the class.

Learners with Special Needs

Additional strategies for supporting learners with special needs can be found on page 177L.

Pronunciation Key

Objectives

- **To recognize and understand the use of the pronunciation key**
- **To identify and use respelling as an aid to correct pronunciation**

Warming Up

- Write this poem on the board and invite a volunteer to read it aloud:

  I closed my eyes and went to sleep
  And had a fearful dream.
  I **dremt** that **wûrdz** in the dictionary
  Wûr not always **hwot** they **sēm!**

- Ask volunteers to offer explanations as to why the words in dark type are written differently than usual.

- Invite students to sound out the phonetically respelled words in the poem, with the help of a pronunciation key. Then have a volunteer spell the words correctly.

Teaching the Lesson

- Display a dictionary page showing the entry for the word **eye.** Draw students' attention to the phonetic respelling (**ī**). Then go to the board and write the words **flow, high,** and **large,** along with their phonetic respellings (**flō, hī, lärj**).

- Show students the pronunciation key on the dictionary page. Explain that the pronunciation key tells you all the symbols used in the phonetic respellings. It tells you the sound each symbol stands for by giving an example word for each symbol. For example, in some pronunciation keys the symbol **ī** is found in or next to the word **ice.** This symbol is used in the phonetic respellings of **eye** and **high.**

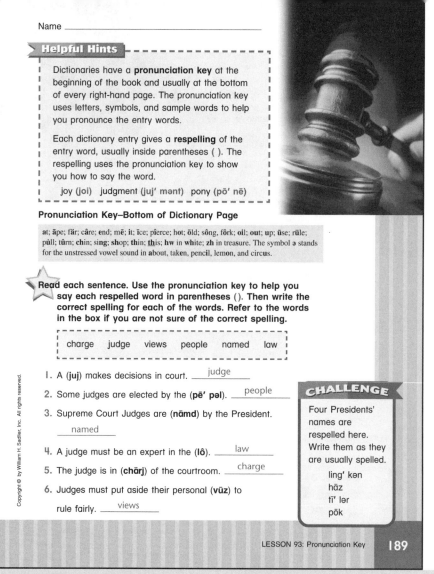

Name _____

▷ Helpful Hints

Dictionaries have a **pronunciation key** at the beginning of the book and usually at the bottom of every right-hand page. The pronunciation key uses letters, symbols, and sample words to help you pronounce the entry words.

Each dictionary entry gives a **respelling** of the entry word, usually inside parentheses ( ). The respelling uses the pronunciation key to show you how to say the word.

joy (joi)   judgment (juj′ mənt)   pony (pō′ nē)

Pronunciation Key–Bottom of Dictionary Page

at; āpe; fär; câre; end; mē; it; īce; pîerce; hot; ōld; sông; fôrk; oil; out; up; ūse; rüle; pull; tûrn; chin; sing; shop; thin; this; hw in white; zh in treasure. The symbol ə stands for the unstressed vowel sound in about, taken, pencil, lemon, and circus.

⭐ Read each sentence. Use the pronunciation key to help you say each respelled word in parentheses ( ). Then write the correct spelling for each of the words. Refer to the words in the box if you are not sure of the correct spelling.

charge	judge	views	people	named	law

1. A (**juj**) makes decisions in court. ___judge___

2. Some judges are elected by the (**pē′ pəl**). ___people___

3. Supreme Court Judges are (**nāmd**) by the President. ___named___

4. A judge must be an expert in the (**lô**). ___law___

5. The judge is in (**chärj**) of the courtroom. ___charge___

6. Judges must put aside their personal (**vūz**) to rule fairly. ___views___

▷ CHALLENGE

Four Presidents' names are respelled here. Write them as they are usually spelled.

ling′ kən
hāz
tī′ lər
pōk

UNIVERSAL ACCESS
Meeting Individual Needs

Visual Learners

Create a set of flash cards with words spelled correctly on one side and written phonetically on the other side. Working in pairs, have one student show the respelling and have the partner pronounce it correctly. Use challenging words like **ferocious, action, multiply, coral, vegetable, consider, anemone,** and so on. Distribute pronunciation keys for students to refer to as they play.

Logical Learners

Students may enjoy finding out more about diacritical marks such as the following: acute accent, grave accent, caret, cedilla, circumflex, dieresis, macron, and tilde. Provide students with a list of terms, and have them create a chart displaying the terms, the diacritical marks, and a brief explanation of their function.

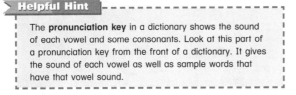

Helpful Hint

The **pronunciation key** in a dictionary shows the sound of each vowel and some consonants. Look at this part of a pronunciation key from the front of a dictionary. It gives the sound of each vowel as well as sample words that have that vowel sound.

★ Read each respelling below. Next to it, write the words from the pronunciation key that have the same vowel sound. Then write the correct spelling for the word. The first one is done for you.

	Respelling	Example Words with Same Vowel Sound	Correct Spelling
1	(boi)	oil, toy	boy
2	(brāv)	ape, pain, day, break	brave
3	(fôrs)	order, fork, horse, story, pour	force
4	(chärm)	father, car, heart	charm
5	(drô)	coffee, all, taught, law, fought	draw
6	(skâr)	care, pair, bear, their, where	scare
7	(bŭk)	put, wood, should	book
8	(wind)	it, big, English hymn	wind
9	(yîr)	ear, dear, here, pierce	year
10	(prün)	rule, true, food	prune
11	(blēch)	equal, me, feet, team, piece, key	bleach
12	(bout)	out, now	bout
13	(rist)	it, big, English, hymn	wrist

Pronunciation Key– Front of Dictionary

a	at, bad
ā	ape, pain, day, break
ä	father, car, heart
âr	care, pair, bear, their, where
e	end, pet, said, heaven, friend
ē	equal, me, feet, team, piece, key
i	it, big, English, hymn
ī	ice, fine, lie, my
îr	ear, deer, here, pierce
o	odd, hot, watch
ō	old, oat, toe, low
ô	coffee, all, taught, law, fought
ôr	order, fork, horse, story, pour
oi	oil, toy
ou	out, now
u	up, mud, love, double
ū	use, mule, cue, feud, few
ü	rule, true, food
ù	put, wood, should
ûr	burn, hurry, term, bird, word, courage
ə	about, taken, pencil, lemon, circus

190   LESSON 93: Pronunciation Key

Home Involvement Activity You will hear the **schwa sound** (ə) in many words. Work together to circle the vowel that makes the schwa sound in these words: **focus, liberty, allow, melon, stencil.**

English-Language Learners/ESL

Students might appreciate knowing where they can find help with their pronunciation of English. If you think students are ready to use a pronunciation key, pair them with fluent speakers and give them a list of words to look up. Have partners work together to decode the respellings.

Gifted Learners

Write the word **ghoti** on the board and tell students that it spells **fish.** Explain that it begins with **gh**, which stands for the sound of **f** in **laugh, o**, which stands for the sound of **i** in **women**, and **ti**, which stands for the sound of **sh** in **nation.** Have students create other words made of unusual letter combinations.

Learners with Special Needs

Additional strategies for supporting learners with special needs can be found on page 177L.

Practicing the Skill

● Read aloud the direction lines on pages 189–190. Point out both pronunciation keys.

● As a group, complete the first item on page 189 and discuss the first answer on page 190.

● Point out on page 190 that students still have to decide which spelling to use, as in the case of **brave.**

Curriculum Connections

Spelling Link

Read these words and sentences aloud. Have students write each boldfaced word. When they finish, have students look up each word in the dictionary to check its spelling.

judge   A **judge** tries to be fair.

people   There were ten **people** in the jury box.

law   Citizens obey the **law.**

force   The police **force** upholds the law.

wrist   Sean broke his **wrist** skating.

Music Link

Display the opening lines of "The Star-Spangled Banner."

> **Oh say, can you see,/by the dawn's early light,/What so proudly we hail'd/at the twilight's last gleaming?**

Have students work in small groups to look up these words and rewrite them phonetically. You might have students who can read music write the phonetic lyrics on a photocopy of the actual sheet music for "The Star-Spangled Banner."

Observational Assessment

Check to see that students can correctly pronounce words based on respellings.

190

Accent Marks

Objectives

- To identify an accent mark in a dictionary entry

- To use accent marks as an aid in pronunciation

- To recognize that homographs may have different pronunciations and meanings

Warming Up

● Write these tongue twisters on the board.

> The **desert** lizard did not **desert** the dune.

> For much more than a **minute**, Minnie made out the motion of a **minute** microbe.

> Peter played the piano to **perfect** his **perfect** pitch.

● Have students find and circle the word that appears twice in each sentence as shown above in boldface.

● Call on volunteers to read the sentences aloud. Ask students what the circled words mean. If they are unsure, have them look up the words in the dictionary.

● Have students underscore the accented syllable for the two circled words.

⭐ Teaching the Lesson

● Write these words on the board.

> **record   object   content**

● Ask students to say each word twice, the first time stressing the first syllable, and the second time stressing the second syllable.

● Display all the dictionary entries for **record**. Point out the two respellings. Have a volunteer point out the accent marks that tell which syllable to stress. Do the same with **object** and **content**.

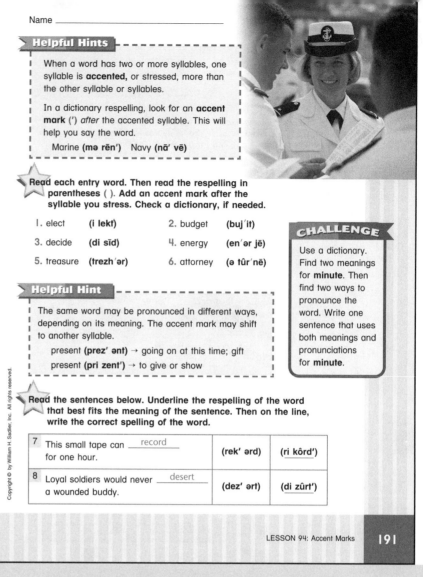

Name _____

▷ Helpful Hints

When a word has two or more syllables, one syllable is **accented**, or stressed, more than the other syllable or syllables.

In a dictionary respelling, look for an **accent mark** (ʹ) *after* the accented syllable. This will help you say the word.

> Marine (mə rēnʹ)   Navy (nāʹ vē)

⭐ Read each entry word. Then read the respelling in parentheses ( ). Add an accent mark after the syllable you stress. Check a dictionary, if needed.

1. elect	(i lekt)	2. budget	(buj it)
3. decide	(di sīd)	4. energy	(en ər jē)
5. treasure	(trezh ər)	6. attorney	(ə tûr nē)

▷ Helpful Hint

The same word may be pronounced in different ways, depending on its meaning. The accent mark may shift to another syllable.

> present (prezʹ ənt) → going on at this time; gift
> present (pri zentʹ) → to give or show

⭐ Read the sentences below. Underline the respelling of the word that best fits the meaning of the sentence. Then on the line, write the correct spelling of the word.

7	This small tape can ___record___ for one hour.	(rekʹ ərd)	(ri kôrdʹ)
8	Loyal soldiers would never ___desert___ a wounded buddy.	(dezʹ ərt)	(di zûrtʹ)

CHALLENGE

Use a dictionary. Find two meanings for **minute**. Then find two ways to pronounce the word. Write one sentence that uses both meanings and pronunciations for **minute**.

UNIVERSAL ACCESS
Meeting Individual Needs

Auditory Learners

Prepare a set of cards for words that have two meanings and two pronunciations, such as:

> **produce   console   upset**
> **minute   rebel   extract**
> **commune   contract   defect**
> **project   permit   desert**

Say the word with the accent on the first syllable and have students make up a sentence for that meaning. Then do the same with the accent on the second syllable. Students may use a dictionary for reference.

Visual Learners

Divide the board into two columns. In one column, write words that have two meanings and two pronunciations. In the other column, in different order, write a brief definition of each word. Call on students to draw a line between the word and its meaning. Then have them look up the word and respell it phonetically.

⭐ **Read** the sentences below. Underline the respelling of the word that best fits the meaning of the sentence. Then on the line, write the correct spelling of the word. Some words from the box will be used more than once.

address	content	perfect	present
progress	refuse	subject	contest

1. I remember thinking that my teacher was
   perfect in every way.   (pər fekt') (pûr' fikt)

2. She wasn't _content_ unless we were
   learning something new.   (kən tent') (kon' tent)

3. She would always _address_ us as "ladies
   and gentlemen," but we were only ten!   (ad' res) (ə dres')

4. I made a remarkable amount of _progress_
   that year.   (prə gres') (prog' res)

5. Ms. Lane loved math, and it became
   my favorite _subject_.   (sub' jikt) (səb jekt')

6. She would hug anyone who would _present_
   her with a homemade card or gift.   (prez' ənt) (pri zent')

7. She helped me _perfect_ my sloppy
   handwriting.   (pər fekt') (pûr' fikt)

8. She also entered my poem in a
   poetry _contest_.   (kən test') (kon' test)

9. She said that she cared about the _content_
   of our hearts as well as our minds.   (kən tent') (kon' tent)

10. She would never _refuse_ to give help to
    anyone who asked for it.   (ref' ūs) (ri fūz')

11. My education would _progress_ rapidly,
    thanks to her.   (prə gres') (prog' res)

192   LESSON 94: Accent Marks

🏠 **Home Involvement Activity** Use the symbols in a pronunciation key as well as accent marks to respell the names of family members. Then write the respellings on name tags to wear.

192

Connecting Spelling and Writing

Objectives

- **To say, spell, sort, and write words relating to dictionary use**
- **To write a set of instructional steps using spelling words**

Warming Up

- Have each student list seven words chosen randomly from different pages of a dictionary. Tell students to mix up the words so that they are not in alphabetical order.
- Direct students to trade papers with a partner and arrange the words alphabetically.
- Have students identify which words belong in the beginning part of the dictionary (**A-I**), which belong in the middle (**J-Q**), and which belong at the end (**R-Z**).

Teaching the Lesson

- Make a three-column chart on the board or on chart paper, using these headings.

Beginning: A–I	Middle: J–Q	End: R–Z

- Have each student come up to the board to write his or her last name in the appropriate column.
- Extend the lesson by asking students this question: *If your last name were in the dictionary, which guide words might appear at the top of the page?*

Practicing the Skill

- Read the directions on page 193. Ask students to read each phrase aloud.
- Have students complete the page. Encourage them to ask questions if they have forgotten the meaning of any of the terms in bold type.

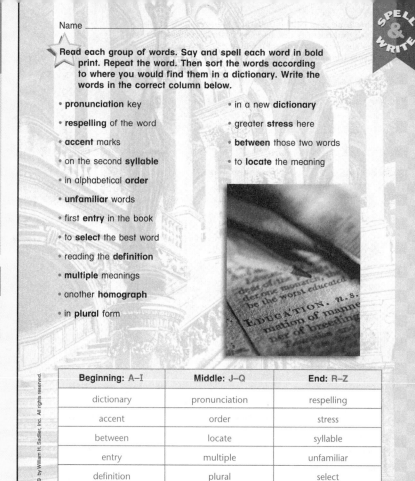

Name _____

Read each group of words. Say and spell each word in bold print. Repeat the word. Then sort the words according to where you would find them in a dictionary. Write the words in the correct column below.

- **pronunciation** key
- **respelling** of the word
- **accent** marks
- on the second **syllable**
- in alphabetical **order**
- **unfamiliar** words
- first **entry** in the book
- to **select** the best word
- reading the **definition**
- **multiple** meanings
- another **homograph**
- in **plural** form

- in a new **dictionary**
- greater **stress** here
- **between** those two words
- to **locate** the meaning

Beginning: A–I	Middle: J–Q	End: R–Z
dictionary	pronunciation	respelling
accent	order	stress
between	locate	syllable
entry	multiple	unfamiliar
definition	plural	select
homograph		

UNIVERSAL ACCESS
Meeting Individual Needs

Visual Learners

Print enough spelling words on cards or paper strips to give each student two words. On a large bulletin board make a three-column chart with these headings: **Beginning: A–I, Middle: J–Q, End: R–Z.** Have each student attach his or her words under the appropriate heading. When all the words have been posted, have students alphabetize them.

Tactile Learners

Have students work in pairs. Give each pair a set of letter cards or tiles. Arrange three containers on a desk, labeled **Beginning: A–I, Middle: J–Q, End: R–Z.** Have students sort the letter cards or tiles by placing them in the correct containers. Next, distribute vocabulary words on index cards and have students sort the words in the same manner.

Learners with Special Needs

Additional strategies for supporting learners with special needs can be found on page 177L.

Suppose a new student has joined your class. On that day, the class is working on dictionary skills. Your teacher has asked you to work as a partner with the new student. However, the student has never used a dictionary before. How would you explain how to use a dictionary?

★ **Plan a set of steps that you would follow in order to find the word *welcome* in the dictionary. Write your instructions in order. Use time-order words, such as *first*, *next*, *then*, and *finally*. Use at least three of these spelling words to write your instructions.**

pronunciation	respelling	accent	syllable	order
unfamiliar	entry	select	definition	multiple	homograph
plural	dictionary	stress	between	locate

Sentences will vary.

_____

_____

_____

_____

_____

_____

_____

_____

Writer's Tip

Check that your instructions work. Give them to a classmate to follow. Have a peer conference to find out how to improve your instructions.

Writer's Challenge

Make a list of "Dictionary Discoveries." Look through a dictionary to find interesting words for your list. Try to find words that are long, hard to pronounce, funny, unusual, or fun to draw. Define all the words. Then respell the words and add accent marks to show how to pronounce them.

194 LESSON 95: Connecting Spelling and Writing

The Writing Process

Tell students that on page 194 they will write a set of steps to find a word in the dictionary. Read the directions and spelling words at the top of the page.

Prewrite Discuss with students how they would go about looking up the word **welcome.** Tell them to break the process down into steps. For example, what would they do first? (note the first letter of the word) What would they do next? (consider where in the dictionary that letter appears) Guide students to develop a step-by-step plan.

Write Call students' attention to the Writer's Tip on page 194. Remind students to include at least three spelling words. Also remind them to use time-order words.

Revise Have students reread their steps and revise as needed. Encourage them to make their writing clear and specific.

Proofread Have students check for errors in spelling, grammar, and punctuation.

Publish Have students copy their final drafts onto page 194 or a sheet of paper. Then have them trade papers with a partner and try each other's instructions.

Computer Connection Share the following tip with students who use a word processor to do their writing.

● You can "cut and paste" text from one place in a document to another or from one document to another.

● Highlight the text you want to move. Then use either the "Copy" command or the "Cut" command. Next, place your cursor at the desired insert point and use the "Paste" command.

● "Cut," "Copy," and "Paste" are all typically found on the toolbar and/or on the Edit menu.

Portfolio Have students add their lists of how to use a dictionary to their portfolios.

English-Language Learners/ESL

Choose several spelling words. Read the words aloud and help students write them on a piece of paper. Then tell students to look up each word in the dictionary. Work with them, using pictures, objects, or pantomime, to help them understand the word's definition. Then have them use each word in a sentence.

Gifted Learners

Challenge students to write an essay or a story that tells at least one way in which a dictionary can help readers and/or writers. Encourage students to consider their own experience using dictionaries as they write their essay.

Reviewing and Assessing
Dictionary Skills

Objective

To review and assess dictionary skills

Warming Up

● Have students write their first names on the board in clusters of four or five names each. Then ask students to put each group of names in alphabetical order.

● You can extend the activity by having the class then put all the names on the board in alphabetical order.

● Choose a number of names at random and ask students whether each one would belong in the beginning part of a dictionary (**A–I**), the middle (**J–Q**), or the end (**R–Z**).

Teaching the Lesson

● Lessons 88–94 (pages 179–192) contain several Helpful Hints for using a dictionary. Have volunteers explain/review each of these Helpful Hints for the class. Stress that students should use their own words. Proceed in order of the lessons, and continue until all hints have been covered.

● List the following terms on the board: **guide words, entry words, homograph, pronunciation key, respelling.** Have volunteers define each term and identify an example of each one in a dictionary.

● Encourage students to ask questions if they feel unsure about anything. Also, remind them that many words with endings, prefixes, or suffixes won't appear as separate entry words (see the Helpful Hints at the top of page 185).

195

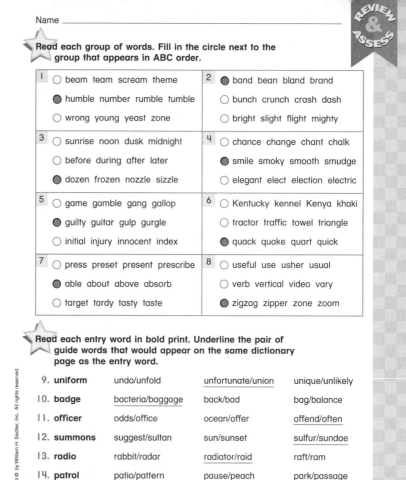

Name _____

Read each group of words. Fill in the circle next to the group that appears in ABC order.

1	○ beam team scream theme
	● humble number rumble tumble
	○ wrong young yeast zone

2	● band bean bland brand
	○ bunch crunch crash dash
	○ bright slight flight mighty

3	○ sunrise noon dusk midnight
	○ before during after later
	● dozen frozen nozzle sizzle

4	○ chance change chant chalk
	● smile smoky smooth smudge
	○ elegant elect election electric

5	○ game gamble gang gallop
	● guilty guitar gulp gurgle
	○ initial injury innocent index

6	○ Kentucky kennel Kenya khaki
	○ tractor traffic towel triangle
	● quack quake quart quick

7	○ press preset present prescribe
	● able about above absorb
	○ target tardy tasty taste

8	○ useful use usher usual
	○ verb vertical video vary
	● zigzag zipper zone zoom

Read each entry word in bold print. Underline the pair of guide words that would appear on the same dictionary page as the entry word.

9.	**uniform**	undo/unfold	<u>unfortunate/union</u>	unique/unlikely
10.	**badge**	<u>bacteria/baggage</u>	back/bad	bag/balance
11.	**officer**	odds/office	ocean/offer	<u>offend/often</u>
12.	**summons**	suggest/sultan	sun/sunset	<u>sulfur/sundae</u>
13.	**radio**	rabbit/radar	<u>radiator/raid</u>	raft/ram
14.	**patrol**	<u>patio/pattern</u>	pause/peach	park/passage
15.	**accident**	acid/acre	<u>accent/acclaim</u>	ache/acorn

LESSON 96: Review and Assess   195

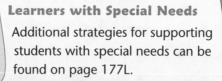

UNIVERSAL ACCESS
Meeting Individual Needs

Logical Learners

List these words on the board: **file, hold, game,** and **flight**. Point to each word, say it, and have students locate it in a dictionary, using guide words. Have a student read aloud the definitions. Invite a volunteer to choose two definitions and use the word in two sentences illustrating the different meanings.

Auditory Learners

List these words on the board: **bow, fair, bass, wind, live.** Have students use a dictionary to find out how to pronounce the words. Do the pronunciations change with different meanings? Have volunteers say each pair of words and give their meanings. Which word's pronunciation doesn't change? (**fair**)

Learners with Special Needs

Additional strategies for supporting students with special needs can be found on page 177L.

The United States Congress has many committees. The words in bold print give the topic of some of these committees. Circle *beginning*, *middle*, or *end* to tell in which part of the dictionary you would find each of these words. Use A–I for the beginning, J–Q for the middle, and R–Z for the end.

1. communication — (beginning) — middle — end
2. taxation — beginning — middle — (end)
3. education — (beginning) — middle — end
4. printing — beginning — (middle) — end
5. technology — beginning — middle — (end)
6. labor — beginning — (middle) — end
7. energy — (beginning) — middle — end
8. agriculture — (beginning) — middle — end

Read each sentence. Underline the respelling that fits the meaning in bold print.

9 A **bear** family used to live in a cave near our farm.	(bâr)	(bîr)
10 Who shall we **elect** for class president?	(u likt′)	(i lekt′)
11 My favorite team is part of the Midwest **League**.	(lēg)	(lig)
12 Many **people** work for the city government.	(pē′ pəl)	(pe′ pül)
13 Camels are well suited for life in the **desert**.	(di zûrt′)	(dez′ ərt)
14 The County Clerk keeps **records** of births and deaths.	(rek′ ərdz)	(ri kôrdz′)
15 What is that shiny **object** in the sky?	(ob′ jikt)	(əb jekt′)
16 Is social studies your favorite **subject**?	(səb jekt′)	(sub′ jikt)

Extend & Apply

Use a dictionary to look up the meaning of these words:
document, **deed**, **certificate**. How are the meanings the same?
How are they different? Write your answers.

196   LESSON 96: Review and Assess

Reteaching Activities

Around the Room

Ask students to suggest various objects around the room (desk, window, chair, etc.). Write their suggestions on the board. Have students look up each word listed on the board to see its phonetic respelling. Then have them find a word in a pronunciation key that has the same vowel sound(s) as the word on the board. For example, the sound of **e** in **desk** is the same sound as **e** in **end** in a pronunciation key.

Race for the Guide Words

Give each student a dictionary and have them work in groups of three. Have one student choose and say a word at random from the dictionary. The other two students race to be the first to identify the guide words on the page containing that word. The winner gets one point. Continue the competition by having students take turns saying words, moving clockwise around their circle. After three or four rounds tally up the results.

Assessing the Skill

Check Up Have students complete the exercises on pages 195–196 to help them review alphabetical order, guide words, respellings, and dictionary usage. You may use the exercises on these pages to help you assess students' dictionary skills.

Go over the directions for each set of exercises. For items 9–15 on page 195, remind students that guide words show the first and last entries on a dictionary page. For items 9–16 on page 196, encourage students to say the respellings softly to themselves.

Observational Assessment Watch students as they work to pinpoint areas of difficulty. Note especially how students handle the second exercise on page 196. Many students are confused by respellings and need review.

Student Skills Assessment Keep track of each student's progress with dictionary skills using the checklist on page 177H.

Writing Conference Meet with students individually to discuss their written work. Point out ways in which dictionary skills can help students become better writers. Students can check the definition of a word before using it in their writing. Students can also check the spelling of words in a dictionary as they edit and proofread.

Group together students who need further instruction in dictionary skills, and have them complete the *Reteaching Activities*. Turn to page 177C for alternative assessment methods.

PASSPORT

United States of America

Synonyms

Objectives

- **To recognize and identify synonyms**
- **To use synonyms in context**

Warming Up

- Write this rhyme on the board and read it to the class.

  When searching your brain for just the right word,

  Remember this important hint:

  There are **synonyms** for many words,

  So pick up a pen and don't stint.

- Ask a volunteer to look up the word **stint** and then discuss what "don't stint" means (don't hold back).

- Ask students to come up with as many words as possible that mean the same as **stint.** Tell students the words on their list are called **synonyms.**

Teaching the Lesson

- Give the students a list of words: **true** (faithful, loyal); **show** (display, demonstrate); **new** (fresh, recent); **take** (grab, seize); **call** (shout, yell); and **little** (small, petite). Have them list as many synonyms as possible for each word.

- Ask the students to create sentences using these words. Then substitute the words using the synonyms. Ask students if the synonyms used improves the sentence or changes the meaning of the sentences in any way.

- Have a student read the Helpful Hint aloud. Then ask: *How does using synonyms help us to express ourselves more clearly in our writing?*

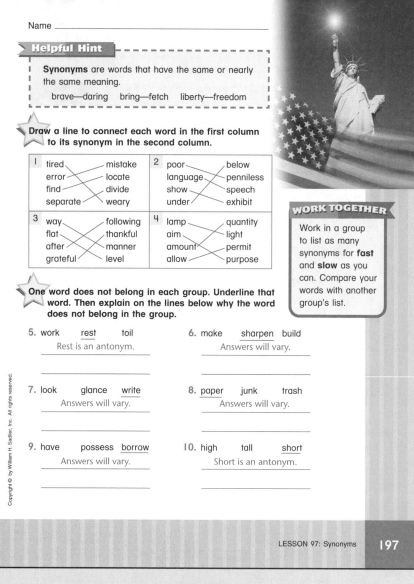

Name _____

Helpful Hint

Synonyms are words that have the same or nearly the same meaning.

brave—daring   bring—fetch   liberty—freedom

Draw a line to connect each word in the first column to its synonym in the second column.

1		
tired		mistake
error		locate
find		divide
separate		weary

2		
poor		below
language		penniless
show		speech
under		exhibit

3		
way		following
flat		thankful
after		manner
grateful		level

4		
lamp		quantity
aim		light
amount		permit
allow		purpose

WORK TOGETHER

Work in a group to list as many synonyms for **fast** and **slow** as you can. Compare your words with another group's list.

One word does not belong in each group. Underline that word. Then explain on the lines below why the word does not belong in the group.

5. work   rest   toil
   Rest is an antonym.
   _____

6. make   sharpen   build
   Answers will vary.
   _____

7. look   glance   write
   Answers will vary.
   _____

8. paper   junk   trash
   Answers will vary.
   _____

9. have   possess   borrow
   Answers will vary.
   _____

10. high   tall   short
    Short is an antonym.
    _____

UNIVERSAL ACCESS
Meeting Individual Needs

Kinesthetic Learners

List pairs of synonyms on index cards. Write a synonym on each card. Mix the cards and place them in a box. Have each student pick a card. Then have students find their "synonym partner" as quickly as possible. To vary the activity, make two identical sets of cards, divide students into two teams, and see which team arranges itself first.

Auditory Learners

Divide the class into pairs. Have the partners play a timed synonym game. One student says a word. The other student says as many synonyms as he or she can while the first student writes them down. Allow sixty seconds per round. Two or three pairs can play at the same time. Use words that generate a number of synonyms, such as **happy, look,** or **new.**

Unscramble the letters of the word in bold print to find a synonym for each numbered word. Then write the synonym on the line.

1. change **ryav** _____vary_____
2. glad **yphpa** _____happy_____
3. decrease **nelsse** _____lesson_____
4. wealth **chries** _____riches_____
5. supply **reodvpi** _____provide_____
6. error **tismkea** _____mistake_____
7. wound **jynuri** _____injury_____
8. occur **phapne** _____happen_____

Read each sentence. Then write the word from the box that is a synonym for the word in bold print.

> updates occupations recent nation difficult neighborhood

9. A census is a count of how many people live in a **country**. _____nation_____

10. A census-taker counts the number of people and finds out their ages and **jobs**. _____occupations_____

11. It is **hard** work to make an exact count. _____difficult_____

12. The number of schools in a **community** is based on the census. _____neighborhood_____

13. The government **revises** its population data after each census is done. _____updates_____

14. A census shows the **new** arrivals to a country. _____recent_____

198 LESSON 97: Synonyms

Home Involvement Activity List as many synonyms as you can for family members. For example, list synonyms for **mother, father, child, grandmother,** and so on.

English-Language Learners/ESL

Make a pair of identical picture cards for each synonym pair:

**curtains/drapes   dish/plate   pants/slacks
car/automobile   coat/jacket   handbag/purse**

Label each card with one synonym. Have students match the pictures and read the labels. Explain that the words are **synonyms:** words that mean almost the same thing.

Gifted Learners

Introduce **connotation:** words that are similar but have different shades of meaning. **(lovely/gorgeous; old/ancient; unclear/doubtful)** Have students list five pairs of synonyms with different connotations and then use the words in a descriptive paragraph.

Learners with Special Needs

Additional strategies for supporting learners with special needs can be found on page 177L.

Practicing the Skill

● Read aloud the direction lines on pages 197–198. Work through the first item in each exercise as a group.

● Remind students that in items 5–10 on page 197, they are looking for the word that does **not** belong.

● Students can benefit from the process of elimination as they complete items 1–4 on page 197 and 9–14 on page 198.

Intervention Strategy

Turn to page 177K for an Intervention strategy designed to help students who need extra support with this lesson.

Curriculum Connections

Spelling Link

● Read the list of words found in the box on page 198: **updates, occupations, recent, nation, difficult, neighborhood.** Have students write each word.

● Then read these words in random order: **corrects, careers, latest, homeland, tough, district.** Have students write each word next to the spelling word for which it is a synonym.

Drama Link

Have students work in small groups to create a humorous skit. Remind students that drama needs a conflict (a problem) which in this case should arise out of a misunderstanding over a synonym. To begin, students should create a list of synonyms and then work them into a dialogue. Encourage students to use a thesaurus or a dictionary for reference.

Observational Assessment

Check to see that students use synonyms appropriately in context.

Antonyms

Objectives

- **To identify antonyms**
- **To use antonyms correctly in context**

Warming Up

- Write the rhyme on the board and call on a volunteer to read it aloud.

    If **winter** is the opposite of **summer,**
    And **first** is the opposite of **last,**
    If **slowly** is the opposite of **quickly,**
    How can **eat** be the opposite of **fast**?

- Invite a volunteer to explain the joke in the poem. Point out that two meanings of the word **fast** are the adverb **quickly** and the verb meaning **to keep oneself from eating.** Encourage students to identify the word that should be the opposite of **fast** in this poem.

★ Teaching the Lesson

- Write these pairs of words on the board.

strange/familiar	near/far
covered/revealed	dry/damp
under/over	dull/sharp
same/different	lose/find
clean/messy	cry/laugh

- Ask students what they notice about each of these pairs. Have students suggest more pairs of opposites and list them on the board. Tell students these opposites are called **antonyms.**

- Have students make up sentences for each antonym pair and say them aloud.

- Have a student read the Helpful Hint aloud. Then ask: *How can understanding antonyms help us in our reading? In our writing?*

Name _____

> **Helpful Hint**
>
> **Antonyms** are words that have the opposite or nearly the opposite meaning.
>
> question—answer   day—night   winter—summer

Circle the two words in each row that are antonyms of the word in bold print.

1. **trust**   assume   (distrust)   believe   (mistrust)
2. **lose**   (win)   fail   (conquer)   misplace
3. **many**   numerous   (few)   several   (scarce)
4. **before**   (after)   next   when   (following)
5. **easy**   (difficult)   simple   (hard)   uncomplicated
6. **boring**   dull   (exciting)   (thrilling)   tiresome

Replace the word in bold print with its antonym from the box.

> rude   damage   over   public   blame   south   win   generous

7. The politician responded to questions about her **private** life. public
8. We drove **north** for ten miles, then turned west. south
9. The man was **stingy** with his money. generous
10. The strike by city workers caused the mayor to **lose** the race. win
11. A debate may **improve** the candidate's chances. damage
12. They were **polite** to the guest speaker. rude
13. The road went **under** the highway and then curved to the right. over
14. Do you **forgive** me for the things I said? blame

> **CHALLENGE**
>
> Write a sensible sentence that has a pair of antonyms in it. Then write another sentence that uses *two* pairs of antonyms.

UNIVERSAL ACCESS
Meeting Individual Needs

Auditory Learners

Pair students and have them play "Antonym Password." Give one partner a list of five words. This student must get his or her partner to guess each word. The only clues allowed are antonyms for the words. Then have partners switch roles.

Visual Learners

Have students work in groups or independently to generate a list of antonym pairs. Then have students choose one pair and illustrate the words' meanings, without labeling the illustrations with the words themselves. When students have finished, have them display their illustrations to see whether classmates can guess which antonym pair the student illustrated.

| amateur | stale | part | gentle | repair | father | cheap | lost |
| empty | subtract | absent | pleasure | sunset | unknown | least |

1. whole — p a r **t**
2. mother — f a t **h** e r
3. pain — p l **e** a s u r e
4. full — e m **p** t y
5. famous — u n k n **o** w n
6. found — l **o** s t
7. fresh — s **t** a l e
8. most — l e **a** s t
9. harsh — **g** e n t l e
10. expensive — c h **e** a p
11. sunrise — **s** u n s e t
12. add — s u b **t** r a c t
13. present — **a** b s e n t
14. professional — a m **a** t e u r
15. break — r e **p** a i r

Question: Rowland Hill was a British civil servant who lived in the 1800s. He was interested in improving mail delivery. He introduced something that we all use today. What did Hill introduce?

Answer: the postage stamp

Home Involvement Activity What is a **philatelist**? Find out together. The post office will be glad to give you information. Do you know any **philatelists**? If so, ask them to tell you about their hobby.

Practicing the Skill

- Read aloud the direction lines on pages 199–200. Work as a group to complete the first item in each exercise.

- For items 1–15 on page 200, remind students to print each letter right on the line, so that they will be able to read the shaded column clearly afterward.

Curriculum Connections

Spelling Link

- Write these scrambled words on the board.

| cultidiff | bringo | teamaur |
| trafe | poteli | gerousne |

- Have students unscramble the words and write them to correctly complete these sentences:

1. An antonym for **simple** is (**difficult**).
2. An antonym for **before** is (**after**).
3. An antonym for **interesting** is (**boring**).
4. An antonym for **rude** is (**polite**).
5. An antonym for **expert** is (**amateur**).
6. An antonym for **stingy** is (**generous**).

Social Studies Link

Have students work in groups to look through social studies textbooks for words they can use to make antonym pairs. Here are some examples: **east/west; win/lose; public/private;** and **mountainous/flat.** Have students use five of their antonym pairs in a mock campaign speech that they would give if they were running for office, whether for class president, U.S. President, or any other elected office.

Observational Assessment

Check to see that students understand what antonyms are and how to verify word meanings.

English-Language Learners/ESL

Give students simple antonym pairs such as **first/last**, **high/low**, and **big/small**. Have students use various classroom objects to demonstrate the meaning of each pair. Then have them use the objects and words to complete a sentence frame such as the following:

This is ____, but this is ____.

Gifted Learners

Students can use antonyms to make analogies such as this one.

wide is to **narrow** as **thick** is to **thin**

There should be a relationship between the first pair of antonyms and the second pair. Have students share their finished analogies with the class.

Learners with Special Needs

Additional strategies for supporting learners with special needs can be found on page 177L.

Homonyms

Objectives

- To recognize that homonyms are words that sound the same but have different meanings and different spellings

- To use homonyms correctly

Warming Up

Write the following dialogue on the board and let half the class read each part:

Terry: I can't **bear** all this homework!

Gerry: How can homework be **bare?**

Terry: Not **bare—bear!**

Gerry: What? We seem to have a **minor** misunderstanding.

Terry: What? I don't work in a mine!

Gerry: Not **miner—minor!**

Terry: What? Now I'm confused, **too.**

Gerry: Well, I'm confused, **three.**

Terry: Not **two—too!**

Gerry: Say that again.

Terry: Not **two—too!** Why are you laughing?

Gerry: Because you sound like a train.

Invite volunteers to explain why Terry and Gerry are so confused.

Teaching the Lesson

- Ask volunteers to identify the three sets of words in the dialogue that sound alike but have different meanings and different spellings. Encourage students to suggest other pairs of such words as you list them on the board.

- Have a student read the Helpful Hint aloud. Then ask: *Why is it important to recognize homonyms?*

Name _____

> **Helpful Hint**

Homonyms are words that sound the same but have different meanings and different spellings.

right—write   eight—ate   fourth—forth

☆ Write the homonym from the box for each word below.

| minor | maid | wait | cymbal | horse | pole |
| their | cruise | him | boar | mist | pail |

1. made _____ maid _____   2. poll _____ pole _____
3. hymn _____ him _____   4. miner _____ minor _____
5. bore _____ boar _____   6. hoarse _____ horse _____
7. weight _____ wait _____   8. crews _____ cruise _____
9. missed _____ mist _____   10. there _____ their _____
11. symbol _____ cymbal _____   12. pale _____ pail _____

☆ Choose the homonym in parentheses ( ) that completes each sentence. Write the word on the line.

13. We usually pay sales (tacks, tax) when we buy something in a department store. _____ tax _____

14. Postal clerks (way, weigh) letters and packages. _____ weigh _____

15. The National (Weather, Whether) Service gives storm warnings. _____ Weather _____

16. Which government agency takes care of clean (air, heir)? _____ air _____

CHALLENGE

To, too, and **two** are homonyms. How many other sets of three homonyms can you name? Make a list.

LESSON 99: Homonyms   **201**

UNIVERSAL ACCESS
Meeting Individual Needs

Kinesthetic Learners

Create pairs of cards with homonyms written on them. Have students each draw a card and hold it up. When you yell "Go!" students must find the classmate whose word is a homonym for theirs. Once students find their partners, have them look up their word in a dictionary.

Auditory Learners

Have students work in pairs to create a dialogue like the one between Terry and Gerry in the *Warming-Up* exercise. Remind students that the dialogue's humor results from the characters confusing words with their homonyms. Encourage students to read their dialogue to the class.

★ **Underline the pair of homonyms in each sentence. Then write a definition for each homonym. Check your definition in a dictionary.**

1. We <u>rode</u> our bikes on the newly paved <u>road</u>.

   rode: sat on and was carried by something in motion

   road: a strip of pavement

2. Congress meets in the <u>Capitol</u> in our nation's <u>capital</u>.

   Capitol: the building in which a legislature meets

   capital: the city in which a government is located

3. I think that the <u>fare</u> for the long train ride is <u>fair</u>.

   fare: the cost of a ride

   fair: good or acceptable

4. We have <u>been</u> putting papers in one <u>bin</u> and jars in another.

   been: the past participle of be

   bin: an enclosed place for holding something

5. Students are not <u>allowed</u> to read <u>aloud</u> during quiet reading time.

   allowed: permitted

   aloud: to be heard

6. They <u>knew</u> all about the <u>new</u> law for keeping dogs on a leash.

   knew: understood clearly

   new: recently made

7. Will she <u>buy</u> the house <u>by</u> the stream, or the one nearer to town?

   buy: to get by giving money

   by: close to

8. I <u>guessed</u> that my <u>guest</u> would stay for dinner.

   guessed: estimated or judged

   guest: a person who is received by another

Home Involvement Activity I towed the toad is a funny sentence that uses a pair of homonyms. Create five of your own funny sentences with homonym pairs.

Practicing the Skill

● Read aloud the direction lines on pages 201–202. Complete the first item in each exercise with students.

● Some students will find it helpful to mask the answer choices alternately in items 13–16 on page 201, to see which one "looks right in the sentence."

Curriculum Connections

Spelling Link

Read the following list of words aloud. Have students write the word plus its homonyms. Then ask students to write sentences to make the meaning of each word clear.

him (hymn)	heir (air)
cruise (crews)	blew (blue)
symbol (cymbal)	plain (plane)
new (knew)	guessed (guest)

Art Link

● Write the following pairs of homonyms on the board.

blue/blew	mist/missed
creek/creak	deer/dear
fir/fur	hare/hair
pear/pair	pale/pail
rain/rein	rays/raise
rose/rows	sea/see

● Have students work together to plan and paint a mural of a realistic or an imaginary scene suggested by the words on the board. Students may wish to include captions or labels on their mural.

Observational Assessment

Check to see that students can recognize the correct definitions of homonyms.

English-Language Learners/ESL

Write the following homonym pairs on the board: **right/write, eight/ate, new/knew.** Have fluent speakers work with English-language learners to demonstrate the difference in meaning of the words in each pair. Suggest that students say each word, point to it, and pantomime its meaning.

Gifted Learners

Invite students to write an original poem using as many pairs of homonyms as they can. Encourage students to illustrate their poems and share their work with the class.

Learners with Special Needs

Additional strategies for supporting learners with special needs can be found on page 177L.

Connecting Reading and Writing

Objectives

- To read a nonfiction piece and respond to it in writing
- To practice making inferences and interpreting
- To write a dialogue

Warming Up

Comprehension Skills

- Tell students that **making inferences** is to form ideas or guesses based on facts, clues, or evidence. Making inferences as you read can help you understand and enjoy what you read more fully, whether it is an article, novel, poem, or textbook.

- **Interpreting** is another skill that can help students as they read. To interpret an article, story, or poem is to make sense of it or to give it meaning.

Teaching the Lesson

- Suggest that students read the first two Reader's Response questions before they read the selection. Then have them read to find the answer to those questions.

- Encourage students to use their imaginations to answer the third question.

Practicing the Skill

- Together, read the directions on page 204. Have volunteers read the boxed words.

- As a class, brainstorm problems about which Sam Wilson might give advice.

Name _____

⭐ **Read about everybody's favorite uncle—Uncle Sam. Then answer the questions that follow.**

Everybody's Uncle Sam

by Lester David

He is better known than any movie star, sports hero, or rock singer, even though he hasn't changed the style of his clothes in more than 100 years. He's everybody's uncle—Uncle Sam.

Uncle Sam is nothing less than the symbol for the United States of America. In fact, he is America. When a newspaper headline reads: "Uncle Sam Wins Gold Medals in Olympics," we know U.S. athletes have won.

But now for a big surprise: Uncle Sam was a real person.

During the War of 1812 against Great Britain, Sam Wilson's company supplied barrels of beef to American soldiers. In October 1812, New York Governor Daniel D. Tompkins visited Wilson's plant with a group of officials. Pointing to several barrels, one of the visitors asked the meaning of the initials "EA-US," which was stamped on top of each. One of the workers replied that "EA" stood for Elbert Anderson, who purchased meat for the Army. Then he jokingly added that the "US" meant Uncle Sam Wilson (it really stood for United States). The story spread, and soon everyone pinned the nickname to Sam Wilson.

Sam Wilson died in 1854. More than 100 years later, Congress passed a resolution saluting him as the original Uncle Sam.

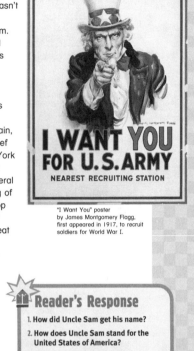

"I Want You" poster by James Montgomery Flagg, first appeared in 1917, to recruit soldiers for World War I.

⭐ **Reader's Response**

1. How did Uncle Sam get his name?
2. How does Uncle Sam stand for the United States of America?
3. What do you think the real Uncle Sam was like?

1. A worker at Sam Wilson's company joked that **US** (for **United States**) stood for **Uncle Sam**.
2. Uncle Sam's name and picture are understood to mean "United States."
3. Answers will vary.

LESSON 100: Connecting Reading and Writing
Comprehension—Make Inferences; Interpret

203

UNIVERSAL ACCESS
Meeting Individual Needs

Visual Learners

Students might get ideas for their dialogues by looking at different images of Uncle Sam. If possible, provide students with posters or cartoons featuring Uncle Sam. Invite students to illustrate their dialogues with their own idea of how Uncle Sam should look.

Auditory Learners

Students may find it easier to begin writing by improvising with a partner. Allow students to complete the assignment in pairs, first improvising their dialogues and then writing them down. Suggest that students read their dialogues aloud with their partner as they work, revising as they go along.

Learners with Special Needs

Additional strategies for supporting learners with special needs can be found on page 177L.

You have probably seen Uncle Sam on posters, in ads, in newspapers and magazines, in parades, at fairs, and as a character in television programs and plays. In fact, the life story of Sam Wilson, the real Uncle Sam, would make a good play. Like Uncle Sam, Sam Wilson was known for his good common sense. From all over the countryside, people would ask him for advice about business, family matters, or arguments with neighbors.

⭐ **Choose a problem that you face or one that you know about. How do you think Sam Wilson would have solved it? Write a dialogue in which Sam Wilson gives advice about a problem to you or another character. Use at least two of these words.**

| concern | improve | argument | progress | advice | leadership |
| suggestion | problem | solve | opinion | believe | consider |

Sentences will vary.

_____

_____

_____

_____

_____

_____

_____

_____

_____

Writer's Tip
Follow the rules for writing a dialogue. Write the first name of each of your characters in capital letters followed by a colon. Do not use quotation marks.

Speaker's Challenge
Work with a partner to practice your dialogue. Then present it to another partner team or to a small group. Speak in the voice that you think Sam Wilson or Uncle Sam would have used.

LESSON 100: Connecting Reading and Writing
Comprehension—Make Inferences; Interpret

The Writing Process

Ask students what makes an effective dialogue. Help them see that when a good dialogue is read or spoken aloud, it sounds the way two people might really speak. In the best dialogues, each character has a distinctive voice. Help students identify elements that can distinguish characters, such as slang, pet phrases, and so on.

Prewrite Encourage students to identify the problem that Sam Wilson will speak about. Suggest that they also imagine the person who is getting the advice. Why does he or she need help?

Write Have students imagine that they can hear two people talk and then simply write down what they say. Remind students that their first drafts don't have to be perfect; they will revise later on.

Revise Have students read their dialogues aloud with a partner. Suggest that they listen for parts in which the speakers don't sound real. Have partners work together to revise these parts.

Proofread Encourage students to read their work carefully to check for errors in grammar, punctuation, and spelling.

Publish Ask students to copy their final drafts onto page 204. Then invite volunteers to perform their dialogues with a partner.

Computer Connection Give the following tip to students who use a word-processing program. Many word-processing programs allow you to create "macros," or repeated groups of characters. You might want to create a macro for a bold-faced version of each character's name plus a colon. Usually, the Tools menu has a feature that enables you to create a macro.

Portfolio Suggest that students add their finished dialogues to their portfolios.

English-Language Learners/ESL
Pair fluent speakers with English-language learners and have them explain the meaning of "Uncle Sam": a character whose name and image represent the United States. Make sure that English-language learners understand the idea of a name and picture representing a country. Invite students to share national symbols from their own cultures.

Gifted Learners
Uncle Sam was created during the War of 1812, almost 200 years ago. Encourage students to invent a new figure to represent the United States, one who can join Uncle Sam and help him. Invite students to create a dialogue between this new figure and Uncle Sam, as the new figure explains who he/she is and how he/she plans to work with Uncle Sam. Students might enjoy staging their dialogues for the rest of the class.

Thesaurus 1

Objectives

- **To understand the purpose of a thesaurus**
- **To use a thesaurus to find synonyms and antonyms**

Warming Up

- Write this song on the board and give students a few minutes to look it over. Then call on a volunteer to sing it (using the tune of "Happy Birthday to You").

  Enjoyable day you were born to you,

  Glad anniversary of the start of your life to you,

  Wonderful celebration of your entry into the world to you,

  Cheery day that marks the beginning of your life to you!

- Students should realize that this verse is a takeoff on the song, "Happy Birthday to You," and that it is awkward on purpose.

- Have students find the synonyms for "happy," and then find the phrases that have been substituted for "birthday."

- If necessary, review with students the meaning of synonyms and antonyms. Ask students to suggest other synonyms for "happy."

Teaching the Lesson

- Tell students that a reference book called a thesaurus is used to find synonyms and sometimes antonyms.

- Call attention to the sample entries on pages 205 and 206. Point out that a thesaurus lists words but does not define words.

- Have a volunteer read aloud the Helpful Hints on page 205 as others follow along silently.

Name _____

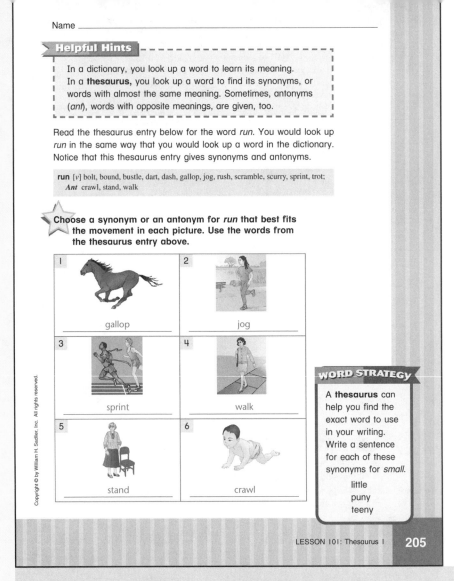

> ### Helpful Hints
>
> In a dictionary, you look up a word to learn its meaning. In a **thesaurus**, you look up a word to find its synonyms, or words with almost the same meaning. Sometimes, antonyms (*ant*), words with opposite meanings, are given, too.

Read the thesaurus entry below for the word *run*. You would look up *run* in the same way that you would look up a word in the dictionary. Notice that this thesaurus entry gives synonyms and antonyms.

run [*v*] bolt, bound, bustle, dart, dash, gallop, jog, rush, scramble, scurry, sprint, trot; *Ant* crawl, stand, walk

⭐ **Choose a synonym or an antonym for *run* that best fits the movement in each picture. Use the words from the thesaurus entry above.**

1	gallop	2	jog
3	sprint	4	walk
5	stand	6	crawl

WORD STRATEGY

A **thesaurus** can help you find the exact word to use in your writing. Write a sentence for each of these synonyms for *small*.

little

puny

teeny

UNIVERSAL ACCESS
Meeting Individual Needs

Kinesthetic Learners

Write several general verbs on the board, such as **go, move,** and **smile** and help students find entries for these words in a thesaurus. List students' findings on the board. Then have students act out the more specific words, emphasizing their differences. Discuss the differences in the meaning of the words with students.

Visual Learners

Display pictures of scenes or events, such as a city street or a political rally. Have volunteers briefly describe the scenes in sentences they write on the board. Then have students suggest how to change the sentences, using synonyms from a thesaurus. For example, students might reword **"Many people are walking"** to read, **"Numerous people are strolling."** Discuss which suggestions seem to work best.

laugh [v] cackle, chuckle, giggle, guffaw, hoot, snort, snicker	throw [v] chuck, flick, fling, heave, hurl, lob, pitch, toss	write [v] compose, draft, enter, jot down, mark, print, scrawl, scribble

1. I gave a loud ____snort____ when the bucket fell on the clown's head.

2. The strong man lifts the heavy rock and ____heaves____ it aside.

3. I've just ____drafted____ a note to my mother.

4. The trainer had me ____toss____ the ball to the excited puppy.

5. We began to ____giggle____ when the funny music began.

6. How old was Mozart when he ____composed____ that piece of music?

7. The Olympic athlete ____hurled____ the ball high over the fence into my friend's yard.

8. We all started to ____cackle____ like chickens.

9. I ____printed____ my name on the line and then neatly wrote my signature below it.

10. I can't read what my little brother ____scribbled____ on the paper.

11. Please ____toss____ that litter into the trash can.

Choose one synonym from each of the three entry words above. Write a sentence for each word you pick.

12. ____Sentences will vary.____

13. _____

14. _____

LESSON 101: Thesaurus 1

Home Involvement Activity Become a "family thesaurus." Together, list as many synonyms as you can for the words **good** and **bad**.

English-Language Learners/ESL

Display pictures of people, places, or events that can easily be described with action verbs, such as a batter hitting a ball or a bird in flight. Have students name a verb to describe each action. Then have students use a thesaurus to find other verbs that are synonyms for the one they named. Have partners work together to list some of the verbs they have found.

Gifted Learners

Challenge students to write poems using antonym pairs, as in the following example.

One girl **stood up,**
Another **sat down.**
One had a **smile,**
The other had a **frown.**

Have them use a thesaurus.

Learners with Special Needs

Additional strategies for supporting learners with special needs can be found on page 177K.

Practicing the Skill

● Read aloud the directions on page 205, and locate the thesaurus entry for **run.** Tell students to compare synonyms or antonyms before they choose one for each picture.

● Read aloud the directions on page 206 and locate the three thesaurus entries. Tell students that more than one synonym may work in the sentences.

Intervention Strategy Turn to page 177K for an Intervention Strategy designed to help students who need extra support with this lesson.

Curriculum Connections

Spelling Link

● Read aloud the following sentences.

1. The mayor **drafted** a speech.

2. She **scribbled** notes in the margins.

3. The crowd **chuckled** at her joke.

4. She **pitched** a ball to open the game.

5. People **scrambled** for cover when it began to pour.

6. When the rain stopped, they **rushed** back to their seats.

● Read the words in bold type again and have students spell them orally. Then have students suggest a synonym for each word.

Writing Link

An author may use a thesaurus to find "just the right word" for a written passage. Have students examine several paragraphs in a work of fiction, paying particular attention to verbs, adjectives, and adverbs. Ask questions such as these: *What other words might the author have used? Why do you think the author chose these words?*

Observational Assessment

Note whether students can find synonyms and antonyms in a thesaurus.

Thesaurus 2

Objectives
- To sort synonyms by meaning
- To replace words in context with more precise synonyms

Warming Up

- Write these pairs of sentences on the board and have volunteers read them aloud.

    We <u>went</u> across country.

    We <u>toured</u> across country.

    We <u>stayed</u> at Yosemite National Park.

    We <u>camped</u> at Yosemite National Park.

- Call students' attention to the underlined words in each pair and discuss with them which word gives more information.

- Remind students they can use a thesaurus when they want to find a word with a more specific meaning.

Teaching the Lesson

- Review synonyms and antonyms with students. Remind students that they are found in a thesaurus.

- Write the paragraph below on the board. Have students suggest synonyms for the underlined words that will make the sentences more interesting and precise.

    When I spotted the bear, I <u>moved</u>.

    Tim was <u>glad</u> to return to the cabin.

- Have a volunteer read the Helpful Hint on page 207. Direct students' attention to how a thesaurus is similar to a dictionary. Discuss how a thesaurus differs from a dictionary.

Name _____

Helpful Hint

A **thesaurus** lists synonyms and antonyms. It can help you use more interesting and more exact words in your writing. Most thesauruses are arranged in **ABC order** like a dictionary.

The box below has synonyms from a thesaurus for the words *big*, *happy*, and *small*. Sort the words by their meaning. Write each word in the correct column.

content gigantic great little roomy tiny vast overjoyed
enormous wee delighted cheerful petite teeny thrilled

1 **big**	2 **happy**	3 **small**
gigantic	content	little
great	overjoyed	tiny
roomy	delighted	wee
vast	cheerful	petite
enormous	thrilled	teeny

Rank each set of words from *least* to *most*. Write the words in the correct order on the lines below.

4. from *least* angry to *most* angry: annoyed, furious, angry

   annoyed, angry, furious

5. from *least* hot to *most* hot: sizzling, hot, warm

   warm, hot, sizzling

6. from *least* noisy to *most* noisy: thunderous, loud, faint

   faint, loud, thunderous

CHALLENGE

Read the words in the **happy** column above. Rank them from *least* happy to *most* happy.

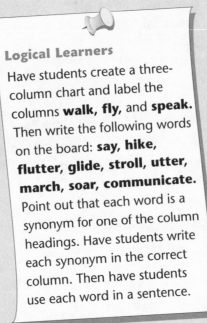

UNIVERSAL ACCESS
Meeting Individual Needs

Logical Learners

Have students create a three-column chart and label the columns **walk, fly,** and **speak.** Then write the following words on the board: **say, hike, flutter, glide, stroll, utter, march, soar, communicate.** Point out that each word is a synonym for one of the column headings. Have students write each synonym in the correct column. Then have students use each word in a sentence.

Auditory Learners

Write this chart on the board:

big	small	happy
roomy	tiny	pleased
vast	stunted	ecstatic
bulky	undersized	delighted

Explain that each column heading is a general word for the synonyms in that column. Have students make up tongue twisters for each group of synonyms. Have them recite their tongue twisters, and challenge classmates to repeat them.

207

⭐ **Replace each word in bold print with a more exact word from the box.**

tiny	roomy	undersized	gigantic	pleased
stunted	delighted	vast	bulky	ecstatic

1. The national park had a **big** number of acres. — vast

2. I needed both arms to carry the **big** package. — bulky

3. The **big** bedroom could hold a chair, two dressers, a desk, and a bed. — roomy

4. The whale is the largest mammal on earth. It is **big**! — gigantic

5. A **small** bug crawled across the paper. — tiny

6. The **small** wrestler was no match for his opponent. — undersized

7. The plant was **small** because it didn't get enough water and light. — stunted

8. We were **happy** when our candidate finally won. — ecstatic

9. She was **happy** with the voting results but not thrilled. — pleased

10. The audience was **happy** to hear her speech. — delighted

Former Texas representative Barbara Jordan speaking at the Democratic National Convention in 1992.

208   LESSON 102: Thesaurus 2

🏠 **Home Involvement Activity** Choose five of the words in the box at the top to describe something or someone in your home.

English-Language Learners/ESL

Have students write three sentences describing what they do on an average day. Here is an example:

I go to school.   **I eat lunch.**   **I do classwork.**

Have students list replacement verbs for each underlined word such as **ride** or **walk** for **go**.

Gifted Learners

Have students research a new program that benefits their community. Then have students write an article that describes the program. Encourage students to find more vivid, precise words in a thesaurus and incorporate them into their article.

Learners with Special Needs

Additional strategies for supporting learners with special needs can be found on page 177L.

Practicing the Skill

● Read aloud with students the directions on pages 207 and 208. Work together to complete the first item in each exercise.

● For the exercise on page 208, remind students that sometimes more than one synonym will work in a sentence; other times only one will work.

● Encourage students to use the dictionary if they encounter words they do not know, such as **petite, stunted,** and **ecstatic.**

● You may wish to have students work with a partner to complete these exercises.

Curriculum Connections

Spelling Link

● Read aloud the following words.

delighted	**pleased**	**little**
undersized	**ecstatic**	**tiny**

● Have students spell the words orally and then write them on the board.

● Ask a volunteer to group words, according to meaning.

Writing Link

● Emergency rescue crews often use special codes to communicate via CB radio. Among these are the following: "10-4" (message received) and "10-70" (fire at [location]). In addition to number codes, there are codes made up of initials, such as "CQ" (seek you).

● Have students work in small groups to research several CB terms and prepare a glossary for their classmates' reference.

● Have students write a simple dialogue and then rewrite it with key terms from the CB glossary.

Observational Assessment

Note whether students use synonyms correctly to convey meaning more precisely.

Connecting Spelling and Writing

Objectives

- **To say, spell, sort, and write synonyms, antonyms, and homonyms**
- **To write a persuasive speech using synonyms, antonyms, or homonyms**

Warming Up

- Write these sentences on the board:

  The mayor said there was too much **rubbish** on the streets and promised to clear the **trash** away.

  The candidates' first debate was **boring,** but the second one was **interesting.**

  I wonder **whether** people will come to the meeting in such rainy **weather.**

- Have volunteers identify the synonyms, antonyms, and homonyms.

Teaching the Lesson

- List these words on the board:

find	tall	happily
separate	flat	laugh
difficult	famous	fix

- For each word, have volunteers write at least one synonym or one antonym.
- List these words on the board: **rode, guest, tacks, hoarse.** Have students write a homonym next to each one and use each word in a sentence.

Practicing the Skill

- Read the directions on page 209. Have students read each phrase aloud.
- Tell students to consider one word at a time. For example, they should start with **country,** seeking a synonym, antonym, or homonym. Once they find a "match," they should write the pair in the chart.

209

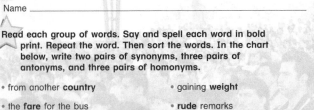

Name _____

Read each group of words. Say and spell each word in bold print. Repeat the word. Then sort the words. In the chart below, write two pairs of synonyms, three pairs of antonyms, and three pairs of homonyms.

- from another **country**
- the **fare** for the bus
- a **polite** smile
- too long to **wait**
- sang a **gentle** lullaby
- made a **mistake**
- did the **right** thing
- go to **private** school
- **error** in judgment
- to **write** a speech
- **public** transportation
- **fair** weather

- gaining **weight**
- **rude** remarks
- **harsh** punishment
- a free **nation**

Synonyms	Antonyms	Homonyms
country	polite	fare
nation	rude	fair
mistake	gentle	wait
error	harsh	weight
	public	right
	private	write

UNIVERSAL ACCESS
Meeting Individual Needs

Logical Learners

Write this story starter on the board: *It was a cold, wet night. Someone knocked loudly on Jeff's door.* Have a volunteer write the next sentence, which must include a synonym, antonym, or homonym for any preceding word. For example, the sentence might use the word **soggy** (synonym for **wet**), **quietly** (antonym for **loudly**) or **knight** (homonym for **night**).

Learners with Special Needs

Additional strategies for supporting learners with special needs can be found on page 177L.

Visual Learners

List these words and have students draw a line from a word in the first column to a synonym, antonym, or homonym in the second column. Have students label each pair accordingly.

injure	**pole**
victory	**answer**
crooked	**rough**
ask	**pale**
gentle	**way**
poll	**triumph**
pail	**straight**
weigh	**damage**

Every few years, the people of the United States get a chance to vote for the candidate of their choice. These candidates use advertisements, public appearances, debates, and speeches to get their points across to the voters.

★ Imagine that you are running for the office of class president. Write a speech that will persuade your classmates to vote for you. Give three strong reasons. Use at least one pair of synonyms, one pair of antonyms, or one pair of homonyms from the box below.

Vote Here

country	fare	polite	wait	gentle	mistake	right	private
error	write	public	fair	weight	rude	harsh	nation

Sentences will vary.

Writer's Tip
Read your speech again. Look in a thesaurus to replace an ordinary word with a more exact synonym.

Speaker's Challenge
Use note cards to jot down the important points of your speech. Practice using your note cards before giving your speech to the class.

Your Vote Counts

210   LESSON 103: Connecting Spelling and Writing

The Writing Process

Explain to students that on page 210 they will write a persuasive speech. Go over the directions and spelling words at the top of the page.

Prewrite Have the class discuss the traits a class president should have. Encourage students to think about what special qualities they, as voters, would look for in a candidate.

Write Encourage students to write three convincing reasons with supporting details or examples that will persuade their audience. Suggest that they look over the spelling words and consider which words will work best in their speech.

Revise Have students read their speech aloud to themselves and revise as needed. Ask: *Have you included specific reasons? Have you used at least one pair of synonyms, antonyms, or homonyms?*

Proofread Have students exchange their speeches with a partner to look for errors in spelling, grammar, and punctuation.

Publish Students can copy their final drafts on page 210 or on a separate paper. Ask volunteers to give their speeches to the class.

Computer Connection

Remind students who use a word processor to take advantage of the following feature.

● Many word-processing programs have a thesaurus. To use this feature, highlight the word for which you would like a synonym. Then scroll down within the "Tools" menu and click on the "Thesaurus" option.

● The computer will display a list of possible synonyms (and sometimes antonyms, too). Choose a word and the computer will insert it for you automatically.

Portfolio Suggest that students add their speeches to their portfolios.

English-Language Learners/ESL

Display labeled pictures illustrating homonyms such as: **eight/ate, made/maid, write/right, pail/pale,** etc. Point to each label, read it aloud, and have students repeat the words after you. Then show students the pictures with the labels masked and have them say the words and write them on the board.

Gifted Learners

Challenge students to write sentences using pairs of synonyms, antonyms, or homonyms, as in the *Warming-Up* activity on page 209.

Reviewing and Assessing

Synonyms, Antonyms, and Homonyms

Objective

To review and assess synonyms, antonyms, and homonyms

Warming Up

- List the following word pairs on the board:

  stingy — generous (antonyms)

  glance — look (synonyms)

  wait — weight (homonyms)

- Have volunteers identify the synonyms, antonyms, and homonyms. As they identify each pair, have students explain the meaning of the terms synonym, antonym, and homonym.

Teaching the Lesson

- On the board or on chart paper, make a chart as follows:

	Synonym	Antonym	Homonym
buy	purchase	sell	by
fair	just	unfair	fare
new	fresh	old	knew
right	correct	wrong	write
pale	colorless	colorful	pail

- Have students fill in at least one synonym, antonym, and homonym for each word. (Examples are shown above.) Then challenge students to make up sentences using one or more of the words in each row.

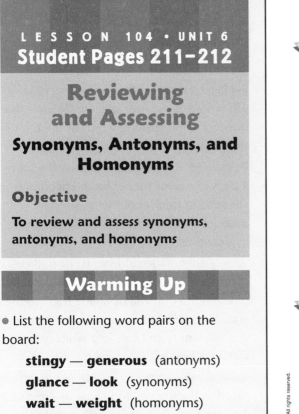

Name _____

☆ Read each pair of words. Write *S* if the words are synonyms. Write *A* if the words are antonyms. Write *H* if the words are homonyms.

1. below—under	S	2. weight—wait	H
3. mist—missed	H	4. wealth—riches	S
5. tall—lofty	S	6. vast—big	S
7. moist—dry	A	8. add—subtract	A
9. part—whole	A	10. hoarse—horse	H
11. pole—poll	H	12. stale—fresh	A
13. permit—allow	S	14. little—tiny	S
15. aloud—allowed	H	16. weather—whether	H
17. many—few	A	18. public—private	A
19. pitch—fling	S	20. boring—thrilling	A
21. tacks—tax	H	22. throw—toss	S

☆ The box below has synonyms for the words *laugh* and *write*. Sort the words by their meaning. Write each word in the correct column.

cackle	compose	chuckle	draft
giggle	guffaw	scribble	jot down

23 Words for *laugh*	24 Words for *write*
cackle	compose
chuckle	draft
giggle	scribble
guffaw	jot down

CHALLENGE

Replace the word in bold print with both a synonym and an antonym.

quiet music
fair weather
good grades

UNIVERSAL ACCESS
Meeting Individual Needs

Visual Learners

Write these words on cards: **aim, purpose, flat, level, error, mistake, occur, happen, win, lose, full, empty, present, absent, whole, part, horse, hoarse, symbol, cymbal, weather, whether, guessed, guest.** Mix the cards and lay them face down. Students take turns turning over two cards at a time, to match synonyms, antonyms, or homonyms.

Learners with Special Needs

Additional strategies for supporting learners with special needs can be found on page 177L.

Auditory Learners

Have students draw three circles on paper and label them: **Synonyms, Antonyms, Homonyms.** Say each of the following word pairs out loud. (You will need to spell out the homonyms.) Tell students to write each pair in the correct circle: **own/possess, rode/road, famous/unknown, hurt/harm, garbage/trash, tax/tacks, pleasure/pain, huge/tiny, made/maid, concern/worry.**

Underline the synonym for each word in bold print.

1. **shut** the gate — paint — close — fix
2. **stroll** in the park — sleep — jog — walk
3. unknown **quantity** — amount — person — quality
4. **aid** for flood victims — sorrow — food — help
5. the day **after** the election — before — of — following
6. **glance** out the window — throw — look — call

Underline the antonym for each word in bold print.

7. likes **winter** sports — team — fall — summer
8. **several** highways — many — few — a lot of
9. **easy** to understand — simple — hard — smart
10. **over** the speed limit — top — obey — under
11. **scurries** away — dashes — jogs — crawls

Underline the correct homonym from the homonym pair in the box to complete each sentence. Then write the word on the line.

bin/been	knew/new	buy/by

12. Has your group ever _____ been _____ to Mount Rushmore?

13. I _____ knew _____ someone who worked there.

14. I asked her to _____ buy _____ me carved stone bookends from the gift shop.

Extend & Apply

Use a thesaurus to revise sentences 12–14. Change one word in each sentence. Choose a word that is more interesting or exact.

Mount Rushmore

Reteaching Activities

Shades of Meaning

Remind students that synonyms have slightly different meanings. Write these verbs on the board: **catch, tell, walk.** Have students use a thesaurus to find synonyms for each. Have them write a few synonyms next to each verb. Then provide a sentence using each verb, such as: *I caught the ball. She told the truth.* Discuss with students which of the synonyms could be substituted in each sentence and how the substitution would affect sentence meaning.

Pair Identification

Have students write the words **synonyms, antonyms,** and **homonyms** on each of three index cards. Select a representative sampling of pairs of synonyms, antonyms, and homonyms from the unit. One at a time, write each pair of words on the board. As you do, have students hold up the index card that correctly names the pair. Then have volunteers use the pair of words in a sentence or two.

Assessing the Skill

Check Up Have students do the exercises on pages 211–212 to help them review what they have learned. You may use these exercises to help you assess students' understanding of synonyms, antonyms, and homonyms.

Go over the directions for each set of exercises. Then have students complete the two pages.

Observational Assessment As long as students understand the basic difference between synonyms, antonyms, and homonyms and take the time to think before writing, they should have little difficulty with the exercises. However, a few of the words, such as **cackle** and **guffaw** on page 211, may challenge some students. Watch students as they work to make sure they understand that words paired as synonyms or antonyms are related by meanings, whereas words paired as homonyms are related by sound.

Student Skills Assessment Keep track of each student's progress in understanding synonyms, antonyms, and homonyms using the checklist on page 177H.

Writing Conference Meet with each student to discuss his or her written work. Discuss how using a thesaurus can help students become better writers and help build their vocabulary.

Group together students who need further instruction in synonyms, antonyms, and homonyms and have them complete the *Reteaching Activities.* Turn to page 177C for alternative assessment methods.

LINCOLN

Clipped Words and Blended Words

Objectives

- **To recognize and write clipped words**
- **To form blended words and use them in context**

Warming Up

- Read this poem aloud.

    Take a snip of one word—a syllable or more.

    Tie it to another word, and send it out the door.

    Or if a word comes on the scene with syllables galore,

    Just say the best and leave the rest, and save yourself a chore.

- Discuss the fact that language is constantly changing, and that spoken language changes more quickly than written language.

- Have students suggest some of the influences that can change a language.

Teaching the Lesson

- Tell students that this lesson introduces clipped words and blended words.

- Point out that a clipped word may be the first syllable of a longer word, such as **gas** for **gasoline.** A clipped word may also be the end of a longer word, as in **plane** for **airplane.** Some clipped words, such as **mike** for **microphone,** have a different spelling altogether.

- Some clipped words can stand for more than one long word. For example, **sub** can mean **submarine** or **substitute.**

- Ask what letters were dropped to make the blended word **smog? (oke** of **smoke** and **f** of **fog)** Discuss how blended words combine meanings as well as letters.

213

Name _____

Helpful Hint

Language changes all the time as people use it. Sometimes, long words get shortened so that they are easier to say and spell. These shorter forms are called **clipped words.**

gasoline→gas   laboratory→lab

☆ Match each clipped word in Column *A* with the long form of that word in Column *B*. Write the long form of the word on the line.

	A		B
automobile _____	1. auto		a. bicycle
airplane _____	2. plane		b. mathematics
veterinarian _____	3. vet		c. influenza
influenza _____	4. flu		d. telephone
gymnasium _____	5. gym		e. gymnasium
bicycle _____	6. bike		f. veterinarian
mathematics _____	7. math		g. automobile
telephone _____	8. phone		h. airplane

☆ Read each sentence. Replace the word in bold print with the clipped word in the box. Write the clipped word on the line.

pro	copter	sub	exam

9. The class is taking a science **examination.**   exam _____

10. Our teacher was once a **professional** bowler.   pro _____

11. He also served on a **submarine** in the Navy.   sub _____

12. Mr. Vargas flies a **helicopter,** too.   copter _____

CHALLENGE

Write the long form of each of these clipped words. Use a dictionary to help you.

    zoo
    ad
    cell phone

UNIVERSAL ACCESS
Meeting Individual Needs

Kinesthetic Learners

Have students do this activity with a partner. Give each pair of students a set of letter cards or tiles. Have students take turns arranging the letters to form one of the unclipped words on page 213 or a pair of words that make up a blended word on 214. The partner must then remove the letters to make a clipped or a blended word.

Auditory Learners

Read aloud pairs of words that are combined to form blended words, such as **sp**oon and **f**ork **(spork), s**moked **p**ork and h**am (spam),** and Inter-**net** cit**izen (netizen)** or the words on page 214. Stress the sounds of the letters that are blended. After you read each pair, have students say the blended word. Then have a volunteer write the blended word on the board and explain which two word parts were combined.

⭐ **Complete each sentence. Combine the letters in bold print in the two words to form one blended word.**

1. If you blend **tw**ist + wh**irl**, you get _____ twirl .

2. If you blend **fl**utter + h**urry**, you get _____ flurry .

3. If you blend **c**hunk + **lump**, you get _____ clump .

4. If you blend **fl**ame + g**lare**, you get _____ flare .

5. If you blend **slo**p + slu**sh**, you get _____ slosh .

6. If you blend **br**eakfast + l**unch**, you get _____ brunch .

7. If you blend **gl**eam + shi**mmer**, you get _____ glimmer .

8. If you blend **tele**vision + mara**thon**, you get _____ telethon .

9. If you blend **mo**tor + ho**tel**, you get _____ motel .

10. If you blend **cam**era + re**corder**, you get _____ camcorder .

⭐ **Write one of the blended words from above to complete each sentence.**

11. My sister taught me how to _____ twirl _____ a baton.

12. On clear nights, you can see the faint _____ glimmer _____ of faraway stars.

13. The captain lit a signal _____ flare _____ to call for help.

14. The _____ telethon _____ for the hospital raised more than $2 million.

15. After the heavy rain, we had to _____ slosh _____ through deep mud.

16. There was a _____ flurry _____ of excitement when the mayor arrived.

Home Involvement Activity You may have a fax machine or a modem at home. **Fax** is a clipped word. **Modem** is a blended word. Work together to find out how each word was formed.

English-Language Learners/ESL

Create pairs of word cards for the following clipped words and the original words or phrases they came from: **movie/moving picture, exam/examination, limo/limousine, fan/fanatic, lunch/luncheon,** and **champ/champion.** Mix the cards. Shuffle the cards. Lay them out face down, Concentration-style. Have students play to match clipped words with the words they came from.

Gifted Learners

Have groups of students create new blended words. Have them pick a topic such as games, foods, or fashion and present their new words to the class in an advertisement encouraging others to use the new words.

Learners with Special Needs

Additional strategies for supporting learners with special needs can be found on page 177L.

Practicing the Skill

● Read aloud with students the directions for pages 213 and 214. Complete the first item in each exercise together.

● Encourage students to use a dictionary for new or unfamiliar words, such as **influenza, flurry, glimmer,** and **telethon.**

Curriculum Connections

Spelling Link

● The following word pairs include both a clipped and a blended word. Read each word pair aloud.

motel	and	**auto**
flu	and	**brunch**
bike	and	**glimmer**
camcorder	and	**twirl**

● Have students repeat the words and spell them orally. Then have students make up sentences that include both words in the pair.

Science Link

● Display a chart of the Food Guide Pyramid and tell students to list healthy foods they like to eat for breakfast and for lunch.

● Discuss the idea of **brunch**—a mid-morning meal served in place of breakfast and lunch. Have students select foods from their lists to develop a tasty but healthy brunch menu.

● If possible, have students cook and serve a class brunch.

Observational Assessment

Note whether students can identify the longer forms of clipped and blended words.

Borrowed Words

Objective

To recognize and correctly use words borrowed from other languages

Warming Up

● Write the following on the board, and have a volunteer read it aloud.

Q: How do you spell **taxi** in French, German, Swedish, Spanish, Danish, Norwegian, Dutch, and Hungarian?

A: T-a-x-i

● Discuss with students the fact that language enables people to communicate, and when people communicate, ideas flow from place to place.

● Have students talk about why the word **taxi** might be the same in so many different languages. Tell students that many languages borrow words from each other and that English has adopted many words from other languages.

Teaching the Lesson

● Display these words: **alligator, balloon, hamburger, mosquito, confetti,** and **tornado.** Explain that all six words come from languages other than English. (Spanish—**alligator, mosquito, tornado;** Italian—**balloon, confetti;** German—**hamburger**)

● Make a three-column chart with these headings: **Spanish, Italian,** and **German.** Help students sort the words into the columns.

● Tell students that they can learn about the history of a word, by reading the beginning of the dictionary entry. Have students do this for the words in the chart.

● Point out that borrowed words often undergo a spelling change when they are absorbed into English.

Name _____

> **Helpful Hint**
>
> Language is always changing. English borrows words from many other languages. Some words stay as they are. Other words change a little. Look at these **borrowed words:**
>
> rodeo (from Spanish)   tea (from Chinese)

Each of the words in the box has been borrowed from another language. Write the correct word from the box to complete each sentence. Begin the word with a capital letter.

ukulele	library	pajamas	menu
pretzel	moccasin	thesaurus	umbrella

1. _____Moccasin_____ is an Algonquian word for a soft leather slipper.

2. _____Pajamas_____ is a Hindi word for clothes for sleeping.

3. _____Menu_____ is a French word for the list of foods at a restaurant.

4. _____Pretzel_____ is a German word for a salty, twisted bread snack.

5. _____Thesaurus_____ is a Greek word for a book of synonyms and antonyms.

6. _____Ukulele_____ is a Hawaiian word for a small guitarlike instrument.

7. _____Umbrella_____ is an Italian word for something that protects you in the rain.

8. _____Library_____ is a Latin word for a place where books are kept.

> **CHALLENGE**
>
> Match each food with the language from which it was borrowed:
>
> bagel   Taino
> potato   Bantu
> gumbo   Yiddish
>
> Learn more about these words and languages by checking the dictionary.

UNIVERSAL ACCESS
Meeting Individual Needs

Visual Learners

Have students work with a partner to look up the word histories of the words on pages 215 and 216. Have partners make a poster that illustrates the history of one or more of the words. Display the posters in the classroom.

Auditory Learners

Explain that some words come from sounds or noises such as **bang, boom, pop, quack, hiccup,** and **tick.** This is called onomatopoeia. Have students say each word so it sounds like the sound from which it comes. Challenge them to invent their own sound-imitating words. Get them started with an example, such as **ker-splish,** a word for the sound of a cookie falling into a glass of milk.

Solve this crossword puzzle that uses borrowed words. All answers appear in the Word Bank. The language from which each word was borrowed appears in the Word Bank, too.

Across

2. machine that can do some of the things a human can do
4. thick tropical forest
8. detective
9. collection of articles, printed each week or month
12. couch
13. grade before first grade
14. opposite of war
16. instrument with a keyboard
17. small, furry rodent pet
18. pale tan color

Down

1. sour yellow fruit
3. circus swing
4. type of American music
5. to rub away pencil marks
6. fish used in sandwiches
7. chess piece
10. child without parents
11. prehistoric animal: woolly _____
13. yellowish-brown cloth used for army uniforms
15. chubby angel child with wings

Word Bank

Arabic: lemon, magazine, sofa
Creole: jazz
Czech: robot
French: beige, trapeze
German: hamster, kindergarten
Greek: orphan, bishop
Hebrew: cherub
Hindi: jungle, khaki
Icelandic: sleuth
Italian: piano
Latin: erase, peace
Russian: mammoth
Spanish: tuna

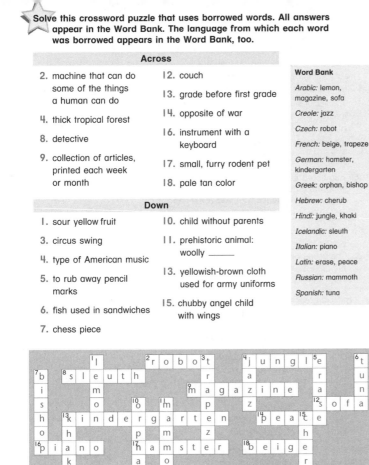

216   LESSON 106: Borrowed Words

Home Involvement Activity Many foods that people eat in the United States have names that are borrowed from other languages, such as **waffle, taco,** and **spaghetti.** Work together to list foods that have borrowed names.

Practicing the Skill

● Read aloud the directions for page 215 and complete the first item together. Then have students work independently to finish the exercise.

● Have students read the directions for page 216. Point out that words in a crossword puzzle are written both across and down. Call students' attention to the numbers in the boxes and show how they are used to find the clues.

● Have students complete the puzzles with a partner, if necessary.

Curriculum Connections

Spelling Link

● Read each word aloud.

ukulele	moccasin
beige	mammoth
sleuth	trapeze
khaki	pretzel

● Call on a volunteer to spell the word orally and write it on the board.

● Have the class copy the words and write a sentence for each one.

Multicultural Connection

● A number of words from Native American languages have made their way into English. Some are place names and some are the names of such North American animals as the **moose, raccoon,** and **skunk.** Even the word **tuxedo** has Native American origins.

● Have students conduct research to learn about Native American words that have been adopted into English. Invite them to share their findings with the class.

Observational Assessment

Note whether students are able to use and spell borrowed words correctly.

English-Language Learners/ESL

Make picture cards of some of the borrowed words in this lesson. Then make a word card for each picture. Have students match the word card to the picture card and pronounce the word. If students know of any words from their language of origin that have been incorporated into English, ask them to share these words with the class.

Gifted Learners

Many English words come from people's names. Have students research and report on the origin of one of the following: **America, Braille, volt, Fahrenheit, leotard, watt, pasteurize, silhouette, teddy bear, saxophone,** or **zeppelin.**

Learners with Special Needs

Additional strategies for supporting learners with special needs can be found on page 177K.

216

Idiomatic Expressions

Objectives

- **To recognize the meaning of idioms**
- **To write sentences using idioms**

Warming Up

- Write the following sentences on the board. Have volunteers read them aloud.

  "Hold your tongue," said the king. "I don't want to hear another word."

  The answer to your question is on the tip of my tongue.

- Ask students what each underlined expression means. Explain that the words have a figurative meaning rather than a literal one. That is, their meaning is different from the meaning of the individual words. For example, the king does not really expect the other person to grab onto his tongue!

Teaching the Lesson

- Explain that English has many such colorful expressions. They are called **idioms,** or **idiomatic expressions.**

- Ask a volunteer to read aloud the Helpful Hint on page 217. Discuss the two examples.

- Provide additional examples of idioms. Some possibilities include: **to give (someone) a break, to go to the dogs, to pull (someone's) leg, by heart, to let the cat out of the bag, in the long run, to hit the sack, to rub (someone) the wrong way.** Discuss each example and have students use it in a sentence.

- Explain that often you can figure out the meaning of an idiomatic expression by using logic and context clues, as in the *Warming-Up* examples.

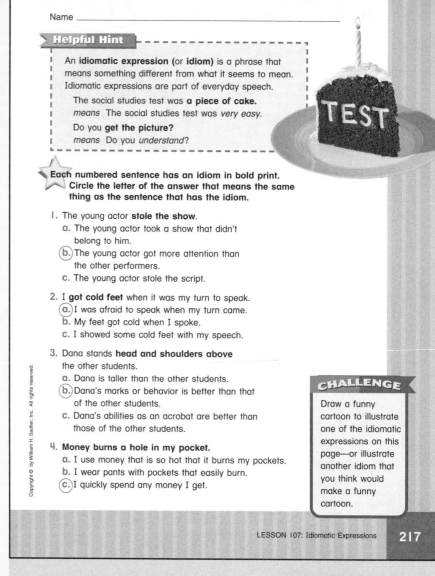

Name _____

Helpful Hint

An **idiomatic expression** (or **idiom**) is a phrase that means something different from what it seems to mean. Idiomatic expressions are part of everyday speech.

The social studies test was **a piece of cake.**
means The social studies test was *very easy.*

Do you **get the picture?**
means Do you *understand?*

Each numbered sentence has an idiom in bold print. Circle the letter of the answer that means the same thing as the sentence that has the idiom.

1. The young actor **stole the show**.
   a. The young actor took a show that didn't belong to him.
   b. The young actor got more attention than the other performers.
   c. The young actor stole the script.

2. I **got cold feet** when it was my turn to speak.
   a. I was afraid to speak when my turn came.
   b. My feet got cold when I spoke.
   c. I showed some cold feet with my speech.

3. Dana stands **head and shoulders above** the other students.
   a. Dana is taller than the other students.
   b. Dana's marks or behavior is better than that of the other students.
   c. Dana's abilities as an acrobat are better than those of the other students.

4. **Money burns a hole in my pocket.**
   a. I use money that is so hot that it burns my pockets.
   b. I wear pants with pockets that easily burn.
   c. I quickly spend any money I get.

CHALLENGE

Draw a funny cartoon to illustrate one of the idiomatic expressions on this page—or illustrate another idiom that you think would make a funny cartoon.

LESSON 107: Idiomatic Expressions   **217**

UNIVERSAL ACCESS
Meeting Individual Needs

Logical Learners

Have students use logic and context clues to figure out the meaning of the underlined idioms below.

When I asked Dad whether I might tell him what happened, he said, "Go ahead—I'm all ears."

Jim refused the lawn-mowing job because he had his hands full with his paper route.

Auditory Learners

Have students work in pairs to write a paragraph using at least three idioms. Encourage students to use idioms that they find in the dictionary, not only ones from the lesson. Ask volunteers to read their paragraphs aloud. Have listeners identify the idioms used. Write them on the board, and discuss their meanings.

Each sentence at the left has an idiom in bold print. Draw a line to match the sentence at the left with the sentence at the right that means the same thing.

1. They are not **out of the woods** yet.
2. They didn't **know the ropes.**
3. They are all **in the same boat.**
4. He **got up on the wrong side of the bed.**
5. He will **drop me a line.**
6. They **hit the roof** when he asked to borrow the car.
7. I was **down in the dumps.**
8. Everything you say to him **goes in one ear and out the other.**
9. I spent **an arm and a leg** on a fan.
10. He told me to **keep it under my hat.**

a. They didn't know how things worked.
b. They all face the same situation.
c. He will write to me.
d. They are not yet free of trouble.
e. He was in a bad mood.
f. He said I should keep it a secret.
g. I bought a very expensive fan.
h. I was unhappy.
i. Everything you say goes through his mind without making an impression.
j. They became angry when he asked to borrow the car.

Choose four idioms from above. Use each idiom in a sentence that shows its meaning.

Sentences will vary.

11. _____
_____
12. _____
_____
13. _____
_____
14. _____
_____

218   LESSON 107: Idiomatic Expressions

Home Involvement Activity Interview an older family member or a neighbor. Ask the person to tell you some idiomatic expressions that he or she used to hear but doesn't hear anymore. Find out what these expressions mean.

Practicing the Skill

● Go over the directions for pages 217 and 218. Have students consult a dictionary if they need to. Explain how to look up an idiom in a dictionary.

● For items 11–14 on page 218, remind students that their sentences should have enough context to show the meaning of the idiom.

Curriculum Connections

Spelling Link

● Since most idioms contain simple words, students will probably have little spelling trouble. However, some of the following words may be difficult, and students will benefit from a review of both their meaning and spelling: **idiom, idiomatic, expression, phrase.**

● Have students use the words in sentences, making sure to spell them correctly.

Math Link

Idioms or idiomatic expressions often involve numbers. Examples include: *at sixes and sevens, on all fours, at the eleventh hour, to put two and two together, one by one.* Have students explain the meaning of these expressions, checking a dictionary when necessary. Challenge students to find other idioms that use numbers.

Observational Assessment

Note whether students are able to use context to help them distinguish between literal and figurative meanings of idioms.

English-Language Learners/ESL

Explain that idioms are phrases that mean something different from what they seem to mean. For example, a French term of endearment meaning something similar to "my little darling" is **mon petit choux**, which literally translates to **my little cabbage.** Help students understand English idioms by explaining ones that evoke vivid images, such as **raining cats and dogs** or **pulling (someone's) leg.**

Gifted Learners

Challenge students to use their imaginations to explain how idioms may have originated. Have them think about common idioms, such as **in the same boat** and **out of the woods.** Then have them reflect on a less obvious one: **to get up on the wrong side of the bed.**

Learners with Special Needs

Additional strategies for supporting learners with special needs can be found on page 177L.

218

Word Analogies

Objectives

- **To recognize relationships between words in word analogies**
- **To complete word analogies**

Warming Up

- Ask students: *How are the gills of a fish like the lungs of a human?* Explain that fish use their gills to breathe, while humans use their lungs to breathe.
- Write the following sentence on the board. Ask a student to read it aloud.

  <u>Gills</u> are to <u>fish</u> as <u>lungs</u> are to <u>humans</u>.

- Explain that this is an analogy, a way of comparing. This comparison is based on how two things are alike. Ask: *How are gills and lungs alike?* Explain that gills and lungs are both used for breathing.

Teaching the Lesson

- Tell students that a specific kind of analogy is a word analogy. Have a volunteer read aloud the Helpful Hints on page 219.
- Discuss the examples in the Helpful Hints. Guide students to understand that each one is based on a different relationship between words.
- Point out that the order of the word pairs in a word analogy may be reversed without changing the analogy. For example:

  toe : foot :: room : house

  is the same as

  room : house :: toe : foot

- Make a large chart on the board with these headings: **Antonyms, Synonyms, Cause/Effect, Parts/Whole, Object/Use.** Provide an example under each heading. Have students add examples to the chart.

Name _____

> **Helpful Hints**
>
> **Word analogies** show how words and ideas are related.
> **High** is to **low** as **big** is to **small**.
> **THINK:** **High** and **low** are *opposites*. **Big** and **small** are *opposites*. The words in both pairs show a relationship. Both are *antonyms*.
> You can also write the analogy like this:
> **high : low :: big : small**
> Here are some other ways that pairs of words are related:
>
> | | |
> |---|---|
> | They are *synonyms*. | **Begin** is to **start** as **stop** is to **halt**. |
> | They show *cause and effect*. | **Hungry** is to **eat** as **tired** is to **rest**. |
> | They show *parts of a whole*. | **toe : foot :: room : house** |
> | They show how objects are *used*. | **pencil : write :: knife : cut** |

⭐ **Read each word analogy. Write how the words in both pairs are related. Choose from these words or word pairs:**
synonyms, antonyms, cause/effect, part/whole, object/use.

1. *Most* is to *least* as *new* is to *old*.
   <u>antonyms</u>

2. *Hard* is to *difficult* as *careful* is to *cautious*.
   <u>synonyms</u>

3. *Finger* is to *hand* as *page* is to *book*.
   <u>part/whole</u>

4. *Study* is to *learn* as *practice* is to *improve*.
   <u>cause/effect</u>

5. *Couch* is to *sit* as *bed* is to *sleep*.
   <u>object/use</u>

> **CHALLENGE**
>
> Make up a word analogy using either synonyms or antonyms. Leave out the last word. Have a friend complete your analogy.

LESSON 108: Word Analogies   **219**

UNIVERSAL ACCESS
Meeting Individual Needs

Logical Learners

Explain that completing a word analogy is like solving a problem. Students must analyze the relationship between the words in each pair. They should focus on the first pair and figure out how they are related. Then they should look at the next word and ask themselves which word would relate to it in the same way. Give students examples to complete.

Auditory Learners

Write this phrase on the board.

_____ **is to** _____ **as**
_____ **is to** _____ .

Write **laugh** in the first space. Then ask a volunteer to write a synonym for **laugh** in the second space. Next, write **weep** in the third space. Ask a student what kind of word must appear in the fourth space to complete the analogy. (a synonym for **weep**) Repeat this for analogies based on antonyms, part/whole, cause/effect, and object/use.

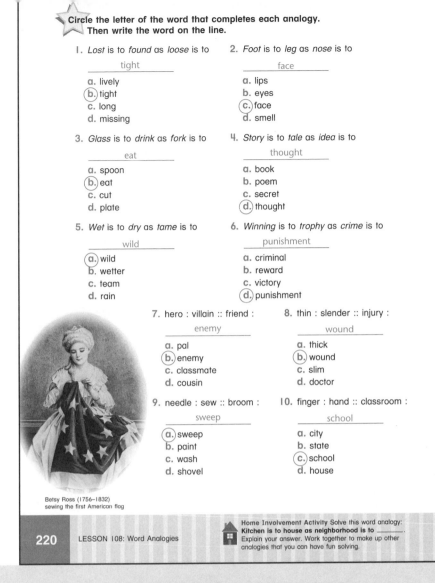

★ Circle the letter of the word that completes each analogy.
Then write the word on the line.

1. *Lost* is to *found* as *loose* is to

_____tight_____

a. lively
(b.) tight
c. long
d. missing

2. *Foot* is to *leg* as *nose* is to

_____face_____

a. lips
b. eyes
(c.) face
d. smell

3. *Glass* is to *drink* as *fork* is to

_____eat_____

a. spoon
(b.) eat
c. cut
d. plate

4. *Story* is to *tale* as *idea* is to

_____thought_____

a. book
b. poem
c. secret
(d.) thought

5. *Wet* is to *dry* as *tame* is to

_____wild_____

(a.) wild
b. wetter
c. team
d. rain

6. *Winning* is to *trophy* as *crime* is to

_____punishment_____

a. criminal
b. reward
c. victory
(d.) punishment

7. hero : villain :: friend :

_____enemy_____

a. pal
(b.) enemy
c. classmate
d. cousin

8. thin : slender :: injury :

_____wound_____

a. thick
(b.) wound
c. slim
d. doctor

9. needle : sew :: broom :

_____sweep_____

(a.) sweep
b. paint
c. wash
d. shovel

10. finger : hand :: classroom :

_____school_____

a. city
b. state
(c.) school
d. house

Betsy Ross (1756–1832)
sewing the first American flag

220   LESSON 108: Word Analogies

Home Involvement Activity Solve this word analogy:
Kitchen is to house as neighborhood is to _____.
Explain your answer. Work together to make up other
analogies that you can have fun solving.

Connecting Reading and Writing

Objectives

- **To read a nonfiction piece and respond to it in writing**
- **To practice identifying main idea and details and synthesizing information**
- **To write notes for a letter**

Warming Up

Comprehension Skills

- Have students think of a story and tell its **main idea**—what it is about. Then have them give **details**—pieces of information—that support the main idea. Here is an example:

<u>Main Idea:</u> A fairy godmother helps Cinderella go to the ball.

<u>Details:</u> a) The fairy godmother changes a pumpkin into a coach.

b) The fairy godmother changes Cinderella's rags into a gown.

- Remind students that **synthesizing** is to put together ideas within a piece of writing and make sense of them.

Teaching the Lesson

Have students reread the article to answer the first Reader's Response question. For the second question, ask them to think about the selection's overall message. Tell students to give reasons for their answers to the third question.

Practicing the Skill

Invite volunteers to read the directions and boxed words on page 222. Bring in some "help-wanted" ads and review them with students, identifying details about various jobs.

221

Name _____

Read about a special kind of government worker. Then answer the questions that follow.

Park Rangers

They wear green and khaki uniforms and unusual hats. They also wear name tags and badges. They work in some of the most beautiful, exciting, and important places in the United States. These government workers care about the past, the present, and the future. They value the environment. They listen and also teach. These men and women lead tours and hikes, and give directions. Who are these people? Can you guess? They are our nation's park rangers.

Park rangers work for the National Parks Service (NPS). The National Parks Service has an important job. It must protect America's natural resources. The Service cares for land that our government owns. It cares for national parks like the Grand Canyon. It takes care of historical sites like Valley Forge. It cares for national monuments like the Statue of Liberty.

It takes a large staff to care for so many places. Our many park rangers come from all fifty states. They learn all about the park or site. Some may even live within the park grounds. These rangers share their knowledge of our nation's beauty and history with anyone who is lucky enough to visit one of these wonderful sites.

1. Park rangers work for the National Parks Service leading tours and hikes.
2. Main Idea: The NPS protects our natural resources through its park rangers. Details: 1) Park rangers care for the parks and sites. 2) They learn about the parks and sites. 3) They teach the public.
3. Answers will vary.

Reader's Response

1. What does a park ranger do?

2. What is the main idea of this selection? Give three details that support the main idea.

3. Would you like to be a park ranger? If so, where would you like to work?

LESSON 109: Connecting Reading and Writing
Comprehension—Main Idea and Details;
Synthesize

221

UNIVERSAL ACCESS
Meeting Individual Needs

Auditory Learners

Have students talk about their notes with a writing partner. Suggest that students discuss specific information about the job they will do, what experience they have, and how their skills and interests relate to the job they wish to do. Have partners help each other recall what they have said so that they can translate their oral work into writing.

Logical Learners

Students think about the requirements of the job they want. What kinds of work does the job involve? What kind of skills does the person need? What kind of person would do this job well? When students have answered these questions, they can then ask themselves: *What qualities, skills, experiences, and interests do I have that fit what the job requires?*

Learners with Special Needs

Additional strategies for supporting learners with special needs can be found on page 177L.

Most park rangers enjoy their jobs. They get to serve their country in important ways. They meet people from the United States and from all over the world. They get an inside look at some of our national treasures. Many park rangers even get to live among nature.

⭐ Choose a national park or a historical site or monument. Imagine that you are applying for the job of park ranger there. Write notes for a job application letter. Tell why you would be right for the job. Use at least two of these words.

public	history	service	information	outdoors	directions
nature	leadership	communicate	site	uniform	friendly

Sentences will vary.

The Place: _____

The Job: _____

Your Experience: _____

_____

Your Skills and Interests: _____

_____

_____

_____

Writer's Tip
Read some "help-wanted" ads in the newspaper to see the kinds of details to include.

Speaker's Challenge

Imagine that you are being interviewed for the job of park ranger. Work with a partner to role-play the job interview. Make a list of the questions beforehand and think about the answers. Then role-play your interview for another partner team.

222 LESSON 109: Connecting Reading and Writing
Comprehension—Main Idea and Details; Synthesize

English-Language Learners/ESL

Invite English-language learners to discuss national parks and historic sites with fluent speakers. Provide students photographs of national parks and historic places. Then help them choose a particular place that interests them. You may wish to have English learners complete the assignment orally, rather than in writing.

Gifted Learners

Invite students to write an adventure story that takes place in a national park or historic site. Students may wish to do research so that they can include realistic details about the location. Encourage students to illustrate their stories and share them with the class.

The Writing Process

Discuss the purpose of a job-application letter—to persuade the person reading the letter that you are the best person for the job. Choose a national park and brainstorm the kinds of work involved in being a ranger there. Then have students identify the kinds of experience, skill, and interests a person would need for that job.

Prewrite Have students begin by choosing a park, site, or monument, and perhaps doing some research about it. Suggest that students make a list of the tasks that will be involved in being a ranger at the place they have chosen.

Write Encourage students to look over the boxed words and to keep them in mind as they write. Remind students to be clear and specific.

Revise: Have students read their notes to a writing partner and ask: *"If you were in charge of this site, would you hire me to be a ranger? Why or why not?"*

Proofread Tell students to read their notes slowly and carefully to check for errors in grammar, punctuation, and spelling.

Publish Have students copy their final drafts onto page 222. Invite volunteers to read their notes aloud.

Computer Connection

Give the following tip to students who use a word-processing program to write.

• All word-processing programs allow you to highlight and move sections of text. If you are prewriting and drafting on your computer, you can copy portions of your work into a final draft.

• Usually, the Edit menu has a feature that enables you to move text.

Portfolio Have students add their notes for a letter to their portfolios.

Reviewing and Assessing

Clipped Words, Blended Words, and Idioms

Objective

To review and assess clipped words, blended words, and idioms

Name _____

⭐ Is it a clipped word or a blended word? Underline your answer. Then write the word or words that make up the clipped or blended word.

		clipped word	blended word	
1.	photo	_clipped word_	blended word	photograph
2.	teen	_clipped word_	blended word	teenager
3.	brunch	clipped word	_blended word_	breakfast + lunch
4.	lab	_clipped word_	blended word	laboratory
5.	smog	clipped word	_blended word_	smoke + fog
6.	vet	_clipped word_	blended word	veterinarian
7.	motel	clipped word	_blended word_	motor + hotel
8.	champ	_clipped word_	blended word	champion
9.	bike	_clipped word_	blended word	bicycle
10.	fax	_clipped word_	blended word	facsimile

⭐ Each sentence below has an idiom in bold print. Circle the letter of the answer that means the same thing as the sentence that has the idiom.

11. Our homework was **a piece of cake.**
    (a.) Our homework was very easy.
    b. Our homework was to bake a cake.
    c. Our homework was to eat a piece of cake.

12. Do you **get the picture?**
    a. Do you get the prize?
    b. Do you have to buy the painting?
    (c.) Do you understand?

13. Some computers **cost an arm and a leg.**
    a. Some computers have hands and feet.
    (b.) Some computers cost a great deal of money.
    c. Some computers can hurt your arms and legs.

LESSON 110: Review and Assess   **223**

Warming Up

● Write the following sentence on the board. Have a student read it aloud.

    The **motel** we stayed at **cost an arm and a leg**, but it had its own **gym.**

● Have students define the terms clipped word, blended word, and idiomatic expression (or idiom).

● Have a volunteer underline the example of the clipped word, circle the blended word, and draw a box around the idiomatic expression from the sentence on the board.

Teaching the Lesson

● Give the class examples of clipped words they have studied. Have students write both the whole word and its clipped form on the board. Then discuss with students which form of each word they have seen or heard more often. Explain the fact that the clipped forms of words are easier to say and spell.

● Ask students for examples of blended words they have learned. Have students write the examples on the board and the two words that have been blended to create them.

● Have students offer examples of idiomatic expressions. Ask volunteers to use each one in a sentence.

UNIVERSAL ACCESS
Meeting Individual Needs

Visual Learners

Explain that idiomatic expressions are often easy to visualize. Have volunteers choose an idiom and describe the mental image it creates. Ask: *How does this image relate to the meaning of the idiom?* Then have students work individually or in small groups to draw an imaginative picture that illustrates the meaning of an idiom.

Auditory Learners

Have students make up riddles for clipped or blended words. Here is an example: *A doctor will give you one—and so will a teacher. It has four letters. What is it? (an exam)* Ask volunteers to pose their riddles to the class. Have the first student who guesses the word correctly write it on the board, explaining whether it is clipped or blended, and giving the original form of the word.

Learners with Special Needs

Additional strategies for supporting learners with special needs can be found on page 177L.

Read the passage. Then answer the questions that follow.

Pilots fly airplanes safely from place to place <u>each</u> day. Yet they do not do their work alone. <u>Crews</u> in the air and on the <u>ground</u> help—so does a government agency. This agency helps keep our airports safe by directing air traffic. Air traffic controllers see to it that <u>planes</u> land and take off in a safe <u>way</u>.

Air traffic controllers work for the Department of Transportation. Their job can be stressful at busy times or in bad weather. They must <u>act</u> quickly if there is a problem. Anyone who has ever flown can thank these important government workers.

Read the passage again to answer these questions. Circle the letter of the correct answer.

1. The correct respelling for <u>each</u> is
   - a. ēch.
   - b. ech.
   - c. əch.
   - d. əsh.

2. A homonym for <u>crews</u> is
   - a. teams.
   - b. cruise.
   - c. staff.
   - d. characters.

3. The best antonym for <u>ground</u> in the passage is
   - a. chopped up.
   - b. air.
   - c. land.
   - d. soil.

4. <u>Planes</u> is a clipped word for
   - a. plains.
   - b. planets.
   - c. planetariums.
   - d. airplanes.

5. The best synonym for <u>way</u> is
   - a. thrust.
   - b. whey.
   - c. weigh.
   - d. manner.

6. The closest meaning of <u>act</u> is
   - a. rehearse.
   - b. call.
   - c. do something.
   - d. turn on the radio.

Extend & Apply

Air traffic controllers report to the **FAA**. Use a dictionary or an encyclopedia to find out what **FAA** stands for.

Reteaching Activities

Shortening Words

List these words on the board: **submarine, gymnasium, telephone, influenza, necktie, veterinarian, helicopter, photograph.** Have students identify the clipped form of each word by circling the appropriate letters. Explain that clipped words sometimes are taken from internal parts of words (as with **influenza**). Point out that sometimes a clipped word involves a spelling change. **(bicycle/bike, tricycle/trike, facsimile/fax)**

Teaching a Lesson

Write the following terms on cards: **synonym, antonym, homonym, respelling, guide words, homograph, pronunciation key, clipped word, blended word, idiom, word analogy.** Have students work in pairs. Mix up the cards, and have students draw one. Ask students to make a class presentation in which they teach the topic shown on their card. Encourage them to use visual aides as necessary

Assessing the Skill

Check Up Assign the exercises on pages 223–224 to help students review what they have learned. The exercises will also help you assess students' progress.

Make sure students understand the directions for the exercises on page 223. Then have them complete the page. Next, have them read the passage on page 224 and answer the questions.

Observational Assessment As students do the exercises, watch for areas in which they may benefit from review or reteaching. Look back at your observational notes from earlier lessons to help you judge both individual and class progress in using the dictionary and thesaurus.

Student Skills Assessment Keep track of each student's progress in applying dictionary and thesaurus skills using the checklist on page 177H.

Writing Conference As you complete the unit, meet with students individually. Review their writing, note improvements, and offer encouragement. Have students share with the class favorite compositions from their Home Portfolios.

Group together students who need further instruction in dictionary and thesaurus skills and have them complete the *Reteaching Activities*. Turn to page 177C for alternative assessment methods.

References for Word Study Research Base

Adams, M. J., R. Treiman, and M. Pressley. 1996. "Reading, Writing, and Literacy." In *Handbook of Child Psychology*. Edited by I. Sigel and A. Renninger, vol. 4, Child Psychology in Practice. New York: Wiley.

Braunger, J. and J. P. Lewis. 1997. *Building a Knowledge Base in Reading*. Portland, OR: Northwest Regional Educational Laboratory's Curriculum and Instruction Services.

Gaskins, I. W. and L. C. Ehri, et al. 1996/1997. "Procedures for Word Learning: Making Discoveries About Words." *The Reading Teacher* 50: 312–336.

Hennings, D. G. 2000. "Contextually Relevant Word Study: Adolescent Vocabulary Development Across the Curriculum." *Journal of Adolescent & Adult Literacy* 44: 268–279.

Morrow, L. M. 1997. *The Literacy Center: Contexts for Reading and Writing*. York, ME: Stenhouse Publishers.

_____. 2001. *Literacy Development in the Early Years: Helping Children Read and Write*. 4th ed. Needham Heights, MA: Allyn & Bacon.

Morrow, L. M. and D. Tracey. 1997. "Strategies Used for Phonics Instruction in Early Childhood Classrooms." *The Reading Teacher* 50: 644–653.

National Institute of Child Health and Human Development. 2000. *Report of the National Reading Panel: Teaching Children to Read and Evidence-Based Assessment of the Scientific Research and Literature on Reading and Its Implications for Reading Instruction*. Washington, DC: National Institute of Child Health and Human Development.

Pearson, D. P., L. R. Roehler, J. A. Dole, and G. G. Duffy. 1992. "Developing Expertise in Reading Comprehension." *In What Research Has to Say About Reading Instruction*. Edited by J. S. Samuels and A. E. Farstrup. Newark, DE: International Reading Association.

Texas Education Agency. 1997. *Beginning Reading Instruction: Components and Features of a Research-Based Reading Program*. Austin, TX: Texas Education Agency.

Vacca, J. L., R.T. Vacca, and M. K. Gove. 2000. *Reading and Learning to Read*. New York: Addison Wesley Longman.

Vacca, R. T. 2000. "Word Study Strategies at the Middle Grades." New York: William H. Sadlier, Inc.

Vacca, R. T and J. L. Vacca. 1999. *Content Area Reading: Literacy and Learning Across the Curriculum*. New York: Addison Wesley Longman.

Wong Fillmore, L. 1991. "When Learning a Second Language Means Losing the First." *Early Childhood Research Quarterly* 6: 323–346.